THE ECONOMY
AND MATERIAL CULTURE OF SLAVES

THE ECONOMY
AND MATERIAL CULTURE OF SLAVES

GOODS AND CHATTELS ON THE SUGAR PLANTATIONS
OF JAMAICA AND LOUISIANA

RODERICK A. McDONALD

LOUISIANA STATE UNIVERSITY PRESS   BATON ROUGE AND LONDON

Designer: Amanda McDonald Key
Typeface: Bembo
Typesetter: G& S Typesetters, Inc.
Printer and binder: Thomson-Shore, Inc.

Library of Congress Cataloging-in-Publication Data

McDonald, Roderick A. (Roderick Alexander), date.
     The economy and material culture of slaves : goods and chattels on
the sugar plantations of Jamaica and Louisiana / Roderick A.
McDonald.
        p.   cm.
     Includes bibliographical references and index.
     ISBN 0-8071-1794-3 (alk. paper)
     1. Slavery—Jamaica—History.   2. Slavery—Louisiana—History.
3. Sugar industry—Jamaica—History.   4. Sugar industry—Louisiana—
History.   5. Plantation workers—Jamaica—History.   6. Plantation
workers—Louisiana—History.   I. Title.
HT1096.M4   1993
306.3'62'097292—dc20   93-392
                                                                    CIP

For my mother, Elizabeth McDonald, and to the memory of my father,
A. G. McDonald

CONTENTS

CONTENTS

ILLUSTRATIONS

MAPS

TABLES

ACKNOWLEDGMENTS

In researching and writing this book, I have been fortunate in the help and encouragement friends and colleagues have given me. Their collegiality and generosity constitute one of the most rewarding aspects of the enterprise and, of course, have improved the work immeasurably. My thanks go to Ira Berlin, Nigel Bolland, Michael Craton, Stanley Engerman, Peter Fearon, Barry Gaspar, Barry Higman, Howard Johnson, David Katzman, Woodville Marshall, August Meier, Philip Morgan, Richard Sheridan, Mary Turner, William Tuttle, Swithin Wilmot, and the late Neville Hall. They are responsible for many of the book's strengths, but, of course, none of its shortcomings.

I have presented aspects of this study at conferences, where again I received thoughtful criticism and unstinting assistance. I should like to thank here the good friends and valued colleagues it is a pleasure to see each year at that finest of all scholarly meetings, the Association of Caribbean Historians conference, as well as the participants in sessions devoted to the independent economic activities of slaves at meetings of the Southern Historical Association (1981 and 1990), the Social Science History Association (1984), and the Association for the Study of Afro-American Life and History (1980). The conference "Cultivation and Culture: Labor and the Shaping of Slave Life in the Americas," held in 1989 at the University of Maryland, let me meet a number of other scholars working on aspects of the internal economy, and thus was particularly valuable.

My participation at NEH summer seminars directed by Orlando Patterson (1983) and Philip Curtin (1991) helped the progress of the book, as did fellowships with the Philadelphia Center for Early American Studies, under Richard Dunn's directorship (1990 and 1992). A Rider College research fellowship (1990), summer research fellowship (1985), and grant-in-aid (1987–1988) supported my work; two University of Kansas summer fellowships

(1978 and 1979) and a University of Kansas dissertation fellowship (1978–1979) provided partial funding for the early research. The educational support staff at Rider College, in particular Celeste Thatcher and Wanda Guarino, were professional and courteous in typing many drafts of the manuscript.

I profited from the expertise and helpfulness of the staffs of the Institute of Jamaica, in Kingston; the Jamaica Archives, in Spanish Town; the West India Collection at the University of the West Indies, Mona, Kingston; the Department of Special Collections and Archives at the University of Aberdeen; the Scottish Record Office and the National Library of Scotland, both in Edinburgh; the British Library and the Public Record Office, both in London; the Department of Archives and Manuscripts of the Louisiana State University Libraries; the Department of Archives and Manuscripts of the Tulane University Libraries; the Department of Archives and Manuscripts of the Earl K. Long Library at the University of New Orleans; the Louisiana Historical Center, at the Louisiana State Museum, in New Orleans; the Historic New Orleans Collection; the Louisiana Historical Preservation and Cultural Commission, in Baton Rouge; the Louisiana Collection of the Louisiana State University Libraries; the Louisiana State Library, in Baton Rouge; the Department of Archives and Manuscripts of the University of Southwestern Louisiana Libraries; the University of Kansas Libraries; the Rider College Library; the Van Pelt Library, at the University of Pennsylvania; and the Library of Congress.

Working with the staff at Louisiana State University Press has been most gratifying. In particular, I should like to thank Margaret Dalrymple, the editor in chief, to whom my debts go back to when she was an archivist with the Department of Archives and Manuscripts at the Louisiana State University Libraries and whose interest and support over the years I have always appreciated. I must also thank Catherine Landry, the managing editor, and Barry Blose, the editor who marked my typescript.

My final acknowledgment is to all my friends, to my family, to my colleagues at Rider College, at the Philadelphia Center for Early American Studies, and elsewhere, to everyone who assisted or encouraged me throughout this project. This book benefited from the efforts of many, and I thank you all.

THE ECONOMY
AND MATERIAL CULTURE OF SLAVES

INTRODUCTION

Slave communities on sugar plantations in Jamaica and Louisiana organized extensive and integrated economic systems, accumulating and disposing of capital and property within internal economies that they themselves created and administered. Such economic systems probably functioned on every sugar estate in Jamaica and Louisiana, and their importance far outweighed the often limited pecuniary benefits slaves derived. The internal economies not only reflected the ways in which slaves organized their efforts to earn and spend money but also influenced the character and development of their family and community life. The slaves' economies thus shaped patterns of slave life, providing the material basis for slave culture in the two sugar-producing regions.

Time and space separated the sugar plantation societies of Jamaica and Louisiana. Jamaica had a well-established sugar culture and was the world's leading producer of the commodity by 1795, when Jean Etienne de Boré first successfully granulated sugar in Louisiana; Louisiana's sugar boom under slavery peaked in the decades that followed full emancipation in Jamaica in 1838.

Although the temporal and spatial distance between the two societies caused their plantation systems to differ somewhat, the characteristics that mature sugar plantation societies shared transcended the differences. Sugar's profitability encouraged its extension to most of the regions of the Americas favorable to its cultivation, but no matter when or where it was grown, from the sixteenth to the nineteenth century, from Brazil in the south through the Lesser and Greater Antilles and elsewhere in the Caribbean basin to Louisiana in the north, the techniques of its cultivation and processing were much alike. The slave system that accompanied the crop and the plantation complex also conformed to a common pattern.

Great Britain turned Jamaica into a sugar plantation society. In 1655, a British military expedition seized the island and Britain assumed its governance, after nearly 160 years of desultory Spanish rule. Thereafter, Jamaica's development as a plantation society proceeded slowly: it was not until well into the next century that it replaced the much smaller but earlier-developed island of Barbados as Britain's leading sugar colony. By the mid–eighteenth century, however, Jamaica dominated the British West Indies in sugar production and acreage as well as in the size of its slave trade and slave population. Notwithstanding recessions during the Seven Years' War (1756–1763) and the American Revolution (1775–1783), the growth of the island's sugar industry continued until the second decade of the nineteenth century. Its sugar economy under slavery peaked in the years 1783–1815. After the collapse of production in St. Domingue in the 1790s, Jamaica became the world's leading supplier. The slave trade to Jamaica was greatest, in both value and volume, between 1783 and 1808, the year Britain abolished the slave trade to its colonies, when 354,000 slaves—the island's largest-ever slave population—lived on Jamaica.[1]

Louisiana was the foremost sugar-producing state in the antebellum South. Between 1824 and 1861, sugarcane, which was climatically unsuited to cultivation on most of the North American continent and grown only sporadically and on a small scale elsewhere along the Gulf coast, became the principal crop in south Louisiana. Although for over a quarter century following Boré's first granulation of sugar there was limited development in the crop's cultivation, Louisiana quintupled its sugar production to more than 500,000 hogsheads annually from 1824 to the outbreak of the Civil War, becoming the only significant region of cane sugar production in the United States at the time. During the same period, the number of sugar estates increased almost sevenfold, from 193 to 1,308, while the state's slave population rose dramatically.[2]

Demographic analyses reflect sugar's preeminence in Jamaica and southern Louisiana. Of a Jamaican slave population that stood at 328,000 in 1800 and peaked in 1808, the last year of the slave trade, at 354,000, at least one-half worked on sugar plantations. Since some 75 percent of all Jamaican slaves lived on plantations with work forces of fifty or more, labor on large

---

1. Seymour Drescher, *Econocide: British Slavery in the Era of Abolition* (Pittsburgh, 1977); Noel Deerr, *The History of Sugar* (2 vols.; London, 1949), I, 158–207; Roderick A. McDonald, "Measuring the British Slave Trade to Jamaica, 1789–1808: A Comment," *Economic History Review,* XXXIII (1980), 253–58; Barry W. Higman, *Slave Population and Economy in Jamaica, 1807–1834* (London, 1976), 61.

2. J. Carlyle Sitterson, *Sugar Country: The Cane Sugar Industry in the South, 1753–1950* (Lexington, Ky., 1953), 28–30, 60.

sugar plantations was clearly the modal slave occupation on the island in the period under study.[3]

Sugar was king, too, in south Louisiana, where there were some of the largest and richest plantations of the South. Although only twenty-three of the state's forty-eight parishes grew sugar, and less than 50 percent of the improved lands in the sugar parishes were ever in cane cultivation, the sugar region had a disproportionate number of both slaves and large estates. Louisiana's total slave population numbered 69,064 in 1820 and rose steadily, reaching 109,588 in 1830, 168,452 in 1840, and 244,809 in 1850. On the eve of the Civil War, it stood at 331,726. Slaves who worked on sugar estates numbered 21,000 in 1827 and by 1830 had reached 36,091, about one-third of the state's total slave population. The number of sugar plantation slaves increased to 50,670 in 1841, 65,340 in 1844, and by 1852 and 1853 it stood at some 125,000, or approximately one-half of all slaves in the state.[4] Land consolidation and the growth of large estates paralleled the sugar boom. Small holdings were common in the 1820s, even in prime sugar land that fronted the rivers and bayous. After 1830, however, small farms gave way to large estates, and by 1860 the average sugar plantation contained 480 improved acres, compared with 128 improved acres for noncane farms. Occasional annual decreases in the number of sugar estates attest to the process of consolidation, in which not only did the average number of slaves on each plantation increase steadily but sugar production soared as well (Table 1). Although smaller farms continued to grow some sugar throughout the antebellum period, production was dominated by the larger estates on which most south Louisiana slaves, like their Jamaican counterparts, lived and worked.[5]

The population and production statistics for St. Mary Parish, one of the state's principal sugar parishes, exemplify the structure of the mature sugar plantation system in Louisiana during slavery. In 1857, slaves numbering 12,019 lived in St. Mary Parish, along with 4,021 whites and 585 free coloreds. The sugar production from the 59,326 acres under cultivation on the

3. Higman, *Slave Population,* 16, 61, 256, 275.

4. Sitterson, *Sugar Country,* 48; *Hunt's Merchants' Magazine and Commercial Review* (New York), VII (1842), 133–47, 242, XXX (1854), 499, XXXI (1854), 675–91, XXXV (1856), 248–49; *De Bow's Review* (New Orleans), I (1846), 54–55; Joseph C. G. Kennedy, *Population of the United States in 1860; compiled from the original returns of the eighth census* (Washington, D.C., 1864), 188–93.

5. Sitterson, *Sugar Country,* 30, 48–50; *De Bow's Review,* I (1846), 54–55, XIX (1855), 354; *Hunt's Merchants' Magazine,* XXX (1854), 499, XXXV (1856), 248–49, XLII (1860), 163.

TABLE 1

LOUISIANA SLAVE POPULATION AND PRODUCTION

	Number of Sugar Estates	Number of Slaves on Sugar Estates	Average Number of Slaves per Estate	Louisiana Sugar Production, in Hogsheads
1827	308	21,000	68	87,967
1830	691	36,091	52	75,000
1841	668	50,670	76	125,000
1844	762	65,340	86	204,913
1852	1,481	ca. 125,000	84	321,934
1853	1,437	ca. 125,000	87	449,324

SOURCES: *De Bow's Review,* I (1846), 54–55, XIX (1855), 354; *Hunt's Merchants' Magazine and Commercial Review,* XXX (1854), 499, XXXV (1856), 248–49, XLII (1860), 163.

171 estates of the parish totaled 31,915 hogsheads. Thus, an average of approximately seventy slaves lived on each estate, the average size of which was 350 acres. In 1857, slave labor produced not only a large sugar crop in St. Mary Parish but also 41,309 barrels of molasses and 401,600 bushels of corn.[6] Throughout sugar's antebellum ascendancy, many sugar estates in Louisiana had work forces considerably larger than the statistical averages. Plantations with slave populations numbering in the hundreds were commonplace in Louisiana as well as in Jamaica.

The years from 1783 to 1815 in Jamaica and from 1824 to 1861 in Louisiana were the time when the two sugar plantation systems reached maturity. The two periods thus represent corresponding stages of economic development and provide a basis for the comparative study of the two slave societies.[7]

6. *Hunt's Merchants' Magazine,* XXXIX (1858), 523, XLII (1860), 163.
7. For comparative methodology to yield what Franklin W. Knight terms "more meaningful generalizations about slave societies," he contends that "the comparative study of slave systems in the Americas . . . should be concerned less with concurrent time spans and metropolitan institutional differences than with equivalent stages of economic and social growth." See his *Slave Society in Cuba During the Nineteenth Century* (Madison, Wis., 1970), 194.

Sugar was the most valuable commodity of world trade in the eighteenth century, and the most valuable plantation crop in the Americas throughout the era of slavery. The development of sugar plantations in the New World during the seventeenth century had changed the diet of Europeans, and what had previously been an expensive rarity was, by the middle of the eighteenth century, a staple of the European diet.

The growth of the sugar plantation system depended on a plentiful supply of workers. Millions of African slaves, and their enslaved American-born descendants, furnished the needed labor and bore the bitter social costs of sweetening the food and drink of Europeans. The labor regimen exacerbated the burden of bondage. Sugar plantation slavery, the most common experience of black slaves in the Americas, exacted more onerous labor than the raising of other plantation staples. Although differences in the geography, climate, and technological sophistication of sugar-growing regions may have caused the techniques of cultivation and production to vary, slaves' work regimens on sugar plantations were everywhere similarly arduous.

The climate is crucial in sugar growing. Sugarcane takes from fourteen to eighteen months to reach maturity, and thus frost-free tropical and sub-tropical climates, with equable year-round temperatures, abundant, well-distributed rainfall, and fertile soil, provide optimal growing conditions. Caribbean islands like Jamaica provide fine conditions for the cane, but Louisiana's climate, where freezing temperatures occur annually, made it at best a marginal grower and necessitated adjustments in the husbandry of the crop. Accordingly, although Jamaica and Louisiana conformed to a common pattern of cultivation and processing, the timetables differed in the two regions. The work schedules of slaves on Jamaican plantations spanned the full growing cycle of sugarcane, whereas Louisiana's winters cut short the crop's growing season, resulting in a labor routine geared to just a twelve-month cycle.

The seasonality of Jamaica's rainfall lay behind the timing of the sugar crop's cultivation. The island's rainfall occurs principally in the latter half of the year, and during this time slaves planted the cane and tended it through the early stages of growth. The first step was to clear the fields and prepare the ground for planting. In Jamaica, slaves dug holes five feet by five feet and some six inches deep, into which they placed short sections of seed cane, set aside from the previous harvest, covering them with a layer of earth. As the plants grew, they added further layers of earth and perhaps a compost fertilizer until the holes were completely filled and the field leveled. The young canes required weeding and care for the first three or four months, after which the crop could be "laid by" and left to grow to maturity, since it had grown tall enough to prevent weed infestation. The ob-

5

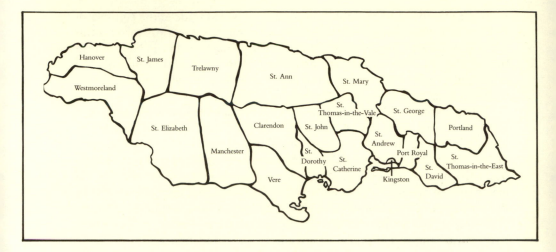

Map 1   Jamaica in the early nineteenth century

jective of the holes was to conserve topsoil. Digging them in soil baked hard by the sun was such a burdensome task, however, that planters often decided to hire jobbing slaves rather than subject their own labor force to the exhausting work (Figures 8, 11).

Sugarcane did not have to be replanted after each harvest, since the stubble left sprouted new shoots, or ratoons, which yielded less sugar than canes grown from seed but demanded less labor than planting and thus permitted a much larger acreage to be kept under crop. Depending on soil fertility, cane would be ratooned for up to three years, after which low sugar yields required redigging and replanting from seed. By ratooning some of the canes, and judiciously spacing the planting schedule throughout the latter half of the year, Jamaican sugar planters could assure an annual harvest.

Harvest occurred during the first half of the year, Jamaica's dry season. Plantation slaves usually enjoyed a brief respite from work around Christmas, but the harvest followed on the heels of the holiday. Wielding long-bladed machetes, slaves cut off each stalk of cane at ground level, lopped the top, stripped the leaves, and cut it into lengths of two to three feet. (Mature canes grew to heights of eight to ten feet.) Slaves loaded the sections onto ox-drawn wagons, to be transported to the estate's sugar mill.

In addition to planting, tending, and harvesting the crop, slaves also processed it. After the harvest, the juices in the cane fermented and soured rapidly. Because, to avoid spoilage, the processing had to be done within twenty-four to forty-eight hours after cutting, it ran concurrently with the harvest, exacerbating the already punishing burdens upon labor. Slaves crushed the cane in a mill driven by water, wind, or animal power, and they boiled the extracted juices. The refining removed impurities, after which the cane juice, by then of a thick, treacly consistency, began to crystallize. At that point the molten sugar was taken from the fire (in refining terminology, "struck"), left to cool, and then placed in hogsheads. In the barrels, a mass of sugar solidified, and the liquid residue, molasses, drained off. That took about a month in the storage shed or curing house to which the hogsheads were removed. When the hogsheads were emptied, the top and bottom layers were low-quality sugar, which went back to the boiling house for further refining, but the middle layer was suitable for final drying and repacking in hogsheads ready for shipment. The molasses was either sold or distilled into rum. Processing involved not only complex technology and organization but also considerable labor. Slaves manned every stage of the process from feeding the newly cut canes through the mill to loading the hogsheads of sugar for shipment. This work was in addition to their labor in the fields.

Field slaves on Jamaican sugar estates worked in gangs. Depending upon the size of the plantation, the main or great gang, consisting of both male and female slaves at peak working ability, was augmented by weaker second, third, and fourth gangs constituted by youths and young adults not yet at full physical development and older slaves past their best working years.

Not all the slaves worked in the field gangs. Domestics attended to the needs of the estates' whites, and skilled slaves worked in trades such as coopering, smithing, masonry, sugar making, and distilling. Slaves also staffed the many services that did not involve field work, acting as stockmen, cooks, watchmen, hospital attendants, water carriers, wainmen, and carters.

Planters expected young slave children to work. They were introduced to the routine of plantation labor early in their lives, participating in "pickaninny" or hogmeat gangs under the direction of elderly slave women known as driveresses. In such gangs, which incorporated all the components of the adult gangs to which they would graduate, they performed tasks like weeding and collecting fodder. Convalescent slaves and pregnant and suckling women were often also assigned lighter labor like weeding and cleaning up around the plantation buildings.

The occupational structure had a sex bias. Men dominated the elite positions as drivers and head craftsmen and the specialized occupations as stockmen, wagoners, watchmen, and skilled sugar-mill workers. Specialized roles for women were more limited, chiefly as domestics, cooks, medical and midwifery aides, and garden and poultry tenders. Consequently women generally made up a larger proportion of the field hands, whose work was the most onerous.

Although the growth cycle of sugarcane ran from a year and a quarter to a year and a half, Jamaican planters instituted a rotation of planting and ratooning that permitted an annual cycle of labor. Planting, the late-summer and fall work, fully occupied the daily schedule of the field hands during its time of the year. In late fall and early winter, the slaves tended the crop during its early growth. That work, which involved weeding, cleaning, hoe-plowing, and thinning and replanting the cane shoots, required less labor than planting. Some of the slaves could turn to other tasks on the estate: planting provision and minor staple crops, working on the maintenance and upkeep of the estate and its buildings, and preparing for the harvest, which usually began early in the new year and lasted four or five months. At harvest, work on the sugar crop again monopolized the slaves' labor.

During planting and tending ("out of crop"), the slaves' daily schedule differed significantly from their work routine at harvest ("in crop"). Out of crop, their plantation work filled the hours of daylight; in crop, they spent their days in the field harvesting, and part of each night at the works processing.

Between four and five in the morning, the plantation overseer sounded a signal that inaugurated the slaves' diurnal work. Every day except Sunday, both in and out of crop, slaves had to respond to the summons. Those who did not or who were late risked a back lacerated by the driver's or overseer's whip. The overseer expected the slaves to be in the field, ready for work, at dawn. Often, however, "before-day-jobs" around the sugar works or stock pens had them working even earlier. William Fitzmaurice, an experienced overseer and bookkeeper on Jamaican sugar estates, testified to a committee of the House of Commons that slaves, prior to going to the fields, had "various works to do which are considered as detached jobs from the field labour, such as hoeing intervals, which they can do before day, as also carrying mould to cattle pens, chopping up dung, or making mortar, or carrying white lime, or making preparations for tradesmen employed in the buildings about the works." Fitzmaurice informed the committee that "these are called before-day-jobs."[8]

The slaves in the fields worked from sunup to sundown. At first light, they assembled with their implements—a machete during harvest, a hoe out of crop—and their breakfasts. From dawn until midmorning the field gangs labored, their work uninterrupted save, perhaps, for the occasional water break when the young boys who worked as water carriers came around. During the midmorning break of a half hour the slaves ate breakfast, sometimes heated for them by field cooks, and rested. After that respite, work lasted until the midday dinner. For two hours the slaves might rest, eat, and even tend their own livestock or cultivate their kitchen gardens or provision grounds. Then they reassembled in the fields and worked without interruption until sunset. Before returning home, however, they often had to perform chores around the estate similar to the "before-day-jobs," such as cleaning out cattle pens and collecting grass for animal fodder. James Stephen, a leading opponent of slavery, calculated that Jamaican sugar plantation slaves worked, on average, "from 5 A.M. till 7 P.M.; deducting two and a half hours for breakfast and dinner." The eleven-and-a-half-hour

8. Testimony of William Fitzmaurice, "Minutes of the Evidence taken before a Committee of the House of Commons, being a Select Committee appointed to take the Examination of Witnesses respecting the African Slave Trade," in *British Sessional Papers: House of Commons*, 1731–1800, Accounts and Papers, XXXIV, 746–47, 217.

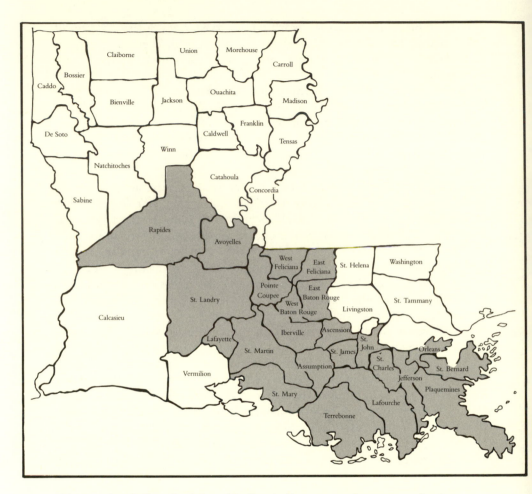

Map 2 Antebellum Louisiana. Shading indicates area of sugarcane planting.

day included only field work and did not count the two hours or more for before- and after-day work and travel time to and from the fields. This out-of-crop routine was the minimum daily work load.[9]

In crop, slaves had to work much longer hours. Throughout the harvest, slaves had to labor at night, processing the sugar, in addition to putting in their regular hours in the field. During the months of harvest, sugar works on Jamaican estates operated around the clock, six days a week, closing only on Sundays. If a plantation had an adequate complement of slaves, they were divided into three spells or shifts, each working one-third of the night. Often, however, plantations were shorthanded. If only two shifts could be adequately staffed, the slaves worked half the night, every night, in addition to their daywork. Slaves on a two-shift system went straight from fourteen hours in the field to five hours in the sugar mill on alternate nights (5 A.M. to 7 P.M. in the fields, 7 P.M. to midnight at the sugar works). On other nights, they worked five hours in the mill immediately prior to their day's work in the fields (midnight to 5 A.M. in the works, 5 A.M. to 7 P.M. in the fields). Under a three-shift system, slaves did an early, middle, or late spell of night work, working each of those shifts every third night—all, of course, in addition to their day's field work.

In Jamaica, the sugar mills closed every Sunday, although planters often "cheated" slaves of this time off by keeping the works in operation into the early hours of Sunday morning and restarting them late Sunday night instead of Monday. Slaves used the day off to recuperate from the six 18- to 20-hour days they had just worked. They also had to find time to go to their grounds to gather provisions that would supplement the rations supplied by the planter.

The cultivation of sugar in Louisiana was a race against time. Because sugarcane cannot withstand the frosts that annually threaten Louisiana, the sugarcane harvest had to come but nine or ten months after planting. The sturdy, fast-maturing Ribbon Cane best suited the abbreviated growing season. Yet the longer the crop stayed in the ground, the higher its sugar content. Louisiana planters thus sought to plant as early as they could and to harvest at the last conceivable moment. In deciding when to start the harvest, the planter had to estimate both the speed with which the crop could be cut and processed, and the date of the first killing frost.

The work routine of Louisiana sugar plantation slaves reflected the compression of the crop's cycle. Especially during the planting and harvest sea-

9. James Stephen, *The Slavery of the British West India Colonies Delineated* (2 vols.; London, 1824–30), II, 150.

sons, slaves labored tremendously. Technological advances in sugar processing, and the topography of southern Louisiana, added to the work. By the time of Louisiana's sugar boom, mills driven by steam engines had replaced those powered by water, wind, or animals. The new engines required fuel. Nearby swamps and forests afforded a plentiful supply of wood, but the slaves had to fell it and drag it to the mills. Because most of Louisiana's sugar estates stood on the Mississippi floodplain, they had to have both levees and extensive drainage systems. Planters incorporated the necessary construction into the routine of the slaves.

The annual work cycle for Louisiana sugar plantation slaves began as early as possible in the new year—although it could be delayed by a late harvest extending into January. Immediately after the Christmas and New Year's holidays, the slaves plowed the fields preparatory to planting the canes. Whereas Jamaican slaves hand-hoed holes for seed cane, Louisiana slaves used plows drawn by animals to open up furrows some six to eight feet apart, into which they placed seed cane set aside from the previous year's crop. Usually Louisiana planters allowed any single cane piece to ratoon for no more than two years before replanting. Slaves accordingly planted about one-third of the estate's acreage each year.

Slaves usually completed planting by the end of February and, after the plant cane and ratoons sprouted, tended the crop through the first months of its growth. That involved hoeing and plowing between the rows to keep the cane pieces free of grass and weeds. By late June or early July the canes had grown tall enough to withstand weeds. Slaves then plowed and hoed ("threw up") the rows of cane in ridges to permit better drainage around the plants' roots. The sugarcane was then "laid by" and left to grow untended until harvesttime.

Tending the crop required less work than either planting or harvesting. During the spring and early summer, therefore, planters could divert some labor to tasks like growing provisions and secondary cash crops, preparing for the harvest, and maintaining and improving the estate. Through the spring and summer, slaveholders had the slaves plant one or two crops of corn, as well as perhaps potatoes, pumpkins, sweet potatoes, and other vegetables. In addition, many planters grew peas in the cane fields. They planted this crop, after the canes had been laid by, in the strips of ground between the cane rows. Slaves harvested these crops and cut hay for fodder before the sugar harvest began. They also mended roads and fences, built and repaired levees, made bricks for the construction and refitting of plantation buildings, dug and cleaned ditches, and gathered wood both for fuel and for use by the estate's coopers. Before the sugar harvest began, planters sought to have everything ready to see them through it: sufficient wood to fuel the sugar mill, enough barrels and hogsheads to hold the crop, and adequate roads to transport the cane from field to works.

The harvest usually began by mid–October. Once under way, the cutting of canes and the processing of the crop continued uninterrupted until completion. The slaves first cut and matlayed the cane that was to be used for the next year's seed: the seed cane was laid out in mats and covered with a layer of earth to protect it from frost. Thereafter, the harvest began in earnest. So as to ensure adequate supplies at the mill, slaves began cutting canes a day or two before the planter started up the works, which he hoped to run nonstop until the harvest was over. Slaves on Louisiana sugar estates, unlike their Jamaican counterparts, worked in crop seven days a week, day and night, although bad weather, impassable roads, or breakdowns at the mill could disrupt their schedule.

Because of the race against frost, harvest proceeded at a furious pace from late October to December. Freezing temperatures were likeliest in the first two months of the new year, so planters tried to finish the crop by Christmas, at which time the slaves had their annual holidays. Often, however, the harvest continued into January.

If frost came early, the normal routine ceased and all hands worked at windrowing the crop. They cut the canes, laid them in the furrows between the ridged cane rows, and covered them with cane leaves and tops. Windrowing gave protection from the weather, but processing had to proceed apace in order to keep the canes from spoiling or rotting.

The harvesting techniques resembled those in Jamaica. Slaves worked in gangs, cutting and stripping the canes with flat-bladed knives. Teams of slaves then loaded the crop onto carts drawn by animals and transported it to the sugar mill for processing. Apart from technological advances in the machinery, the processing of the crop was also similar to that in Jamaica. The slaves on the estate performed all the labor, from feeding and stoking the mill to loading hogsheads of sugar and barrels of molasses onto the river steamers at the plantation wharf, and they did that in addition to their field work. The planters enforced a system of shifts whereby slaves had to work in the sugar mill part of the night, every night, for the duration of the harvest.

The gang system prevailed in Louisiana, as in Jamaica, with the delegation of tasks reflecting disparities in the physical capabilities of the gangs. The principal gang, made up of the strongest slaves on the estate, performed the most arduous work, such as plowing, hoeing, and harvesting. For the two most strenuous tasks on the estate, ditching and wood gathering, a sexual division of labor emerged: usually only the men of the great gang did that work.

The gangs of slave children on Louisiana plantations were similar to the "pickaninny" gangs on Jamaican estates. As there, a female slave driver, the driveress, initiated the children into labor routines by assigning them light tasks like cleaning up around the sugar works and picking fodder. The work schedule of women with unweaned children accommodated their babies' feeding needs. Such women either had additional time off from labor in the gangs or worked in a "sucklers' gang."

The workday of Louisiana slaves resembled that of their Jamaican counterparts as well. Slaves worked from sunup to sundown, with a half hour off for breakfast and a midday dinner break lasting from one and a half to two hours. Out of crop, the slaves worked five and a half to six and a half days a week, having time off on Saturdays and Sundays. But during harvest, they enjoyed no respite: they worked sixteen or more hours a day, seven days a week. Captain Thomas Hamilton, a traveler, commented in 1833 that "the crop in Louisiana is never considered safe till it is in the mill, and the consequence is that when cutting once begins, the slaves are taxed beyond their strength, and are goaded to labour until nature absolutely sinks under the effort."[10]

Louisiana sugar plantations earned a dreadful reputation "as the most terrifying of all the various hells of the deep South to which blacks from the older slave economies of the tidewater states could be sold." One antislavery traveler remarked, "The cultivation of sugar in Louisiana is carried on at an enormous expense of human life. Planters must buy to keep up their stock, and this supply principally comes from Maryland, Virginia, and North Carolina." Frances Trollope, another abolitionist, asserted that "to be sent south and sold [was] the dread of all the slaves north of Louisiana." E. S. Abdy, an Englishman who traveled through the South in 1833 and 1834, related how planters in the Old South disciplined slaves by threatening to sell them "down the river to Louisiana." Slaves incorporated the Louisiana sugar region's unenviable reputation in the chorus of a song:

> Old debble, Lousy Anna,
> Dat scarecrow for poor nigger,
> Where de sugar-cane grow to pine-tree,
> And de pine-tree turn to sugar.[11]

10. Captain [Thomas] Hamilton, *Men and Manners in America* (2 vols.; Edinburgh and London, 1833), II, 229–30.

11. C. Duncan Rice, *The Rise and Fall of Black Slavery* (London, 1975), 287; Hamilton, *Men and Manners*, II, 229; Frances Milton Trollope, *Domestic Manners of the Americans* (1832), ed. Donald Smalley (New York, 1949), 246; E. S. Abdy, *Journal of a Residence and Tour in the United States of North America, from April 1833, to October 1834* (3 vols.; London, 1835), III, 103–104.

The curse of Cain similarly marked sugar slavery in Jamaica. Throughout the sugar boom, the island's slave population failed to reproduce itself naturally. The work schedule on the plantations, in combination with excessive punishment and inadequate rest, food, shelter, and medical care, proved destructive to slaves' lives. Like elsewhere throughout South and Central America and the Caribbean, in Jamaica slaves put to cultivating sugar died faster than they bore progeny. Only the slave trade, the Black Mother, could maintain and increase the size of the slave populations. While Jamaica relied on slave traffic across the Atlantic, for Louisiana the Black Mother was interstate traffic, the slave states of the Old South supplying the men, women, and children the sugar planters needed.

Sugar plantation slavery in Jamaica and Louisiana, as elsewhere in the Americas, earned its reputation as the Sweet Malefactor. To please the palates of white Western Europeans and Americans, black slaves suffered and died within a system characterized by undernourishment, overwork, harsh punishment, poor housing, inadequate clothing, high infant mortality, ill health, despair, and life-spans shortened by a grim regime. As victims of a system that deprived them of their liberty, transported them against their will, and sold them as chattels at the behest of others, the slaves on sugar estates passed most of their working lives in toil creating wealth for those who held them in bondage. These slaves, however, struggled to transcend the wretchedness of their lot. Slave community life throughout the reign and dominion of King Sugar displayed extraordinary creativity; the hundreds of thousands of men and women who lived and died as slaves showed resourcefulness, aspiration, dignity, and courage—the full array of humanity's most prized attributes, which even as coercive a system as slavery could not suppress. Slaves triumphed over the adversity of their bondage, as they proved in their art and music, family and community development, and religion, as well as in their economic activities and material culture. As their houses, gardens, and grounds provided the focus for their family and community life, so too were these the basis of their independent economic systems.

1

THE SLAVES' ECONOMY IN JAMAICA

Despite the hardships that sugar production imposed, the slave communities on sugar plantations in Jamaica had thriving and dynamic internal economies. Slaves who in law were defined as chattels, the property of a master, had property of their own and controlled the accumulation and disposition of earnings and possessions. Their right to an internal economy was something they claimed and the planters acknowledged. Although statutory law neither created nor recognized a body of slave rights, they existed de facto in the slaves' informally negotiated conditions of life and labor. Slaves could exercise significant control over their work and lives, for example, by manipulating labor productivity. Despite planter coercion, slaves could work within the limits of the plantation power relations to extract concessions regarding their personal lives and autonomy. For the internal economy, legal provisions were less important than entrenched custom. There was no protection in law for slave-held property, whether real estate, animal stock, or crops and manufactures, or for the earning of pay for labor or the accumulation of money and goods. Slaves had no legal right to the land they cultivated or the revenue deriving from the sale of crops, no legal right to own or dispose of poultry, pigs, goats, and other livestock, and no legal right to sell their labor on any occasion. But planters recognized the peril of trespassing upon what the slaves conceived as customary rights, and of breaking what had the effect of a compact.

The Jamaican planter Ezekiel Dickinson illustrated this, albeit as an absentee owner. Time and again he counseled his nephew Caleb, manager of his St. Elizabeth sugar plantations, to accommodate the inclinations of the slaves. He was "very desirous of . . . all our People having ev'ry reasonable indulgence," and he asked "that no care or attention . . . be wanting to the Negroes," inasmuch as "the Gang of Negroes is the Planter's riches: the attention and care of them was one means that enabled our ancestors to settle and cultivate their Estates with such success." Dickinson insisted that all whites on the estate become aware of the need for solicitude toward the slave labor force. He contended that an overseer who dealt inhumanely with slaves was "not fit to run an Estate."[1]

In 1815 and 1816, the novelist Matthew Gregory Lewis visited his sugar estate in Jamaica, which an attorney had managed in his absence. His journal leaves no doubt that the slaves on his plantation knew their customary rights and acted in concert when they felt justice violated. "On the Sunday after my first arrival," he recorded on February 24, 1816, "the whole body of Eboe negroes came to me to complain of the attorney, and more particularly of one of the book-keepers. I listened to them . . . for about an hour and a half; and finding some grounds for their complaint against the latter, in a few days I went down to their quarter of the village, told them that to please them I had discharged the book-keeper, named a day for examining their other grievances, and listened to them an hour more."[2]

Lewis not only addressed disputes on his own plantation but was also presented with the grievances of slaves from nearby estates. In a journal entry dated January 19, 1816, he wrote that "a young mulatto carpenter, belonging to Horace Beckford's estate of Shrewsbury, came to beg my intercession with his overseer." A few days later he was again approached: "A large body of negroes, from a neighbouring estate, came over to complain of hard treatment, in various ways, from their overseers and drivers, and requesting me to represent their injuries to their trustee here, and their proprietor in England." It happened one time that Lewis had no sooner tried to resolve a dispute on his own estate than he was called to act on complaints of slaves from another: "I went down to hear the whole body of Eboes lodge a complaint against one of the book-keepers, and appoint a day for their being heard in his presence. On my return to the house, I found two women belonging to a neighbouring estate, who came to complain of cruel treatment from their overseer, and to request me to inform their trustee how ill they had been used, and see their injuries redressed."[3]

James Colquhoun Grant and John R. Webb, who managed Joseph Foster Barham's sugar plantation in Westmoreland Parish, advised the owner

1. Ezekiel Dickinson to Caleb Dickinson, August 19, 1786, November 28, 1786, February 10, 1787, all in Letterbook of Ezekiel Dickinson, Papers of Caleb and Ezekiel Dickinson, West India Collection, University of West Indies, Mona, Kingston.

2. Matthew Gregory Lewis, *Journal of a West India Proprietor* (London, 1834), 187–88.

3. *Ibid.*, 115, 129–30, 144.

against depriving his slaves of their customary perquisites even where these contravened Jamaican law. In a letter to Barham dated September 4, 1809, Grant and Webb observed that "by the Consolidated Slave Law amended in 1807 Clause 33 No Slave is permitted to have in his possession any Horse, Mare, Mule or Gelding: Notwithstanding this law in many instances it is evaded and some of your Negroes have a few stock of this description kept in free people's names, as for Horned stock they have upwards of 100 Head amongst them, to compell them to sell off would not be for your Interest. Your Negroes have been long indulged in the same way and it would make them very discontented." These slaves were property owners who would protest the abridgment of their status, clearly assuming that their "owners" not only recognized this status but also knew that their own interests were best served by preserving and protecting it.[4]

The internal economy had its basis in the customary rights claimed by slaves, and it took form through the ownership and control of property and through the slaves' prerogative of deriving personal gain from their labor. Slaves could garner profit from property in the way of land, livestock, or manufactures. In Jamaica, as in Louisiana, they had de facto control of certain land on the plantation—gardens and grounds. The occupant of each house in the slave village had the use of the small garden area adjacent to the dwelling; in addition there were allocations of more sizable areas from tracts set aside for the slaves' use elsewhere on the plantation.

In Jamaica, the estate furnished little food. Planters distributed only a meager protein ration, usually salt herring, and expected the slaves to obtain the rest of their food from their provision grounds. That practice enabled the plantation population to work for themselves, generate a surplus, and keep the profit. Slaves received both land and time off to cultivate their crops, and many succeeded in achieving the surplus that meant gain. Planters agreed to this practice, and accepted that slaves retain the profits, for avoiding the costs of a fully dependent work force was to the owners' advantage. But the profits also permitted the slaves a degree of independence at odds with the notion of being chattels. The slaves controlled both the crops and the land on which they were grown, and the planters recognized and respected that reality.

Government records testify to the extent of slave control over provision grounds. *The Minutes of the Proceedings of the Committee of Secrecy and Safety*

4. J. C. Grant and J. R. Webb to J. F. Barham, Westmoreland, September 4, 1809, in Barham Family Papers, MS, Clarendon dep. c. 358, Bundle 1, Jamaica Correspondence, 1809–1816, Bodleian Library, Oxford University.

in the Parish of St. James for February, 1792, referred to a Mr. Whitaker who "had sold a property called Windsor Castle and told his Negroes that as they were to leave the place he would pay for their Grounds which he did at the valuation which the Negroes themselves put upon them, although that valuation amounted to several hundred Pounds more than the valuation that had been put on them by the Gentlemen who had been appointed to estimate the value of the property and on whose estimation the place had just been sold." The deponent explained, "I understand that the Negroes grounds were valued at about £280, and that Mr. Whitaker paid them for their grounds, for some stock and to compensate their inconveniences on leaving the place near £1000."[5]

In 1807, John Blackburn, a thirty-five-year resident of Jamaica and the manager of thirty sugar estates, testified before a government committee on the commercial position of the West Indies. Blackburn's testimony, although couched in typically inflated planter rhetoric, acknowledged the control that slaves exercised over the provision grounds. "In the infancy of a Plantation," he explained, "the Negro provision-grounds are near their houses, which again are close to the works; that in the extension of the Plantation, it becomes necessary to cultivate in cane the Negro provision-grounds, and give them others at some farther distance, and in doing so, it is a matter of great delicacy to be done with much leisure and caution; you must give them other grounds of better quality, and well stocked with provisions fit for use, and pay them money to get their consent to make the exchange." Clearly the planters Blackburn described recognized the slaves' stake in the provision grounds. He went on to delineate the proprieties of the required negotiations, and the consequences if they were not observed: "You must particularly take care, by bribery or otherwise, to get the sanction of the head people, or your slaves would probably get discontented, and careless of their own property and of yours." Blackburn pointedly referred to "their houses, their provision grounds, their gardens and orchards, (which they consider as much their own property as their Master does his Estate)."[6]

Because, as Blackburn mentioned, provision grounds on established estates were usually some distance from the slave village, they were not suited

5. Minutes of the proceedings of the Committee of Secrecy and Safety in the Parish of St. James, Jamaica, February, 1792, in C.O. 137/90, Secretary of State, November, 1791, to October, 1792, Public Record Office, London.

6. Testimony of John Blackburn, in *Report from the Committee on the Commercial State of the West India Colonies* (Ordered to be printed July 24, 1807; London, 1807), 40, 43.

either for keeping livestock that required daily attention or for working at odd moments. Slaves kept most of their livestock closer to the quarters, usually in the plots by their houses. They also used these plots as kitchen gardens and orchards, cultivating both of these for domestic consumption and sale.

In the kitchen gardens, also called shell-blow grounds, the slaves might spend the spare hour during the work week, especially at the midday dinner break and at sundown. The name "shell-blow grounds" came about because the slaves could work there during the daytime break and still be able to hear the signal blown on a conch shell that summoned them for the afternoon's labor.

Some of the kitchen gardens appeared prosperous. William Beckford saw slave houses whose gardens contained fruit trees, and he mentioned that they often had a hut for animals and storage. In addition, some gardens had enclosed pigsties. "Most negroes in Jamaica," Beckford concluded, "have either fowls, hogs, or cattle; some have all." Hector McNeill, a staunch defender of the plantocracy, traveled around Jamaica and reported seeing slave houses whose kitchen gardens contained plantain groves, banana and orange trees, hogsties, and flocks of fowl. Typically, however, the gardens were less well accoutred than those McNeill and Beckford described. McNeill also noted that the slaves kept some larger livestock, probably cattle, in the plantation pen, although owning cattle was rarer than owning poultry and smaller livestock. The attorneys for Barham's plantations wrote to him that "each [slave] possessing stock consider[s] them as much their own Property (using their own words 'as Massa does Plantation')."[7]

The fowl were free ranging. "Poultry houses are not wanted," observed a Jamaican resident, Alexander Barclay, "the chickens are carefully gathered at night and hung up in baskets, to preserve them from the rats." Attesting to the prevalence of poultry in the slave quarters, Barclay recalled that "the noise which some hundreds of cocks make about day-dawn in a negro village, amidst the usual stillness of a tropical morning, cannot easily be imagined by those who have not heard it."[8]

The kitchen gardens' bounty, in both livestock and provisions, could

7. William Beckford, *A Descriptive Account of the Island of Jamaica* (2 vols.; London, 1790), I, 229; William Beckford, *Remarks upon the situation of Negroes in Jamaica* (London, 1788), 91; Hector McNeill, *Observations on the Treatment of Negroes in the Island of Jamaica* (London [1788?]), 3–4; J. C. Grant and J. R. Webb to J. F. Barham, September 12, 1813, in Barham Papers.

8. Alexander Barclay, *A Practical View of the Present State of Slavery in the West Indies* (London, 1826), 315, 317.

"not only furnish [the slaves] with sufficient food for their own consumption, but an overplus to carry to market." According to the Reverend John Riland, a sugar planter in northern Jamaica, the plantations depended upon products slaves grew or raised on their own. From the pigs and poultry of the kitchen gardens, he noted "the master usually purchase[d] the provisions of his table, paying the Negroes the common price for which they would sell at the market." Various plantation records show this to be normal practice. For example, plantation accounts of Charles Gordon's Georgia estate for 1788 included the entry, "To cash paid Mason Prince for a young Steer raised by him on the Estate £8:10:0." David Ewart, the agent on Lord Penrhyn's King's Valley estate, also bought stock belonging to the plantation slaves. "I make it a practice to buy the Calves when they are a year old at a Doubloon each," he told Penrhyn. "I think it is a fair bargain for both parties, the Negroes are satisfied with it." Early in December, 1807, Ewart reported that he bought the slaves' livestock, comprising "bullkins and heifers," for 140 pounds. He paid the slaves cash, since "money is more acceptable to them at this Period of the year as they wish to lay it out in little matters of finery etc. for Xmas." Ewart limited the number of livestock each slave could have, probably because they were kept in the plantation pen. He wrote to Lord Penrhyn, "I found several negroes had 4 or 5 head of Stock and I expressed a wish that each negro shall have but one meaning that they should distribute them amongst their children and relations or sell them to the Estate to which they readily agreed and several were transferred from one negro to another." None of the slaves availed themselves of the option of selling to the estate. Ewart did not tell whether slaves who received the cattle paid those who had owned them. It may be that those who divested themselves transferred the animals to members of their family and retained control over them.[9]

The fruit trees of the kitchen gardens may have included coconuts, oranges, mangoes, akees, and avocados. In some cases there may have been small stands of bananas and of the local staple, plantain, and various other vegetables such as yams, eddoes, okra, and calalu. Records of Lord Seaford's two sugar plantations in St. James Parish document both the acreage used

9. John Stewart, *A View of the Past and Present State of the Island of Jamaica; with Remarks on the Moral and Physical Condition of the Slaves and on the Abolition of Slavery in the Colonies* (1823; rpr. New York, 1969), 267; Rev. John Riland, *Memoirs of a West India Planter* (London, 1827), 151; Charles Gordon, Account Current with Francis Grant, 1788, in Gordon of Buthlaw and Cairness Papers (1160/6/61), University of Aberdeen Library; David Ewart to Lord Penrhyn, October 26, 1807, December 8, 1807, both in Penrhyn Castle Papers (MSS 1479, 1495), West India Collection.

for kitchen gardens and the number of livestock owned by the slaves (see Appendixes 1, 2). In 1825, Old Montpelier estate had a slave community of 400 people, of whom 190 were male and 210 female (65 males and 61 females were African-born, the remainder were Creoles, that is, born in the West Indies), and they shared land for kitchen gardens measuring approximately 17.2 acres. On New Montpelier estate, the slave population numbered 320 (156 males, of whom 56 were African-born, and 164 females, 71 of whom had been born in Africa), and between them they worked kitchen garden allotments totaling 22.5 acres.[10] Slaves on the two plantations kept most of their livestock on these modest plots (on Old Montpelier the allocation averaged some 200 square yards per person—man, woman, or child—and on New Montpelier it averaged approximately 340 square yards). The Old Montpelier slaves owned 173 head of cattle, 190 hogs, and 856 head of poultry altogether, while those on New Montpelier had 70 head of cattle, 211 hogs, and 718 head of poultry. On the two estates, all but a very few households owned some livestock and cultivated kitchen gardens. A number of those who had neither livestock nor gardens were watchmen without houses, living instead on the premises they guarded, or invalids or "runaways."[11]

The garden and livestock holdings of individual households varied substantially. On Old Montpelier, for example, the Warren/Tomlinson/Thompson household, which had eight members, cultivated a sizable kitchen garden of 1.5 acres (7,260 square yards) and owned 6 head of cattle, 13 hogs, and 30 fowl, whereas the four members of the Ellis/Howard/Cross household had only 4 head of poultry, 1 hog, and a garden of 300 square yards. Similarly, on New Montpelier, the four members of the Ellis/Thompson household gardened a 1.2-acre plot (5,800 square yards) and owned 10 head of cattle, 16 hogs, and 32 fowl, whereas the five people the Williamson/Brown/Lee household comprised had only 750 square yards of garden and 2 fowl.[12]

Slaves controlled cash crops elsewhere on the plantation as well. On John and Charles Ellis' Caymanas estate, they harvested the coconut trees, and since the yield from marketing the fruit of a single tree was about £5.6.8 (one doubloon) a year in 1818, this abundant plant translated into substan-

10. "Minutes of Evidence taken before the Select Committee of the House of Lords appointed to inquire into the Law and Usages of the several West India Colonies in relation to the Slave Population . . . ," in *British Sessional Papers: House of Lords,* 1831–32, CCCVI, 82–89, 1376–93.
11. *Ibid.*
12. *Ibid.*

tial earnings. The slaves evidently exercised de facto rights to the crop, since when some coconut trees had to be felled to make way for an overseer's house, the slaves who collected fruit from them were indemnified although the trees did not grow in their gardens. Barclay also related how slaves on Simon Taylor's Holland estate were recompensed for some coconut trees near the planter's house that were felled.[13]

It was on the provision grounds, though, that the slaves had most of the crops they consumed and marketed. Plantain was by far the most important there, and much of the land was laid out in groves (known as walks) of that staple. Other crops on the provision grounds were yams, cocoas, and corn. Though slaves kept little livestock that far from their houses, since it would have made it hard to give the animals sufficient attention, Thomas Cooper, who had spent some time on Robert Hibbert's estate, recounted that they did, however, keep some goats there, presumably tethered or hobbled.[14]

The Consolidated Slave Acts of Jamaica (1792) decreed that planters were to "allot and appoint a sufficient quantity of land for every slave." The laws did not call for the land to be ceded to the slaves as their property but mandated only that a certain acreage be assigned for growing provisions: property rights assumed by slaves were worked out in situ. According to John Stewart, a Jamaican planter, the amount of land allocated to an adult slave in compliance with the laws was "about half an acre." Those with families got "an additional portion of land." The records of Lord Seaford's Montpelier estates contain an exact tabulation of the provision grounds awarded the 720 slaves who lived there. In 1825, 310.2 acres were allotted to 400 slaves on Old Montpelier, and the 320 slaves on New Montpelier worked ground totaling 157 acres. The allocation on Old Montpelier thus averaged about three-quarters of an acre for every man, woman, and child, and on New Montpelier one-half acre. A list of allotments of provision ground by family reveals, however, considerable differences in the amount of land worked by households of similar size (see Appendix 3). Further, although the slaves grew similar crops, primarily the staples of plantains, cocoas, and yams, the condition of their plots varied markedly.[15]

13. *Jamaica Journal* (Kingston), I (1818), 312–18; Barclay, *A Practical View,* 53–54.

14. Thomas Cooper, *Correspondence between George Hibbert, Esq., and the Rev. T. Cooper relative to the condition of the Negro slaves in Jamaica* (London, 1824), 37.

15. Bryan Edwards, *The History, Civil and Commercial, of the British Colonies in the West Indies* (3 vols.; 1793; rpr. New York, 1972), II, 145, 158; John Stewart, *A View,* 267; *British Sessional Papers: House of Lords,* 1831–32, CCCVI, 82–89, 1376–93.

Differentials in the land worked (both as provision grounds and as kitchen gardens) and the livestock owned favored certain groups within the community. On the Montpelier estates, the status and skills of the holders helped determine the differentials. "Coloured and skilled slaves," Barry Higman avers in his analysis of the households on the two plantations, "generally had the use of relatively large areas of provision grounds and possessed considerable numbers of livestock." Patterns of inheritance and land consolidation through marriage also influenced the size of gardens and grounds.[16]

The land for the provision grounds was unused or unfit for sugar cultivation. Plantations in their early years put the land closest to the sugar works into cane and gave slaves provision grounds on more remote tracts. But as the plantations developed, the allotment of provision grounds was determined not only by distance but also by the fields' quality. Mature sugar estates put into cane as much of the suitable land as possible. Slaves therefore received for their own use the less fertile scrublands and uplands. Consequently, the provision grounds often stood at the periphery of, or even outside, the estates, and at a considerable distance from the slave villages. William Hylton, a North American who settled in Jamaica as a sugar planter, lamented that travel from home to provision ground fatigued the slaves; another planter expressed similar misgivings, pointing out that the provision grounds were sometimes miles from the plantation. The long trip to, and the arduous work at, the grounds proved a heavy burden to the slaves, as Beckford testified. If slaves got Saturday off and wanted to work their land, they sometimes had to travel as much as five to seven miles. There they spent the day, returning in the evening with enough provisions for their own consumption during the week ahead and for sale at the following day's market. Sunday was market day throughout Jamaica. If the slaves got only Sunday off, they had to go first to the provision grounds and then to the market, traveling the considerable distances as well as laboring in their grounds all in one day.[17]

16. Higman, *Slave Population,* 168–69.

17. John Stewart, *A View,* 267; Letter from William Hylton (in response to an undated circular letter from the bishop of London concerning the condition of slaves), June 26, 1808, MS 670, in Institute of Jamaica, Kingston; *Observations Upon the African Slave Trade, and on the Situation of Negroes in the West Indies,* by a "Jamaica planter" (London, 1788), 29; Beckford, *A Descriptive Account,* II, 152–53. Barry Higman, in *Jamaica Surveyed: Plantation Maps and Plans of the Eighteenth and Nineteenth Centuries* (Kingston, 1988), provides a detailed delineation of the physical layout of numerous sugar plantations of the slavery era, including information on the size and location of slave gardens and grounds.

The Consolidated Slave Acts provided each slave "sufficient time to work the [provision grounds], in order to provide him, her or themselves, with sufficient provisions for his, her or their maintenance"; this was stipulated to be "one day in every fortnight . . . exclusive of Sundays, except during time of crop." Actual practice, however, varied. Slaves did no plantation work on Sundays. Those able and willing went to their provision grounds and to market. The number of other so-called Negro days was not as uniform, as the plantation journals attest. The five-month harvest work schedule for Rose Hall plantation, for example, listed slaves "taking days" in their grounds only on Sundays. For the rest of the year, the slaves were "taking days" twice a week, on Sunday and, in addition, Thursday, Friday, or Saturday. On Braco estate, in Trelawny, the work book of James Galloway, the overseer, showed an eight-week spell of harvest labor assignments from May 8 to June 26, 1796, during which work was recorded for every day except Sundays. Nothing was entered for the eight Sundays, when the slaves were "taking days," but in the following year, throughout the harvest, the notation for every Sunday read, "in their grounds." In the twelve weeks, all out of crop, between October 1 and December 18 of that year, however, the slaves had days for themselves six times on both Saturday and Sunday, four times on both Friday and Sunday, and twice on only Sunday. Apparently they received compensatory time out of crop for missing days off during harvest, more than a decade before any legislation on the question. It was not until 1809 that an act for the "better order, regulation, and government of slaves" incorporated the principle applied on Braco estate, mandating twenty-six Negro days a year, an average of one every other week both in and out of crop. Slaves on Braco were accustomed to another aspect of compensatory time as well. Slaves working in the mountains who were unable to tend their provision grounds were accommodated on their return, the work schedule for Friday, August 22, 1797, recording regular plantation work for all slaves on the plantation "except those who lost their day while in mountains [who were] in their grounds."[18]

It was, of course, in the planters' interest that the provision grounds be well kept and productive, since they supplied the slaves with most of their food. That partly explains the sanctity of Negro days; extant plantation records consistently show that slaves received at least one day off a week

18. Edwards, *The History, Civil and Commercial,* II, 158; Rose Hall Journal, 1817–1822, in IB/26, No. 1, Jamaica Archives, Spanish Town, Jamaica; Braco Estate Journal, May, 1795–November, 1797, in 4/2, Jamaica Archives; "An Act for the protection, subsisting, clothing, and for the better order, regulation, and government of Slaves," passed on December 14, 1809, in *British Sessional Papers: House of Commons,* 1816, XIX, 375–93.

throughout the year. Besides, the slaves would have resisted attempts by the planters to abridge the number of Negro days, since the full number were needed to generate the surpluses, and profits, on which they counted. Because the slaves could sabotage the plantation's operations if provoked, they could shape their work relations to a considerable degree.

The development of the internal economies of the slave communities on Jamaican sugar estates depended on earnings accumulations arising from the surpluses. The process of accumulation occurred, however, within a context provided by both plantation and island societies.

In the first place, a terribly exacting work routine, over and above the labor expected by the planter, confronted slaves who undertook to raise a surplus for market. Before dawn, and in the evening after a full day's labor, they had to tend their livestock and gather fodder for them. They spent the midday mealtime—the dinner break, in plantation terminology—in their shell-blow grounds, forgoing what little rest they might have gained from their morning's exertion before returning to the cane fields until sunset. They spent Negro days and Sundays traveling to, and working in, their provision grounds and at market. At the provision grounds, they had little time to work their land, which was usually less fertile and harder to cultivate than the acreage in cane, for in the brief time available to them, they had to harvest and market their production as well. The time constraints resulted in a division of labor. Women in Jamaica have traditionally dominated the retail side of the still flourishing market system, the pattern of which, as Sidney Mintz has pointed out, was formed during slavery. Probably women became the market retailers in what were family endeavors not only because of the difficulty of one person's tending crops, harvesting them, and transporting them for use and sale, all in one day, but also because practices in the region from which most Jamaican slaves came, the Guinea Coast, placed women in central roles in various economic activities, especially planting and marketing.[19]

The division of labor took husband, wife, and children—or in a female-headed household, mother and children—to the provision grounds, where together they quickly harvested the produce to be sold. Since retailing was consistent with the other roles of women, such as child rearing, the woman carried the stock to market, spending the rest of the day selling it, while others in the family—either husband or grown children—tended the plot and harvested enough for the family's consumption.

19. Sidney W. Mintz, "The Jamaican Internal Marketing Pattern," *Social and Economic Studies,* IV (1955), 95–103.

Yet not all the slaves participated. The Jamaican planter Gilbert Mathison contended that "every well-conditioned Negro on a plantation keeps one or more pigs, and poultry, or trafficks in tobacco, or sells his surplus provisions at market," but he noted that "those less fortunate suffered from poverty." Mathison recognized that not everyone could profit from raising surpluses, and he deplored the poverty and poor diet of the many slaves who could not raise even enough to supply themselves. This group, he noted, comprised the idle, the sick, the old, and those with a large number of children—the very people least able to withstand poverty and want. Slaves who did not grow surplus produce were excluded from at least the horticultural dimension of the internal economy. The nonparticipants can be divided into two categories: the unfit and the unwilling.[20]

Willing or not, the aged, the infirm and disabled, the sick, and the young were physically unable to take part fully in marketing produce. Some were able to contribute to the effort: the elderly and the children often looked after livestock and worked in the kitchen gardens. The extent to which they benefited was often limited to the extent of their involvement, though the family orientation of the endeavors could mitigate the correlation. Some could not contribute at all, and on the whole they fared worst.

Some slaves not directly involved in this arduous branch of the internal economy took part in other of the internal economy's dynamics, and some, by virtue of kinship or community ties, were even incidental beneficiaries of the sale of provisions. Kin incapable of full participation in growing and marketing produce nevertheless might share in the family's profits.

The investment in time and energy of even the most industrious slaves could go for naught, since horticultural practices and fierce tropical weather often combined to destroy plantings. When that happened, the slaves found themselves unable even to feed themselves. The slaves customarily put most of their time and acreage into raising plantains; provision grounds were often little more than extensive groves of that staple. Plantain, like its relative the banana, grows on a tall, delicate tree, which the autumn storms of the hurricane season could devastate. When bad weather destroyed the plantain crop, the slaves had to live largely on the foods that had escaped destruction, especially root crops. If those resources proved inadequate, however, the population faced starvation unless it received supplementary rations from the plantation.

As the overseer on Nathaniel Phillips' Pleasant Hill estate wrote, a gale

20. Gilbert Mathison, *Notices Respecting Jamaica in 1808–1809–1810* (London, 1811), 30, 39–40.

27

in early November, 1791, caused so much damage to the slaves' agriculture that he was "obliged to purchase for the support of the Negroes." Only in mid–April of the next year was he ready to venture "that the period is nearly arrived again when they'll be able to go to market with Plantains, as usual." Two months later, and more than seven months after the storm, he could at last reassure Phillips that the slaves were "now selling Plantains on Sundays as usual."[21] In 1812, on Charles Gordon Gray's sugar estate in St. James Parish, a storm damaged the provision grounds to the extent of menacing the food supply. Although the slaves spent additional days in the provision grounds and plantain walks trying to save their crops, their situation remained dire. Even three months later, Gray had to acknowledge, "The Negroes are complaining of Hunger as Plantain is a rarity."[22]

A large part of the slaves' economic activity as buyers and sellers took place in the weekly market. There they not only offered for sale the commodities they had raised, made, or appropriated but also purchased consumer goods. The labor of slaves resulted in the "vast quantities of provisions, vegetables, and fruits" that William Sells saw "brought to Kingston market"; Mathison observed that slaves were that market's exclusive suppliers of such commodities as poultry, pigs, fruit, and vegetables. As suppliers of most of the island's fresh produce, the slaves were pivotal to the commerce of Jamaica, but here, in contrast to their role with sugar, they not only created the wealth but also accumulated it and controlled its application.[23]

Since such a large proportion of Jamaica's fresh produce was distributed through the weekly markets, they drew purchasers of all classes. Retail transactions involved either barter or cash. With other tradespeople the slaves bartered, but the people who came solely to buy had to pay cash.

In addition to fresh provisions, artifacts manufactured on the plantation, especially basketwork, pottery, and woodwork, found customers at the markets. Thus slaves who were averse to working their own plots, or who had an aptitude for craftwork instead, could still participate in the market. Although Bryan Edwards disparaged the quality of the cottage industries' goods, they fabricated some fine articles. The incapacitated and elderly, who spent much of their time at the slave village, could also manufacture goods

21. Thomas Barritt, Pleasant Hill, Jamaica, to Nathaniel Phillips, London, November 2, 1791, April 10, 1792, June 13, 1792, all in Nathaniel Phillips Papers (MSS 8384, 8392, 8397), West India Collection.

22. Charles Gordon Gray to his father, November 26, 1812, February 18, 1813, both in MST 163, Institute of Jamaica.

23. William Sells, *Remarks on the Condition of the Slaves in the Island of Jamaica* (London, 1823), 11; Mathison, *Notices*, 1.

for the market. Other members of the slave community, even those active in the provision grounds, might devote some spare time to craftwork.[24]

Accounts of the Sunday markets from the period describe both the variety of goods on sale and the slaves' domination of the trade. Edwards, for example, observed that besides dealing in foodstuffs, slaves made "a few coarse manufactures, such as mats for beds, bark ropes of a strong and durable texture, wicker chairs and baskets, earthen jars, etc. for all which they [found] ready sale." He continued, "Sunday is their day of market, and it is wonderful what numbers are then seen, hastening from all parts of the country, towards the towns and shipping places, laden with fruits and vegetables, pigs, goats, and poultry, *their own property.*" He estimated "that upwards of 10,000 assemble every Sunday morning in the market of Kingston, where they barter their provisions, etc. for salted beef and pork, or fine linen and ornaments." Edwards shared an article of faith typical of planters in fancying an idyllic slave life, but he and others, like Mathison, are consistent in describing the weekly markets, and other letters and journals corroborate them.[25]

The slaves were not the only sellers at the markets. The Reverend Richard Bickell saw in Kingston market "Jews with shops and standings as at a fair, selling old and new clothes, trinkets, and small wares at a cent, per cent, to adorn the Negro person; there were some low Frenchmen and Spaniards, and [free] people of colour, in petty shops and with stalls; some selling their bad rum, gin, tobacco, etc.; others salt provisions, and small articles of dress; and many bartering with the slave or purchasing his surplus provisions to retail again." Another commentator amplified on the involvement of traders other than slaves. "The Sabbath was," he remarked, "almost the only time plantation negroes had for the culture of their grounds and vending their commodities at the public markets, which are held on this day; from which irreligious and impolitic custom the lower Jews who keep shops are particularly benefitted: the negroes taking the sole opportunity of being in town to supply themselves with cloth, and foreign provision."[26]

When slaves did not personally attend market, they traded with higglers. The ubiquitous higglers were the only group apart from the plantation slaves and the retailers mentioned by Bickell that was involved in the vending side of the weekly market. Nonplantation slaves, free blacks, and free

---

24. Edwards, *The History, Civil and Commercial,* II, 125.

25. *Ibid.,* II, 125 (my emphasis); Mathison, *Notices,* 1.

26. Rev. Richard Bickell, *The West Indies As They Are* (London, 1825), 66; "Characteristic Traits of the Creolian and African Negroes in Jamaica," *Columbian Magazine; or, Monthly Miscellany* (Kingston), III (1797), 168.

coloreds constituted the group, essentially playing the role of intermediary. Higglers journeyed around the island, buying up produce, manufactures, and stolen property, which they sold at market on Sundays. Their margin of profit was the difference between the sale price acceptable to plantation slaves in order to be freed from the work of transporting and selling the goods themselves, and the higher price that the goods commanded when retailed. Higglers also bought up produce when the slaves arrived in town with it on Sundays; the slaves were apparently willing to give up some profit in order to have time in town for other purposes.

Higglers dealt with the slaves in either barter or cash. A somewhat jaundiced description from the time shows clearly the scope of their activities: the anonymous observer described higgling as attractive "to the indolent and desultory disposition of the negroes. They are sent abroad by their owners, to work out as it is called, for which liberty they are obliged to pay a certain rate per week or month. . . . Turned loose on the community, they are guilty of every kind of fraud and forestalling, to make up their respective allotments. They are the receivers and venders of stolen goods and occasionally thieves themselves; the most honest part of their employment being to monopolize roots, greens, fruit, and other edibles, which they purchase from the country negroes, and retail at exorbitant prices."[27]

Slaves on Taylor's Holland estate, some miles from Kingston, were enterprising in bringing their produce to market. "Slaves of Holland Estate," related Barclay, "have, or had lately, a coasting-vessel, which they employed in carrying plantains, yams, eddoes, and corn, from the estate's wharf to Kingston, a distance coastwise of sixty to seventy miles." He added that "the register of the vessel, of course, was in the name of a free person." Other ships plied the piers of estates along the coast; Barclay was aware that slaves sold plantains and yams "to one of the coasting vessels that supply the Kingston market."[28]

The weekly markets were the principal route by which cash entered the internal economy of plantation slaves. Cash purchasers included planters or their representatives buying for their own table or supplementing their imported provisions, as well as ship chandlers, army quartermasters, and townspeople. Kingston was a large city by the late eighteenth century, and a number of other ports and administrative boroughs on the island had sizable urban populations. The markets held each week in the environs of every town of any size played an integral part in meeting Jamaica's food needs.

27. "Characteristic Traits," *Columbian Magazine,* II (1797), 702.
28. Barclay, *A Practical View,* 272–73.

TABLE 2

COIN IN JAMAICA, 1774

	£	s.	d.
Circulating among Negro slaves (chiefly in small silver)	ca. 10,437	10	0
Circulating among rest of inhabitants	39,562	10	0
Total circulating	50,000	0	0
Inert or uncirculating, in the chancery chest, treasury, and private hoards	ca. 15,000	0	0
Total circulating and uncirculating	65,000	0	0

SOURCE: Edward Long, *The History of Jamaica* (3 vols.; 1774; rpr. New York, 1972), I, 537.

The markets were well patronized by town dwellers, who bought what they needed with ready money.

Edward Long, the planter-historian whose *History of Jamaica* was published in 1774, calculated that the slaves held approximately 20 percent of Jamaica's circulating coin at that time, this being about 16 percent of all coin then on the island (Table 2).[29] Long did not reveal the source of his data, and he acknowledged the speculative nature of the calculations. Still, they were part of an extensive and informed consideration of the economy of the island, which in the absence of any other data at least offers a general indication of the magnitude of the cash component of the slaves' internal economy in relation to the overall economy of the island. His figure of £10,437.10.0 incorporated the cash holdings of all 170,000 slaves on the island, though, not just the approximately 105,000 who worked on sugar plantations.[30]

Long bemoaned the shortage and debasement of Jamaica's coin, and expressed concern over the growing scarcity of the small denominations in which slaves traded. He condemned the intra-Caribbean livestock trade, in

29. Edward Long, *The History of Jamaica* (3 vols.; 1774; rpr. New York, 1972), I, 537.
30. *Ibid.*, 496.

which Jamaica was primarily a purchaser, because it adversely affected the island's currency supply. "This trade," he observed, "drains away much of the old hammered silver, and the milled ryals; and indeed renders them so scarce, that it is to be feared, the want of them must some time or other prove very distressful to the Negroes, who would fall into a miserable state, if ever the island should be deprived of small silver."[31] Long wanted to solve the crisis in small currency so as to assist the slaves' internal economy, and his statement of the steps needed affords insight into that economy's scope and structure. He wanted to help slaves "carry on their marketing for butcher's meat, poultry, hogs, fish, corn, eggs, plantains, and the like" by ensuring an adequate supply of small coin that would both "supply to a great extent, the necessities of the internal commerce" and "establish a measure for the lowest kinds of barter, or traffic, that can be carried on by the Negroes." As it was, he noted, slaves were "put to great difficulty and loss, by having no other than a silver currency, of too high value for their ordinary occasions . . . the lowest denomination whereof is equal to fivepence sterling."[32]

Long claimed that the slaves suffered loss not only through the shortage of small currency but also through the debasement of the silver coinage circulating. He referred to the "notorious clippers" who trimmed off part of the coin's silver before exchanging the coin at face value rather than at the lesser value by weight left after the clipping. If the slaves were among the "notorious clippers," they were also victims of it. Long accused white traders of accepting debased coins at their value by weight and then returning them to circulation at the face value. According to Long, slaves lost out at both ends of this deal. "Debased currency circulate[d] chiefly in the retail branch of internal commerce; in which its passage from one person to another [was] so rapid, that its imperfections escape[d] notice." That affected slaves above all, "for they have their dealings chiefly with the retail shopkeepers, who are a sort of middle-men between them and the merchant importers." He added that

> these shopkeepers, who, for the major part are Jews, look with great circumspection on the coin they receive, knowing, that if it is too much depreciated, it will not pass on the merchant; whenever therefore they take diminished money from the Negroes, it is with design to profit upon them; and this is usually managed, by giving but a trifling value of their goods for it; and then, by watching for oppor-

31. *Ibid.,* 549.
32. *Ibid.,* 562, 571.

tunities to change it for heavy money; and, as the light money reverts into circulation, and can have no outlet by trade, so it continues to run current so long as any heavy money can be picked up; when this is exhausted, the shopkeepers begin to cry down the light and counterfeit coins; the Negroes are unable to carry on their traffic; and a general confusion ensues.

One has to suspect, however, that the trading and financial acumen of slaves regularly dealing at market was more refined than Long conceived, but whether or not he was right, his analysis does reaffirm the extensive involvement of slaves in Jamaica's cash economy.[33]

Invariably the plantation slaves were at the weekly market also as consumers buying goods either by barter or with cash. Among their purchases were clothing and accessories, food, alcohol, tobacco, and housewares. Since they could raise their own domestic provisions, they were primarily interested in purchasing imported foodstuffs. Mathison listed commodities such as salt pork and beef, cod, meat, rice, flour, and bread. Edwards also mentioned that slaves purchased salt beef and pork. In addition, they bought clothing and the finery—jewelry and accessories—they wore on holidays and Sundays. According to Barclay, when the coasting vessel of the Holland estate's slaves returned from taking their provisions to Kingston, it "brought in Irish salt-pork, butter, mackerel, cod-fish, linens, printed cottons, muslins, handkerchiefs and crockery-ware."[34]

Many slaves enjoyed smoking and used some of the money they made from marketing provisions to buy tobacco and pipes. A commentator observed that "Negroes of both sexes regale themselves with smoking tobacco." They used pipes that often had leather caps covering the bowl and fastened to the stem, to prevent tobacco and embers from falling out.[35] The housewares and personal items they bought included the goods other slaves had taken to market—bowls, furniture, bed mats, baskets, and the like—besides the imported manufactures in jewelry, pocket knives, and other metalware.[36] They took some of the alcohol they bought back to the plantation for consumption during the week, perhaps transporting it in receptacles similar to those described in a Kingston journal, the *Columbian Magazine,* in 1797: "The most common utensil is a calabash bottle, stopt with the stem

33. *Ibid.,* 573.

34. Mathison, *Notices,* 1; Edwards, *The History, Civil and Commercial,* II, 125; Barclay, *A Practical View,* 273.

35. "Characteristic Traits," *Columbian Magazine,* III (1797), 108–109.

36. Edwards, *The History, Civil and Commercial,* II, 125; Sells, *Remarks,* 11.

on which the Indian corn grows. A cane is sometimes used for this purpose, to fit it for which they clear it of the membranes at the joints and cork the upper end: a large cane will hold a considerable quantity, and serves the double purpose of a bottle and walking stick." Slaves also drank liquor while socializing at market. Many studies have documented that the consumption of alcohol is central to market-day activities in many rural communities; Jamaican slaves were no exception to the rule.[37]

Weekly markets were the setting for the principal social activities of Jamaican slaves off the plantation. On their weekly excursions to town they stepped beyond the regulatory plantation authority, distancing themselves from the white overseers and bookkeepers. The markets were bustling, crowded affairs, which afforded the slaves anonymity and a broader scope for autonomous activity than they had, day in, day out, laboring in a gang under the eye and whip of overseer, bookkeeper, and driver. As a result, the markets served to loosen, both physically and psychologically, the bonds of servitude. The diurnal plantation regulations limited interplantation contact. Nocturnal mobility in part compensated for that, and planters repeatedly complained of the ramblings of slaves from plantation to plantation to visit friends and relatives at night. Apart from such night excursions and holiday visits, however, slaves from different plantations had few occasions for contact with one another. The weekly markets gave them the chance for closer contact with friends and kin. The laxity of regulation and of surveillance at market permitted them to indulge, with little restriction, in whatever activities they chose.

The slaves' attitudes to market day are evident in the way they prepared for it. Going to market was a reason for some to dress up in their Sunday best—clothes they had acquired by their own efforts (Figure 1). They not only put the plantation behind them physically but also divested themselves

---

37. "Characteristic Traits," *Columbian Magazine,* III (1797), 109. Included in the extensive body of anthropological work on this are Paul Bohannon and George Dalton, eds., *Markets in Africa* (Evanston, Ill., 1962); Thomas F. De Voe, *The Market Book: A History of the Public Markets of the City of New York* (1862; rpr. New York, 1970); Enrique Mayer, Sidney W. Mintz, and G. William Skinner, *Los campesinos y el mercado* (Lima, Peru, 1974); and Robert H. T. Smith, ed., *Market-Place Trade: Periodic Markets, Hawkers, and Traders in Africa, Asia, and Latin America* (Vancouver, 1978). Scottish literature provides the example of Tam O'Shanter:

> Frae November till October
> Ae market-day [he] was nae sober
>
> (Robert Burns, *The Complete Works*
> [Boston, 1863], 172)

of the identifiable accoutrements of slavery that their plantation garb constituted. Mathison stated that many of the slaves who went to market were "dressed in finery." Others of them, who either had no finery or were unwilling to wear it in going from plantation to provision grounds to market and back, wore work clothes.[38]

The behavior of slaves at market differed little from that of other rural populations in Africa, Europe, the Americas, and elsewhere. The slaves spent the early part of the day, a time of great bustle, acting as purveyors and purchasers. Mathison remarked on the noise of the loud and extended bargaining. In the later hours of the day, as the commercial activity wound down, social activities took over. Once the slaves had completed their transactions, they could spend time visiting with friends and perhaps using some of the money they had gained to buy food and drink in the nearby rum shops. "Many houses are kept for [the slaves'] entertainment," an observer noted, "where they have a meal of coarse bread, salted fish and butter, and a bowl of new rum and water for one ryal, which is about fivepence sterling."[39]

The fervor with which the planters condemned market-day drinking and socializing attests to its popularity among the slaves. Bickell complained that very often slaves spent the money they realized from selling provisions on "new destructive rum, which intoxicate[d] them, and drown[ed] for a short time, the reflections that they [were] despised and burthened slaves." He grumbled that "the drunkenness of some with the imprecations and obscenities of others put one in mind of a pandemonium." Dr. John Williamson, who practiced on a St. Thomas-in-the-Vale estate, owned by the Earl of Harewood, mentioned that market day was "concluded by scenes of excess and brutal debauchery." Another observer commented that, after the slaves sold their goods, they frequently went to "regale and debauch" themselves before returning to the plantation. Long also complained of the latter part of Sunday "being uselessly dissipated in idleness and lounging, or (what is worse) in riot, drunkenness, and wickedness."[40]

Gambling also occurred at the close of the market. The author of an anonymous article that appeared in a Kingston journal in 1797 asserted that

38. Mathison, *Notices*, 3.
39. "Characteristic Traits," *Columbian Magazine*, III (1797), 108.
40. Bickell, *The West Indies*, 66; *Negro Slavery; or, a View of Some of the More Prominent Features of that State of Society as it Exists in the United States of America and in the Colonies of the West Indies, especially in Jamaica* (London, 1823), 57; "Characteristic Traits," *Columbian Magazine*, III (1797), 170–71; Long, *The History of Jamaica*, II, 492.

male slaves were "addicted" to gambling and that many gambling houses in Kingston welcomed them. Because gaming houses were illegal in Jamaica, the proprietors had to take precautions, but apparently few were discovered or suppressed. Another option for slaves was to gamble in secluded open-air venues: Kingston's burial ground was one such place. The article's author noted that the slaves played a number of games, including not only cards and dice but also some of their own devising in which they bet sums of money against stolen goods.[41]

No doubt Bickell accurately perceived that slaves got drunk to drown their sorrows and, for the moment, put the realities of slavery behind them. In addition, though, the rum shops offered conversation and camaraderie in an atmosphere less readily found on the plantation.[42]

The whites viewed the slaves' comportment on market day with distaste and, in times of unrest on the island, with alarm. They recognized that large assemblies of slaves over whom there was little surveillance were a threat to their safety and to the security of the island. The slave rebellion of the Haitian Revolution in the early 1790s caused Jamaican planters to reconsider the security of the island. They were especially unhappy that the male slaves who attended market carried cutlasses and machetes. Since those work tools were also potential weapons, the decision was to deal with the problem head on, perhaps by confiscating or banning cutlasses, on the next market day. The slaves came to market that day, however, without their cutlasses, discomfiting the whites by demonstrating not only the bondsmen's unwillingness to be disarmed but also the rapid dissemination of information among them.[43]

Many of the activities proscribed on the plantation which the slaves could participate in at the weekly market depended on financial competence, that is, on the success of the slaves' trading efforts earlier in the day. Grog cost money, and it took money to gamble. "In this island," as Long pointed out, the slaves "have the greatest part of the small silver *circulating among them,* which they gain by sale of their hogs, poultry, fish, corn, fruits, and other commodities, at the markets in town and country." Those who had readiest access to the market and the greatest stock of commodities to offer stood to profit most. That meant that many were economically disadvantaged.[44]

Market sales were not, however, the only way that slaves accumulated money. Gifts, thefts, and gambling contributed to their assets.

41. "Characteristic Traits," *Columbian Magazine,* III (1797), 168–69.
42. Bickell, *The West Indies,* 66.
43. C.O. 137/90, Correspondence, Public Record Office.
44. Long, *The History of Jamaica,* II, 411 (my emphasis).

Money, sometimes in significant amounts, entered the slaves' internal economy as gifts and incentive payments from planters and their agents. A few slaves on Phillips' plantation received an "Xmas Box" containing a small sum of money. In December, 1788, twenty-one out of a slave population of about three hundred, all male, received cash gifts ranging from six shillings and eightpence to two shillings and sixpence. The following year, fifty-four slaves, both male and female, got from thirteen shillings and four-pence to one shilling and eightpence, the average gift being about five shillings. The presents probably went to privileged slaves: drivers, sugar boilers, distillers, craftsmen, perhaps domestics, and others in positions of influence and authority. But not all planters followed the practice of Phillips' estate. James Chisholme told the overseer on his Trouthall estate that he never gave slaves money at Christmas nor would he ever countenance doing so. His need to declare his opposition to the policy, of course, indicates its existence elsewhere.[45]

When planters distributed cash, they had the ulterior motive of influencing and rewarding slaves' behavior. Slaves received cash payments, for example, out of the planters' concern over slave fertility. The net natural decrease of the slave population greatly worried the owners. Especially when the abolition of the slave trade became a possibility and then a reality, they undertook expedients to increase births. Some began to pay incentives to mothers and medical attendants. In a letter to Lord Penrhyn, the attorney Rowland Fearon described the practice he employed on Penrhyn's plantations. "To encourage the Midwives to perform their duty with attention and ability," he explained, "every Child she brings me one Month old, as a reward, I give her 6/8 and the Mother of the infant 3/4 to buy the stranger a Fowl to commence its little stock in life." The concluding phrase is a telling one, confirming that for at least this representative of the plantocratic elite, the concept of property rights, all-important and all-pervasive within that group, extended to an autonomous realm for the slave population. The agent on Penrhyn's King's Valley estate followed a similar practice. "As soon as the Month is out [that is, when the baby is a month old]," he told Penrhyn, "every Mother comes to me with the Child, and I give her two dollars in Money, with some other little thing for the Child—I also give the Grandee, or Midwife, two dollars—for in this Country I have observed that a good deal depends upon her attention and good will—Since I took charge

---

45. Diaries, 1788, 1789, in Phillips Papers (MSS 9418, 9419); James Chisholme, Bath, to James Craggs, Vere, Jamaica, December 5, 1803, in Letterbook of James Chisholme, William and James Chisholme Papers (MS 5476), National Library of Scotland, Edinburgh.

of Kings Valley [two to three months ago] I have had the pleasure of paying two in this way, and I hope I may have many more—I also give the Mother two dollars when she weans the Child." Planters offered rewards for weaning children because of the slave women's abstinence from sexual relations, according to a practice widespread in West Africa, as long as their infant was breast-feeding. Taboos on intercourse while nursing, which in African societies spanned two to three years, functioned as a means of birth control by limiting the time women of childbearing age were at risk of pregnancy. The observance of the African practice on Jamaican sugar plantations, however, exacerbated that population's negative reproduction rate.[46]

The code of regulations that Mathison's overseers followed awarded the midwife ten shillings for every child she delivered who reached the age of one month. By that age, the child had survived the period of greatest vulnerability to tetanus, the principal cause of infant mortality.[47]

The private papers of Jamaican planters abound in similar references to bonuses in support of childbearing. Dickinson counseled his nephew Caleb to make "it in the Interest and Wealth of breeding Women to be particularly attentive to Nursing and breeding up their children." He desired "that the Breeding Women and Midwives [have] some pecuniary reward." The attorneys of Barham's sugar plantation in Westmoreland recommended "giving the Mothers something handsome" (a "couple of Doubloons"), and a year later mentioned that "every woman bringing up a Child, attended by the Midwife, commonly about the expiration of the Month receives 26/8 and . . . the Midwife of late receives the same sum of money."[48]

Inducements might also take the form of food, clothing, and other gifts. On Barham's plantations, as part of a vain attempt to check the net natural decrease of the slave population, the attorney's plan to give "encouragement to the Women in rearing their Children" made provision for "those mothers who are deserving to keep a Cow or two for the benefit of themselves and children—this can be done by my purchasing a Heifer for each instead of

46. Rowland W. Fearon, Clarendon, Jamaica, to Lord Penrhyn, January 26, 1805, David Ewart to Lord Penrhyn, August 6, 1807, both in Penrhyn Castle Papers (MSS 1361, 1477).

47. Mathison, *Notices*, 107–17.

48. Ezekiel Dickinson to Caleb Dickinson, May 6, 1786, in Papers of Caleb and Ezekiel Dickinson; J. C. Grant and J. R. Webb to J. F. Barham, August 11, 1810, J. R. Webb to J. F. Barham, September 14, 1811, both in Barham Papers; Herbert S. Klein and Stanley L. Engerman, "Fertility Differentials Between Slaves in the United States and the British West Indies: A Note on Lactation Practices," *William and Mary Quarterly*, XXXV (1978), 357–74.

giving them money, this I have suggested to them with which they are very well pleased—I have also indulged them in having the Stone wall rebuilt round their Houses for the benefit of their raising hogs."[49]

Less common than either Christmas presents or rewards to mothers of newborns and to midwives were premiums for having learned a trade and emoluments aimed at influencing the actions of newly purchased slaves. Dickinson, concerned by the high cost of hiring men who knew trades, recommended that his nephew recompense slaves for apprenticing to a craft on the plantation. He was aware of the "large payments made Barton Estate for Tradesmen's Labour," and pointed to the "great advantage arising from bringing up Young Slaves under experienced tradesmen either White or Black, which I recommend to your notice by giving them a yearly consideration for their encouragement."[50] Dickinson, who owned four plantations in St. Elizabeth Parish, also wanted to reward slaves who assisted in seasoning recent arrivals from Africa (called bozales), whom he had purchased to supplement the plantations' labor forces. The seasoning of bozales involved not only acclimatizing them to Jamaica's weather and disease environment but also acquainting them with the system of slavery and, the planters hoped, reconciling them to a life of bondage. In trying to achieve that, planters meted out punishments and rewards, and Dickinson emphasized as well the importance of the bozales' peer group, the slave community already on the plantation, in molding their behavior. A letter to his nephew intimated his displeasure with the socialization of previously purchased slaves and proposed to influence the new bozales by sending a trusted slave to the pen in the mountains where the newcomers underwent acclimatization. Dickinson recommended that the "trusty" should receive "some reward for his fidelity." Similar references elsewhere show that it was a common practice for planters to signify their approval or appreciation by small cash gifts. On Chisholme's Trouthall estate, for example, slaves received a three-dollar payment as an inducement to complete the construction of housing.[51]

Opportunities occurred on the plantation for slaves to sell their labor. Although planters purchased and held sole title to the slaves, there were limits to the quantity and quality of the time and labor they realized. Slaves on the Braco estate who lost their Negro days while doing plantation work

49. J. R. Webb to J. F. Barham, September 2, 1812, in Barham Papers.

50. Ezekiel Dickinson to Caleb Dickinson, November 23, 1784, in Papers of Caleb and Ezekiel Dickinson.

51. Ezekiel Dickinson to Caleb Dickinson, May 11, 1785, in Papers of Caleb and Ezekiel Dickinson; William Anderson, Trouthall Estate, to James Chisholme, March 9, 1811, in Chisholme Papers.

received compensatory time off (see above, p. 25), but on other estates they got cash payments. The accounts for Hugh Hamilton's plantations record payments "to the Negroes attending the [indigo] Vatts on a Sunday." Slaves could thus profit monetarily from the indigo making that was a sideline on the sugar plantation.[52]

Slaves also received cash awards from agencies off the plantation. The Consolidated Slave Acts mandated payments where slaves acted in the interests of the plantocracy. Slaves who caught runaways or assisted in their capture by supplying information got a bounty "not exceeding twenty shillings." Slaves who killed others of their number "in actual rebellion" received three pounds, and if they took the rebels alive, the reward was five pounds "and a blue cloth coat, with a red cross on the right shoulder."[53]

As in any economy, theft and other officially unlawful involvements provided a revenue source that was an alternative to regular work. Plantation records, an extensive body of published literature, and voluminous government records substantiate the widespread incidence of theft among the slave population. The prevailing philosophical and religious condemnation of theft was reflected in the codes and behavior of both the slave and nonslave communities. What is clearly seen in the laws of Jamaica and the weltanschauung of the plantocracy vis-à-vis theft may also be discovered in the ways of the slave community. Stewart made reference to various uses of obeah, an African-derived fetishistic religious belief credited with the capacity among other things to prevent or avenge crimes against a person whom its powers protected. Stewart noted that an obeah fetish placed in the gardens or grounds of slaves became an "excellent guard or watch, scaring away the predatory runaway and midnight plunderer with more effective terror than gins and spring-guns." Robert Renny, another Jamaican planter, corroborated Stewart's account. His *History of Jamaica* tells how slaves who had been robbed by members of their community went to the obeah men to discover the culprit. An aggrieved slave bought an obi—a compound of materials such as blood, feathers, parrots' beaks, dogs' teeth, alligators' teeth, broken bottles, grave dirt, rum, and eggshells—which when "stuck in the thatch, hung over the door of a hut, or up on the branch of a plantain tree," instilled such fear in the thief that he was certain to "tremble at the very sight of the ragged bundle, the bottle or the egg shells." Edwards too referred to the use of obeah to detect a thief among the slaves' fellows.[54]

52. Accounts, Hugh Hamilton and Company, Settled December 31, 1784, Indigo Account, in Hamilton of Pinmore Papers, Scottish Record Office, Edinburgh.

53. Edwards, *The History, Civil and Commercial,* II, 149–50.

54. John Stewart, *A View,* 278–79; Robert Renny, *An History of Jamaica* (London, 1807), 172; Edwards, *The History, Civil and Commercial,* II, 82.

But in certain circumstances theft was condoned. Neither the slave nor the nonslave community condemned it universally. This study is not concerned, though, with the grand larceny the plantocracy perpetrated, to paraphrase Eric Williams, in stealing Africans to work lands they had stolen from the Indians.[55] Among slaves, how theft was judged hinged on the status of the victim. Slaves on sugar plantations lived in a social system bifurcated into slave black and free white. The slaves condemned intragroup theft and condoned intergroup theft to the extent that the perpetrator was a member of the slave community. John Stewart's history of Jamaica mentioned the duality: "To pilfer from their masters they consider as no crime, though to rob a fellow slave is accounted heinous."[56]

The common slave attitude, according to Stewart, was, "What I take from my master, being for my use, who am his slave, or property, he loses nothing by its transfer." This rather glib rationale captured a kernel of the slaves' philosophy regarding such acts, insofar as their outlook condemned both the person and the institution responsible for depriving them of their liberty. What the owners deemed theft, therefore, should be viewed in part as resistance to the slaveholders and the system they embraced. But it carried the additional advantages of improving the perpetrators' diet and life-style and contributing to the growth of the internal economy.[57]

Undoubtedly slaves committed both intragroup and intergroup thefts, and the planters' records establish that the latter sort were widespread. Intragroup stealing would have been less fully documented. Through obeah, slaves had an internal authority structure to deal with crime, so much of the intragroup theft remained beyond the ken of whites. Nonetheless, evidence of intragroup theft exists. Edwards, Renny, and John Stewart referred to it, after all, in their descriptions of obeah. Their observations and similar testimonies by other planter-historians indicate that the slave gardens and the provision grounds were the most frequent targets when slaves stole from slaves. James Stewart, a planter in Trelawny, maintained that slaves would "steal the provisions of their neighbours at the time their own grounds yield abundance," and an anonymous article on the condition of slaves published in the *Quarterly Review* contended that improvident slaves subsisted by stealing from their "owner, neighbours, or fellow-slaves." Theft against other slaves could not be carried out with impunity, however. Slave grounds were sometimes protected by obeah fetishes and were often guarded by

55. Eric Williams, *Capitalism and Slavery* (London, 1944), 9.
56. John Stewart, *A View,* 249. On some plantations, a small number of free blacks and free coloreds may have been present.
57. *Ibid.*

members of the slave community. Beckford, though, held the caliber of slave policing in low esteem. He saw ailing, crippled, and superannuated slaves sent to watch the provision grounds. But some plantations were efficiently guarded. On Tydixton Park estate, "one of the Watchmen . . . named Watty" shot and killed a slave from Worthy Park, the neighboring estate, who was "in their Negroe grounds stealing provisions." A slave named Tom from Phillips' Pleasant Hill estate was killed on the nearby Winchester plantation "of a chop in the head received . . . in the act of stealing a hog." Since slaves raised most of this kind of livestock on the estate, it is likely that the hog Tom was stealing belonged to a fellow slave.[58]

The inference must be that if slave guards had guns, thefts from "Negroe grounds" were more than a minor annoyance. Nevertheless, even discounting for the planters' greater reporting of what they personally experienced, the frequency with which slaves committed intergroup theft seems to have been considerably greater than that of their involvement in intragroup stealing.

Planters constantly referred to slaves' propensity to steal. James Stewart and John Stewart used precisely the same phrase here: they maintained that the slaves were "addicted to theft." Renny viewed slaves as "thievish," and J. B. Moreton referred to them as "born thieves." Even the abolitionist Thomas Cooper asserted that they were "addicted to thieving," and the anonymous fictional piece *Marly; or, A Planter's Life in Jamaica* affirmed that "whenever you see a black face you see a thief." Extant court proceedings, such as those in the record book of the court of St. Ann Parish, bear witness to the widespread incidence of theft. There, robbery, along with running-away, assault, and arson, are the most frequently cited crimes.[59]

The preponderant evidence on the extent of stealing by slaves rests on the most impressionistic of the records left by the planters: their published

58. James Stewart, *A Brief Account of the Present State of the Negroes in Jamaica* (Bath, 1792), 18; "Condition of the Negroes in our Colonies," *Quarterly Review* (London), XXIX (1823), 489–90; Beckford, *Remarks,* 17; Increase and Decrease of Negroes, 1793, Worthy Park Plantation Book, 1791–1811, in Worthy Park Estate Records, 4/23-3, Jamaica Archives; Increase and Decrease of Slaves on Pleasant Hill, in Phillips Papers (MS 9502).

59. James Stewart, *A Brief Account,* 18; John Stewart, *A View,* 249; Renny, *An History of Jamaica,* 166; J. B. Moreton, *West India Customs and Manners* (London, 1793), 161; Thomas Cooper, *Facts Illustrative of the Condition of the Negro Slaves in Jamaica* (London, 1824), 17; *Marly; or, A Planter's Life in Jamaica* (Glasgow, 1828), 36; Record Book of the Court of the Parish of St. Ann, 1787–1814, Slave Court, MS 273, in Institute of Jamaica.

histories and recollections. From the consistency with which slaveholders throughout the Americas referred to the "thievery" of slaves, it would seem to have been endemic to the peculiar institution of black slavery. A different picture emerges, however, if the slaves' taking of their owners' property is viewed not as theft but as resistance to slavery, and as the appropriation and redistribution of illicitly accrued wealth. Slaves' clandestine stealing from the planter and plantation attacked the institution of slavery by diminishing its profitability to the slavocracy. The coerced labor of slaves created the wealth of the plantation, and the colony functioned to protect the system of forced labor. Jamaica's wealth, based on slave labor, went to those who coerced the work, not those who performed it. Thus, theft from planters by slaves represented a reallocation of wealth by those who created it. As a strategy of resistance, that had considerable advantages over other methods. Stealing was clandestine, it was relatively easily perpetrated, and it was difficult to prevent and to detect. It led not only to the diminution of the victim's wealth but also to the aggrandizement of the perpetrator's. As such it held practical benefits not present in other acts of resistance, like arson or the poisoning of livestock.

Not all surreptitious property transfers fell into the category of resistance, however, nor did their proceeds all enter the internal economy. Much of the appropriation of plantation goods reflected the desperation of deprived and hungry slaves. A series of statements by the attorney on Georgia estate to Gordon, the absentee owner, illustrated this. "We are making a little rum from the Molasses on hand, but they will yield very little," Francis Grant wrote Gordon in the autumn of 1781, "and the Negroes, impelled by hunger, have lessened the quantity considerably by frequently breaking into the Curing house. For sometime past they have had nothing to support them of their own." He continued, "I believe I shall be forced to cut canes sooner than I could wish to prevent their being destroyed by Negroes, for not only your own but your Neighbour's are making very free with them of late notwithstanding some of the best and [obscured] People belonging to you are watching them." A month later he attributed the low sugar yield "to the Negroes stealing the Canes which it was impossible wholly to prevent." Even into the next year he asserted that the harvest was slow because "the Canes were mostly destroyed by Negroes during the late Scarcity of Provisions."[60]

Slaves could suffer deprivation even during relatively good harvests. For

60. Francis Grant, Georgia Estate, to Charles Gordon of Cairness, near Fraserburgh, Scotland, August 27, 1781, September 23, 1781, January 23, 1782, all in Gordon of Buthlaw and Cairness Papers (6/14[2], 6/15[1], 6/21).

whatever reason, some slaves always needed supplies they could not provide for themselves. Their provision grounds may have failed, or they may have been unable to get their grounds planted or too sick to tend them. One solution was to appropriate supplies from the plantation, as the slaves on Gordon's Georgia estate did. Some planters showed concern over food shortages in the slave community. Mathison's regulations for his overseer directed that slaves who, for whatever reason, abandoned or neglected grounds be fed "abundantly" from the plantation store. Nevertheless, slaves elsewhere frequently suffered malnutrition and dietary deficiency. Any assessment of the impact of intergroup theft on the internal economy must be tempered by the recognition that not everything taken could enter the economy. Some stolen goods, particularly foodstuffs, were used directly to avert pain and starvation.[61]

But additionally, appropriations of plantation property contributed to the growth of the internal economy. According to *Marly,* slaves came up with the metaphor of the "Calibash Estate" for their depredations on the goods of the plantation. Slaves used calabashes as containers into which to divert quantities of the plantation's rum, sugar, and other output. To extend the metaphor, the capitalization of the Calibash Estate's property occurred at the weekly markets.[62]

Planters were at a disadvantage in their battle against unauthorized appropriations. Not only were whites tremendously outnumbered by slaves but in addition they could look for little assistance from anyone outside their own community in identifying who had taken missing belongings. Since the slave community for the most part sanctioned the abstraction of plantation property, it shielded slaves sought for theft. Gray, in a letter to his father from his plantation in St. James Parish, wrote that slaves "lately broke open my Fowl House and took away 12 Fowls. I have not found out the thief." Nor on a plantation with 171 closemouthed slaves and only a handful of whites, was it likely that he would. What is more likely is that when he stocked his larder with purchases from the market that week, he bought back his own chickens, perhaps neatly plucked and trussed.[63]

The principal defense of planters against thefts by slaves was vigilance, preferably by fellow whites. When supervision over slaves diminished, theft of the plantation's property rose proportionately. Nathaniel Phillips' over-

61. Mathison, *Notices,* 107–17.
62. *Marly,* 43.
63. Charles Gordon Gray to father, July 17, 1810, in MST 163, Institute of Jamaica.

seer, Thomas Barritt, bemoaned the continuance of martial law at the time of the Trelawny Maroon Rebellion, in 1795, which required military service by the white people of the plantation who normally supervised the harvest. "If this Military Duty should continue during Crop," Barritt complained, "we shall be much puzzled how to take [the canes] off, and there will be great pilfering going on, as we shall be obliged to trust much to the Negroes." Here was a clear recognition of how slaves regarded the plantation's property.[64]

The plantocracy, unable to protect their property, instituted punishments whose severity was intended to discourage theft. Slaves convicted received hard labor in the workhouse, and whipping. The records of the St. Ann Parish Slave Court show stipulated terms in the workhouse from a few days or months up to life for theft. A specified number of lashes—for example, thirty-nine each week for a set length of time—invariably accompanied the sentences. The *Columbian Magazine* recorded the proceedings against a slave, William Wynter, of Hampshire estate, in St. Thomas-in-the-Vale. Wynter was found guilty of breaking into the estate's stillhouse and stealing rum, and he was sentenced to two years at hard labor in the workhouse, with thirty-nine lashes every three months until the expiration of his term. Colonial Office documentation of slave trials includes the sentence of three months in the workhouse, with twenty-five to thirty-nine lashes on both arrival and departure, for receiving stolen coffee. Other sentences meted out imposed transportation off the island for stealing sheep and execution for stealing steers. In cases where slaves were transported or executed, the planter received in cash the valuation the court placed on the slave.[65]

But court trials were atypical; more often planters dealt directly with those who had been caught purloining the estate's property. Plantation justice invariably meant that the slave was whipped, and there could also be some form of detention. Slaves might be shackled and confined to the hothouse except for when they were taken to work in the fields.

The paucity of sources precludes an accurate assessment of the volume and profitability to the slave community of intergroup theft. Given its pervasiveness, one can reasonably infer that it made a significant contribution to the slaves' cash accumulation and, by extension, to the internal economy as a whole. Drawing on the efforts of tens of thousands of slaves, the theft-based Calibash Estate was one of the most lucrative operations on the island.

64. Thomas Barritt to Nathaniel Phillips, November 13, 1795, in Phillips Papers (MS 9210).

65. Record Book of the Court of the Parish of St. Ann, in Institute of Jamaica; *Columbian Magazine,* VII (1799), 126; C.O. 137/147, Trials of Slaves, July 1, 1814–June 30, 1818, Public Record Office.

Neither do the sources reveal which slaves took part in intergroup theft. Presumably not all slaves were prepared or motivated to accept the attendant risks. Such theft did affect the lives of a much larger group than just the slaves directly involved, however, since it was a substantial source of profit and had a corresponding impact on the internal economy.

All slaves living on plantations belonged to communities that had internal economies where cash was invariably one of the mediums of exchange. The internal economies affected more slaves than were involved in the Sunday markets. If those markets were the source of much of the revenue that fueled the internal economy, the plantation community was the base of much of its activity.

Edwards maintained that slave owners never interfered with the wealth accumulated by slaves at market or elsewhere—that those who had property or capital could dispose of it in any manner they thought fit. Through bartering and buying and selling at market, the slaves converted a large portion of their earnings and resources into consumer goods. Some of the profit accrued at market, however, returned with the slaves to the plantation as cash. Slaves spent that money at subsequent markets or on the plantation, or saved it.[66] Jamaican slaves based their plantation economies, in part, on that cash.

Slaves other than those directly involved in the market dimension of the internal economy were able to share in it by providing services and commodities on the plantation. The capture and sale of rats were a source of income. Rats infesting the cane fields caused extensive damage to the sugar crop. Planters either employed slaves as ratcatchers or offered a bounty for trapped rats. The bounty on some plantations was a "quantity of rum, proportioned to the number taken, which is known by the number of tails." The rest of the rat's body was also a marketable commodity, since slaves ate rat meat. One commentator claimed that the bounty for catching rats was unnecessary: "The animals themselves are sufficient inducement for taking them, as [the slaves] eat them with as much satisfaction as [planters] should some species of game." On the plantation of the novel *Marly,* the slave assigned to catching rats sold them to other slaves for food. Slaves, incidentally, nicknamed rats Sir Charles Price after a leading Jamaican planter. Plantation records contain few references to ratcatching and selling, and it is therefore difficult to determine their extent. If, however, slaves controlled the sale of the twenty rats a day caught by one slave on Gray's estate in St. James Parish, there was a lucrative potential.[67]

66. Edwards, *The History, Civil and Commercial,* II, 125.
67. "Characteristic Traits," *Columbian Magazine,* III (1797), 107; *Marly,* 46; Charles Gordon Gray to father, August 16, 1810, in MST 163, Institute of Jamaica.

Fishing, shrimping, and crabbing permitted slaves to improve their diet and earn some money. Alexander Barclay, a longtime Jamaican resident, remarked on the extensive participation of slaves in the capture and sale of land crabs, which "are caught by torch light at night, and put into covered baskets. Crowds of negroes from the neighbouring plantations pass my house every evening with their torches and baskets, going to a crab wood on the other side, and return before midnight fully laden." According to Barclay, a successful evening's crabbing could result in a fair profit. "Their baskets will contain about 40 crabs," he estimated, "and the regular price is a five-penny piece, our smallest coin, equal to about 3 1/2d. sterling, for five or six crabs. At this rate a negro will make 2s.6d. currency in an evening." Barclay mentioned that slaves whose provision grounds were unproductive relied on this as an alternative source of income. "The more improvident, who will not cultivate provision grounds, depend on some measure upon catching crabs, and selling them to the others. A hundred plantains usually sold at five shillings, will purchase from sixty to seventy crabs," he calculated, "and two of these, eaten with plantains or yams, make an excellent meal." Land crabs apparently formed a regular source of protein for slaves, since as Barclay explained, "Almost every negro family has an old flour barrel pierced with holes, in which their crabs are kept. They are fed with plantain skins, etc.; and taken out and thrown into the pot as wanted." Barclay noted too the various devices slaves used to catch shrimp and fresh- and saltwater fish. "At shell-blow," he observed, "numbers of the negroes are seen making traps or examining those they have got in the water." Here again slaves had the opportunity to sell their catch.[68]

Barclay also asserted that on the estate slaves bought and sold goods that had been purchased at market. Articles that slaves bought at Kingston market, Barclay said, were "regularly retailed in the plantation villages."[69]

When slaves attended community celebrations and festivities, they purchased food and drink from others who had prepared it. Moreton said in *West India Customs and Manners* that, on those occasions, such fare as "strong liquors" and dishes of swine, poultry, salt beef, pork, herrings, vegetables, and roasted rats were served in calabashes that sold at a bit and a half bit each.[70]

An anonymous article on the condition of slaves published in the *Quarterly Review* in 1823 affirmed that slaves who were "too improvident to cultivate their provisions" sometimes worked in the provision grounds of

68. Barclay, *A Practical View*, 324, 329.
69. *Ibid.*, 273.
70. Moreton, *West India Customs*, 155–56.

others and in return received a "small allowance for their present wants."
They were not involved in marketing and had no control over the grounds
or the crop but exchanged their labor for a share of the proceeds.[71]

Obeah involved the transfer of money. The value of the rare and obscure
components of the amulets, fetishes, and charms was compounded by the
magical qualities vested in them by the obeah practitioner. Hesketh Bell
mentioned in his post–Emancipation study of obeah in the West Indies that
"the most valuable of the sorcerer's stock, namely, seven bones belonging
to a rattlesnake's tail—these I have known sell for five dollars each, so
highly valued are they as amulets or charms." He went on to comment on
"how profitable was the trade of Obeah-man." A similar buying of charms
and fetishes must have existed on sugar plantations seventy or a hundred
years earlier.[72]

Reports relating to slave deaths offer further evidence of the vitality of the
internal economy. Both Edwards and Long said that slaves made bequests
of capital and property on their deaths. "They are permitted," Edwards
wrote, "to dispose at their deaths of what little property they possess: and
even to bequeath their grounds or gardens to such of their fellow-slaves as
they think proper." Long explained that

> the black grandfather, or father, directs in what manner his money,
> his hogs, poultry, furniture, cloaths, and other effects and acquisi-
> tions, shall descend, or be disposed of, after his decease. He nominates
> a sort of trustees, or executors, from the nearest of kin, who distribute
> them among the legatees, according to the will of the testator, without
> any molestation or interruption, most often without the enquiry, of
> their master; though some of these Negroes have been known to pos-
> sess from 50 l to 200 l at their death; and few among them, that are at
> all industrious and frugal, lay up less than 20 or 30 l. For in this island
> they have the greatest part of the small silver circulating among them,
> which they gain by sale of their hogs, poultry, fish, corn, fruits, and
> other commodities, at the markets in town and country.[73]

John Stewart's *View of the Past and Present State of the Island of Jamaica*
offered evidence from burial ceremonies that slaves incurred financial debts:

71. "Condition of the Negroes," *Quarterly Review*, XXIX (1823), 489–90.
72. Hesketh J. Bell, *Obeah: Witchcraft in the West Indies* (1889; rpr. New York, 1970), 16.
73. Edwards, *The History, Civil and Commercial*, II, 125; Long, *The History of Jamaica*, II, 410–11.

Previous to the interment of the corpse it is sometimes pretended that it is endowed with the gift of speech; and the friends and relatives alternately place their ears to the lid of the coffin, to hear what the deceased has to say. This generally consists of complaints and upbraidings for various injuries, —treachery, ingratitude, injustice, slander, and, in particular, the non-payment of debts due to the deceased. This last complaint is sometimes shown by the deceased in a more *cogent* way than by mere words; for on coming opposite the door of the negro debtor, the coffin makes a full stop, and no persuasion nor strength can induce the deceased to go forward peaceably to his grave till the money is paid; so that the unhappy debtor has no alternative but to comply with this demand, or have his creditor palmed upon him, as a lodger, for some time.[74]

The internal economies were fluid, as Long made clear in referring to the rapid circulation of small currency "in the retail branch of internal commerce." Slaves were less likely to accumulate significant savings than they were to spend what they had earned. Some slaves saved enough to purchase their freedom, but typically these were not plantation slaves, or if they were, they held positions of privilege on the plantation—as skilled workers, domestics, and the like. The engagement of most plantation slaves in the internal economy was on a smaller scale. Agricultural pursuits epitomized the pattern, involving nothing more than a variety of staples suitable for consumption and sale, and a few head of small livestock. Slaves spent most of their money more or less as it was earned, on clothing, food, furniture, tobacco, and other consumer goods. Orlando Patterson contends that "very few [Jamaican] slaves managed to save anything," and Long correctly indicated the atypicality of slaves who left fifty to two hundred pounds at their death. He overstated the reality, however, in asserting that bequests of twenty to thirty pounds were the norm.[75]

74. John Stewart, *A View*, 275–76.
75. Long, *The History of Jamaica*, I, 573, II, 410–11; Orlando Patterson, *The Sociology of Slavery: An Analysis of the Origins, Development, and Structure of Negro Slave Society in Jamaica* (London, 1967), 229.

2

THE SLAVES' ECONOMY IN LOUISIANA

The internal economies of Louisiana estates, in which slaves accumulated and disposed of money and property, showed the same vitality as those developed by Jamaican slaves. In both plantation societies, the internal economy was central to slave family and community life. Louisiana law, however, offered no protection to slaves participating in the internal economy; local statutes, like those in Jamaica, gave planters extensive power over slaves.

As in Jamaica, the modus vivendi on Louisiana sugar estates was not defined solely by the power of the planters. Slaves exercised power by affecting productivity. Although they risked punishment, they applied what control they had to the processes of production, withholding their labor or laboring less efficiently—or more specifically, running away, malingering, working slowly, feigning sickness, ignoring orders or responsibility, and sabotaging crops, tools, and livestock. They thereby got planters to concede better working conditions and more adequate clothing, food, and shelter. The slaves of Louisiana's sugar plantations sought protection for their economic activities and secured as a customary right the opportunity, during time off from plantation labor, to work on their own, to market the fruits of their labor, and to keep the proceeds. Their internal economy expanded steadily until the Civil War.

Louisiana slaves, like their Jamaican counterparts, controlled the use of some land on and around the plantation, where they raised livestock and grew crops for their personal consumption and sale. Although the staple of Louisiana's slaves was corn rather than plantain, they held and cultivated the land similarly to the slaves of Jamaica.

In the slave villages of Louisiana estates, land surrounded the houses, so that the occupants could have kitchen gardens and keep some livestock. Travelers sometimes commented on the gardens. "In the rear of each cottage, surrounded by a rude fence," Thomas Bangs Thorpe wrote in 1853, "you find a garden in more or less order, according to the industrious habits of the proprietor. In all you notice that the 'chicken-house' seems to be in excellent condition." William Howard Russell, a correspondent for the London *Times,* included a description of a slave village on a Louisiana sugar plantation in his *Diary North and South.* He mentioned the "ground round the huts . . . amidst which pigs and poultry were recreating" and added that "the negroes rear domestic birds of all kinds." On another plantation, Russell noted that "behind each hut are rude poultry hutches, which, with geese, turkeys and a few pigs form the perquisites of the slaves." A former slave, Elizabeth Ross Hite, confirmed the travelers' accounts: "We had a garden right in front of our quarter. We planted ev'rything in it. Had watermelon, mushmelon, and a flower garden." Similarly, the former slave Catherine Cornelius remembered the "garden patch, wid mustard greens, cabbage, chickens too."[1]

Louisiana slaves put their kitchen gardens to diverse uses, raising a variety of fruits and vegetables, and small livestock, especially poultry and hogs. The close proximity of the gardens to the slave village meant that slaves could work them at odd times through the week as Jamaican slaves worked their shell-blow grounds—during the midday break and in the evenings. Moreover, elderly slaves, who did little plantation work and spent most of their time in the quarters, labored in the kitchen gardens. One former slave recalled that her grandmother did not go to work in the fields but "would tend to the lil patch of corn, raise chickens, and do all the work around the house."[2]

Besides kitchen gardens, slaves had more extensive allotments of land

1. Thomas Bangs Thorpe, "Sugar and the Sugar Region of Louisiana," *Harper's New Monthly Magazine* (New York), VII (1853), 753; William Howard Russell, *My Diary North and South* (London, 1863), 371, 396; Elizabeth Ross Hite, interviewed by Robert McKinney, *ca.* 1940, under auspices of the Slave Narrative Collection Project, Federal Writers' Project, Works Progress Administration, in Louisiana Writers' Project File, Louisiana State Library, Baton Rouge; Catherine Cornelius, interviewed by Octave Lilly, Jr., *ca.* 1939, under auspices of Slave Narrative Collection Project organized by Dillard University using only black interviewers (a project that developed alongside the Federal Writers' Project), in Marcus Bruce Christian Collection, Department of Archives and Manuscripts, Earl K. Long Library, University of New Orleans.

2. Melinda [last name unknown], interviewed by Arguedas, *ca.* 1940, in Federal Writers' Project Interviews, Federal Writers' Project Files, Melrose Collection, Archives Division, Northwestern State University of Louisiana Libraries.

elsewhere on the plantation. There they generally cultivated a cash crop, most commonly corn. Some of the crops raised in the kitchen garden were eaten at the slaves' table, but most crops in their provision grounds, commonly known as "Negro grounds," were sold. In addition to corn, they grew other market staples like pumpkins, potatoes, and hay. Usually located on the periphery of the plantation, beyond the land in sugar, the Negro grounds were less accessible than the kitchen gardens. On Houmas estate, an Ascension Parish sugar plantation belonging to John Burnside, it was "on the borders of the forest" that the slaves "plant[ed] corn for their own use."[3]

Distance kept the slaves from working their Negro grounds during the workweek. Only on weekends—primarily on Sunday, but also sometimes for part of Saturday—when slaves did no work for the plantation, were they able to tend those more distant fields. At the sugar harvest, when there was an attempt to gather the crop as swiftly as possible to avoid the dangers of frost, the slaves worked every day without respite, but they sometimes got days off at the end of the harvest equal to the number of Sundays worked. The plantation journal for Elu Landry's estate in 1849 recorded that, after completion of the sugar harvest on November 20, slaves had the following three days off in compensation for the Sundays they had worked.[4] Out of harvest, the slaves had Sundays to work in their grounds, and on some plantations they got additional time off. On a sugar plantation that Russell visited, the slaves had "from noon on Saturday till dawn on Monday morning to do as they please." But on other plantations, the slaves did regular plantation labor for six days and some light work for part of Sunday. Hite recalled that "de Sunday wurk was light. Dey would only pull shucks of corn." On Sunday, the work usually addressed a specific task, after which the slaves had the rest of the day to themselves. Entries in the plantation journal for Samuel McCutcheon's Ormond estate, in St. Charles Parish, recorded that on Sunday, August 5, 1838, the slaves worked shelling corn and gathering fodder till 10 A.M.; on September 23, the men branded oxen and the women made hay until noon; and a month later, on October 28, the slaves shelled corn until 8 A.M. On each occasion the slaves had the rest of the day off. Cornelius recalled a similar arrangement on Dr. William Lyle's Smithfield plantation, in West Baton Rouge Parish. On that estate, the task work was on Saturday; the slaves invariably had Sunday off except during the harvest: "Dat [Saturday] was de day fo' ourselves," Cornelius explained.

3. Russell, *My Diary,* 399.
4. Elu Landry Estate Plantation Diary and Ledger, in Department of Archives and Manuscripts, Louisiana State University Libraries.

"We all had certain tasks to do. If we finished dem ahead of time, de rest of de day was ours."[5]

The slaves also spent some time during the annual holiday periods working for themselves. Holidays usually came at Christmas and New Year's—although they could be delayed by a late harvest—as well as at the end of planting, when the crop was laid by in midsummer, and immediately prior to the harvest. The holiday before the harvest was particularly important to the slaves, since it allowed them to bring in their own crops before laboring full-time cutting and grinding cane. On Isaac Erwin's Shady Grove plantation, two days of holiday—September 28 and 29—were allowed before the sugar harvest began on October 1, 1849. The slaves devoted those days to "diging their Potatoes & Pinders." On Valcour Aime's plantation in St. James Parish the slaves had a "free day to dig their potatoes" just preceding the sugar harvest of 1851.[6]

The slaves practiced a diversified system of agriculture in their provision grounds. Some land was put into pumpkins, which sold for one to two cents each. On Benjamin Tureaud's estate, a slave named Big Mathilda received ten dollars for the seven hundred pumpkins she sold to the plantation in 1858; slave accounts for the Gay plantation, in Iberville Parish, show that in 1844 seven of the seventy-four slaves recompensed by the plantation for goods and services derived part of their earnings from the sale of pumpkins at two cents apiece. In the previous year, the plantation's record book includes an entry for "Pumpkins 4000 bought of our Negroes . . . $80."[7] Slaves also raised potatoes, and their hay crops found a ready market on the plantation. In 1844, the proportion of the Gay plantation slaves selling hay to the estate was about the same as that selling pumpkins. The retail price of the hay stood at three dollars a load. A year before, the total crop of hay sold by the slaves on the Gay estate was ten loads (three thousand pounds), for which they received thirty dollars, or one cent per pound.[8] Still, all of the other crops were of lesser consequence than corn. Corn was the most

5. Russell, *My Diary,* 399; Hite interview; Plantation Diary, Volume I, 1838–1840, in Samuel McCutcheon Papers, Department of Archives and Manuscripts, LSU Libraries; Cornelius interview.

6. Isaac Erwin Diary, in Department of Archives and Manuscripts, LSU Libraries; Plantation Diary of Valcour Aime, in Louisiana Historical Center, Louisiana State Museum, New Orleans.

7. Ledger, 1858–1872, in Benjamin Tureaud Papers, Department of Archives and Manuscripts, LSU Libraries; Daybook, 1843–1847 (Vol. V), in Edward J. Gay and Family Papers, *ibid.*

8. Plantation Diary of Valcour Aime; Daybook, 1843–1847 (Vol. V), in Gay Papers.

lucrative sector of the internal economy of the Louisiana sugar plantation slaves, and its growth and retailing occupied the largest proportion of the slave population. Plantation records abound with references to slaves growing corn in their grounds and selling it, primarily to the plantation, but often elsewhere.

Both slaves and planters benefited from retailing corn within the confines of the plantation. By selling to the plantation, slaves could avoid the expense and effort of shipping and marketing their crop; the planters were saved the fees they would otherwise have had to pay an agent. Cornmeal, along with meat, constituted the standard slave rations, and thus the planters had a constant need for the corn raised on their estates. When the slaves marketed their crop off the plantation, they sometimes used the estate's transportation. Elu Landry recorded in his plantation diary for October 7, 1849, that he "gave [the slaves] permission & pass to sell their corn in the neighborhood—lent them teams for that purpose." In 1859, slaves on the estate of Mr. Ventress, a sugar planter of Bayou Goula, sold their crop of 1,011 barrels of corn to John H. Randolph, of Nottoway estate, and received a cash payment of $758 (seventy-five cents a barrel).[9]

On the plantation, the purchase price of corn ranged from 37.5 cents to 75 cents a barrel. Slaves on George Lanaux' Bellevue estate received the top price of 75 cents a barrel for the corn they harvested in 1851 and 1852, as did twenty slaves on William T. Palfrey's Ricohoc estate, who sold 275 barrels to the plantation in 1861 at "6 bits" each. Through the 1830s, slaves on Lewis Stirling's Wakefield and Solitude estates, both located on Bayou Goula, in West Feliciana Parish, sold their corn at 62.5 cents ("5 bits") a barrel, except in 1831. A successful crop in 1830 realized $189.565 for the 306 barrels grown by thirty-seven slaves on the Solitude estate, but the 1831 crop yielded only 109.25 barrels for the twenty-two slaves involved, and sold for only 31.25 cents a barrel. A note appended to the account explained the drop in price: "I allow but 2 1/2 bits a barrel for Corn this year because there was a great deal of rotten corn amongst it." In subsequent harvests, however, the price rose again to five bits: in 1838, forty-nine slaves on the two estates owned by Stirling sold a total of 621 barrels at this price, realizing $388.13. Through the 1850s, corn sold for 50 cents a barrel at Nottoway estate, and slaves regularly harvested a crop totaling 200 to 300 barrels. Slaves on the Gay family's plantation received 50 cents a barrel for their corn in 1844; a year before, they had sold their crop of 900 bushels for $375.00,

9. Landry Estate Plantation Diary and Ledger; Plantation Book, 1853–1863 (Vol. VI), in John H. Randolph Papers, Department of Archives and Manuscripts, LSU Libraries.

or 41.5 cents per bushel. In the years from 1857 to 1859, the price that slaves received for their corn on Stirling's Wakefield estate stood at 50 cents a barrel: they harvested 384.5 barrels in 1857, 322.25 barrels in 1858, and 456 barrels in 1859. The price was 12.5 cents above what a barrel commanded in 1856. The price fluctuation is unexplained in the sources but likely resulted from conditions beyond the plantation, in the regional corn market.[10]

The prices slaves received on the plantation were somewhat below the commodity's market price in New Orleans, where from 1847 through 1860 the cost per barrel fluctuated between 45 cents and $1.40. Shipping, handling, and commission charges could account for the price differential; the plantation price would be the equivalent of a local market price. The large fluctuations on the New Orleans market during these fourteen years stemmed partly from the lack of an organized retail market for corn. The crop was grown throughout the sugar region, and most growers sought to be self-sufficient while giving little thought to retailing their surplus as a cash crop. Sam Bowers Hilliard has pointed out that the retail trade in corn was local in nature, with prices fluctuating significantly when a bad harvest created strong local demands. Moreover, the undeveloped market probably accounted for part of the variation in what the plantations paid their slaves.[11]

The slaves sometimes managed to obtain indemnification when their crops were lost or damaged. The accounts for Stirling's Wakefield estate record that in 1859 twelve slaves "lost all their corn," a total of forty-seven

10. Journal, 1851–1860 (Vol. XIV), in George Lanaux and Family Papers, Department of Archives and Manuscripts, LSU Libraries; Plantation Diary, 1860–1868, 1895 (Vol. XVIII), in William T. and George D. Palfrey Account Books, *ibid.;* Ration Book, 1828, 1830–1838 (H-13), in Lewis Stirling and Family Papers, *ibid.;* Plantation Book, 1853–1863 (Vol. VI), in Randolph Papers; Daybook, 1843–1847 (Vol. V), Estate Record Book, 1842–1847 (Vol. XII), both in Gay Papers; "Negroes Corn for 1857," in Box 9, Folder 54, Stirling Papers; "Negroes Corn Sept. 18, 1858," in Box 9, Folder 56, Stirling Papers; "Negroes Corn 1859," in Box 9, Folder 57, Stirling Papers; "Negroes Corn [1856]," in Box 8, Folder 52, Stirling Papers; "List of the Negro Corn [1852]," in Box 7, Folder 44, Stirling Papers.

11. The average price per barrel of corn sold in New Orleans was $1.10 in 1847; $0.60 in 1848; $0.45 in 1849; $0.90 in 1850; $0.90 in 1851; $0.70 in 1852; $0.75 in 1853; $0.90 in 1854; $1.40 in 1855; $0.80 in 1856; $1.25 in 1857; $0.50 in 1858; $1.00 in 1859; and $1.00 in 1860, according to *De Bow's Review,* IV (1847), 393, VI (1848), 436, VII (1849), 420, IX (1850), 456, XI (1851), 496, XIII (1852), 512, XV (1853), 528, XVII (1854), 530, XIX (1855), 458, XXI (1856), 368, XXIII (1857), 365, XXV (1858), 469, XXVII (1859), 477, and XXIX (1860), 521. See also Sam Bowers Hilliard, *Hog Meat and Hoecake: Food Supply in the Old South* (Carbondale, Ill., 1972), 155.

barrels. They were, however, compensated by the planter at the full price of fifty cents a barrel. Two years earlier, six slaves had "lost their corn by the hogs" but received payment of twenty-two dollars. The records do not reveal the grounds for the planters' making good the lost or damaged crops. Their willingness, however, shows the extent to which planters would go to ensure their slaves' continued involvement in private agriculture.[12]

The slaves had to devote the greatest amount of their free time to the corn crop when planting in spring and harvesting in the fall. Sometimes, particularly during the harvest, they secured additional time off from the regular plantation schedule in order to take in the corn and market it. The hectic corn harvest immediately preceded the sugar harvest. On Duncan Kenner's Ashland plantation, slaves on Sunday, October 10, 1852, "gathered their corn, made a large crop." Two days later, on Tuesday, "all but a few hands went to Donaldsonville," a nearby town, presumably to market their crop or, if they sold it to the plantation, to spend their earnings. The next day, the sugar harvest began. From October 13 until the journal ended, on December 31, the slaves worked at the sugar harvest every day, including Sundays and Christmas.[13]

Poultry and hogs, the livestock most commonly raised by the slaves, found their principal market on the plantation, although river traders were also buyers and the slaves sometimes sold at the town markets. Few travelers failed to comment on the proclivity of slaves to keep poultry. Descriptions of slave villages on Louisiana sugar plantations usually mention the chickens, ducks, turkeys, and geese ranging through the quarters.[14] Raising poultry was ideally suited to the economy of the slave community, since fowl needed little attention and the eggs could generate income until the birds were ready to sell. Except, perhaps, for the initial expense of buying fledglings, raising poultry required minimal capital outlay while providing a steady income. The prices paid by planters for fowl varied little throughout the period of the sugar boom. Chickens sold at anywhere from 10 cents to 25 cents each, and the price of eggs was from 12.5 cents to 15 cents a dozen. On Colonel W. W. Pugh's Woodlawn plantation, in Assumption Parish, muscovy ducks fetched 37.5 cents each in the early 1850s.[15]

12. "Negroes Corn for 1857"; "Negroes Corn 1859."

13. Ashland Plantation Record Book, in Department of Archives and Manuscripts, LSU Libraries.

14. Thorpe, "Sugar and the Sugar Region," 753; Russell, *My Diary,* 373.

15. Thomas Haley (overseer), Grande Cote, to Mary Weeks, New Iberia, April 11, 1841, in Box 9, Folder 29, David Weeks and Family Papers, Department of

Ellen McCollam, who with her husband, Andrew, owned a small sugar plantation in Assumption Parish, listed in her diary her transactions with slaves. "I bought all their chickens in the Quarters," she noted in August, 1847. "From Little Jack 5 for 2 bits, 5 for 4 bits and 4 hens one dollar, Molly 3 hens 6 bits 1 pullet 20 cents, Barrel 1 hen 2 bits 3 little chickens 15 cents—Big Isaac 2 hens 4 bits 1 chicken 5 cents little Isaac 9 young chickens 10 cents a piece and one rooster 11 cents Mary one pullet 20." Somewhat over a year later she recorded that she "bought of little Isaac 5 hens 2 roosters [and] a little chicken [for] $1.00." [16]

Judging from a scene Russell witnessed, slaves in their dealings with planters over poultry showed the trading acumen of independent retailers. "An avenue of trees runs down the negro street," he observed when visiting Burnside's Houmas plantation, in Ascension Parish, "and behind each hut are rude poultry hutches, which, with the geese and turkeys and a few pigs, form the perquisites of the slaves." When slaves transacted business, Russell continued, "their terms are strictly cash." He narrated a transaction he witnessed while in the company of Burnside:

> An old negro brought up some ducks to Mr. Burnside and offered the lot of six for three dollars. "Very well, Louis; if you come tomorrow, I'll pay you." "No massa, me want de money now." "But won't you give me credit, Louis? Don't you think I'll pay the three dollars?" "Oh, pay some day, massa, sure enough. Massa good to pay de tree dollar; but this nigger want money now to buy food and things for him leetle family. They will trust massa at Donaldsonville, but they won't trust this nigger." I was told that a thrifty negro will sometimes make ten or twelve pounds a year from his corn or poultry. [17]

This slave knew both the value of his commodity and the terms he wanted for the transaction. Indeed, Louis did not hesitate to contradict the planter in the course of the negotiations. Although he had a market for his goods on the plantation, he apparently planned to spend his proceeds off the estate,

---

Archives and Manuscripts, LSU Libraries; Notebook, 1853–1857 (Vol. IX), in David Weeks and Family Papers—The Weeks Hall Memorial Collection, *ibid.;* Daybook, 1843–1847 (Vol. V), in Gay Papers; Ledger, 1851–1856 (Volume XVIII), in Lanaux Papers; Cashbook for Negroes, 1848–1855 (Volume VI), in Col. W. W. Pugh Papers, Department of Archives and Manuscripts, LSU Libraries.

16. Diary and Plantation Record of Ellen E. McCollam, in Andrew and Ellen E. McCollam Papers, Department of Archives and Manuscripts, LSU Libraries.

17. Russell, *My Diary,* 396.

in Donaldsonville, where he must have traded before, given his familiarity with the merchants' attitudes. Burnside was to have no influence in determining how Louis spent his money.

Other livestock brought much more than the fowl. In 1845, on the Gay family's estate, the selling price for a breeding sow stood at three dollars.[18]

Technological developments in the sugar industry gave Louisiana slaves an opportunity to earn money that Jamaican slaves did not have. Mechanization of the grinding and milling of sugar allowed Louisiana planters a higher yield and made possible larger harvests than the water-, wind-, or animal-powered mills in late-eighteenth- and early-nineteenth-century Jamaica could process. The machines used in Louisiana, however, required fuel—almost without exception huge quantities of locally gathered wood. Experiments with imported coal and sugarcane from which the juice had been extracted—trash or bagasse—usually proved unsuccessful: there was the expense of coal, and the technological development of the bagasse burner proceeded slowly.[19]

Wood collecting was tedious, unpleasant work. The wood had to be taken from swamps and bayous abutting the riverfront plantations. The slaves either worked from flatboats or had to stand in the water for long periods. The wood they cut was floated or boated out. Invariably, only men did the work, which was well paying. In 1849, slaves who cut wood on Stirling's plantations received six bits, or seventy-five cents, per cord; three years before, slaves on Uncle Sam estate, in St. James Parish, got fifty cents a cord. The price paid on Uncle Sam plantation remained constant through the rest of the antebellum period: a journal entry for October 25, 1859, read, "Payé aux nègres pour 2018 Cordes Bois—$1009.25," and in the fall of 1861, 61 of the 130 slaves on the plantation cut 1,598 cords of wood and received $799. In 1861, the greatest amount of wood cut by one slave was eighty cords, and the least was three cords. The majority of the sixty-one slaves cut between fifteen and forty cords. The Gay estate, in Iberville Parish, also paid slaves fifty cents a cord for cut wood, as did Colonel Pugh at Woodlawn plantation in the years 1848–1855; throughout the 1850s, Lanaux paid sixty cents a cord to slaves at his Bellevue estate.[20]

18. Daybook, 1843–1847 (Vol. V), in Gay Papers.

19. Plantation Diary, 1842–1859, 1867 (Vol. XVII), in Palfrey Account Books. In 1842, 225 barrels of "Pittsburg Coal," costing ninety dollars, were purchased for the Gay family's sugar estate (Box 11, Folder 81, in Gay Papers).

20. Box 7, Folder 39, in Stirling Papers; Box 1, in Uncle Sam Plantation Papers, Department of Archives and Manuscripts, LSU Libraries; Joseph K. Menn, *The Large Slaveholders of Louisiana, 1860* (New Orleans, 1964), 353–54; Plantation Rec-

In 1853, slaves on the Stirling family's plantation harvested 306 acres of cane, which yielded 533 hogsheads of sugar, 953 barrels of molasses, and 59 barrels of cistern sugar. In processing the crop, the sugar house burned 1,350 cords of wood. The following year, the crop of 500 hogsheads of sugar, 833 barrels of molasses, and 44 barrels of cistern sugar required 1,125 cords of wood. William T. Palfrey's sugar mill was much less efficient than the Stirling plantation's. In the harvest of 1857, Palfrey ran out of wood, with eleven arpents of cane still to be ground, after the mill "used at least 1800 cords of wood" to make around 440 hogsheads of sugar. In the following year, after the "bagasse burner proved a failure," he used 1,520 cords of wood to make 385 hogsheads of sugar but still had 130 arpents to grind. He had to buy an additional 253.5 cords at four dollars a cord from his son in order to complete the harvest.[21] The overall magnitude of the wood requirements for Louisiana plantations can be estimated from the need of two to four cords of wood to make one hogshead of sugar and the knowledge that twice in the decade preceding the outbreak of the Civil War the sugar crop topped 400,000 hogsheads. Although wood collecting was part of the plantation routine, it proved insufficient to the estates' needs. But contracting for wood off the plantation, as Palfrey found out in 1858, was an expensive proposition.[22] Slaves consequently could spend their days off in the summertime and the early fall collecting wood and selling it to the planter. That still let them tend and weed their own crops in the spring. By summer the provision-ground crops had grown high enough to be laid by and left until harvest. By gathering wood, the slaves let the planters effectively and efficiently supplement their fuel supply and at the same time earned substantial money.

Planters paid a below-market price—fifty or sixty cents per cord. On the other hand, the slaves used the plantation's axes and saws and had access to the estate's flatboats, work animals, and tackle for bringing the wood out of the swamp and back to the mill. Moreover, the planters owned the land and held title to the felled trees.[23]

Planters also paid slaves to dig ditches. Sugar estates needed a well-maintained irrigation system because of the topography of that region of

ord Book, 1849–1860 (Vol. XXXVI), in Gay Papers; Journal, 1851–1860 (Volume XIV), in Lanaux Papers.

21. Plantation Diary, 1851–1863, in Stirling Papers; Plantation Diary, 1842–1859, 1867 (Vol. XVII), in Palfrey Account Books.

22. L. Bouchereau, "Statements of the Sugar and Rice Crops Made in Louisiana" (New Orleans, 1871), in Box 1, Folder 1, UU-211, No. 555, Pharr Family Papers, Department of Archives and Manuscripts, LSU Libraries.

23. Plantation Diary, 1842–1859, 1867 (Vol. XVII), in Palfrey Account Books.

Louisiana and its proximity to the Mississippi River. As with woodcutting, the amount of ditching done as part of the plantation labor routine proved insufficient to the estates' needs, and planters often contracted ditchers—gangs of slaves hired from an outside agent (so-called jobbing slaves) or free white, often Irish, wage laborers. Many planters, either as an alternative or in addition, were willing to pay slaves on the plantation for any ditching they chose to do on their time off.

The amount paid slaves for this work varied according to the kind of ditches dug, as frequent citations in plantation records confirm. For example, on Kenner's plantation, slaves got three dollars per acre for digging a ditch six feet deep, while the pay for ditches one to two feet deep went from fifty cents to a dollar an acre. The records of Colonel Pugh's Woodlawn plantation show that digging 344 yards of "cross-ditching" earned the slaves $5.50.[24]

Wood cutting and ditching were the most arduous paid work slaves did for the plantation. But plantation records abound also with lists of other kinds of jobs the slaves did in their spare time for which they received pay. On Colonel Pugh's estate, making shingles earned $3.00 per thousand, staves paid $5.00 per thousand, pickets $1.25 per hundred, and boards 2.5 cents per four-foot length. Pugh bought slave-made shuck collars for 37.5 cents each and hogsheads for 75 cents each. Hauling wood paid 75 cents a day, since driving a cart was light work. Slaves who wanted to do regular work for the plantation on Sundays or holidays got from $1.00 to $1.25—which, incidentally, matched the cost of jobbing slaves.[25]

Jobs on the Gay family's sugar estate that slaves could do for pay in their time off from plantation labor included sugar potting, making hogsheads and barrels at $2 each, fixing and firing kettles, collecting fodder for 1 cent per bundle, making iron hoops, mending shoes at 12.5 cents a pair, counting hoop poles for 50 cents a day, and serving as watchmen at $1 a month. Skilled slaves were paid for their services during the sugar harvest. In the mid-1840s the sugar maker received $30, while his deputy got $15; the chief engineer and the kettle setter each got $10. The firemen, kettle tenders, and the second engineer all got $5 for their work during the harvest season.[26]

24. Diary, 1847 (Vol. I), in Kenner Family Papers, Department of Archives and Manuscripts, LSU Libraries; Plantation Record Book, 1849–1860 (Vol. XXXVI), in Gay Papers; Cashbook for Negroes, 1848–1855 (Vol. VI), in W. W. Pugh Papers.

25. Cashbook for Negroes, 1848–1855 (Vol. VI), in W. W. Pugh Papers; Plantation Record Book, 1849–1860 (Vol. XXXVI), in Gay Papers.

26. Daybook, 1843–1847 (Vol. V), Plantation Record Book, 1849–1860 (Vol. XXXVI), both in Gay Papers; "Memorandum relative to payments to negroes Dec. 1844," in Box 11, Folder 81, *ibid*.

Tureaud paid slaves on his estate for such work as making bricks, hogsheads, shuck collars, and baskets; on the Wilton plantation, in St. James Parish, estate accounts catalog cash payments to slaves for ditching, "levying," and making rails and handbarrows.[27] Skilled slaves had an especially wide range of opportunities for independent work. Slave carpenters, coopers, and blacksmiths could use their training for their own profit and undertake large-scale lucrative projects. On the Gay family's plantation, a slave named Thornton got $20 for making a cart.[28]

On some estates, the slave artisans did piecework, whereby each worker had to produce a specific number of items. On Nottoway plantation, on Bayou Goula, coopers received cash payments for producing more than an agreed-upon number of barrels. In December, 1857, a cooper, Henry, received a payment of $19.50 for making twenty-six barrels and thirteen hogsheads above his quota; his fellow coopers William and Jack earned $16 and $8 for their extra production of twenty-two barrels and ten hogsheads, and ten barrels and six hogsheads, respectively. It is uncertain, but it may have been that the coopers worked for themselves during regular plantation hours after completing their set tasks.[29]

Many paying jobs, for example, woodcutting and ditching, required great physical stamina if not trained skills. Apart from a few jobs such as counting hoop poles and collecting fodder, slaves without either strength or skills had few opportunities to work for pay on the plantation in any capacity but as day laborers. Such work took into consideration the abilities of the individual slaves, since it was voluntary: if the work did not suit them, they would not do it. Many slaves chose not to do paid work for the plantation, preferring to tend to their farming, gardening, livestock raising, and domestic crafts. Others combined work for themselves with work for the plantation.

Many sugar plantation slaves found profit in nearby swamps and streams apart from the wood they yielded. Hunting and fishing brought some variety to the diet of pork and corn supplied by the planters and also offered a possible source of income, since slaves could sell or barter some of their catch to fellow slaves, traders, or planters.

At Christmas, some slaves expected to receive holiday bonuses. Through the early 1850s, regular entries in the books of Nottoway estate show

27. Ledger, 1858–1872, in Tureaud Papers; S-124 (9), No. 2668, in Bruce, Seddon, and Wilkins Plantation Records, Department of Archives and Manuscripts, LSU Libraries.

28. Plantation Record Book, 1849–1860 (Vol. XXXVI), in Gay Papers.

29. Plantation Book, 1853–1863 (Vol. VI), in Randolph Papers.

money paid for the "Negroes' Christmas" (Table 3). The records do not tell precisely how or to which of the 150 slaves on the plantation the Christmas money was distributed.[30]

Plantation manuscripts contain numerous references to cash paid slaves without giving the reason for the payments. In the Stirling family's plantation records, there is a "Memorandum of Money Paid or Given to the Negroes in 1854" (Table 4), which shows that ninety-five slaves—fifty women and forty-five men—got cash payments ranging from fifteen dollars to ten cents; one slave on the list, George Austin, apparently received no money. The total paid was $314.55. Although some of the payments may have been gifts, it is likely that most compensated slaves for goods and services. Some of the larger went to partners in some moneymaking venture such as woodcutting. A similar list, probably dating from the following year (Figure 2), shows that seventy-eight slaves received a total of $258.50. In the early 1840s, there were a number of unexplained cash payments to slaves on the Gay family's plantation: from September 24 to December 28, 1840, the planter paid some six hundred dollars, and a year later, between December, 1841, and January, 1842, thirty-four men received a total of some two hundred dollars, the individual amounts ranging from a dollar to twenty dollars. The timing of the payments indicates that they were either for some of the slaves' crops or for work performed during harvest, or perhaps for Christmas.[31]

Occasionally slaves received money for catching runaways. The estate accounts of Magnolia plantation for 1829 include the payment of two dollars to one of the slaves on the plantation for stopping a fugitive. Randolph entered in his journal for 1850, "Paid Gus for catching Ben—$3.00." Both Gus and Ben were slaves on Randolph's plantation. Eight years later, Randolph paid "To Cropper's [an Iberville Parish sugar planter] Negro Man for Catching Runaway—$25.00."[32]

Notwithstanding the dominance of a marketing pattern that centered on the plantation and the planter, slaves usually had the opportunity to trade outside it. The home plantation was not the only source of revenue, since slaves could bypass it and sell their commodities elsewhere. Some were in-

30. Journal—Plantation Book, 1847–1852 (Vol. V), Plantation Book, 1853–1863 (Vol. VI), both in Randolph Papers.

31. Box 8, Folder 49, Box 8, Folder 51, both in Stirling Papers; Estate Record Book, 1832–1845 (Vol. VIII), Cashbook/Daybook, 1837–1843 (Vol. XVIII), both in Gay Papers.

32. Book of Accounts of the Magnolia Plantation, 1829–1853, in Louisiana Historical Center; Plantation Book, 1853–1863 (Vol. VI), in Randolph Papers.

TABLE 3

"CHRISTMAS MONEY" PAID TO SLAVES ON JOHN H. RANDOLPH'S NOTTOWAY ESTATE

December 25, 1850	"Paid Negroes Christmas"	$150
December 27, 1851	"Paid Negroes Christmas"	175
December 25, 1852	"Paid Negroes Christmas"	200
January 9, 1854	"Paid Negroes for Christmas money"	300
December 25, 1854	"To Cash Paid negroes for corn & Extra money"	500
December 21, 1855	"To Negroes as Christmas money"	188
December 25, 1856	"Paid out to the Negroes about"	200

SOURCES: Journal—Plantation Book, 1847–1852 (Vol. V), Plantation Book, 1853–1863 (Vol. VI), both in John H. Randolph Papers, Department of Archives and Manuscripts, Louisiana State University Libraries.

volved in marketing at major ports on the Mississippi River, as well as at local town markets, and in the neighborhood of the plantation. They also transacted business with the traders who plied the waterways of south Louisiana.

Throughout the sugar region, slaves worked for themselves collecting and drying a very marketable crop, Spanish moss, that grew in profusion in that part of Louisiana. Spanish moss (*Tillandsia usneoides*) is indigenous to the area. The grayish green moss, whose hairlike strands festoon trees, was one of the principal stuffings for upholstered furniture before synthetic fibers took its place. The moss was much in demand, but in North America it grew only in Louisiana and a few other parts of the southern United States. The slaves in Louisiana could sell as much Spanish moss as they could gather, and they were excellently placed to gather a lot of it.

Picking moss from the trees was relatively easy, requiring only some agility and application. With the assistance of a long staff the nonparasitic plant could readily be detached from a tree's trunk and limbs. After drying it in the sun, the slaves bound the moss into bales weighing 250 to 350 pounds, ready for shipment. Using the estate's draft animals and wagons, they transported the bales to the riverside wharf, where steamers took the cargo on. The slaves consigned the dried moss to major entrepôts on the Mississippi, chiefly St. Louis, New Orleans, and Natchez, whose retail agents they dealt with.

T ABLE 4

"Memorandum of Money Paid or Given to the Negroes in 1854," Lewis Stirling and Family Estate

Wesley	$6.35	Clarinda	$4.00	Lewis	$2.00	Catrine	$4.75
Allen	11.00	Ellen	4.00	Baptiste	2.00	Maretta	2.50
Jack White & Wash.	15.25	Liddy	4.75	Robert	1.50	Sarah	2.00
Adam & Jack D.	11.35	Nanny	4.00	Wiley	2.00	Lucy	1.50
Sam Brown	6.10	Cecile	4.00	Luke	0.50	Liddy	1.00
Long George	6.65	Marinda	3.00	Edmund	0.40	Affy	2.50
Ervin	6.60	L. Charlotte	4.00	Primus	0.30	Fanny	2.00
Alfred	15.00	Frozene	4.00	L. Joe	0.30	O. Charlotte	2.00
William	8.85	Maria	3.75	Sampson	0.30	Margaret	2.50
Isaac	4.00	Rose	4.00	Stephen	0.10	Amy	0.30
George Austin	—	Eliza	4.00	Henry	0.10	Ann	0.30
Sam Jackson	5.00	Eveline	4.00	Old Joe	1.50	L. Margaret	0.30
Levin	3.00	Jane	4.00	Tompo	2.00	Judy	0.30
Julius	3.00	Celia	4.00	Wilson	5.00	Harriet	0.30

Primus	3.00	Francoise	4.00	Spencer	3.00	Caty	1.50
Sambo	3.00	Nelly	4.00	Anderson	3.00	Sophia	2.50
Joseph	4.75	Clara	4.00	Joe J.	4.00	H. Louisa	2.00
Little George	4.35	Isabell	4.00			Suckey	2.00
Old Barrica	4.00	Delila	4.00			Hannah	2.00
Harry	4.00	Serella	4.00			Nannette	2.00
Bartlett	2.50	Esther	3.00			Josaphene	0.50
Nelson	5.70	Phoebe	3.50			Kitty	0.50
Lige	4.00	Rosabell	3.00			O. Lindu	1.50
Monday	4.00	Harriet	4.00				
Joe Clay	2.00	Louisa	2.50				
L. Barrica	2.35	Henrietta	2.50				
L. Leven	2.00	Lindu	4.00				
Totals	$147.80		$102.00		$28.00		$36.75
Total $314.55							

SOURCE: Box 8, Folder 49, in Lewis Stirling and Family Papers, Department of Archives and Manuscripts, LSU Libraries.

Hunton Love, who for the first twenty years of his life had been a slave on John Viguerie's sugar plantation on Bayou Lafourche, testified to the importance of the collection and sale of the moss. "Once I heard some men talking," he recalled when interviewed in the 1930s, "an' one sed, 'You think money grows on trees,' an' the other one say, 'Hit do, git down that moss an' convert it into money,' an' I got to thinkin' an' sho' 'nuff, it do grow on trees." [33]

On Robert Ruffin Barrow's sugar estates on Bayou Lafourche, slaves set aside Sundays for collecting and processing their moss crop, and the accounts of Magnolia plantation, a relatively small sugar estate with a slave population of between forty and fifty, also recorded payments to slaves for moss. [34] The records of the Gay family's sugar estate, in Iberville Parish, contain much more extensive documentation of moss gathering, concerning the collection and marketing pattern, and including payment schedules. In the mid-1840s, Colonel Andrew Hynes and John B. Craighead ran the plantation while Edward Gay lived in St. Louis and acted as agent for the estate's produce. In 1844, Gay wrote to Hynes and Craighead suggesting that the slaves pick moss and send it to St. Louis, where he could guarantee it would sell for a good price. Within a few months, they sold their first shipment there at two cents a pound, with twenty-two slaves, two of them women, sending in all 9,705 pounds and receiving a total of $162.03 ($196.10 less $34.07 for freight and commission). Individual payments ranged from the $26.55 Jacob Young received for 1,490 pounds of moss, to $4.30 Thornton earned for one bale weighing 260 pounds. [35] Up until the Civil War, slaves on the Gay estate continued to send their bales to St. Louis for sale. The price per pound dropped from 2 cents to 1.25 cents between 1849 and 1851 but returned to 2 cents from 1852 through 1861. They shipped moss, on average, four or five times a year. After it was sold, Gay sent a receipt of the transaction to Hynes, listing the name of the slave, the

33. Hunton Love, interviewed, *ca.* 1940, in Louisiana Writers' Project File, Louisiana State Library.

34. J. L. Rogers (overseer), Caillou Grove, to Robert Ruffin Barrow, residence, October 29, 1853, in Box 2, Folder 1850s-20, Robert Ruffin Barrow Papers, Department of Archives and Manuscripts, Tulane University; Residence Journal of R. R. Barrow, January 1, 1857–June 13, 1858 (copied from original in Southern Historical Collection, University of North Carolina, Chapel Hill), *ibid.;* Book of Accounts of the Magnolia Plantation, 1829–1853.

35. Edward Gay, St. Louis, to Hynes and Craighead, Iberville, April 6, 1844, in Gay Papers; "Account 1844, Memorandum, Sale of moss for the negroes," in Box 11, Folder 81, *ibid.*

number of bales, and the poundage, price, expenses, and net proceeds. Hynes then distributed the profit to the slaves.[36]

The Barrow and Gay records show that the slaves paid for the cartage aboard ship and the agent's sales commission, which totaled from 75 cents to $1.25 a bale. The net proceeds of the moss usually came to four to five dollars a bale. The planter took no cut, though the moss came from his land and the bales were hauled to riverside by his draft animals.[37]

The extent of the slave community's involvement in moss gathering is evident from a record book of the Gay plantation for the years 1849–1861. The data found there show that in the thirteen-year period, 160 slaves, 41 of whom were women, sold a total of 1,101 bales of moss, with individual slaves selling from 1 to 48 bales during that time (see Appendix 4). But more than the 160 sellers were engaged in collecting and drying the product. Some of the shipments were sent jointly by a husband and wife, whose children and kin assisted them in the project. Since the total slave population on the estate in 1850 was 224 and in 1860 stood at 240, it is likely that most of the adult slaves on the plantation participated. During the period at least four thousand dollars from moss entered the internal economy, an average of some three hundred dollars a year.[38]

Another commodity the slaves sold was molasses. On Kenner's Ashland plantation, the overseer, W. C. Wade, recorded, in January, 1852, that after he "sold the negroes molasses," he bought flour for them with the proceeds. Slaves on the Gay plantation regularly shipped molasses to St. Louis, where it fetched eight to twelve dollars a barrel through the 1840s. The net returns to slaves for molasses sold in St. Louis on April 29, 1845, included $11.80 to Ned Teagle for the barrel he sent, and $11.18 and $10.00 to Martin and Big Maria respectively for their one barrel each. In the next months, nine slaves sent a total of 6.5 barrels, which sold for a comparable price. The largest shipment from the Gay plantation at this time was the 19.5 barrels sent on the *Highlander* to W. H. Belcher, an agent in St. Louis. That shipment, sold in January, 1847, netted fifteen slaves a total of $148.89. The plantation records reveal that throughout the late 1840s, shipments of molasses regularly accompanied the bales of moss that went to St. Louis by steamer. The records do not make clear whether the slaves grew cane in

36. Moss Record Book, 1849–1861 (Vol. XXXV), Boxes 11–13, Folders 81–96, all in Gay Papers.

37. Residence Journal of R. R. Barrow; Boxes 11–13, Folders 81–96, in Gay Papers.

38. Moss Record Book, 1849–1861 (Vol. XXXV), Estate Record Book, 1848–1855 (Vol. XXXIV), both in Gay Papers; Menn, *The Large Slaveholders*, 244–45.

their grounds and processed it in the estate's mill or whether they received molasses in payment for services rendered the plantation. The second explanation is perhaps the more likely, since slaves did not sell any of the other cane products—sugar or cistern sugar.[39]

Consignment was not the only way for slaves to market their crops and goods. Some transacted business close to the home plantation. Slaves on the Ventress estate contracted with Randolph for the sale of their corn crop of 1,011 barrels, at seventy-five cents a barrel, and slaves on Landry's plantation borrowed the estate's draft animals and wagons to sell their crops throughout the neighborhood (see above, pp. 54). Slaves living near towns could trade, as their Jamaican counterparts did, at the village markets on Sundays. The Reverend P. M. Goodwyn, who was living on the sugar plantation of his brother-in-law, Edward Gay, in Iberville Parish, was appalled at the prevalence of Sunday trading. He saw "going to and from the place of trade—wagons & carts, loaded and empty—servants walking and riding, carrying baskets—bundles—packages etc.—and I ask, why all this?—Can it be possible that there is a necessity for it?—If so, then it is excusable,—and, vice versa,—Has the Master gone, or is he going to the house of God today?—How will he—how *ought* he to feel—as the thought comes up while he is attempting to worship—My Servant, or Servants, have a *permit* from me,—and *now*, while I am here, they are trading and traficing in the stores of the town [probably Plaquemine]."[40]

Despite Goodwyn's misgivings about violating the Sabbath, Sunday remained the principal day for slaves to go to town to sell their goods and spend their earnings. The slave Louis, who sold his ducks to the owner of Houmas estate (see above, p. 57), was obviously well acquainted with the retail outlets in the nearby town of Donaldsonville, since he knew that "they will trust massa [with credit] but they won't trust" somebody like him.[41]

The Louisiana sugar slaves, like their Jamaican counterparts, used market day to shake off the routine and restrictions of the plantation. When going to market, slaves may have donned their best clothing, the "strangely cut [and] wonderfully made" Sunday clothes that Russell observed they had. They followed the market-day custom of spending some of their earnings

39. Ashland Plantation Record Book; Daybook, 1843–1847 (Vol. V), Box 12, Folder 86, both in Gay Papers; "Sales of Moss & Molasses belonging to the Negroes," in Box 13, Folder 100, *ibid.;* Box 12, Folder 93, Box 13, Folder 96, both in Gay Papers.

40. Plantation Book, 1853–1863 (Vol. VI), in Randolph Papers; Landry Estate Plantation Diary and Ledger; Rev. P. M. Goodwyn, St. Louis Place, to Edward Gay, August 27, 1860, in Box 29, Folder 255, Gay Papers.

41. Russell, *My Diary,* 396.

on alcohol. A letter from P. E. Jennings, the mayor of Plaquemine, to Edward Gay, expostulated that "several Negroes were lately caught in this town drunk and gambling on Sunday in the day time in the house of a Free Negro woman." Illicit "shebeens" were no doubt a feature of market towns throughout the sugar region.[42]

Even when the Sabbatarian scruples of either slave or planter militated against Sunday trading, slaves could still find a retail outlet for their goods in town markets. In 1853, William Weeks, of Grande Cote Island sugar estate, reported that a slave named "Amos has heard of the flat boats [trading vessels] being in New Town & has asked my permission to spend a portion of his crop on them—In consideration of his faithful services on all occasions, and his really conscientious scruples about trading on Sunday, I have concluded to let him go tomorrow." On Monday, a working day on the plantation, Amos went to town to trade on his own behalf.[43]

Townspeople and other residents of the area, including the planters themselves, purchased the fresh produce the slaves sold, and the slaves bought goods from the towns' merchants. But it is probable that a smaller percentage of the sugar slaves of Louisiana than of Jamaica had the opportunity of marketing in the towns. On the relatively small island of Jamaica, the distances from all but the most remote sugar plantations were short enough to allow the slaves to walk to market, to trade, and to return to the plantation on the same day. The twenty-three parishes of Louisiana's sugar region not only encompassed three times the area of the island of Jamaica but also included towns that were more scattered. Nevertheless, by transacting business with itinerant peddlers—the traveling traders who plied the highways and waterways of the Louisiana sugar region—the slaves established trade networks over which the planters had no control. Frances Doby, who as a child was a slave on Lucius Dupré's sugar plantation, in St. Landry Parish, recollected that "some time de banana wagon come or de dago man selling pom cake. We run to de wagon to buy wid de picayons." The former slave Martha Stuart recalled the salesmen who "come thru the country," and Cornelius remembered how the slaves on the plantation where she lived would "git down to de ped'lers on de riber at nite tuh buy stuff."[44]

42. *Ibid.*, 373; P. E. Jennings, mayor of Plaquemine, to Edward Gay, August 25, 1858, in Box 25, Folder 221, Gay Papers.

43. William F. Weeks, Grande Cote, to Mary C. Moore, January 31, 1853, in Box 31, Folder 82, Weeks Papers.

44. Frances Doby, interviewed by Arguedas, McKinney, 1938, in Federal Writers' Project Files, Northwestern State University of Louisiana Libraries; Martha Stuart, interviewed by Octave Lilly, Jr., *ca.* 1938, Dillard Project, in Marcus Bruce

River traders had more extensive contact with plantation slaves than highway traders did. Inadequate roads made travel by land difficult, but the large sugar plantations had direct access to navigable waterways. Moreover, river traders could move in and out of areas quietly and quickly and thus trade clandestinely in illicit goods. The bayous and rivers of southern Louisiana formed a trading network for the river traders, most of whom were white, and the sugar plantation slaves. On the eve of the Civil War, William Kingsford, a Canadian traveler, left an excellent description of river traders. From the deck of a steamer heading to New Orleans from Natchez, Kingsford observed

> the small vessels which, owned by pedlars, pass from plantation to plantation, trading with the negroes principally, taking in exchange the articles which they raise, or, when the latter are sold to the boats, offering to their owners the only temptations on which their money can be spent. These vessels are generally unwieldy and ill-built, got up cheaply, for they are intended but for one trip. As a rule, they are constructed on the Ohio, passing down that river to Cairo, when they turn into the Mississippi, proceeding to New Orleans, where they are broken up and sold for lumber. Now and then you come upon one of them, moving sluggishly down stream, or moored inshore, where the owner is dispensing his luxuries, in the shape of ribbons, tobacco, gaudy calicoes, and questionable whiskey.[45]

The trading network, lying outside the control of planters, allowed slaves to sell goods the planters would not buy and to buy goods the planters would neither sell nor order. River traders sold slaves alcohol, whereas planters rarely did. Throughout the period under study there were laws banning the sale of alcohol to slaves unless approved by the slaveowner, under penalty of fine and imprisonment. Traders would also buy commodities, including stolen goods, not traded between slaves and planters.[46] Slaves thus divested themselves of some of the constraints of the plantation and engaged in an independent economic system in which they made their own marketing decisions.

Christian Collection; Cornelius interview. *Picayon* or *picayune* was a term used in Louisiana to refer to small-denomination coins. The words come from *picayune,* a Spanish half-real piece formerly current in Louisiana.

45. [William Kingsford], *Impressions of the West and South during a Six Weeks' Holiday* (Toronto, 1858), 47–48.

46. *The Revised Statutes of Louisiana,* comp. U. B. Phillips (New Orleans, 1856), 48–65.

A letter by Maunsell White, a sugar planter of Deer Range estate, in Plaquemines Parish, clearly shows, on the one hand, the divergence of interests between planters and river traders, and on the other, the coincidence of interests between slaves and river traders. Writing to George Lanaux, the owner of the nearby Bellevue estate, White related how some of his slaves

> were caught stealing molasses to sell to a Boat or "Capota" & were watched until they were found on Board the Boat, where they had hid themselves & were secreted by the owner; a man who called himself "Block," a German & another who called himself "Bill." On searching the Boat, another negro was also found, who said he belonged to the Boat as did also the Men who owned it; but we soon found on arresting the whole of them, that the Boy confessed or said he belonged to you, & when I questioned him again this morning said He had been gone away from you for 4 months;* the whole of which time he said he spent in the City [presumably New Orleans] at work. Thirty five dollars and 50/100 were found on his person, & a Silver Watch. . . . * he afterwards said it was only 2 1/2 months.[47]

In this case the river trader harbored a runaway and concealed from the planter slaves who had stolen goods from the plantation on which they lived. White went on to mention the possibility of conferring with Lanaux "in regards to the prosecution of the offending parties," but there is no record of what happened to Block and Bill.[48]

Transactions in stolen goods between slaves and peddlers were a commonplace throughout the South, according to Frederick Law Olmsted. They had a higher incidence in the Louisiana sugar region, however, because the sugar estates had navigable waterways that let the peddlers more easily transport and conceal themselves. Their necessarily clandestine dealings were usually carried out under the cover of darkness. Olmsted observed that "the traders . . . moor at night on the shore, adjoining the negro-quarters and float away whenever they have obtained any booty, with very small chance of detection." Unless caught in the act, they could always dispose of evidence of wrongdoing by dumping it over the side of the boat.[49] Consequently, they probably also had few inhibitions regarding what they would purchase. The character of the trade dictated against bulky

47. Maunsell White, Deer Range, to George Lanneau, April 15, 1859, in Box 3, Folder 1, Lanaux Papers.

48. *Ibid*.

49. Frederick Law Olmsted, *A Journey in the Seaboard Slave States* (New York, 1856), 674.

consignments, the loading of which would have required time and increased the likelihood of detection. Aside from what caused logistical problems, however, the peddlers were willing to purchase a wide variety of goods; few of the planters' possessions or the plantations' appurtenances were safe from the depredations of those involved in the trade.

A large part of this trade was probably in the plantations' output of molasses and sugar, and perhaps in some of the minor crops like corn. The slaves also must have found a market for the small livestock they could lay their hands on. But the image of the plantations' "movables" gives an idea of the variety of articles that slaves and river peddlers were ready to take. It appears that anything that could be carried off might find its way to the river peddlers. One planter, according to Olmsted, had "a large brass cock and some pipe . . . stolen from his sugar-works." The planter "had ascertained that one of his negroes had taken it and sold it on board one of these boats for seventy-five cents, and had immediately spent the money, chiefly for whisky, on the same boat." It cost the planter thirty dollars to replace the machinery. Another sugar planter told Olmsted "that he had lately caught one of his own negroes going towards one of the 'chicken thieves' (so the traders' boats are called) with a piece of machinery, that he had unscrewed from his sugar works, which was worth eighty dollars, and which very likely might have been sold for a drink."[50]

In both Jamaica and Louisiana, the internal economies had a trading nexus outside the confines of the plantation. Whereas Jamaican slaves relied on the higglers who crisscrossed the island and on weekly markets, the slaves of Louisiana had access to market towns or, if they were distant from markets, could trade with peddlers.

Theft was as prevalent in Louisiana as it was in Jamaica. Every kind of source—slave narratives, plantation records, newspapers and journals, travelers' accounts, and government documents—indicates its widespread occurrence on Louisiana sugar estates, where, as in Jamaica, many slaves were unconstrained by any value system that proscribed it when it was directed against the planter or plantation.

Plantation records confirm that most thefts involved the plantations' production, including its livestock. Slaves on White's Deer Range plantation stole molasses to sell to river traders (see above, p. 71), and Weeks reported from his family's Grande Cote Island estate on "Simon that prince of runa-

50. *Ibid.*, 675.

ways & troublesome negroes [whose] last offence was to go into the sugar house & steal a portion of the little sugar I had kept for home use."[51]

Unlike other agricultural output, which was often stored in locked buildings, livestock ranged free. Time and again plantation records mentioned thefts of the easy prey. The diary of Joseph Mather, the superintendent of Judge Morgan's Aurora plantation, remarked on the "theft of chickens," and Ellen McCollam, in a diary entry dated August 15, 1847, noted that she had "had 8 hens stowlen out of the yard since the first of March." The threat of having livestock purloined prompted White to urge his overseer to make a picket pen "in order to save our hogs, pigs & sheep from all sorts of 'Varmints' two-legged as well as four." The planter J. E. Craighead complained that "the negroes steal our sheep as we have no safe place to keep them." A Louisiana song testifies that the problem was rife:

> Négue pas capab marché san maïs dans poche,
> Ce pou volé poule—
>
> Negro cannot walk without corn in his pocket,
> It is to steal chickens—[52]

On at least two occasions the planter Andrew McCollam and his wife, Ellen, lost items from their laundry. One time they had "8 shirts stolen out of the wash," and a year later they "had a pair of sheets table cloth stollen out of the garden." A visitor to Colonel Hynes's plantation suspected the slaves there of stealing a trunk full of clothing while his luggage was being loaded onto a riverboat at the estate's wharf.[53]

A large part of plantation theft must have gone unrecorded and undetected. For the most part, slaves chose to make off with what was either readily disposed of or hard to track down. Livestock could be slaughtered,

51. William F. Weeks to Mary C. Moore, June 20, 1860, in Box 36, Folder 180, Weeks Papers.

52. Joseph Mather Diary, 1852–1859, in Department of Archives and Manuscripts, LSU Libraries; Diary and Plantation Record of Ellen E. McCollam; Maunsell White to James P. Bracewell, August 10, 1859, in Maunsell White Letterbook, Department of Archives and Manuscripts, LSU Libraries; J. E. Craighead, Plaquemine, to John B. Craighead, Nashville, September 11, 1847, in Box 14, Folder 102, Gay Papers; Lyle Saxon et al., comps., Gumbo Ya-Ya: A Collection of Louisiana Folk Tales (Boston, 1945), 430.

53. Diary and Plantation Record of Ellen McCollam; Nicholas Phipps, Donaldsonville, to Colonel Andrew Hynes, February 1847, in Box 13, Folder 97, Gay Papers.

butchered, and cooked; stolen poultry could be added to a flock where it would become indistinguishable from the rest; stolen cloth and clothing could be made up or altered; and the river traders were waiting for readily transported goods.

Those caught were overwhelmingly men—a pattern that prevailed in both Jamaica and Louisiana. The relative frequency with which male slaves were held for theft does not necessarily correlate with the relative extent of their involvement. Women may have been more careful, or they may have been more involved in lower-risk operations, or men may have assumed culpability if detection became likely. It may also be that there was a division of responsibilities. Men may have assumed the task of carrying off the goods, leaving to women that of concealing the act: slaughtering and cooking livestock, sewing up or altering clothing. In that case, men stood a greater likelihood of detection.[54]

Mather, the plantation superintendent, took action against all the slaves on the estate when he could not identify individual thieves. He set everybody to labor on a Sunday as punishment for poor work and the "theft of chickens." Either he thought that punishing the entire community would deter those he sought to stop or he blamed an integrated network within the slave community for the theft.[55]

As in Jamaica, some stolen property went to supplementing an inadequate diet. F. D. Richardson, a sugar planter in Jeanerette, acknowledged this in a letter he wrote to a fellow planter. He referred to slaves "committing depredations in the way of roberies" but gave his opinion that "the whole matter is no doubt attributable to the high price of pork—for many planters will not buy at the present rates & depend upon a little beef and

54. In the plantation records for this study that cite specific slaves deemed guilty of theft, the culprit was in each case male; in none of the records are women cited as felons. These records include Landry Estate Plantation Diary and Ledger; Ashland Plantation Record Book; Diary and Plantation Record of Ellen E. McCollam; William F. Weeks to Mary C. Moore, June 20, 1860, in Box 36, Folder 180, Weeks Papers; John Palfrey, plantation, Atakapas, to William C. Palfrey, Franklin, July 16, 1833, in Box 2, Folder 9, William T. Palfrey and Family Papers, Department of Archives and Manuscripts, LSU Libraries; Maunsell White to George Lanneau, April 15, 1859, in Lanaux Papers; A. J. Robinson, Chaseland plantation, to Charles L. Mathews, Bayou Sara, September 21, 1856, in Box 2, Folder 16, Charles L. Mathews and Family Papers, Department of Archives and Manuscripts, LSU Libraries; Captain John De Hart, Orange Grove plantation, Indian Bend, to Sarah Evans, Pinckneyville, Miss., October 6, 1832, in Box 4, Folder 27, Nathaniel Evans and Family Papers, Department of Archives and Manuscripts, LSU Libraries.

55. Mather Diary, 1852–1859.

other things as a substitute." Martha Stuart, the former slave, recalled that "ma Marster had a brother, they called him Charles Haynes and he was mean and he didn't feed his people . . . he didn't give 'em nuthin; 'twas the funniest thing tho; his niggers was all fat and fine cause dey'd go out and kill hogs—dey'd steal dem from de boss."[56]

In some cases, slaves would have had to eat the food and livestock they raised if they had not stolen from the plantation. As a consequence, theft contributed to the internal economy by freeing their own goods for sale. But more often stealing food to fill their bellies and the bellies of their families was the only alternative to undernourishment and starvation. Thefts of clothing and other necessities of life must have stemmed from similar exigencies—stolen cloth, for example, supplementing an inadequate clothing ration.

Runaways often subsisted on the food they could steal from plantations. When a slave named Anderson ran away from John Palfrey's sugar plantation, he ate fresh corn and a "quantity of peaches which he purloin'd from Mr. Seraphim Indius' plantation." Albert Patterson, who had been a slave on a sugar plantation, recalled that "if a nigger hide in de woods, he'd come in at night, an' to get a meal. They bore a little hole in the floor an' they break into de meat house, too."[57]

Slaves also probably dealt in stolen goods with others on their own and on nearby plantations, and also perhaps with free blacks and poor whites in the neighborhood. The patterns resembled those in Jamaica. Slaves on Louisiana plantations condoned thefts against outsiders and condemned thefts against members of their own community. Some Louisiana slaves did not consider their own property secure from theft. The presence of locks and lock-fast places in the slaves' houses indicates that (see below, pp. 145–46). Still, the incidence of thefts and the manner in which they were perpetrated suggest that theft seemed to slaves less a menace than a component of their internal economy, and a means by which they could augment their resources.[58]

56. F. D. Richardson, Jeanerette, to Moses Liddell, July 18, 1852, in Safe 12, Folder 3, Moses and St. John Liddell and Family Papers, Department of Archives and Manuscripts, LSU Libraries; Stuart interview.

57. John Palfrey, plantation, Atakapas, to William T. Palfrey, Franklin, July 16, 1833, in Box 2, Folder 9, William T. Palfrey and Family Papers; Albert Patterson, interviewed by Maud Wallace, 1940, in Louisiana Writers' Project File, Louisiana State Library.

58. For patterns of theft on Jamaica sugar plantations, see above, Chapter 1. The presence of locks in the houses of Louisiana sugar plantation slaves is a topic in Chapter 4. For a general discussion of slave theft in the antebellum South, see Eugene D. Genovese, *Roll, Jordan, Roll: The World the Slaves Made* (New York, 1974), 599–609.

Recalling the cash economy of the slave community on Dr. Lyle's sugar plantation, Catherine Cornelius acknowledged, "We got money several ways."[59] But the amount of money within the internal economy fluctuated. Earnings potential varied from slave to slave and plantation to plantation, as well as from season to season and year to year.

A large proportion of the capital entered the Louisiana slaves' economy in the fall or the early winter. Slaves usually gathered and sold their cash crops prior to the beginning of the sugar harvest, in late September or early October, and wood collecting continued till the start of the harvest. In both cases the slaves received payment either immediately before or immediately after the sugar harvest, or else at Christmas. During the harvesting and processing of the crop, they had other opportunities to earn money, by tending the sugar kettles and serving as firemen, sugar makers, and engineers. Stealing from the sugarhouse was also seasonal, since it had to be carried out between the time the crop was processed and when it was shipped off the estate. Gifts from the planters were usually distributed at Christmastide or at the end of harvest. Christmas, according to Thorpe, was the "season when the planter makes presents of calico of flaming colors to the women and children, and a coat of extra fineness to patriarchal 'boys' of sixty-five and seventy. It is the time when negroes square their accounts with each other, and get 'master' and 'mistress' to pay up for innumerable eggs and chickens which they have frome time to time, since the last settling day, furnished the 'big house.' In short, it is a kind of jubilee, when the 'poor African' as he is termed in poetry, has a pocket full of silver, [and] a body covered with gay toggery."[60]

The sudden injection of large sums of money into the internal economy of a slave community during the fall and winter is illustrated by the payment by Aime of $1,300 to the slaves on his plantation for their 1848 corn crop. On October 25, 1859, the slaves on Uncle Sam sugar estate received $1,083.25 for cutting wood and making barrels and bricks. The following year, the slaves on Uncle Sam plantation earned $506 for wood, bricks, and barrels, and the year after that, the total was $843. In these years, as in 1859, all the slaves were paid at the same time. Similar payments, involving sums from a few dollars to hundreds of dollars, appear regularly in plantation records.[61] Poultry, however, provided year-round earnings, as did theft, day labor, and moss collecting.

59. Cornelius interview.

60. Thomas Bangs Thorpe, "Christmas in the South," *Frank Leslie's Illustrated Newspaper* (New York), December 26, 1857, p. 62.

61. Plantation Diary of Valcour Aime, 1847–1852; Boxes 1 and 2, in Uncle Sam Plantation Papers.

The labor schedule seven days a week during the sugar harvest meant that the slaves of Louisiana lacked time to devote to their own economic interests in those weeks of the year. Louisiana planters assumed greater responsibility than their Jamaican counterparts for providing the slaves with food and consequently during the sugar harvest did not give them time off such as the Jamaicans had on Sundays to work their grounds. In addition, the race against the weather in Louisiana required a schedule in which the slaves worked seven days a week.

During harvest, the slaves in both Louisiana and Jamaica had to devote most of the time they had off to the basic necessities of survival—food and rest. Apart from slaves who were paid for their specialized services during the harvest—kettlemen, firemen, sugar makers, and engineers—and those who received or were able to divert to themselves some of the sugar and molasses they made, there was little opportunity at this time of year to do much to advance individual economic positions.

The earnings of slaves fluctuated considerably, since the labor demands of sugar slavery overlaid the seasonal income variations typical of rural populations dependent on the growing and marketing of crops. There were also the fluctuations from year to year, with the vagaries of the weather. Even within a single plantation, wide income disparities were the rule. The money accumulated by individual slaves on Tureaud's estate for 1858–1859 ranged from $170 to $1: 104 slaves earned a total of $3,423. Some slaves, including 22 of the 30 women and 2 of the 98 men listed in the ledger, earned no money, although presumably there was the expectation that some of these would have earnings in the future, since they were granted goods on credit. In 1844, the slaves on the Gay family's plantation collected sums ranging from $82 to $1, with some slaves also getting credit: 66 slaves earned a total of $864.125, and 10 slaves got a total of $32.00 in credit in that year. Spanish-moss accounts for the Gay plantation from 1849 to 1861 show that individual slaves gathered totals of from one to forty-eight bales in the period. The 23 slaves paid for cutting wood on the Stirling family's sugar estate in 1849 received amounts from $10.50 to $1.12 as their share of the $103.48 paid; a "Memorandum of Money Paid or Given to the Negroes in 1854," taken from the same records, lists payments of from $15.25 to 10 cents, for a total of $314.55 paid the 50 women and 45 men named.[62]

Plantation records, however, offer only a partial depiction of slaves' earn-

62. Ledger, 1858–1872, in Tureaud Papers; Daybook, 1843–1847 (Vol. V), Moss Record Book, 1849–1861 (Vol. XXXV), both in Gay Papers; "List of Wood Cut by Slaves and Payment Made," in Box 7, Folder 39, Stirling Papers; Box 8, Folder 39, *ibid.*

ings. Often they list only payments for certain commodities or certain work. Nor do they record income earned off the plantation. Undoubtedly, the earnings omitted would also have been unevenly distributed, but not necessarily in the same ways. Slaves who derived large profits from dealings with river traders or who stole from the plantation may not, after all, have been the ones who made the most money in transactions with the planter.

Participation in an internal economy offered slaves not only material, but also less tangible, benefits. Slaves who worked for themselves and accumulated money and property were in a position to make purchases that could supplement the supplies given by planters, but they could also derive satisfaction from organizing the economic system and acquiring power and control over aspects of their own lives.

The slaves chose the manner and extent of their involvement in the internal economy, making decisions about marketing, agronomy, working, and so forth. The slaves thus decided which crops to grow and how to raise them, how to distribute their time between their small-holding agricultural pursuits and work for which the planters paid them, when to sell, and what to buy—the sorts of decisions not normally associated with an enslaved people whose very being was defined in law by reference to an owner. The important qualification is that the slaves' internal economy operated within the constraints imposed by the "peculiar institution's" structure, and primarily within the confines of the plantation on which the participants lived. The internal economy had to accommodate the sugar plantation's onerous labor regimen and the control planters exercised over slaves. The slaves' economic activities, therefore, were but one facet of plantation life.

Still, the slaves exhibited a remarkable commitment to participation in their internal economy. Its importance to the slaves involved, and to understanding slave life, transcends the obstacles to its development, as well as its size and extent: its mere presence gave slaves a degree of control and independence in tension with the prerequisites for servitude. Slaves qua slaves, at least in their working role as field hands in the omnipresent gang system, operated within a structure of social and labor relations that deprived them of personal rights, autonomous actions, decision-making roles concerning planting, harvesting, and marketing, and self-motivated work disciplines. As participants in the internal economy, however, the slaves determined how to structure their efforts. They controlled, for example, "their" land and the manner of its cultivation, deciding how to market produce and dispose of the accumulated profits.

The plantation journal of Mavis Grove estate, in Plaquemines Parish, graphically brings out the disaccord between slaves' lives as slaves and their activities within the internal economy. The journal entry for Sunday, September 13, 1857, notes, "Boys not cutting wood today, resting from the fatigues of last night's frolic." Normally, slaves on Mavis Grove spent Sundays cutting wood for sale to the planter, but they exempted themselves from doing so on the day following a dance. Their choice was between work on Sunday and merrymaking on Saturday night. Slaves in their internal economy determined how to order their own time and labor in keeping with the priorities they weighed.[63]

A comparison of the labor system in the internal economy with the ideal type of slave labor and with that of free small-holding agrarian labor further demonstrates the divergence between slaves' lives as slaves and their personal economic activities. Field hands in the gang system had virtually no say in how their efforts were to be organized. Planters decided what work to do (planting, hoeing, cleaning, laying by, cutting) and where to do it, what to plant and when and where to plant it, when to harvest, and how to process and market. Field hands performed within this system as followers of commands, working at a specific pace on a preassigned task that they themselves had no part in determining. On the other hand, free small-holding agrarian labor, perhaps best represented in a landed peasantry, could decide how to organize its work, such as planting, harvesting, and marketing. The structure of the slaves' internal economy resembled more closely the latter ideal type; it differed significantly from the other ideal type, which their labor for the planter more closely approximated.

The *process* of the internal economy doubtless proved cathartic to slaves. The dimensions of independence, responsibility, and decision making inherent in the system would, in themselves, have held rewards. If the internal economy had potentially deleterious effects, such as its participants' physical stress and a diminution of the time they could spend on other things, such as resting or being with their family, it was also a source of satisfaction. It allowed the slaves to work for themselves, pace their own work, and take responsibility for the organization of their efforts, as well as to control the disposition of and to profit directly from the fruits of their labor.

Nevertheless, attention to what the slaves bought permits a fuller explanation of why slaves worked and operated an internal economy. Even given that working for themselves afforded gratification, their motivation for involvement undoubtedly rested largely with the internal economy's end product, the purchase and acquisition of goods. Purchasing patterns disclose how slaves defined themselves, what their priorities were in the ac-

63. Journal of Mavis Grove Plantation, 1856, in Louisiana Historical Center.

quisition of "coveted commodities," and how those priorities translated into aspirations and perceptions of "betterment." There can be little doubt as to the slaves' desire to use their earnings for self-improvement—to eat and dress better, to live in more comfortable homes, to care both for themselves and for members of their families. Although their earnings were often small and their purchases modest, what they bought reflects their independent actions as consumers, and as such offers a unique insight into the way they dealt with their lives in bondage.

The purchases by Louisiana slaves fell principally into six categories: food and drink, pipes and tobacco, clothing and other personal items, housewares, implements, and livestock. Although the categories are few, each contains a wide variety of goods. Plantation records provide the most complete cataloging of slaves' purchases, but even they leave much out.

Estate records indicate that slaves usually withdrew some of their plantation earnings in cash. Money withdrawn played no further role in the dealings between slaves and planters, save in the rare instances that the slaves redeposited cash previously withdrawn. Normally they spent the cash elsewhere. When slaves sold goods away from the plantation—to river and highway traders, at town markets, or in the neighborhood of the estate—they spent some of their earnings where they transacted their sales. Off-plantation traders also enabled the slaves to spend cash they had withdrawn from their accounts on the plantation.

What slaves bought outside the estate, however, probably resembled what they bought through the planter, with one notable exception: alcohol. Planters only infrequently supplied slaves with liquor (they occasionally distributed it on holidays, like Christmas) and rarely allowed them to buy it through the plantation accounts—although Stuart recalled that on the plantation where she was a slave "you had whiskey. . . . Our boss didn't care how much you want—sent to town to git it—and git it cheap den, 20 cents a gallon, and twas whiskey."[64]

Slaves spent money off the plantation on gambling as well, as the complaint by the Plaquemine town mayor that slaves were "drunk and gambling" on Sundays demonstrates. For Afro-slave cultural and religious items and locally crafted articles by slave artisans—tools, household implements,

64. Slaves on the Gay family's estate, for example, were occasionally given whiskey. On December 28, 1846, "whiskey for Negroes dinner" cost $1.50, and on December 25, 1850, "Whiskey for Negroes" cost $2.50. The planter paid for these items. See Estate Record Book, 1842–1847 (Vol. XII), Estate Record Book, 1848–1855 (Volume XXXIV), both in Gay Papers; and Stuart interview.

furnishings, and the like—the slaves also went off the estate, or purchased them within their own community. In either case, planters were not involved in the transactions.[65]

The river traders William Kingsford saw sold "ribbons, tobacco, [and] gaudy calicoes" as well as whiskey; V. Alton Moody asserted that these traders sold both whiskey and "cheap finery." Catherine Cornelius recalled that on the plantation where she lived, the planter, Dr. Lyle, "wouldn't gib us combs en brushes, but we got some from pedlin." But in most cases, the slaves could also obtain such goods, except for the whiskey, through their plantation accounts.[66]

Within the six general categories of purchases, the slaves bought such foodstuffs as flour, molasses, meat, coffee, herring, mackerel, ham, beans, pork, rice, biscuits, potatoes, apples, and cordials. They purchased a variety of cloth, from which they made their "best clothing," worn when not at work. Among the fancier finished clothing they bought were "Elegant Bonnets," a "fine Summer Coat," a "Fine Russian Hat," white and colored shirts, roundabouts (short jackets) and waistcoats, black shoes, a fur hat, white "cambrice" and silk dresses, gloves, an oilcloth winter coat, and oilcloth and "log cabin" pantaloons. More usually, however, they purchased lengths of calico, checked, plain, and striped cotton, linen, cottonade, "domestic," blue drilling, and thread, as well as simpler ready-made attire like dresses, hose, shirts, pants, hats, shoes and boots, kerchiefs, suspenders, and shawls. (For a more detailed look at slaves' clothing purchases, see below, Chapter 4.) They bought personal items like pocketknives, combs, fiddles, and umbrellas. Patrick, a slave "Engineer and Overseer" on the Gay family's plantation, paid fifteen dollars for a watch; on Colonel Pugh's Woodlawn estate one slave spent three dollars to repair his watch. Their houseware purchases included blankets, baskets, tin cups and buckets, cutlery, soap, sheets of tin, locks, mosquito bars, bedspreads, "furniture," coffeepots, tallow and spermaceti candles, portable ovens, copper kettles, chairs, bowls, and pots. (For a fuller description of the housewares slaves bought, see below, Chapter 4.) Louisiana slaves also made widespread use of chewing and pipe tobacco, which they bought along with pipes.

Some of the purchases slaves made were capital goods—implements and gear, such as shovels, saddles, bridles and bits, wire, twine, fishing hooks

65. P. E. Jennings, mayor of Plaquemine, to Edward J. Gay, August 25, 1858, in Box 25, Folder 221, Gay Papers.

66. [Kingsford], *Impressions,* 47–48; V. Alton Moody, *Slavery on Louisiana Sugar Plantations* (New Orleans, 1924), 68; Cornelius interview.

and line, "mud boots," and mitts. They also invested in such livestock as pigs and shoats, and poultry, although the records do not tell whether those purchases were for home consumption or for breeding for sale later. No plantation records list purchases of seed, and it is possible either that those slaves who had a crop the previous year sold part of the seed they kept back for the next year to those who had not raised anything the year before, or, perhaps, that slaves received seed from the planters' stock as a perquisite. (For itemizations of slaves' expenditures, see Appendixes 5–7.)

Obviously, not every slave or even every slave community bought as wide a range of goods as this. The tabulation here derives from the records of some twenty Louisiana sugar plantations in the years from 1834 to the beginning of the Civil War. The list does, however, capture the overall trends in slave purchases during the sugar boom in Louisiana.

The slaves' buying patterns underwent little change over time. Throughout the sugar boom, the slaves placed a high priority on a rather limited number of commodities, specifically flour, cloth, and tobacco, and on goods such as shoes and a few items of ready-made clothing. The general patterns held not only over time but also from plantation to plantation. When the slaves had only limited purchasing power, they tended to purchase these few staples; slaves with larger earnings purchased additional goods.

Rations distributed by the planters could alter buying habits; slaves obviously did not have to buy goods they were given by the planter. On the Gay family's plantation, slaves received a regular ration of tobacco, and hence an extensive itemization of purchases on that estate reveals them buying none (Table 5; see also Appendix 6).[67]

The buying habits show that the slaves wanted to improve their diet, furnish themselves with better clothing to be worn when not at work, and smoke tobacco and drink liquor. They considered more elaborate personal wares, housewares, and the like of secondary import. They bought such goods only if they had money left over after buying the staples.

A ledger that lists slave earnings and expenditures on one of Tureaud's plantations shows that of the ninety-three men who bought goods through the plantation, seventy-six (82 percent) spent part of their earnings on tobacco, seventy-seven (83 percent) bought shoes, and seventy (75 percent) bought either meat or flour (see Appendix 5). In addition, more than half the slaves—fifty-one (55 percent)—bought some cloth or clothing other

67. P. O. Daigre (overseer) to Edward J. Gay, August 15, 1858, in Box 25, Folder 221, Gay Papers.

TABLE 5

EARNINGS AND EXPENDITURES OF SLAVES ON THE GAY FAMILY'S ESTATE IN THE
LATE 1850s

Payments to Slaves for:

Ironing Carts	Holiday work ($0.75 to $1.00 per day)
Firing kettles	Ditching ($0.50 to $1.00 per acre)
Fireman's work	Slabs of wood ($0.25 per cord)
Sugar potting	Making a cart ($20.00 [Thornton])
on holiday	Fixing kettles
Moss	Making hogsheads
Hay	
Woodcutting ($0.50 per cord)	

Expenditures by Slaves for:

Coffee	Flour	Fish	Shovels
Shoes	Mitts	Boots	Socks
Mackerel	Calico cloth	Cotton cloth	Beans
Linen cloth	Pork	Checked cloth	Dresses
Cottonade cloth	Flannel cloth	Pants	Saddle
Knives	Shawls	Domestic cloth	Gloves

SOURCE: Plantation Record Book, 1849–1860 (Vol. XXXVI), in Edward J. Gay and Family Papers, Department of Archives and Manuscripts, LSU Libraries.

NOTE: There was also cash withdrawn, with distribution to earners and their wives and daughters.

than shoes. Only a minority bought mosquito bars, locks, buckets, and sheet tin. The records of the Weeks family's Grande Cote Island sugar plantation provide substantiating evidence of the pattern. The principal commodities slaves bought there with money earned from the sale of eggs and chickens were striped cotton, handkerchiefs, tobacco, flour, and coffee. The records of other Louisiana sugar plantations are in the same vein.[68] The slave accounts of the Gay family's plantation for 1844 show that the slaves there placed a similar emphasis on cloth and foodstuffs (see Appendix 6). The

68. Notebook, 1853–1857 (Vol. IX), in Weeks Collection.

records of the Gay and Tureaud estates also show the extent to which slaves withdrew at least part of their earnings in cash; a sizable number of slaves on the Gay plantation bought nothing at all through the planter, withdrawing in cash every penny they earned. How slaves spent that money is, of course, unknown, but perhaps some slaves, though they used their plantation accounts to buy staple goods, were inclined to buy "luxury" goods, such as housewares and personal items, off the plantation, where they could select from a range of goods rather than leave the choice to an intermediary, the planter.

Both the Tureaud and Gay records show slaves putting cash into their plantation accounts. They do not, however, document where the money came from. Some of it may have been the unspent balance of sums previously withdrawn. It is also possible that slaves who made money selling goods on the river or elsewhere off the plantation banked their earnings in their plantation accounts. Money from intracommunity transactions, such as Thorpe referred to ("the time when negroes square their accounts with each other"), could also be deposited with the planter. In view of the extent to which slaves withdrew and deposited cash, they were familiar with the medium of hard currency, if just in small denominations, and thus with the structure not only of a barter or trade system but also of a cash economy.[69]

Some slaves also were conversant with the operation of a credit economy. The accounts for the Gay plantation in 1844 show that nine slaves received a total of thirty-two dollars in credit. Six of the slaves used their advances to obtain flour and coffee, two withdrew theirs in cash, and one slave, Elias, applied part of his four-dollar loan to a "Fine Russian Hat bt. in N. Orleans" that cost him three dollars. The other dollar went to pay off a balance he owed on clothes. On the Tureaud estate, two slaves, Nash and David Big, got flour, meat, handkerchiefs, checked cloth, shoes, and tobacco on credit, while another slave, Charles Yellow, who had earned only two dollars cutting wood, bought tobacco, flour, shoes, hose, meat, handkerchiefs, cotton cloth, and a hat. Since the bill for these goods came to $15.50, the planter apparently extended credit to Charles Yellow for the balance of $13.50 (see Appendixes 5, 6).

Few slave women accumulated earnings and transacted business in accounts registered in their own names. On the Tureaud estate ninety-eight men had accounts, and all transacted business in 1858–1859, whereas of the thirty women in the ledger, only eight accumulated any earnings for which they received goods and cash, and the other twenty-two had neither debits

69. Thorpe, "Christmas," 62.

nor credits (see Appendix 5). Similarly the Gay plantation records show that very few women had accounts, either in comparison with the men (six women and seventy men) or in comparison with the seventy adult women living on the estate (see Appendix 6). Other records conform to that. The accounts of slaves on John Randolph's Nottoway plantation for 1851 show that only eight women, as against forty-seven men, received items such as boots, shoes, and flour (see Appendix 7). Of these eight, only two had their own accounts. Three of the other six apparently were not charged for their shoes, since the journal entry reads "Gave Dicey, L Anny, Silla, a pair of shoes," and no cost was entered. The other three women each had the purchase amounts deducted from the account of a male slave. Two of these women, Mahala and Susan, received shoes at the cost of a dollar, for which the accounts of George and Gus were respectively debited a dollar; in the other case, the journal records, "Long William got 1 pr. Shoes (for Leana)— $1.00." A "List of Negroes" for 1864 shows that George and Mahala were husband and wife, and one may assume that Gus and Susan, and Long William and Leana, were also married, or closely related, although it is also possible that they had some sort of non-kin working or contractual relationship.[70]

The small number of accounts held by women implies neither their lack of involvement in the system nor their enjoyment of fewer benefits from it. The accounts of slaves on the Gay plantation further illustrate how wives made purchases through accounts in their husbands' names. In 1840–1841, William Sanders had his account debited to pay for a "White Cambrice dress for wife." In 1839, Little Moses' account was debited for shoes for his wife, Charity, and five years later, Ned Davis was charged for "Coffee by your wife." The accounts of slaves on the Gay plantation for the late 1850s show account holders as well as their wives and children making withdrawals (Table 5). A slave named Willis paid for children's shoes out of his account on the Tureaud estate, and Kenawa Moses, a slave on the Gay estate, paid for "meat for [his] children" from the money he earned. Other slaves on the Gay estate who were charged for goods for family members included Harry Cooper, who bought shoes for his wife and his daughter Tulip, and Alfred Cooper, who purchased calico for his daughter Louisiana, and two "Elegant Bonnets" costing two dollars each, presumably for his wife, Dido, and his daughter (Table 5; see also Appendixes 5–7).[71]

70. Ledger, 1862–1865 (Vol. VIII), in Randolph Papers.
71. Memorandum Book, 1840–1841 (Vol. XXVIII), Estate Record Book, 1831–1845 (Vol. VIII), both in Gay Papers.

The purchases for wives and children are evidence that these were family accounts. Even where the records make no mention of kin relationships, as in the debit of $12.50 from the account of Woodson, a slave on Colonel Pugh's estate, for a "Silk Dress for Rachel," and in the "cash [paid] to Aunt Julia" from Patrick's account on the Gay plantation, it seems likely that the men and women were kin. A comparison of slave accounts on the Gay family's plantation for 1844 with other slave lists compiled around the same time for the purpose of recording rations distributions and work schedules shows the familial relationships of the account holders. Seventy-six people earned money and held accounts, seventy of whom were men. Of those seventy, thirty-seven were heads of households, six were sons in male-headed households, three were sons in female-headed households, and eighteen were single males without family affiliation. The status of the remaining six males is less clear: one may have been a male head of household and one a son in a male-headed household, while two appear to have been single males and the other two cannot be traced elsewhere in the records. Of the six women holding accounts, two were heads of households, one was a daughter in a female-headed household, and one a single female. The two other women held joint accounts: Clarissa with her husband, Toney, who also held an account with another slave, Ned Teagle, a son in a female-headed household; and Anna with William, neither of whom can be traced elsewhere in the records (Table 6; beyond the information reproduced schematically in the table, there are notations on specific individuals in Appendix 6).[72] Many of the slaves recorded as single and without family affiliation had families who drew on their accounts. The slave Kenawa Moses, for example, who was listed as single, paid from his account for "meat for [his] children." Slaves on the Gay plantation worked on either the Front Place or the Back Place, and rations and labor were allocated according to whether they were on one or the other. Slaves from both parts of the plantation lived together, however, so it may be that a number of those recorded as single males in the various slave lists in fact lived with their family but worked on a different part of the estate and thus were listed separately. Alternatively, some of the single male slaves may have had families on nearby plantations or, as was possible in the case of Kenawa Moses, lived apart from their families, the members of which continued to contribute to and draw from the accounts.

The accounts held by sons in either male- or female-headed households

72. Estate Record Book, 1831–1845 (Vol. VIII), Cashbook/Daybook, 1837–1843 (Vol. XVIII), both in Gay Papers.

TABLE 6

FAMILY STATUS OF SLAVES HOLDING ACCOUNTS ON THE GAY FAMILY'S ESTATE, 1844

Male	
Head of household	37
Son in a male-headed household	6
Son in a female-headed household	3
Single male	18
Head of household (?)	1
Son in a male-headed household (?)	1
Single male (?)	2
Unknown	2
Female	
Head of household	2
Daughter in a female-headed household	1
Single female	1
Joint Male/Female	
Husband and wife	1 couple
Unknown	1 couple

SOURCES: Daybook, 1843–1847 (Vol. V), Estate Record Book, 1831–1845 (Vol. VIII), Cashbook/Daybook, 1837–1843 (Vol. XVIII), all in Gay Papers.

suggest a coming-of-age pattern. Young adults may have been listed individually, for example, when they assumed sole responsibility in a specific moneymaking endeavor.

Records of other plantations, though less complete, suggest a similar structure of account holding, with male heads of households invariably the largest group under whom accounts were listed but with some of the goods purchased going to named persons other than the account holders, usually members of the account holders' families. Other purchases, although debited to the account holders, obviously were not solely for their benefit. The staple foodstuffs slaves bought—meat and barrels of flour—served the family; the lengths of cloth they bought could provide garments for the entire family. The housewares purchased obviously were for the

TABLE 7

PURCHASES BY SLAVES ON BRUCE, SEDDON, AND WILKINS' WILTON ESTATE WITH
MONEY MADE CUTTING WOOD, 1848

Shoes	Tobacco	Soap	Knives
Combs	Hats	Blankets	Baskets
Pipes	Suspenders	Tin cups	Hooks
Line	Cotton cloth	Calico cloth	Checked cloth

SOURCE: Wilton Plantation Daily Journal, 1853, in Bruce, Seddon, and Wilkins Plantation
Records, Department of Archives and Manuscripts, LSU Libraries.

NOTE: There was also cash withdrawn.

whole household: candles, furniture, cutlery and other tableware, coffeepots, blankets, locks, mosquito bars, soap, and cooking utensils. The purchases by slaves on Wilton plantation, Lanaux' Bellevue plantation, Colonel
Pugh's Woodlawn plantation, and Alexis Ferry's estate encompass a range
of commodities, both household and personal, that undoubtedly went to
improve the lives and comfort not only of the slaves who were debited for
the goods but also of members of their families. What Louisiana slaves
bought substantiates a focus upon family and improvement to home, con-
cerns around which many of the economic activities of Jamaican slaves also
revolved (Tables 7–10; see also Appendixes 5–7).[73]

73. Recent scholarship provides evidence for the existence of internal economies
within slave communities throughout the Americas. See, in particular, the special
issue of *Slavery and Abolition,* XII (May, 1991), reprinted as *The Slaves' Economy:
Independent Production by Slaves in the Americas,* ed. Ira Berlin and Philip D. Morgan
(London, 1991).

TABLE 8

EARNINGS AND EXPENDITURES OF SLAVES ON GEORGE LANAUX' BELLEVUE ESTATE, 1851–1854

Payments to Slaves for:

Corn	$0.75 per barrel	Chickens	$0.25 each
Wood	$0.60 per cord	Sunday work	$0.30–$0.60 per day
Eggs	$0.15 per dozen	Holiday work	$0.60 per day

Expenditures by Slaves for:

Flour	$5.00 per barrel	Oilcloth winter	
Knives	$0.25 each	coats	$2.50 each
Sheet tin	$0.35	Oiled pantaloons	$1.10 per pair
Boots	$3.50 per pair	"1 paire	
Fiddles	$2.00 each	Brodequins"	
Biscuits	$3.15 per barrel	(laced boots)	$1.15 per pair
Potatoes	$2.10 per barrel	Denim	
Rice	$7.00 per barrel	pantaloons	$1.10 per pair
Spoons	$0.50 per dozen	"Log Cabin"	
Tobacco		pantaloons	$1.25 per pair
Locks	$0.75 each	"I piece collette	
Portable ovens	$0.85 each	30 yds."	$0.125 per yard
Flannel dresses	$1.25 each	"1 serrure	
Copper kettles	$0.40 each	francais de 6	
"Mouchoirs		pces" (six-piece	
de tete"		French lock)	$1.00
(kerchiefs)	$0.15 each		

SOURCES: Journal, 1851–1860 (Vol. XIV), Ledger, 1851–1856 (Vol. XVIII), both in George Lanaux and Family Papers, Department of Archives and Manuscripts, LSU Libraries.

NOTE: There was also cash withdrawn.

TABLE 9

EARNINGS AND EXPENDITURES OF SLAVES ON W. W. PUGH'S WOODLAWN ESTATE, 1848–1855

Payments to Slaves for:

Wood	$0.50 per cord	Shingles	$ 4.50 per 1,500
Pickets	$1.25 per 100	Staves	$ 4.50 per 900
Sunday or holiday work	$1.00–$1.25 per day	Shuck collars	$ 0.375 each
Hauling wood	$0.75 per day	Cross-ditching	$ 5.50 per 344 yards
Muscovy ducks	$0.375 each	Boards	$ 0.025 per four-food board
Chickens	$0.20–$0.25 each	Burning kiln bricks	$12.00
Hogsheads made during holidays	$0.75 each	Ditching	

Expenditures by Slaves for:

Flour		Boots	$ 4.00 per pair
Shoes		Blankets	$ 0.75 each
Tobacco		Small shoats	
Apples	$ 2.25 per barrel	"Silk Dress for Rachel"	$12.50 (debited to a slave named Woodson)
Bottles of cordial		"Mending Watch"	$ 3.00

SOURCE: Cashbook for Negroes, 1848–1855 (Vol. VI), in Colonel W. W. Pugh Papers, Department of Archives and Manuscripts, LSU Libraries.

NOTE: There was also cash withdrawn.

T A B L E 10

PURCHASES BY SLAVES ON ALEXIS FERRY'S SUGAR ESTATE WITH MONEY MADE
CUTTING WOOD, 1848

Tobacco	"Bolle Jaune" (yellow bowl)
Cottonade pantaloons	"Gobelets" (cups)
Shoes	"Secousse de Tasse" (saucers?)
Dresses	"Contenit" (containers?)
Hats	"Robe Bontenit" (fine dress?)
Chairs	"Tignons" (head scarf, turban)
Flour	"Pot Jaune" (yellow pot)
Handkerchiefs	"Aunes Coutes" (expensive lengths of cloth?)
Plates	"Aunes Jingus" (lengths of thin [ginguet] cloth?)
Meats	"Aunes Con Teint" (lengths of dyed cloth?)
Cottonade cloth	"Bleuecroisée" (blue twill?)
"Bolle Lustre" (glazed bowl)	"Fublonis" (?)
"Bolle Doré" (gilt bowl)	"Colletes" (?)

SOURCE: Journal, 1842–1865, 1877 (Vol. I), in Alexis Ferry Journals, Department of Archives
and Manuscripts, Tulane University Libraries.

3

MATERIAL CULTURE IN JAMAICA

The stability and security of the internal economy in Jamaica rested on the modus vivendi established between slaves and planters on the plantation. Notwithstanding what slaves did off the estate, they based the operation of their economic activities on the plantation. In the slave houses, gardens, and grounds—the focus of family and community life—slaves established and developed their economic systems.

The houses that sugar plantation slaves lived in were typically made of wattle, or wattle and daub. To build and repair their houses, the slaves employed materials that were readily available and techniques that were, in part, of African derivation. At times, however, planters purchased lumber and other building materials, particularly for finishing and repairs or when the plantation was too distant from woodlands, mountains, and other sources of supply.

The slaves first cleared the land, then lined out and framed their houses. Forked posts provided the middle and end supports; shorter posts framed the house and served as floor joists. Frequently slaves burned the part of the post that was to be sunk below ground level, giving the wood a protective coat to retard rot. A ridgepole placed along the notches of the main supports, and wall plates either notched or nailed into place on the shorter posts of the external frame, completed the skeleton of the house. Rafters, connected in pairs by wooden pins, straddled the ridgepole, and withes (*Heliotropium fruticosum*) bound laths to the rafters.

The walls, which at that point consisted of only the horizontal wall plates and crossbeams, were then wattled. Vertical sticks between every two wall plates, and others attached to each side of every post, provided a lattice into which wattles—either small round sticks or sturdy slivers stripped from larger timbers—were woven by being bent around the perpendiculars, each wattle curving either in or out so that no two adjacent wattles curved in the same direction. Slaves often daubed the wattles with clay or mud combined with vegetable fiber, such as plantain leaves, which acted as a binding agent. Daubing filled the cracks between the wattles, and when smoothed onto both inner and outer walls, provided a hard, plasterlike surface when dry.

Although some slaves used shingles for roofing, most thatched their houses with any of a variety of available plants, the best of which were the mountain cabbage palm (*Roystonea oleracea*) and other thatch palms, all so durable they reportedly lasted for more than thirty years. The leaves of the thatch palms, which are long, narrow, and monocotyledonous, were plaited together, and slaves put several layers of these plaits on the roof laths and tied them there with withes, thus rendering the roof watertight. When they could not get thatch palms, they used inferior substitutes such as sugarcane leaves, grass, and other species of palm.

The slaves constructed doors to their houses by joining a few plain boards together that they hinged with leather straps or wooden pivots. Windows were similarly shuttered. In most cases, the floors of the houses remained uncovered, and the earth in the course of time dried and hardened (Figures 3, 4).[1]

Most slaves lived in wattle-and-daub houses, but not all did. The records of Lord Seaford's two Montpelier sugar estates reveal some variety in slave housing (see Appendix 8).[2] Of the 123 slave dwellings on Old Montpelier in 1825, 11 were built of stone, 17 had board walls, 1 had shingle walls, and 4 were Spanish walled, with pieces of broken stone mortared with clay, or stone covered with lime or earth that was then plastered or whitewashed. Of the remaining houses, 62 were wattled. No description of the walls was given for the other 28. Most of the last group probably also had wattled walls. In the same year, New Montpelier slave village included 101 houses, of which 24 were stone, 2 had Spanish walls, and the remainder were wattled. Thatched roofing predominated, although a number of houses on both estates had shingled roofs. Only seven houses at Old Montpelier and none at New Montpelier had wood flooring.

1. The description of construction techniques here is based on "Characteristic Traits of the Creolian and African Negroes in Jamaica," *Columbian Magazine,* III (1797), 249–52.

2. "Minutes of Evidence taken before the Select Committee of the House of Lords appointed to inquire into the Law and Usages of the several West India Colonies in relation to the Slave Population . . . ," in *British Sessional Papers: House of Lords,* 1831–32, CCCVI, 82–89, 1376–93; Barry W. Higman, "A Report on Excavations at Montpelier and Roehampton," *Jamaica Journal,* VIII (1974), 44.

The size of the houses and their internal layout, though partly dependent on the number of occupants, were also fairly uniform. The "shell" commonly measured from fifteen to twenty-four feet in length, ten to fifteen feet in width, and according to the Jamaican planter-historian Bryan Edwards, was "barely sufficient to admit the owner to walk in upright." The house usually contained two rooms or two rooms and a passageway. The passageway—or if there was none, one of the rooms—was the place for an unvented fire around which people could sit and talk, smoke, and perhaps cook. The other room or rooms were used for sleeping.[3]

The fittings of the cabins varied. William Beckford was aware that occasionally one of the rooms in the cabin had wooden flooring, and he also commented that sometimes one room had a louvred window that operated on the principle of a venetian blind. It is likely, however, that few slave houses displayed those features.[4]

If planters participated at all in the building of houses for the slaves, the most limited form their contribution could take was the supply of some building materials—most important, nails, and less commonly, lumber and shingles. On James Chisholme's Trouthall estate, after each field slave had lined out a house and erected the basic frame, the overseer gave him one hundred nails and promised three dollars for finishing the house. At the next degree of involvement, the planters made the estate's slaves and free craftsmen available to assist with construction. And at the highest degree of involvement, the planters supplied finished housing to the slaves.[5] The planters were more likely to assist with construction if building materials were not available in the neighborhood. But some rendered assistance out of concern for the health and welfare of the labor force.

In response to the high mortality of imported African slaves during the "seasoning period," some planters adopted the policy of providing the newcomers with basic necessities upon their arrival in Jamaica. Besides supplying them with provision grounds ready planted, those owners arranged for shelter in one of three ways. Sometimes the arrivals were boarded out in the existing slave community until they received or built their own houses. Edwards referred to that procedure, which was also used on Nathaniel Phillips' sugar plantations, in St. Thomas-in-the-East. Or as on Lord Penrhyn's plantations, the new slaves were given "tight temporary Huts, until a leisure

3. Edwards, *The History, Civil and Commercial*, II, 126.
4. Beckford, *A Descriptive Account*, I, 229.
5. William Anderson, Trouthall estate, to James Chisholme, March 9, 1811, in Chisholme Papers.

opportunity offer[ed] of erecting Houses for them" and while they were put to "preparing wood for their houses." Or the planter constructed housing before taking on the slaves.[6]

The planters' concern with the housing of the resident slave population on their estates heightened in the last decades of slavery in Jamaica, particularly after the abolition of the slave trade. With the external source of slaves lost, the planters looked to improvements in the treatment and living conditions of their gangs in the hope of maintaining the size of the labor force by natural increase. The planters believed that improved housing would favor an increase in the number of live births and a decrease in the infant mortality rate by promoting better overall health. Thus they instituted various measures that they styled "amelioration," making the slave quarters more weatherproof and building them in safer and healthier locations, supplying both materials and the skilled help of the estate's artisans, and sometimes even helping with the restoration of houses that had suffered weather damage.

Nevertheless, the involvement of the planter in house construction continued peripheral. The primary responsibility for building houses rested with the people who wanted to live in them, and in the main they had to rely on construction materials gathered locally. That had a significant impact on housing quality, architectural design, and residential patterns. Since the slaves exercised considerable autonomy concerning where and how the houses were built, their decisions offer insights into the structure and values of their community.

The houses varied in size and construction according to the number and status of the occupants. In Jamaica, where the housing consisted primarily of family dwellings, that meant that the size of the family had a heavy bearing on the size of the house. But housing for head slaves, including drivers and practitioners of the skilled trades, was often larger than that of field hands, and better in finishing and appointments.

Consanguineal and affinitive relatives residing on the same plantation usually dwelt together as a family unit. Adult slaves not living with family stayed either alone or with other single persons of the same sex. The latter arrangement was common when slaves arrived from Africa to supplement a plantation's labor force. In one such instance, the attorney in charge of

6. Edwards, *The History, Civil and Commercial,* II, 119; Thomas Barritt, Pleasant Hill, Jamaica, to Nathaniel Phillips, July 4, 1793, in Phillips Papers (MS 8419); Rowland W. Fearon to Lord Penrhyn, February 6, 1806, in Penrhyn Castle Papers (MS 1415).

Phillips' plantations informed the owner that he would "get a house or two made for the Men." When the female slaves purchased for Phillips' estates were boarded out with existing households, the ties that developed could become adoptive. The boarders were particularly likely to be adopted as family members if they possessed commonalities with slaves already living on the plantation—if they were from the same part of Africa, belonged to the same African national or linguistic group, or had been transported across the Atlantic on the same vessel. Phillips' attorney said of the slaves he had purchased that "most of the old people here such as Winsor, Ben, Frank etc., are of the same country. . . . The old people are glad to see them, and have taken them in their houses."[7]

Although houses were normally nuclear one-family units, their grouping could reflect an extended family network. A number of adjacent slave houses on the Hope estate, just outside Kingston, belonged to members of the same family and were surrounded by a common fence. The slaves living in that compound used a common gateway. On Old Montpelier, too, the eight people of the Warren, Tomlinson, and Thompson households had a compound of three houses, as well as an acre and a half of kitchen gardens that they worked in common. Enclaves of that sort were the result of choices by the slaves, since the planter designated only the general areas of slave housing and left the precise location of individual dwellings to the discretion of the people building them.[8]

There was generally little regularity in the layout of housing sites in the slave villages on Jamaican plantations, in contrast to Louisiana, where the typical settlement consisted of orderly rows of houses with streets down the middle. Where formal order of that kind existed in Jamaica—as, for example, on Roehampton estate, in St. James Parish—the hand of the planter was evident. The usual Jamaican pattern had houses clustered throughout a general area among fruit trees, vegetable gardens, and livestock pens.

7. Barritt to Phillips, July 4, 1793, in Phillips Papers (MS 8419).

8. *Jamaica Journal,* I (1818), 15–25; *British Sessional Papers: House of Lords,* 1831–32, CCCVI, 82–89, 1376–93. Jamaican slave family organization continues to be debated. Barry Higman, in his analysis of slave families on the island, asserts that since "almost 50 percent [of the slaves in his sample] lived in units approximating the elementary family . . . the woman-and-children household was far from dominant" (*Slave Population,* 159), but Orlando Patterson disagrees, contending that "the typical household was one in which women dominated . . . including those which had grown sons and dependent, emasculated lovers" ("Persistence, Continuity, and Change in the Jamaican Working-Class Family," *Journal of Family History,* VII [1982], 141–43).

The irregular spacing impeded surveillance, whereas in Louisiana, where planters determined the siting of slave housing, a primary consideration was to let the overseer's house look out upon an easily observed slave village.[9]

An anonymous contributor to a Kingston journal remarked that "the groundwork of all Negro habitations in Jamaica was as in Sierre Leone, the Negro huts of Africa." An illustration of Jamaican slave housing (Figures 3, 4) shows the African influence not only in the positioning of the buildings relative to one another but also in the shape and structure of the walls and roofs, and in the techniques of wattling, daubing, and thatching.[10]

Another commentator of the time noted that house construction had its place assigned in the Jamaican slave family's division of labor, in that the husband was expected to do the work necessary for providing shelter. J. B. Moreton observed, "Those who live in pairs together, as man and wife, are mutual helpmates to each other: the men build the huts, and assist to work in their grounds; the women prog for food, boil pots at noon and night, louse their heads, extract chiggers from their toes and wash their frocks and trowsers." The same allotment of responsibilities was seen on Chisholme's Trouthall estate. A letter to Chisholme from the attorney in charge mentioned one of the slave carpenters, his wife, and the "fine House [he] had made her."[11]

During the abolition and emancipation movements, there was considerable inquiry, and much disagreement, concerning the quality of slave housing. Legislative debates raged over the condition of the slaves in the British West Indies. William Fitzmaurice, earlier a bookkeeper and overseer in Jamaica, gave evidence on slave dwellings to the House of Commons Select Committee on the Slave Trade, testifying that "the greater part of them are open, and exposed to the weather—their houses are made of wattle, without being plastered—they lie at night on a board on the ground close to the fire, and after the fire goes out they suffer by cold and damp." Robert Renny supported that testimony in his *History of Jamaica* when he described the slaves as living in wretched habitations barely sufficient to keep the weather out. Dr. John Quier, the resident physician on the Worthy Park

9. For a detailed analysis of the spatial context of Jamaican plantation development, accompanied by plans, maps, and descriptions of the physical layout of numerous sugar estates, and including a discussion of slave housing and villages, see Higman, *Jamaica Surveyed,* esp. 243–48.

10. *Jamaica Journal,* II (1818), in Patterson's *The Sociology of Slavery,* 54.

11. J. B. Moreton, *Manners and Customs in the West India Islands* (London, 1790), 150; William Anderson to James Chisholme, September 6, 1800, in Chisholme Papers.

estate, presented a similar picture in his testimony to the Jamaica House of
Assembly Committee on the Slave Trade: he blamed the inadequacy of
lodgings, and their smokiness, dampness, and cold, for causing respiratory
ailments among the slaves.[12]

Other sources from the period offer a contrasting view. Hector McNeill's
defense of slavery and the slave trade represented the housing of slaves as a
comfortable and commodious arrangement of apartments, with ample furniture, utensils, and apparel. A description of the slave village on Hope
estate compared the quality of its clean and neat houses to English cottages,
and Dr. John Williamson's experiences during his residence in Jamaica from
1798 to 1812 left him with the impression that slaves "in their own
houses . . . have their snug warm fireside, and little air admitted to it."[13]

The conflicting testimony, of course, fit the views of the opposing sides
of the slavery debate. In as extensive a system as sugar slavery in Jamaica, it
is likely that all of it could be substantiated, if not in general, then at least
in specific cases. Citation of a slave carpenter's fine house by the attorney
on Trouthall estate could be combined with the Reverend Thomas Cooper's
observation that some of the slave houses were built in a superior style to
show that the condition of slave housing was not uniformly bad. Properly
constructed wattle-and-daub houses certainly could provide adequate shelter and lodging in the tropical Jamaican climate, and some must have done
so.[14] Edwards, for example, stated that "tradesmen and domestics are in
general vastly better lodged and provided. Many of these have larger houses
with boarded floors." When planters assumed responsibility for constructing houses, they gave slaves in positions of authority and privilege lodgings
that were superior in size or appointments. According to the Jamaican sugar
planter Gilbert Mathison, some slaves spent earnings accumulated through

12. Testimony of William Fitzmaurice, "Minutes of the Evidence taken before a
Committee of the House of Commons, being a Select Committee appointed to take
the Examination of Witnesses respecting the African Slave Trade," in British Sessional Papers: House of Commons, 1731–1800, Accounts and Papers, XXXIV, 745
(1790–91), 206; Renny, An History of Jamaica, 178; Testimony of John Quier, in Two
Reports (one presented on the 16th of October, the other on the 12th of November, 1788)
from the Committee of the Honourable House of Assembly of Jamaica . . . on the Subject of
the Slave Trade, and the Treatment of Negroes . . . (London, 1789), 31.

13. McNeill, Observations on the Treatment of Negroes, 2–3; Jamaica Journal, I
(1818), 15–25; John Williamson, Medical and Miscellaneous Observations Relative to the
West India Islands (Edinburgh, 1817), 147.

14. Anderson to Chisholme, September 6, 1800, in Chisholme Papers; Thomas
Cooper, Facts Illustrative of the Condition, 22–23.

the internal economy to keep their houses in good repair. The weight of the evidence, however, is on the side of the general inadequacy of slave housing on the sugar plantations.[15]

The vast body of the slave population lacked the advantages accorded the drivers, artisans, and other elite slave groups. Field slaves did not have the construction skills necessary to build and repair houses, nor could they accumulate money as readily. Their subordinate position in the labor hierarchy denied them the favors of the planter. Consequently, their housing conditions were apt to be poor.

Appraisals of the buildings' value reflect the standard of slave housing. An inventory of Phillips' Pleasant Hill estate taken in May, 1784, valued at four hundred pounds the "Negro Houses" for a slave population totaling 315. Although the inventory does not state the number of houses, the slaves on this plantation lived for the most part in single-family dwellings that probably averaged four or five occupants each. By way of comparison, the inventory evaluated the 315 slaves themselves at £22,160, the total valuation of the plantation was £73,693, and a single framed "Hot House," or hospital, with stone walls and a shingled roof was valued at two hundred pounds. Although John Blackburn, who had managed Jamaican sugar estates, commented in 1807 before the House of Commons Committee on the Commercial State of the West India Colonies that "their houses are in great measure, of their own building, and may be worth twenty, twenty-five or thirty pounds each," only the best slave housing would have been valued that highly.[16]

The detailed descriptions of over two hundred slave houses on Lord Seaford's Montpelier estates reveal both the range in quality of housing and its general inadequacy (see Appendix 8). The dismal hovels described as "very bad, falling down," "old and ruined," "very indifferent," and "tumbling down" outnumber apparently adequate housing such as the "good stone house, shingled," and the "good house, wattled and plastered, boarded floor," that housed two families on Old Montpelier, and the "three houses, all good: one of stone, one Spanish walled and one wattled," in which one New Montpelier family lived. The quality of housing on Old Montpelier appears to have been inferior to that on New Montpelier. Age may account

15. Edwards, *The History, Civil and Commercial*, II, 127; Gilbert Mathison, *Notices*, 39–40.

16. Testimony of John Blackburn, in *Report from the Committee on the Commercial State of the West India Colonies*, 43; Inventory and Valuation of Pleasant Hill Estate, May 24, 1784, in Phillips Papers (MS 11524).

for the difference, since some of the inadequate slave houses on Old Montpelier, which was settled in 1739, probably predated the establishment of New Montpelier in 1775.[17]

Dr. Collins pointed out in his description of West Indian sugar plantations that for the great majority of slaves—the field hands—"the erection, or repair of their houses, becomes a very heavy task, when it is to be effected alone as is the case on most estates, and, of course, the business advances slowly, and is imperfectly done." Attesting to the inadequacy of the "generality of negro houses," he conceded that "a few [were] much more solidly and artificially constructed by the sensible negroes on most estates." Indeed, *house* may be too grand a word for the structures in which most slaves lived. The words *hut* and *shed,* which Cooper used, may capture better the crude constructions.[18]

Much of the housing was unable to protect its inhabitants from the vagaries of a maritime tropical climate. Jamaica's latitude gives protection against excessively cold weather, but the rather small, mountainous island experiences more wind and rain than the continental tropics do. The weather readily penetrated the chinks between the wattles of houses without daub or plaster; prolonged rains drenched inadequate thatching and caused damp to rise from bare floors. Phillips' estate manager recognized the shortcomings of slave housing, especially in wet weather, when he had to deal with an outbreak of measles on Pleasant Hill plantation. He reported that "the late wet weather is much against Measels Negroes, who are required to be kept warm, we have got the overseers house nearly filled with them." Although the manager put the ill together there in part because of quarantine considerations, he also realized that the slaves' own housing was not suitable for keeping them dry and warm. In a letter to Phillips he explained he had a policy of supplying all measles victims with dry accommodation and warm clothing.[19]

Severe weather often damaged slave housing. A storm in 1815 hit Lord Penrhyn's sugar estates, causing widespread destruction of slave houses, but it was not of sufficient force to harm any of the other buildings on the estate, which had been more substantially constructed by expert workmen.

17. *British Sessional Papers: House of Lords,* 1831–32, CCCVI, 82–89, 1376–93; Higman, "A Report on Excavations," 40.

18. Dr. Collins, *Practical Rules for the Management and Medical Treatment of Negro Slaves in the Sugar Colonies* (1811; rpr. New York, 1971), 117; Cooper, *Facts Illustrative of the Condition,* 22–23.

19. Thomas Barritt to Nathaniel Phillips, April 25, 1795, May 27, 1795, both in Phillips Papers (MSS 9203, 9205).

Similarly, Phillips' Pleasant Hill and Phillipsfield estates suffered storm damage on November 2, 1800. The storm injured crops, but as the manager reported, "few Buildings were hurt Excepting the Negroe Houses." Reports of weather damage to slave housing were so frequent in the records of planters and their agents in Jamaica as to be virtually a perennial phenomenon, occurring with the onset of the hurricane season in the autumn. The damage, however, was often due more to the fragility of the houses than to the severity of the storms. When really severe weather brought significant damage to the sturdier buildings on the plantation, such as the sugar works and the white people's housing, it devastated the slave quarters.[20]

Prolonged rains posed another threat to the slaves' housing. Slave quarters near watercourses could be inundated if the streams burst their banks. This occurred on one of Lord Penrhyn's plantations when "a small Rivulet that is contiguous to the Negroe Houses . . . rose also to a great highth which has done some injury to the Negroe Houses and swept away some of the Negroes Cloaths, Hogs and a little poultry."[21]

Slave housing was particularly susceptible to fire. Dr. Collins, in his *Practical Rules,* detailed preventive measures that attested to the prevalence of this destructive force. He went so far as to say that "fire . . . seldom fails to do more or less mischief on every plantation, once in two or three years, sometimes scarcely leaving the vestige of a house." The chief causes of the frequent fires were combustible building materials, the closeness of the slaves' houses to one another, and the presence of open flames.[22] Wattled, thatched houses, constructed on a skeleton of wood, were both easily ignited and quick to burn. Almost invariably, fire, once begun, spread, consuming nearby houses. A report in the *Jamaica Magazine* of May, 1813, told of the destruction of forty-five slave houses on the Holland estate, apparently the result of a failure by field cooks to extinguish a fire in the cookroom after preparing the hands' breakfast. On Duckenfield Hall estate, seven slave houses burned during very dry weather in April, 1797. Chisholme urged the manager on his Trouthall sugar plantation to guard against fire by ensuring that slaves did not build their houses too close together. The threat of conflagration was ever present because, as Beckford was aware, the slaves kept fires burning constantly in their cabins.

20. J. Shand, Spanishtown, to G. H. D. Pennant, November 6, 1815, in Penrhyn Castle Papers (MS 1542); Thomas Barritt to Nathaniel Phillips, November 26, 1800, in Phillips Papers (MS 11615).

21. Rowland W. Fearon to Lord Penrhyn, June 6, 1806, in Penrhyn Castle Papers (MS 1424).

22. Collins, *Practical Rules,* 121.

The crude torches they fashioned to light their dwellings increased the menace.[23]

What is more, the slaves resorted to arson as a form of resistance: one of the most prevalent covert acts was igniting the cane fields. In dry weather, flames could race through the tinderlike canes wreaking destruction, and since intensive land use meant that the cane fields abutted plantation buildings, the burning canes also threatened the sugar works and houses, as well as endangering neighboring plantations downwind. On Pleasant Hill estate, in St. Thomas-in-the-East Parish, during a dry spell in May, 1796, the estate manager reported "cases of fire breaking out among Negroe Houses, d[itt]o. Grounds or Cane Pieces. —last night this Estate was very near being burnt down, by some evil minded, or Runaway people, setting fire to Stoakes Hall Canes [an adjoining plantation]."[24]

Whatever the susceptibility of slave housing on Jamaican sugar plantations to damage and destruction and whatever the frequency with which that occurred, the responsibility for repair and reconstruction rested primarily with the occupants. Continued deterioration of the housing was the result, since buildings, poorly constructed from the first, had to be repaired by men and women who, more than likely, lacked the essentials for proper maintenance—time, skill, and materials.[25]

Some plantations, however, adopted policies of assisting slaves whose houses were damaged or dilapidated. For example, the attorney on Duckenfield Hall estate, in St. Thomas-in-the-East Parish, explained in a letter to the plantation's absentee owner, Jacob Franks, that

> it is always generally usual after crop time, to give the assistance of the estates carpenters to do such jobs at the negroe houses & is much a matter of course, that I thought you were well aware of it, & therefore did not particularly specify it, in my letters to you. Now as to expence, permit me to assure you, that absolutely no positive expence was the estate put to, but in the few nails, used in the repairs & construction of the houses, & the few feet of common white pine boards, used in repairing old doors & windows, & when necessary, making new ones,

23. *Jamaica Magazine* (Kingston), III (1813), 349; Thomas Barritt to Nathaniel Phillips, April 6, 1797, in Phillips Papers (MS 11580); James Chisholme to William Anderson, August 6, 1810, in Chisholme Papers; William Beckford, *A Descriptive Account*, I, 229; *The Columbian Magazine*, III (1797), 252–53.

24. Thomas Barritt to Nathaniel Phillips, May 20, 1796, in Phillips Papers (MS 11573).

25. Collins, *Practical Rules*, 116–17.

& not only was the expence of both very trifling indeed, in effect, but surely it seems not a moment to be put in competition, with the great satisfaction it was, and is, to the negroes, to have their cottages, (& they are nothing else), weathertight & comfortable, exclusive of the benefit, which their health may accrue from those circumstances.[26]

When a storm devastated the slave village on Pleasant Hill estate in July, 1784, Phillips instructed his overseers to encourage the slaves to repair the damages, "by assisting them in rebuilding their houses." On the same plantation in May and June, 1793, severe rains damaged the slaves' houses, and again the estate manager helped in their repair. A storm that struck G. H. D. Pennant's Denbigh estate in October, 1815, wrecked the slaves' houses, "but," the overseer reported, "the carpenters [were] assisting in repairing them." The same storm also hit Pennant's Kupius estate, where the overseer "allowed the negroes some time to repair their houses," observing that, "a number of [them] are entirely blown down."[27]

When a stream burst its banks on one of Lord Penrhyn's sugar plantations, inundating slave housing, the estate's manager informed him that "the Houses must be repaired for the present, but they must be removed to prevent the like from happening again." On William Dickinson's Appleton estate, in St. Elizabeth Parish, sickness among the slaves prompted the manager to remove their houses to a healthier location. Planters assisted slaves in relocating their settlements, with materials, labor, or time off.[28]

Most slave houses were sparsely furnished. Although McNeill in 1788 saw slave houses with what he called a "propriety" of furniture and utensils, published accounts by Edwards and by John Stewart disclosed deficiencies in the quality and quantity of the furnishings in slave houses; they mentioned only a table and chairs or stools, and perhaps a few items of crockery, calabashes, and containers. Edwards, Stewart, and Dr. Collins concurred in

26. John Kelly, Green Castle, Jamaica, to Jacob Franks, Islesworth, near London, December 10, 1809, in Duckenfield Hall Plantation Records, Acc. 775, 928/5, West India Collection.

27. Nathaniel Phillips to Thomas Barritt and Robert Logan, October 24, 1784, in Letter Book from June, 1778, Phillips Papers (MS 11484); Thomas Barritt to Nathaniel Phillips, June 5, 1793, in Phillips Papers (MS 8419); Extracts from Overseers' Letters, October 25, 1815, October 26, 1815, in Penrhyn Castle Papers (MS 1541).

28. Fearon to Penrhyn, June 6, 1806, in Penrhyn Castle Papers (MS 1424); William Dickinson, Upper Harley Street, London, to Thomas J. Salmon, Jamaica, May 24, 1788, in Dickinson Family Papers, West India Collection.

describing the one other important piece of furniture in slaves' houses: the bed, a wooden frame or board covered with a mat and blanket.

Privileged slaves may have had beds and other furniture of better quality, but Collins reported that some did not have even the most rudimentary pieces. Despite the paucity of data, it is clear that many sugar plantation slaves, especially field hands, experienced serious deprivation in how their dwellings were outfitted.[29] In the main, the slaves had to provide their own household furnishings, planters supplying little at their own expense. Mathison contended in his *Notices Respecting Jamaica* that "well-conditioned Negroes" on sugar plantations used the proceeds from the sale of livestock and provisions to keep their houses in good repair and furnish them. Cash income similarly would have been necessary to provide the books and prints that William Sells related seeing in some of the slave houses he visited. The profitability of the internal economy influenced the quality of slave accommodation, but only beyond a certain threshold of income. Until the slaves had provided themselves and their families with sufficient food and clothing, they did not consider buying more than the bare essentials in household goods.[30]

Many furnishings could be crafted from materials gathered in the surrounding countryside, although that demanded skill, time, and inclination. An article in the *Columbian Magazine* described slave-made chairs "bottomed with flags and rushes," the construction of which required both basketry and carpentry skills. Slaves who made sleeping mats also had to be skilled in basket weaving: the mats were made of "plantain leaf ribs stripped of dry foliage placed close together and confin[ed] . . . so by strips of the bark of trees." Slaves needed woodworking skill to construct tables and benches, and to make the beds described as "cabbins or platforms, (frequently made of cleft cabbage-tree stems), supported by rails placed on four short posts fixed in the earth." Slaves who manufactured furniture and household goods could, of course, use them in their own homes as well as sell or barter them at market.[31]

The one other piece of bedding slaves had—blankets—the planters sometimes provided. Even here, though, slaves were not treated equally. The House of Commons heard in 1789 that a blanket was included in the

29. Hector McNeill, *Observations on the Treatment of Negroes*, 4; Edwards, *The History, Civil and Commercial*, II, 126; John Stewart, *A View*, 266–67; Collins, *Practical Rules*, 120–21.

30. Mathison, *Notices*, 39; Sells, *Remarks*, 36.

31. "Characteristic Traits," *Columbian Magazine*, III (1797), 251.

slaves' annual clothing allowance: "All receive a piece of woollen cloth or blanketting." Three yards of such material was the usual distribution, but drivers and head craftsmen got a double ration. Cooper asserted, however, that many slaves did not receive even the meager three yards. He observed that "they lie on boards, or on a door covered with a mat of their own making, and sometimes a blanket for covering, but they have not all blankets. A woman with children has a blanket, and also the aged men; but many men have none." Later testimony in the House of Commons clarified the normal practice: whereas women got a blanket at the expense of the plantation, men were given a "Welch blanket or Woollen Jacket." The woolens distributed to male slaves were expected to function as both outer garments and bedclothes. The cloth thus wore out more rapidly, leading to the deprivation Cooper saw.[32]

Dr. Collins in his *Practical Rules* drew a stark picture of the lot of field slaves. He understood that "with negroes, half whose time is devoted to the service of others, the little which is not given to sleep, must necessarily be employed in obtaining or cooking their food, which exhausts almost the whole of their short remissions from labour." The punishing labor routine of sugar slavery greatly limited the free time available to those suffering under it and enervated both their spirits and their strength. Any incentive or inclination toward home improvement or the manufacture of furnishings, like any participation in the internal economy, was tempered by the overwhelming fatigue slaves suffered, by their need to provide themselves with sustenance, by the inadequacies of their shelter, and by the despondency of bondage. Erecting and repairing houses well required higher levels of skill than the building of rudimentary pieces of furniture, but any such endeavor required time and motivation in addition to skill. How bare the homes of generations and thousands of slaves who lived and died on the sugar plantations of Jamaica must have been. The evidence of J——— M———, at one time a bookkeeper on Bushy Park estate, in St. Dorothy Parish, confirmed the bleak scene of indifferent huts, frequently devoid of furniture, that served as the setting of slave life.[33]

The kitchen garden surrounding the individual slave house was some-

32. *British Sessional Papers: House of Commons,* 1731–1800, Accounts and Papers, XXVI, 646A, Pt. 3 (1789), 6; List of Slaves on Harmony Hall Estate, Trelawny, June 10, 1797, and June 6, 1799, in Harmony Hall Estate Papers (7/7-1, 7/56-1), in Jamaica Archives; Cooper, *Facts Illustrative of the Condition,* 23; *British Sessional Papers: House of Commons,* 1731–1800, Accounts and Papers, XXVI, 646A, Pt. 3 (1789), 5.

33. Collins, *Practical Rules,* 116; *Negro Slavery; or, A View,* 67.

times fenced off, but occasionally, as on Hope estate, family compounds containing a number of houses and their gardens were set off together. Poultry ranged free in the gardens which sometimes contained a partitioned section of pens or sties for small livestock, principally poultry and hogs. A journal of the day described how slaves constructed "inclosures of pales, sticks placed near [their] houses to confine stock." Hog sties were located on the sides of hills when possible, so as to permit drainage of moisture and effluent. The sties consisted of logs piled pyramidally in squares, crossing at the ends and covered with boughs at the top. The slaves constructed stock pens from "upright posts placed very near each other, sustaining a slight roof of thatch." Both William Beckford and McNeill noted the presence of pens and sties in the kitchen gardens, and Beckford also maintained that a hut often stood behind the house and functioned as a buttery, storehouse, stockhouse, or enclosed pigsty. Despite the word *often,* however, such outbuildings were not especially common. As with other improvements in housing, privileged slaves were more likely to have the outbuildings than ordinary field hands were.[34]

The fertile soil and tropical climate of Jamaica permitted even the small patches of ground that made up the kitchen gardens to yield an abundance of fruits and vegetables. Observers frequently remarked the many fruit trees, coconut palms, and vegetable plots of the slave villages. But if the slaves, for whatever reason, did not work their gardens, the fecundity of the soil quickly turned them into overgrown weedy patches. References to "showplace" examples of slave houses and gardens, as in the *Jamaica Journal* of 1818, should not conceal that these were but one side of the coin. The idyllic view, which saw slave houses nestled like English cottages among trees bearing coconuts, cashews, oranges, shaddocks, mangoes, avocados, akees, neesberries, and other fruits, and standing in fenced gardens that contained poultry and pigs, and vegetables and pineapples, must be tempered by the dismal, and equally common, picture of squalid hovels surrounded by plots gone to seed.[35]

Close to the cabin was the kitchen area. Despite the fire inside the dwelling, slaves usually did their cooking outside, either in the open air adjacent to the house or in a lean-to abutting it. The slaves were responsible for building the shelter, for providing most of the necessary utensils, and for constructing a suitable fireplace.

34. *Jamaica Journal,* I (1818), 15–25; William Beckford, *A Descriptive Account,* I, 229; McNeill, *Observations on the Treatment of Negroes,* 3–4; "Characteristic Traits," *Columbian Magazine,* III (1797), 253.

35. *Jamaica Journal,* I (1818), 15–25, 312–18.

Apart from the implements for working the sugar crop, the owners gave their slaves few tools, although they did sometimes issue cooking utensils. The slaves customarily received cane knives, which they used in the cane fields and in their grounds as well as in their kitchens. *Marly,* the fictional account of plantation life and society in Jamaica, made reference to the distribution of a clasp knife to each slave as part of the annual allowance.[36]

James Stewart's account of slavery in Jamaica related that planters provided slaves with iron cooking pots and knives. The knives were work tools that the slaves took home for their own use; the iron pots were the kitchen utensil most frequently supplied by the planter at his expense. A list of articles provided the slaves on Harmony Hall estate, in Trelawny Parish, in February, 1798, shows that of the twenty-two men on the list, three received pots; of the twenty-one women, one received a pot; none of the sixteen boys or six girls got a pot; and the only other issued at that time went to a cook. Clothing was issued the slaves annually on this plantation, but pots were issued less frequently, perhaps only when one wore out or broke. Since the Harmony Hall list gives no reason for supplying the pots, however, it may also have been a reward or incentive payment. The "Negro Accounts" on Hugh Hamilton's Pemberton Valley estate itemized the purchase of ten iron pots at 3s.9d. each and recorded that "New Negroes" received "calabashes" at the plantation's expense. But slaves received little kitchenware from the planter aside from pots and, according to a passing comment in Renny's *History of Jamaica,* the small wooden spoons slaves got immediately after they had been sold at dockside.[37]

Except for what the slaves could purchase out of their earnings, they depended primarily on country materials to make what kitchen utensils they needed. The principal raw materials available were clay and gourds. They used the clay to make earthenware pots, urns, and bowls, and cut gourds or calabashes to form containers, plates, ladles, and spoons. John Stewart said that slaves also carved wood to make bowls, mortars, pestles for grinding corn, and other such articles.[38] Some slaves were skilled in fashioning clay into glazed, convex-bottomed pots called yabbas, which they sold or bartered for provisions and other wares at the weekly markets. Pots made by less-skilled slaves for domestic use were of similar but probably cruder de-

36. *Marly,* 64.

37. James Stewart, *A Brief Account,* 10; "Served with Cloath . . . ," February 22, 1798, in Harmony Hall Estate Papers (7/56-1); Negro Account, Accounts of Hugh Hamilton and Company, Settled December 31, 1784, in Hamilton of Pinmore Papers (B1755); Renny, *An History of Jamaica,* 176.

38. John Stewart, *A View,* 266–67.

sign and construction. Yabbas, whose name may derive from the West African Igbo word *oba,* meaning "calabash" or "pot," were made following traditional African methods, casting the vessels by montage, that is, by adding successive rings of clay, and either firing them over an open flame or just leaving them to dry. Surviving examples of slave-made yabbas show the strong influence of Asante pottery design (Figure 7). Making gourd or calabash containers was much easier. Calabashes with one end cut off and a stick pushed through the side served as water cups; cut from one end to the other, the hard fruits became spoons. Besides using African techniques in making the yabbas, Alexander Barclay suggested the slaves used African designs to decorate their calabashes. "Every negro has his calabash," he observed, "and many have them carved with figures like those which are tattooed on the skins of the Africans." The slaves' utensils of daily use no doubt ranged from the most crudely fashioned gourd or coconut-shell dipper to earthenware of truly artistic construction and design. In this realm the slaves sometimes transcended, through their own talents, both the deprivation of supplies and a white-created infrastructure of privilege. For other slaves, however, the planters' failure to supply kitchen implements exacerbated the destitution of their lives in bondage.[39]

The slaves probably cooked their meals in much the way a late-eighteenth-century account in the *Columbian Magazine* laid out:

> The trivet for supporting the vessel in which [the slave] prepares his food, consists of three large stones: when he cannot get so many old gun or pistol barrels, broken augers or bill handles to drive into the earth, racks, spits and dripping pans when requisite are soon collected. Two forked sticks placed in the earth at a due distance from each other, are substitutes for the first; or a longer and slender one serves for the second. The last is compounded of half a cylinder taken from the stem of a plantain tree, and placed before the fire under the meat, with one end depressed to convey the gravy into a calabash placed to receive it.

Because the diet of the slaves contained little meat, they must have used the spit less frequently than the trivet; they also occasionally constructed crude ovens by scooping a hollow in a cutbank and placing hot coals in it.[40]

The slaves stored food and water in their houses in gourds and earthen-

39. Beatrice F. Welmers and William E. Welmers, *Igbo: A Learner's Dictionary* (Los Angeles, 1968); Michel Leris and Jacqueline Delange, *African Art* (London, 1968), 448; "Characteristic Traits," *Columbian Magazine,* III (1797), 251–52; Barclay, *A Practical View,* 315.

40. "Characteristic Traits," *Columbian Magazine,* III (1797), 251–52.

ware jars, some of which were suspended from the ceiling to prevent rats from getting at the grain or fish. As an additional precaution against pests, they built a device from a "half cylinder of bark with the round side uppermost, the rope to which their food [was] appended passing thro' this up to the ridge pole."[41]

The general neglect by planters and their delegates of the slaves' housing was a two-edged sword. It could subject the slaves to discomfort and could even threaten their health and lives, yet it also gave them a measure of autonomy. The neglect permitted them considerable liberty within their quarters. As a result, the slave's house became the focus and base for activities inherently inimical to the institution of slavery and largely independent of the plantation system and those who controlled it. The slaves had no legal rights to the privacy or sanctity of their homes, and some planters ordered their overseers and bookkeepers to visit the slave houses regularly; nevertheless, the sequestration of the quarters was generally maintained as a consequence both of the attitudes the slaves shared and of the antipathy, acquiescence, laziness, and unconcern of the whites.

The slaves developed a territorial and proprietary attitude to their houses and gardens. Testimony in the House of Commons' *Report from the Committee on the Commercial State of the West India Colonies* in 1807 included a Jamaican sugar estate manager's reference to the slaves' "houses, their provision-grounds, their gardens and orchards, (which they consider as much their own property as their Master does his Estate)." Compensation to slaves when their grounds were relocated owing to the expansion of the sugarcane fields attests to de facto proprietorial rights, as do the actions of Lord Penrhyn's agent, Rowland Fearon, who, when flooding damaged slave housing and "swept away some of the Negroes Cloaths, Hogs and a little poultry [was] obliged to help them out by replacing their little losses to make them satisfied."[42] The slaves demonstrated a sense of proprietorship by their use of homemade wooden locks, keys, and bolts to secure their dwellings. In Louisiana, lists of purchases by slaves show they spent some of their financial resources on locks. Although the possession and use of locks by slaves were antithetical to the whole notion of slave subjugation, they were also widespread, indicating a degree of slave autonomy.[43]

41. *Ibid.*

42. Testimony of John Blackburn, in *Report from the Committee on the Commercial State of the West India Colonies,* 40; Fearon to Penrhyn, June 6, 1806, in Penrhyn Castle Papers (MS 1424).

43. "Characteristic Traits," *Columbian Magazine,* III (1797), 251; Ledger, 1851–1856 (Vol. XVIII), in George Lanaux and Family Papers.

Slaves were, and viewed themselves as, property holders, with the right to keep, protect, and bequeath their possessions and territory. They invested their houses and grounds with the hallmarks of ownership, and these were normally, though tacitly, recognized by the planters and their agents. The uses to which the slaves put their own land reveals their sense of territoriality. In the garden near the house, they had a burial plot where they interred their kin, sometimes erecting a grave marker on the spot. J. B. Moreton's description of slavery noted that families sometimes even buried the deceased under their beds within the house itself. The plantation manager Blackburn testified to the Committee on the Commercial State of the West India Colonies in 1807 that the slaves considered their home and adjacent grounds hallowed and sacrosanct because of the interments. He asserted that "every [slave] house has a garden round it, of a quarter or half an acre or more; they are attached to the spot, and they are attached to the graves of their forefathers." Similar burial patterns existed in various West African societies.[44]

The pervasive religious practice of obeah reinforced the property and ownership status of the slaves' grounds and houses. The planter John Stewart observed in his history of Jamaica that obeah charms, when placed on slave property, were credited with affording protection from plunder and theft. A charm, he wrote, "loses its power, however, when put to protect the gardens and plantain walks of the Buckras." The system of obeah made distinctions consonant with the bifurcated structure of slave and white property and ownership.[45]

On levels less esoteric than the sepulchral and religious, the attitudes and actions of slaves illustrated the importance of the sanctuary that houses and grounds embodied. Slaves preferred, when sick, to remain in their own houses rather than go to the estate's hospital, or "hot house." According to William Beckford, the "better kind of negroes" were allowed to do so. Slaves invested much time, effort, and money in their homes, which served as the repository for their possessions, no matter how meager, such as "best clothes" and artifacts of utility and comfort: "The under-

44. Moreton, *Manners and Customs,* 162; Testimony of John Blackburn, in *Report from the Committee on the Commercial State of the West India Colonies,* 43. On West African burial customs, see J. Olumide Lucas, *The Religion of the Yorubas* (Lagos, 1948), 225; for a more general treatment, see Edward G. Parrinder, *West African Religion* (London, 1949).

45. John Stewart, *A View,* 278–79.

parts of eaves [which] project to shelter walls from rain afforded [slaves] places to bestow sticks, pipes, whips, hunting and fishing spears, cutlasses etc."[46]

The slave quarters, of course, were the venue for social activities. Family and friends gathered around the fires in the kitchen and inside the house or, more usually, weather permitting, in the "yard" outside. Planters complained that runaways skulked around and were fed in the slave villages. Superannuated slaves were left to their own devices there. The houses and grounds of the slaves were the prime setting for their autonomous action and decision making and were the nucleus of slave community and family development, within which a form of independence was asserted, and was conceded by the whites despite its fundamental dissonance with the basic premises of slavery.

The autonomy of Jamaican sugar plantation slaves was sufficient to permit them personal possessions acquired through their own efforts. As the examination of their internal economy shows, slaves sought to purchase for themselves and their families a wide range of goods, of which clothing and personal accessories, housewares, food, and drink were the most important. No matter how limited the independent economic activities in a particular slave community, the acquisition of these commodities was central in the pattern of slave expenditures. But rather than just supplementing supplies allocated by planters, the goods that slaves secured for themselves often gave expression to the autonomy they had wrested from their state of bondage.

Under Jamaican law, slaveholders bore the expense of clothing the slaves. In 1792, the Consolidated Slave Acts of Jamaica required "that every master, owner, or possessor of slaves, shall, once in every year, provide and give to each slave they shall be possessed of, proper and sufficient clothing, to be approved of by the justices and vestry of the parish where such master, owner, or possessor of such slaves resides." As a general rule, the planters each year gave the slaves either a suit of ready-made clothes or corresponding lengths of material.[47]

Marked disparities between the clothing of the slaves arose from differences in both the clothing the planters supplied and the apparel the slaves themselves purchased. The clothing distribution varied from estate to estate and often even on the same plantation, where privileged slaves might re-

46. William Beckford, *A Descriptive Account,* II, 18; "Characteristic Traits," *Columbian Magazine,* III (1797), 251.
47. Edwards, *The History, Civil and Commercial,* II, 148.

ceive allotments beyond the regular issue given field hands. Moreover, the clothes that the slaves obtained by their own efforts and that they never wore at work on the plantation introduced still more variety. These garments they purchased with money they had earned, or they traded for them, or they stole them.

Slaves on Jamaican plantations commonly wore clothes of osnaburg cloth. This coarse, hard-wearing linen fabric—named for its German town of origin, Osnabrück—was what slaves wore at work throughout the Caribbean. Other textiles issued in Jamaica included baize, kersey, peniston flannel, and other coarse woolens, as well as fustian (a cotton-and-flax mixture), linsey-woolsey (a wool-and-flax mixture), and various cottons. Customarily, Jamaican planters purchased the cloth or clothing they issued to the slaves, and they bore the entire expense. When the planters supplied ready-made garments, they included, besides the main items—trousers, jackets, frocks, coats, and shirts—certain accessories, for example, hats, caps, and kerchiefs. Since the Jamaican planters did not supply field hands with shoes, most slaves worked barefoot.

But Jamaican slaves usually received an annual issue of lengths of cloth, which they themselves sewed into clothing, using needles and thread that also came from the owner. On Peeke Fuller's Thetford plantation, in St. John Parish, the standard allotment for adult slaves in the clothing distribution of 1800 was a cap, seven yards of osnaburg, and three and a half yards of baize. Adolescent girls and boys received a cap, five yards of osnaburg, and two and a half yards of baize, while younger children were allocated two yards of osnaburg and a yard and a half of baize. A few minor variations aside, the only consistent divergence from this pattern was that drivers and head craftsmen received an additional one to five yards of osnaburg.[48]

The annual allowance of clothing on Hinton East's Somerset plantation for 1793 showed a similar pattern, but with a much more complex breakdown. Not only did privileged slaves receive more and children less than the normal ration but also distinctions existed between, and even within, the work gangs, reflecting differences in the capabilities of individual slaves. Slaves in the first or great gang received a larger allowance than those in the weaker and less productive second gang, who received more than slaves working in the still weaker third gang. Superannuated slaves, watchmen, and others with lower productive capacities received reduced allowances

48. Thetford Plantation Book, 1798–1799, in Worthy Park Estate Records, 4-23/9, Jamaica Archives.

(Table 11). The 1799 clothing list for Harmony Hall estate (Table 12) shows age, occupational, and gender differences in distribution. Michael Craton's compilation of the clothing issued slaves on Worthy Park estate in 1793 (Table 13) manifests a similar pattern.[49]

Through the early years of the nineteenth century, especially after the closure of the slave trade, the amount of material furnished Jamaican slaves increased. A comparison of the quantities given the slaves on Harmony Hall estate in 1799 with the quantities for 1811 and 1813 clearly shows that (Table 14). The ration for 1811 was significantly larger than that of 1799, and the ration for 1813 showed similar increases but with slightly larger quantities overall. The coincidence of the more liberal clothing allocations with the agitation against and the ultimate abolition of the slave trade suggests that the largess was one of the ameliorative measures the planters hoped would cause the slave population to increase naturally, thus obviating the need for reinforcements from Africa.[50]

Although the combination of osnaburg linen and baize woolen was the usual issue, planters substituted a variety of other materials when market pressures or the preferences of either slaves or planters pushed in that direction. An important market influence was the emergent cotton industry in Great Britain, which was challenging the dominance of European-manufactured linens such as osnaburg. International conflicts, especially the blockades of Europe during the Napoleonic Wars, contributed to shifts in market and product, again adversely affecting the trade in osnaburg.[51]

Slaves voiced their opinions on the cloth they received, indicating their likes and dissatisfactions. The absentee sugar planter Nathaniel Phillips, in a letter written to the overseer of his Jamaican sugar estate in October, 1789, revealed the slaves' preferences: "Agreeable to my promise to my black friends, I have sent them Blue Cottons, and also some striped d[itt]o. for the Women." A letter from Barritt, the overseer, to Phillips in April, 1793, related that the slaves "have not been well pleased with their Oznabrig, Hats & thread this year," and seven years later the theme recurred, when slaves complained that the osnaburg and thread were both of poor quality. The chief problems seemed to have been the coarseness and openness of the

49. Journal of Somerset Plantation, MS 229, in Institute of Jamaica; List of Slaves on Harmony Hall Estate, Trelawny, June 6, 1799; Michael Craton, *Searching for the Invisible Man: Slaves and Plantation Life in Jamaica* (Cambridge, Mass., 1978), 176–79.

50. List of Slaves on Harmony Hall Estate, Trelawny, June 6, 1799; Harmony Hall Estate Account Book, MS 1652, Vol. I, in Institute of Jamaica.

51. Grace Lovat Fraser, *Textiles by Britain* (London, 1948), 64–75.

TABLE 11

"A LIST OF SOMERSET NEGROES SERVED WITH THEIR ANNUAL ALLOWANCE OF CLOTHING FOR 1793"

	Osna-burg to each (yds.)	Baize to each (yds.)	Thread to each (skeins)	Needles to each	Hats to each
First gang					
46 men, 50 women	8	4	4	4	1
2 men	12	4	8	6	1
3 men	10	4	4	4	1
Second gang					
8 men, 21 women	6	4	4	4	1
1 man	12	4	6	6	1
Third gang					
11 men, 9 women	4	2	3	2	1
1 man	8	4	4	4	1
Carpenters					
6 men	10	4	4	4	1
1 man	12	4	6	6	1
Watchmen					
18 men	8	4	4	4	1
1 man	12	4	6	6	1
Domestics (6 men, 5 women)					
2	10	4	4	4	1
1	6	3	4	4	1
8	8	4	4	4	1
Superannuated slaves					
9 men, 11 women	6	4	4	4	1
Children unfit to work					
19	3	1.5	2	0	1
24	3	1.5	2	0	0

Continued on next page

SOURCE: Journal of Somerset Plantation, Hinton East, Proprietor, 1782–1796 (MS 229), in Institute of Jamaica, Kingston.

TABLE 11—*Continued*

	Osnaburg to each (yds.)	Baize to each (yds.)	Thread to each (skeins)	Needles to each	Hats to each
Stockkeepers					
5 men	8	4	4	4	1
2 men	6	3.5	4	4	1
Others (status unknown)					
4 men	8	4	4	4	1
1 man	4	2.5	4	4	1
1 woman	4	2.5	4	4	1

TABLE 12

CLOTHING ISSUED TO EACH SLAVE ON HARMONY HALL ESTATE, TRELAWNY, JUNE 6, 1799

	Osnaburg (yds.)	Blanketing (yds.)	Hats	Caps
2 men	10	3.5	1	
3 men	10	3	1	
22 men	6	3	1	
26 men	6	3		1
10 boys	3	2		
1 boy	3	2.5		1
36 women	6	2.5		1
6 women	6			1
8 girls	6			1
3 female children	3			

SOURCE: List of Slaves on Harmony Hall Estate, Trelawny, June 6, 1799, in Harmony Hall Estate Papers (7-1), Jamaica Archives, Spanish Town.

NOTE: Also listed are "1 boy runaway" and "1 infant boy," neither of whom received a clothing ration.

Table 13

Clothing Rations to Each Slave on Worthy Park Estate, 1793

	Number	Osnaburg (yds.)	Baize (yds.)	Checked cloth (yds.)	Hats	Caps	Coats	Blankets
Drivers, driveresses	7	10–12	3	3	1	0	1	0
Head housekeepers	2	10	3	0	1	0	1	0
Head cooper	1	10	3	3	1	0	0	0
Head potter	1	7	2.5	3	1	0	0	0
Second boilerman	1	7	2.5	3	1	0	0	0
Head mason	1	10	3	3	1	0	0	0
Head sawyer	1	10	3	3	1	0	0	0
Head carpenter	1	10	3	3	1	0	0	0
Head blacksmith	1	10	3	3	1	0	1	0
Head cattleman	1	10	3	3	1	0	0	0
Head muleman	1	10	3	3	1	0	0	0
Head home wainsman	1	7	2.5	3	1	0	0	0
Head road wainsman	1	10	3	3	1	0	0	0
Head watchman	1	10	3	3	1	0	0	0
Waiting boys	2	7	2.5	3	1	0	0	0
Groom	1	7	3	3	1	1	0	0
Seamstresses	2	10	3	0	1	1	0	0
Washerwomen	2	10	3	0	1	1	0	0
Cook	1	10	3	0	1	1	0	0

Midwife	1	7	3	0	1	1	0	0
Hothouse nurses	2	7	3	0	1	1	0	0
Black doctor	1	12	3	3	1	1	0	0
Coopers	6	10	3	3	1	1	0	0
Boilers	9	7	3	3	1	1	0	0
Distillers	4	7	3	3	1	1	0	0
Potters	2	7	3	3	1	1	0	0
Sugar guards	2	10	3	3	1	1	0	0
Carpenters	9	7–10	3	3	1	1	0	0
Sawyers	3	10	3	3	1	1	0	0
Masons	2	10	3	3	1	1	0	0
Under blacksmith	1	7	3	3	1	1	0	0
Home wainsmen	6	7	2.5	3	1	1	0	0
Road wainsmen	7	10	3	3	1	1	0	0
Mulemen	14	7	2.5	3	1	1	0	0
Hog tenders	3	7	2.5	3	1	1	0	0
Poultry tenders	2	7	2.5	3	1	1	0	0
New Negro tenders	3	7	2.5	3	1	1	0	0
Cattlemen and boys	8	5–10	2–3	3	1	1	0	0
Ratcatchers	2	7	2.5	3	1	1	0	0
Great or first gang	147	7	2.5	0	1	1	0	0

Continued on next page

SOURCE: Stanley L. Engerman and Eugene D. Genovese, eds., *Race and Slavery in the Western Hemisphere: Quantitative Studies*. Copyright © 1975 by the Center for Advanced Study in Behavioral Sciences, Stanford, Calif. Used by permission of Princeton University Press.

TABLE 13—*Continued*

	Number	Osnaburg (yds.)	Baize (yds.)	Checked cloth (yds.)	Hats	Caps	Coats	Blankets
Second gang	67	7	2.5	0	1	1	0	0
Third gang	68	5–6	2	0	1	1	0	0
Grass or weeding gang	21	3–5	2	0	1	1	0	0
Vagabond gang	13	5–7	2.5	0	1	1	0	0
Pen negroes	48	7	0	0	1	1	0	0
Watchmen	25	7	3	0	1	1	0	0
Grass gatherers	7	7	2.5	0	1	1	0	0
Hopeless invalids	18	5–7	2.5	0	0	1	1	1
Child watchers	3	5	2	0	1	1	0	0
Pad menders	2	5	2	0	1	1	0	0
Superannuated slaves	2	2.5	2	0	0	0	0	0
Infants	37	2–4	1–2.5	0	0	0	0	0
Women with six children	3	10	3	0	1	1	0	0

TABLE 14

CLOTHING RATIONS TO EACH SLAVE ON HARMONY HALL ESTATE,
1799, 1811, 1813

	Osnaburg (yds.)	Baize (yds.)	Hats
1799			
Men	6	3	1
Women	6	2.5	1
Boys	3	2	0
Girls	6	0	1
1811			
Men	8	5	1
Women	7	6	1
Children	5	3	1
1813			
Men (24)	8	5.5	1
Men (16)	7	5	1
Women	7	6.5	1
Children	6	4	1

SOURCES: List of Slaves on Harmony Hall Estate, Trelawny, June 6, 1799; Harmony Hall Estate Account Book, MS 1652 (Vol. I), in Institute of Jamaica.

weave of the cloth. The slaves on Phillips' plantations also found fault with the heavier material given them. Barritt wrote to Phillips in May, 1791, "I had [the slaves] served the 22nd Inst with their Blanket Clothing, when the women in general mentioned that they wished you would send them out Blue Blanks. to their coats, instead of the linsey woolsey, as it lasts much longer."[52]

52. Nathaniel Phillips to Thomas Barritt, October 20, 1789, in Letter Book from June, 1778, Phillips Papers (MS 11484); Thomas Barritt to Nathaniel Phillips, April 10, 1793; Thomas Barritt to Nathaniel Phillips, May 25, 1791, both in Phillips Papers (MSS 8413, 8374).

Aesthetic considerations were important as well. In October, 1791, Phillips apologized because "the Striped Woollens were shipped for the Women before I understood that they preferred the Blue." In trying to rectify the mischoice, he observed, "You will find by the Invoices that I have sent an additional quantity of Blue Cotton . . . & some Gray (for a trial) in all 550 yards—so that you may keep that quantity of the Striped for the year following." Either Phillips confused the cloths, or else he expected slaves to choose the color they preferred even though it was in a different material.[53]

In clothing the slaves, Jamaican planters probably considered cost first. Only a small expenditure, however, was required to supply a slave with the quantities of material that made up the normal allocation. Charles Gordon, in calculating various expenses on his Georgia estate, estimated that a slave's "clothing and feeding [cost] £10" annually. The "Negro Accounts" of Hugh Hamilton's estate showed the purchase, in July, 1784, of 447 yards of osnaburg at the cost of £14.13.5 1/2 (about 8*d*. per yard). By December, 1787, the price of osnaburg had risen to 10 1/2*d*. per yard, 428 yards being bought at the cost of £18.14.6. At that time, Hamilton also purchased three pounds of osnaburg thread at 3*s*.9*d*. per pound, and "5 Dozn. Negroe Hats" at £1.2.6 per dozen (1*s*.10 1/2*d*. each). The price of osnaburg continued to rise, and in 1789 the Duckenfield Hall estate's accounts record that the cost of osnaburg was 1*s*.3*d*. per yard. Cost was not, however, the only factor; planters also showed concern over whether the cloth would adequately protect the slaves and prove durable.[54]

Normally only special-status slaves received made-up apparel. Sick slaves often received ready-mades, as did slaves in positions of authority and privilege. Childbearing women also received clothes, either for themselves or for their infants, as an incentive to raise large families, and other slaves were allocated clothes as bonuses. Chisholme, for example, sent word to his resident overseer, James Craggs, that he was shipping eight bedgowns for slave women with young children, twelve checked shirts for children one month old, and an old coat, waistcoat, and breeches of his which were to be given to "the most deserving negro." Four years later, his concern for stimulating the growth of slave families prompted him to extend incentive payments to the nurses: he sent a trunk containing "72 yards of printed cotton for the

53. Nathaniel Phillips to Thomas Barritt, October 12, 1791, in Letter Book from June, 1778, Phillips Papers (MS 11484).

54. Charles Gordon to Francis Grant, May 19, 1787, in Gordon of Buthlaw and Cairness Papers (1160/6/86); "Negro Account," 1784, "Negro Account," 1787, both in Hamilton of Pinmore Papers (B1755); Acc. 775, 943/6, in Duckenfield Hall Plantation Records.

breeding women . . . several parcels marked for the Children's Nurses," and a sizable quantity of his old clothes for deserving slaves at the overseer's discretion.[55]

A report on the condition of pregnant women on one of Lord Penrhyn's sugar estates, submitted by the resident agent, indicates both the solicitous attitude taken toward "breeding" on some plantations and the widespread inadequacy of infant clothing elsewhere. The agent, David Ewart, reported to Penrhyn,

> I have always, My Lord, given great encouragement to Breeding, without reference to the late measures of the abolition, and I hold out several little rewards to the Women, which few others do—Your Lordship will observe a dozen suits of Baby Linen written for in the List of Supplies, after their arrival every Child will have one given to it—The Mothers can hardly be expected to have those things, particularly the poorer sort of Negro Women, and the old Sheets, Table Cloths etc of many Estates do not afford a sufficient supply—Osnaburghs are too coarse for such infants.[56]

Mathison was equally solicitous. He drew up a formal "Code of Regulations" for the overseer on his estate, which was issued on January 1, 1810, one provision of which stipulated that each woman who delivered a child was to be given a calico or linen frock for herself, in addition to two of the same for her child when it reached the age of one month. On some other plantations, women who had just borne children received additional lengths of cloth, sometimes of superior material. On the Hope estate, near Kingston, as on Chisholme's estate, mothers of young children received lengths of calico and printed cotton.[57]

The Duckenfield Hall estate accounts show a payment of 6s.8d. being made for a "Frock for sick negro named Tryal"; Jacob Israel Bernal, the proprietor of Richmond New Works sugar plantation, in St. Ann Parish, spent £1.2.6 in October and November, 1792, to furnish a sick male slave with a "warm Jacket," a "check shirt," and a "pair of shoes." The policy on

55. James Chisholme to James Craggs, Vere, Jamaica, December 10, 1793, James Chisholme to James Craggs, December 3, 1797, both in Letterbook of James Chisholme (MS 5476), Chisholme Papers.

56. David Ewart, Westmoreland, to Lord Penrhyn, August 6, 1807, in Penrhyn Castle Papers (MS 1477).

57. Gilbert Mathison, *Notices,* 107–17; *Jamaica Journal,* I (1818), 15–25; Chisholme to Craggs, December 3, 1797, in Letterbook of James Chisholme.

Phillips' plantations was to supply all measles victims with dry housing and warm clothing.[58]

In the 1798 clothing distribution of Harmony Hall estate, the driver, Spize, received an additional five yards of osnaburg beyond the standard ration of seven, and a "Jacket & Pantaloons." According to the anonymous author of the novel *Marly,* head slaves received a woolen jacket as well as their regular issue of osnaburg and baize.[59]

James Stewart recorded in his *Brief Account of the Present State of the Negroes in Jamaica* that some planters, when distributing clothes, made special provision for "indolent" slaves. The annual clothing allowance, distributed at Christmas, was equivalent to two suits of osnaburg and one suit of Kendal cotton. Stewart asserted that "the intelligent [slaves] receive their quantums of cloth which they make up at leisure after any fashion they please." He added, however, that planters had to give made-up clothing to other slaves, and he allowed himself the exaggeration that "it [was] often necessary to cloath the indolent and careless, five or six times during the year." Stewart's observations certainly do not square with those of Renny, who observed that the clothing given to slaves by the planters was coarse and scanty, "it being in many instances, two years, before new osnaburg frocks [were] allotted to them."[60]

Sometimes a broader section of the plantation community received ready-made clothing, either as the regular or a supplemental allocation. Chisholme wrote to his overseer that he was sending a slave domestic, a maid, to his Trouthall estate "to make new Negro clothes." The clothing distribution list for Harmony Hall estate in 1798 recorded a number of slaves receiving ready-made clothing and not lengths of cloth (see Appendix 9). This list showed that only women received needles. Possibly, couples were given cloth, the wives receiving needles to sew clothing for themselves and their husbands, while planters gave the single slaves ready-to-wear garments. Phillips, for reasons not revealed in the letter, intended to give the slaves on his plantation gifts of clothing: Barritt wrote, "I have been consulting Old Betty and some others of the good people to know what present from Young Massa & Missus will be most pleasing to them, and they seem to hint that a shirt of cotton check to the Males, and a coat of D[itto]o. to the

58. Acc. 775, 945/9 (1791), in Duckenfield Hall Plantation Records; MS 1073, Accounts of Jacob Israel Bernal, Esq., Proprietor of Richmond New Works, Sugar Plantation, St. Ann Parish, Middlesex, 1792, in Institute of Jamaica; Barritt to Phillips, May 27, 1795, in Phillips Papers (MS 9205).
59. Harmony Hall Estate Papers (7/56-1), in Jamaica Archives; *Marly,* 64.
60. James Stewart, *A Brief Account,* 12; Renny, *An History of Jamaica,* 179.

females with a Handkerchief each would make them say Thankey grandee to both."[61]

Newly purchased African slaves also usually received made-up clothing. On arrival in Jamaica, those slaves would be clothed, at most, in a loincloth or shift, and planters would supply them with clothes either immediately after purchase or on reaching the plantation. One source mentions that when the slaves were taken on shore, they were immediately clothed, men in osnaburg trousers and frocks and woolen caps, women in osnaburg shifts and coats and checkered kerchiefs. Edwards corroborated that procedure, noting that African slaves, after purchase, were clothed in osnaburg and given hats or kerchiefs and knives. But the records of Worthy Park plantation mention that a female slave, Cuba, received "12 yds OZ [osnaburg] to make 4 Pair Truses [trousers] for the New Negroes—Falmouth, Homer, Samson, Philip." Apparently these slaves did not receive the full clothing allotment until their arrival at the plantation.[62]

Clothing rations often proved inadequate. When planters showed an indifference to the slaves' clothing needs, there were few sanctions that could be brought to bear on them. As sentiment grew in favor of amelioration, though, the clothing supplies apparently improved somewhat. "Of clothing," Edwards observed in 1793, "the allowance of the master is not always so liberal as might be wished, but much more so of late years than formerly." John Stewart agreed that after the closure of the slave trade, planters treated slaves better, and one of their ways was to improve the clothing ration. But despite the desire for conditions that would let the slave population maintain, and even increase, its numbers, many planters failed to supply it with the legally mandated "proper and sufficient clothing."[63]

Inadequate apparel may have been less detrimental to the health of most slaves than it would have been elsewhere. Jamaica's benign climate meant that they, even scantily clothed, were not likely to suffer from exposure. The ragged clothing slaves wore was sufficient for most of the year. Lightly clad slaves may have been healthier than the planters, who, in conformity with their perception of status and rank, felt obliged to affect an attire more

61. Chisholme to Craggs, December 10, 1793, in Letterbook of James Chisholme; "Served with Cloath . . . ," February 22, 1798, in Harmony Hall Estate Papers (7/56-1); Barritt to Phillips, June 5, 1799, in Phillips Papers (MS 11603).

62. "Characteristic Traits," *Columbian Magazine*, II (1797), 700–701; Edwards, *The History, Civil and Commercial*, II, 118; Plantation Book, 1783–1787, in Worthy Park Estate Records, 4/23-1.

63. Edwards, *The History, Civil and Commercial*, II, 127, 148; John Stewart, *A View*, 230–31.

suited to Britain's cool, temperate climate. Light clothing was cooler and more comfortable, less apt to become damp with perspiration, and easily washed and dried. Nonetheless, shoes and more adequate clothing would have helped prevent the cuts, bruises, and insect bites that afflicted slaves, especially when they worked in the fields.

Jamaica's dependence on imports from Europe had a bearing on clothing rations. Sea routes were often temporarily severed, especially during wartime, when European adversaries preyed on one another's shipping. At times like that, local stocks of provisions were likely to be overtaxed or exhausted, as one overseer lamented in a letter to his employer in England. Discouraged that the fleet outward bound from Britain had had to put back after fifty days at sea, he admitted, "We are in great want of W. Hoops [sic], Oil, Grease, Copper Nails, Candles, and the Negro Cloathing, all of which articles, wth. many others, sells here at three times the price that they formerly cost."[64]

Dry goods in Kingston were consistently more expensive than those bought in the United Kingdom and shipped directly to the estate; planters preferred to buy at the source when they could. Circumstances, however, sometimes forced the planter to buy in Kingston. "If there is not a sufficient quantity of warm Cloathing shipt to supply the aged People on the Estate and Breeding Women (who I am very desirous shall have all reasonable indulgence particularly such as may be descendants from those who were resident on my late Patriot Colonel Gomersals time)," Ezekiel Dickinson wrote to a nephew who ran one of his estates, "I desire you will purchase what further may be wanted in Kingston."[65]

Barritt assured Phillips that "every attention is paid to [the slaves'] Houses, Clothing & feeding," and Phillips expressed his "earnest wish to have adopted every reasonable plan to make [them] comfortable and happy." A few years later Barritt wrote to Phillips blaming the slaves' attitudes, and not the inadequacy of their clothing, for sickness among them: "I believe oweing to the North winds prevailing at this time of year, many of them are troubled with colds and fevers and it is impossible to make any of them put on their warm clothing."[66]

64. Thomas Barritt to Nathaniel Phillips, April 15, 1796, in Phillips Papers (MS 11571).

65. Ezekiel Dickinson, Bowden House, Wiltshire, to Caleb Dickinson, November 28, 1786, in Letterbook of Ezekiel Dickinson, Papers of Caleb and Ezekiel Dickinson.

66. Thomas Barritt to Nathaniel Phillips, September 8, 1790, in Phillips Papers (MS 8363); Nathaniel Phillips to Thomas Barritt, November 1, 1790, in Letter Book

Needless to say, not all planters or their delegates shared the solicitude of Phillips and of Penrhyn's agent. Nor was Jamaica's climate so equable that clothing did not matter at all. During the autumn and spring rains, and on winter nights, especially at the higher elevations, temperatures could be cool and the atmosphere damp. Then all slaves, but especially the weak, the elderly, the young, and the sick, were adversely affected by inadequate apparel. While some plantations made special accommodation for the worst-affected groups, on others "scanty" clothing undoubtedly caused sickness and death. William Beckford lamented the lot of slaves working as watchmen—traditionally the elderly—especially on plantations and pens at higher elevations. He understood that cold winds were particularly hard on them, for they were obliged to be on hill summits all night "without raiment perhaps, and without food."[67]

Evidence that the privileged slaves often obtained an ample supply of superior-quality clothing is available in plantation records and in the visual testimony of some artists who painted scenes of plantation life. Prints of the era depict drivers wearing much more elaborate outfits than the field hands (Figures 8–11). Items such as frock coats, shoes, collars and cravats, and glazed hats, along with the omnipresent whips or swagger sticks, distinguished the drivers in their position of privilege. Still, an idealization or stylization may have been made of the subjects in these prints, since even the field hands seem to be overdressed for the arduous tasks of holing, loading, and cutting that they are performing.

Slaves arriving from Africa underwent a rite of passage immediately after sale to a planter. Two key constituents of it were the assertion of power by virtue of ownership, and the process of acculturation by which the plantation imposed and reinforced slave status. Slave ownership was legally established by purchase, but in seeking to assert control and dominance, the planters branded the slaves and limited their movements and activities. Slaves could be separated from relatives and companions, shackled, and forced to walk or be transported to the destination the planter dictated: the sugar plantation where they would probably spend the rest of their lives in bondage. Such hardships were legitimated, justified, and reinforced both by the immediate sanction—the ubiquitous whip—and by the formal legal structure of the society.

Clothing was one of the most important instruments planters had in the acculturation process that asserted and defined slave status. The clothes that

from June 1778, Phillips Papers (MS 11484); Thomas Barritt to Nathaniel Phillips, November 20, 1793, in Phillips Papers (MS 8424).
67. William Beckford, *A Descriptive Account*, I, 198–99.

slaves arriving in Jamaica received were foreign to all their previous experience. The style and material derived from the heritage of the slaveholding Europeans, but at the same time the cut immediately identified the wearer's status. The men wore trousers and a loose shirtlike frock or smock covering their upper body; the women wore a full-length shift and a half- to three-quarter-length coat. Headgear consisted of woolen caps, glazed or felt hats, and kerchiefs. Men wore hats or caps; women usually wore kerchiefs. Children had little clothing, both sexes wearing only simple one-piece shifts if they wore anything at all. But although the material and style were European, the osnaburg trousers, frocks, shifts, and coats were the clothing of slaves and slaves alone.

The clothes of drivers and other privileged slaves brought them closer to the whites: their clothes more closely resembled those of the planters. Planters created a hierarchy of privilege that was affirmed by tangible, visible rewards such as better housing and food, as well as power and influence. Clothing was one of the most visible perquisites. In the clothing of the elite slaves is visible a continuation of the Europeanizing—or in the case of Jamaica, the Anglicizing—of the slaves that was started with the rite of passage at the dockside sale. Anglicizing was embedded in the privileges sought by some members of the slave community. Drivers, occupying a middle ground between field slaves and planters, adopted attitudes not only of dress but also of manners and speech that came closer to white attitudes than did those of field hands. Edward Brathwaite uses the evocative image of "snow . . . falling on the canefields."[68]

Outside the sway of the planters, Jamaican slaves spent a large part of any money they accumulated purchasing clothing for Sunday and holiday wear, the styles of which reflected three influences: European, African, and Creole.

Slaves often invested in ready-made clothing, tailored either locally or in Europe, that followed European styles. If they bought material, they made it up to resemble, even to the point of caricature, current European fashions. John Stewart wrote,

> Neither sex wear shoes in common, these being reserved for particular occasions, such as dances, etc., when all who can afford it appear in very gay apparel—the men in broad-cloth coats, fancy waistcoats, and nankeen or jean trowsers, and the women in white or fancy muslin gowns, beaver or silk hats, and a variety of expensive jewellry. . . .

68. Edward Brathwaite, *The Development of Creole Society in Jamaica, 1770–1820* (London, 1971), 300.

All of them who can afford to buy a finer dress, seldom appear, excepting when at work, in the coarse habitments given them by their masters.

Some years earlier, James Stewart commented on the finery that the slaves "sport[ed] on holidays or extraordinary occasions." Female slaves wore fine linen, cambric, and muslin, and were bejeweled with costly ornaments; the dress of the men included cocked hats, waistcoats, breeches, and "preposterous ruffles and coats." A similar pattern, to which plantation slaves probably aspired but which few can have attained, was manifested by urban slave artisans and described in a contemporary journal: "Mechanics are generally able from their own labour to buy good cloathing: Broadcloth coats, linen waistcoats and breeches, a smart cocked hat, with a gold or silver loop, button and band, are common with them in the holidays; to which they sometimes add shoes and stockings. They frequently have their cloaths made in the newest English fashion and sometimes exceed it fantastically." John Stewart described slaves dressed for holidays wearing "fine clothes and a profusion of trinkets."[69]

The language in all this underscores that, despite the element of emulation or adoption of various modes of European dress by slaves, the effect was not completely European. Creole clothing incorporated adaptations of other styles and combined garments in ways that to European or African eyes seemed incongruous and clashing.

Perhaps the most common article of clothing of African descent was the turban, worn by the women both as part of their work dress and—as prints of the time portraying slaves at their leisure show (Figures 8–16)—as part of their finery. Edward Long referred to the predilection of slave women to wear turbans "at all times," and Michael Scott, in a description of women in finery during a holiday celebration, touched on "their nice showy, well put on toques, or Madras handkerchiefs, all of the same pattern, tied round their heads, fresh out of the fold."[70]

Slaves wore jewels and ornaments as an integral part of their best cloth-

69. John Stewart, *A View*, 269–71; James Stewart, *A Brief Account*, 10–11; "Characteristic Traits," *Columbian Magazine*, III (1797), 7. Since slave finery was described most fully in records and histories written by planters, the descriptions incorporate certain biases. Besides stressing the benignity of slavery, the planters, as a result of their conviction of their own cultural superiority, probably overemphasized the extent to which slaves mimicked their clothing and other ways.

70. Long, *The History of Jamaica*, II, 412–13; Michael Scott, *Tom Cringle's Log* (1838; rpr. London, 1915), 245.

ing. William Beckford commented on the slaves' liking for beads, coral, glass, and chains, which they wore on their necks and wrists. The styles worn by slave women, although partly incorporating European styles, were also of African derivation: "Besides the usual European ornaments of ear-rings and necklaces, the women have at different times used as beads, the seeds of Jobs-tears, liquorice, and lilac; the vertebrae of the shark; and lately red sealing wax, which in appearance nearly resembles coral. Sometimes they sportively affix to the lip of the ear, a pindal or ground nut, open at one end; at other times they thrust through the hole bored for the ear-ring, the round yellow flower of opopinax." The African heritages also appeared in the adornments, the "party-coloured beads tied around their loins," that Scott saw slave children wearing, and they can be inferred from the "profusion of beads and corals, and gold ornaments of all description" with which Matthew Lewis saw slave women bedecked at the commencement of a festival on his plantation.[71]

Many slaves on Jamaican sugar plantations, however, wore little besides what the planters issued. Some had few opportunities to own more, since not all slaves benefited equally from the internal economy. Material poverty, sufficiency, or well-being, depended on two primary factors: the planters' largess and the internal economy. The institutional character of slavery was compatible with vast differences in both the responsibilities assumed by the planter and the profitability of individual efforts within the internal economy. The internal economy, however, markedly enriched the material existence of the Jamaican slave population.

71. William Beckford, *A Descriptive Account,* II, 386; "Characteristic Traits," *Columbian Magazine,* III (1797), 109; Scott, *Tom Cringle's Log,* 141; Lewis, *Journal of a West India Proprietor,* 74.

4

MATERIAL CULTURE IN LOUISIANA

Slave housing on sugar plantations in Jamaica and in Louisiana differed physically in construction materials and in site placement, as well as in the degree of control exercised by slaves and planters.

Typically, slave houses in Louisiana were built of wood or brick. Wooden houses were simple frame structures—clapboards nailed to a wooden skeleton—and the two principal types were double and single cabins. In double cabins, which accommodated two slave families or households, the structure was partitioned down the middle, and each apartment had its own front entry. These cabins often had a built-in front-roof overhang, and the gable faced sideward. Each living unit was itself divided into two rooms, front and back. A chimney stood in the middle of the building, thus serving both households, their fireplaces being built into the central partition. Single cabins had a front-facing door, side-facing gables; they were divided into a front and back room, with the fireplace and chimney in one of the side walls (Figures 17, 18).

Brick houses, though generally constructed according to the same plan, occasionally varied dramatically from it. A notable example was the row of four two-story brick houses on the Woodland plantation, in Plaquemines Parish. In a design unusual for Louisiana, this structure provided lodging for four households. A central chimney served the fireplace in each of the four units. The row is still standing, and two of the apartments were still occupied in 1965 (Figure 19).[1] On other Louisiana plantations, too, the slave quarters differed from the general pattern for wood or brick houses. On the McCollam plantation, in Assumption Parish, brick pillars provided the skeleton to which the weatherboards were secured, and on the Weeks family's plantation, at Grande Cote Island, the overseer recorded that he had

---

1. William Darrell Overdyke, *Louisiana Plantation Homes: Colonial and Ante Bellum* (New York, 1965), 204.

built log cabins, adding parenthetically that they were the best that could be made under the circumstances.[2]

The roofs of the houses invariably were of shingle nailed to wooden rafters and battens. Raised wooden floors, wooden-shuttered windows, and occasionally, a porch, completed the single-story dwellings, which usually lacked any loft space. Sometimes double cabins were built with a fireplace at each end of the building, and with two end chimneys rather than the more usual central flue.

The decision whether to build of wood or brick depended on considerations of convenience, durability, cost, and personal preference. Normally the materials at hand were used. Many of the plantations along the Mississippi, its tributaries, and other south Louisiana waterways had either a sawmill or a brickyard, or both. Those that did not had such works near at hand and readily accessible by river. River driftwood and the abundant stocks waiting to be felled in the swamps at the rear of the riverfront plantations assured a plentiful supply of lumber, and the clay for brickmaking needed only to be dug. The overseer on the Weeks family's plantation built log cabins because the estate lay in what was, at that time, a frontier area. Logs were plentiful, but there was no ready access to either of the improved materials, board or brick.

Despite the greater durability of brick, many more slave houses were built of wood than of it. Readily available, wood called for construction skills more common among plantation craftsmen. Moreover, an address given in 1845 on construction materials affirmed that planters believed brick houses to be damp and to cause illness and debility among the slaves. That belief reputedly led the planters to use wood in building slave quarters even sometimes when they used brick in their own more elaborate and better-constructed dwellings.[3]

The size of the cabins was fairly uniform. On J. E. Craighead's plantation, in Iberville Parish, double cabins measured thirty-two feet by sixteen feet; in West Feliciana Parish, one of the Butler estates had cabins which measured thirty-two and a half feet by sixteen feet. Single cabins measured anywhere from sixteen to twenty feet by sixteen feet. But Solon Robinson, a noted agriculturist from Indiana, described an uncommon construction design. While traveling in the South in 1849, he visited Trufant and

2. John Merriman, Grande Cote, to Mary Weeks, New Iberia, July 5, 1840, in Box 8, Folder 28, Weeks Papers.

3. Judge P. A. Rost, *Sugar, Its Culture and Manufacture: Discourse before the Agricultural and Mechanics Association of Louisiana, May 12, 1845* (Hahnville, La., 1876).

White's Myrtle Grove sugar plantation, in Plaquemines Parish, and reported that "the negro houses [were] built of brick, with elevated floors, 32 feet square, divided into four rooms with chimney in the centre." Twelve such structures accommodated the plantation's slave population of 139, of whom 80 were field hands. Other slave houses built of brick, such as those on Evan Hall plantation, conformed to the regular rectangular pattern (Figures 20, 21).[4]

The cabins generally had front and back rooms of different sizes. The front room was usually the larger of the two, although in the slave houses on Laurel Valley estate, near Thibodeaux, the back room was the larger. The fireplace was in the room of greater size, which served as kitchen, parlor, sitting room, dining room, and bedroom. Slaves used the smaller room primarily for sleeping. In double cabins, of course, both partitioned sections were similarly divided.[5]

The slave houses in Louisiana, with their small plots that could be cultivated as kitchen gardens, differed from Jamaican slave quarters by invariably standing, regularly spaced, in straight lines on either side of a dirt road. On larger estates, such as Uncle Sam plantation, in St. James Parish, there were more than two rows of houses, each regularly spaced with a road in front (Figures 22, 23).[6] The quarters were often distant from the great house, but the overseer usually lived near the slaves. The overseer's house, of similar design to the slave houses though larger and more elaborate, stood so that it commanded a view of the slave village. Standing on a promontory, or else at right angles to the rows of slave houses, it looked down the dirt road between the cabins.[7]

In Jamaica, most of the responsibility for construction and repair devolved on the slaves; in Louisiana, it rested principally with the planter. The evidence of that is in the contractual arrangements the Louisiana planters

4. J. E. Craighead, Plaquemine, to John B. Craighead, Nashville, September 11, 1847, in Box 14, Folder 102, Gay Papers; The Cottage, in National Register of Historic Places, Louisiana Historical Preservation and Cultural Commission, Department of Culture, Recreation, and Tourism, Baton Rouge; Herbert Anthony Kellar, ed., *Solon Robinson, Pioneer and Agriculturalist: Selected Writings* (2 vols.; Indianapolis, 1936), II, 181; Henry McCall, "History of Evan Hall Plantation" (1899; MS in Department of Archives and Manuscripts, Tulane University Libraries).

5. Laurel Valley plantation, in National Register of Historic Places.

6. Madewood plantation, in National Register of Historic Places; Uncle Sam plantation, in Historic American Buildings Survey, LA 74, Department of Archives and Manuscripts, LSU Libraries.

7. Uncle Sam plantation, in Historic American Buildings Survey.

made. A contract between John H. Randolph, of Nottoway plantation, in Iberville Parish, and C. A. Thornton, of Wilkinson County, Mississippi, for example, stipulated that Randolph supply land on his estate for sugar cultivation and a mill to process the sugar. Thornton promised, in exchange for one-third of the proceeds, to provide a slave labor force of approximately twenty-five hands, to pay one-third of the plantation expenses, and to erect six slave cabins and a hospital. A similar contract between Mary C. Moore and her husband, John Moore, both of whom, prior to their marriage, owned sugar estates, stated:

> John Moore furnishes, the use of his plantation situate in the Parish of St. Mary below Franklin also the labor of his Slaves named on the Schedule herewith, estimated equivalent to twenty-two working hands, and puts in the moveables, described on the Schedule at the value there Stated
>
> Mrs. Mary C. Moore furnishes the labor of her Slaves named on the Schedule estimated equivalent to Fifteen working hands and puts in the moveables described on the Schedule at the value there Stated—She is to have Cabins made for the use of her Slaves at her individual cost, which will belong to her and may be removed at the expiration of the Partnership.[8]

Planters either hired an outside contractor, who may have been assisted by the estates' laborers, or depended solely on the skilled and unskilled workers on their estates, to construct slave housing. On the McCollam plantation, in Assumption Parish, two white artisans were hired to erect slave cabins; William T. Palfrey contracted with Addison Pumphrey to build slave cabins on his plantation in St. Mary Parish. J. E. Craighead recorded, in a letter to his father, the financial obligation he had assumed for the construction of slave houses: "I have paid $34 each for 5 double cabins framed 32x16 $170 For 13 single cabins framed lumber & all put up at $20 each $260." Undoubtedly he contracted to have these cabins built by an outside agent, though he did not state that. By comparison, the contract between Palfrey and Pumphrey, undertaken in 1857, ten years after Craighead's transaction, required two cabins to be built at the cost of $25 each.[9]

8. Contract Between J. H. Randolph, Iberville Parish, and C. A. Thornton, Wilkinson County, Miss., January 1, 1846, in Box 1, Folder 6, Randolph Papers; Contract Between Mary C. Moore and John Moore, January 23, 1847, in Box 14, Folder 40, Weeks Papers.

9. Diary and Plantation Record of Ellen E. McCollam, August 10, 1847, Au-

Responsibility and control over the construction of slave housing remained in the hands of the planters even when slaves performed the labor. When the estate's skilled and unskilled slaves did the work, it was as part of the plantation's daily labor schedule under the direction and supervision of the planter and overseer. The residence journal of Robert Ruffin Barrow's sugar plantation in Lafourche Parish confirms that throughout the early months of the year, when the field hands were planting the cane crop, the estate's carpenters mended old cabins and framed new ones. Elizabeth Ross Hite, formerly a slave on Pierre Landreaux' Trinity plantation, in Assumption Parish, recalled that "de houses was like little doll houses made by de carpenters on de farm."[10]

Even when planters contracted out for the construction of new houses, they often left repairs to the estate's craftsmen. Sugar planter Mary Weeks's overseer told her, "I have renewed all the cabins since I have been here and put good shingle ruffs on them." Joseph Mather, superintendent of Judge Morgan's Aurora plantation, in St. James Parish, employed some of the hands in shingling slave cabins in June, 1855. The carpenters mentioned in the residence journal of Barrow's plantation were employed in repair as well as in construction.[11]

Because of involvement with construction, Louisiana planters bore more direct responsibility for the quality and condition of slave quarters than did Jamaican planters. The construction practices employed on Louisiana sugar plantations, if prosecuted with suitable care and consideration, could have provided adequate, though unlavish, housing. The usual result, however, was cheaply built dwellings of materials lacking durability, on a simple, somewhat flimsy design. In order for such rude and insubstantial houses to shelter their occupants adequately, they had to be continuously repaired and refurbished, or else the rapid deterioration they were bound to suffer accelerated. Whereas the inadequacy of slave housing on Jamaican sugar plantations sprang from the planters' virtual abdication of responsibility for construction and maintenance, the quality of Louisiana slave dwellings varied according to whether or not planters assumed responsibility for their upkeep.

On the whole, the houses on Louisiana sugar plantations, constructed

---

gust 25, 1847, in McCollam Papers; Plantation Diary, 1842–1859, 1867 (Vol. XVII), March 9, 1857, in Palfrey Account Books; J. E. Craighead to John B. Craighead, September 11, 1847, in Box 14, Folder 102, Gay Papers.

10. Residence Journal of R. R. Barrow, February 2, 1857; Hite interview.

11. Merriman to Weeks, July 5, 1840, in Box 8, Folder 28, Weeks Papers; Mather Diary, June 16, 1855; Residence Journal of R. R. Barrow, February 2, 1857.

and repaired by skilled workers using finished materials, were of somewhat better quality than those on Jamaican estates. The crude huts erected by Jamaican field slaves probably provided less adequate shelter than the slave housing on Louisiana estates where craftsmen had time allotted for building and maintenance. Comparing slave housing in Jamaica and Louisiana, however, must take other conditions into account. The two regions differ, of course, in topography and climate, and those variables have consequences for the kinds of shelter required. Housing that provided shelter in the frost-free climate of Jamaica, where winter temperatures average in the low seventies Fahrenheit, would be inadequate in Louisiana, where snow and freezing temperatures occur occasionally during the winter months. It is doubtful whether, in general, the wood and brick houses of Louisiana functioned any better in their environment than the wattle-and-daub houses did in Jamaica. Evidence of the inadequacy of slave houses can be seen in a letter from John Palfrey, of Forlorn Hope plantation, in the Atakapas District, to his son William T. Palfrey. Although Palfrey bemoaned the shortage of hands on his plantation during the 1836 harvest, he outlined a plan for a large crop the following year. But at the same time that he was projecting an extensive commitment of his labor force, a time that coincided with the severest weather of the year, he noted, "My negro cabins are to be completed, the present ones affording scarcely a shelter." Palfrey recognized the need to build houses but had permitted the job to be put off until what housing remained was dilapidated, even though the slaves most depended on shelter and protection from the elements during winter and when they worked hardest—in the grinding season.[12]

In Louisiana, as in Jamaica, the flimsiness of slave housing not only exposed the occupants to dampness, cold, and drafts, and consequently debilitated them, but also had difficulty withstanding rough weather. In August, 1831, on Wakefield plantation, in West Feliciana, strong winds blew the roofs off most of the slave cabins. Although other buildings were located near the quarters, only the slave houses suffered damage.[13]

Some estates did provide well-built housing, however. After visiting a Louisiana sugar plantation, Frederick Law Olmsted wrote that the slave

12. J. Palfrey, Forlorn Hope plantation, Atakapas District, to William T. Palfrey, Franklin, December 5, 1836, in William T. Palfrey and Family Papers.

13. Plantation Diary, August 28, 1831, in Box 12, No. 24, Stirling Papers. The destruction wrought by this storm closely paralleled the devastation to buildings on Nathaniel Phillips' Jamaican estates some thirty years earlier, when the slaves' houses suffered severe damage but the rest of the buildings on the estate were unscathed. See above, p. 101.

houses were "neat and well-made." Still, any superiority in Louisiana sugar plantations' slave houses, when compared with those in Jamaica, likely did little more than compensate for the harsher climate they had to face.[14]

"One family to a Cabin," was how the former slave Catherine Cornelius remembered life on the Lyle plantation. Her recollection confirms the tendency of slaves on Louisiana estates to live in nuclear family groupings. If slaves had no established marriage or family connections, they lived alone or in households made up of members of the same sex.[15] Plantation records provide ample evidence that family ties weighed heavily in shaping occupancy patterns. The Gay plantation, in Iberville Parish, in 1856 had 167 slaves living in forty-nine household groups that occupied the apartments in twenty-five double cabins; one apartment was vacant (Table 15). The two single-occupant dwellings housed slaves named Bill Chase and Jim Banks. Four years previously, the harvest work schedule recorded that both Chase and Banks were field hands, so it seems unlikely that they were living alone because they held a privileged position in the labor force. More likely they were widowers whose families were no longer staying with them. That possibility, which the virtual absence of any extended families in the listing may itself render probable, seems still likelier in view of two slave lists recorded in 1842. At that time, Banks was fifty years old and living with his wife, Amy Gilchrist, who was the same age, and another person, Susan, for whom no age was given but who may have been their daughter. In 1842, Chase, who was then thirty-three years old, apparently lived on his own. In his case, there is the possibility of a wife and family living on another plantation (see Appendix 10).[16]

The forty-nine slave dwellings on the Gay plantation each measured approximately sixteen feet by sixteen feet, thus providing the occupants limited living space. Chase and Banks, living on their own, and the fifteen households made up of two persons each, must have had relatively uncrowded quarters, but the same cannot be said for the ten male slaves who shared a cabin, each with approximately twenty-five and a half square feet of shelter—a little over six feet by four feet. Ceceil George, who had been a slave on a Louisiana sugar plantation, attested to the crowded conditions. She commented that "all de houses [were] packed wid people."[17]

14. Olmsted, *A Journey,* 659.
15. Cornelius interview.
16. Plantation Record Book, 1849–1860 (Vol. XXXVI), in Gay Papers.
17. *Ibid.;* Ceceil George, interviewed by Maude Wallace, 1940, in Louisiana Writers' Project File, Louisiana State Library.

TABLE 15

SLAVE HOUSEHOLD COMPOSITION ON THE GAY FAMILY'S ESTATE, 1856

	Number of Units	Number of Slaves
Husband, wife, five children	1	7
Husband, wife, four children	2	12
Husband, wife, three children	4	20
Husband, wife, two children	14	56
Husband, wife, one child	6	18
Husband, wife	10	20
Father, two children	2	6
Mother, two children	1	3
Mother, one child	3	6
Mother, child, grandchild	1	3
Ten male slaves[a]	1	10
Two male slaves	2	4
One male slave	2	2
Total	49	167

SOURCE: Plantation Record Book, 1849–1860 (Vol. XXXVI), in Gay Papers.

[a]Notation next to this entry: "House for old men and young men without homes."

On some estates planters promoted a hygienic regimen in the quarters that called for the slave houses to be regularly whitewashed, inside and out. Cornelius recalled that on the Lyle estate "de cabins was white." Painting often coincided with a general cleanup around and under the cabins, usually in the spring or summer. That included the removal of the trash, refuse, and also probably human excrement that had accumulated in the vicinity of the cabins.[18]

Some plantations provided the slaves with latrines. On Barrow's estate the "Residence Journal" for 1857 recorded that, on one day in November,

18. Cornelius interview.

"Jerry and 3 hands [were] building negro privies over ditch." Slaves, however, were not normally provided with privies. The usual practice in Louisiana, which also prevailed in Jamaica, was, in the patois of the island, to "go a bush." Both privies and the alternative, however, were unsanitary and likely to harm the slaves' health: the use of primitive facilities could spread disease when the seepage contaminated drinking water, and "going a bush" led to the accumulation of excrement around the quarters. Even if cleanups were carried out annually, they were probably too infrequent to deal adequately with the potential health risks.[19]

On estates where planters mandated cleanups and whitewashing, slaves did the chores as part of the regular work schedule. The tasks may have been delegated to some of the weaker hands, or done as Saturday or Sunday light work. On Charles Oxley's Roseland plantation, in St. Charles Parish, the latter alternative was adopted: the diary for 1847 recorded that slaves cleaned their quarters on Sunday, August 8. There is no indication of how they disposed of the refuse, nor of whether the collected excrement served as night soil. It is unlikely, however, that such cleanup operations were effective against the dysentery, bowel complaints, worms, and related maladies that afflicted people who live with insanitation. The slaves of Louisiana themselves bore much of the responsibility for keeping their quarters clean, but they had little time and few resources to devote to that objective because of the prodigious labor demands placed upon them, especially during planting and harvest.[20] Often only a serious and immediate health threat moved planters to improve the hygiene of the houses. Yet, even then, they did little more than clean up superficially in and around the houses and whitewash them inside and out. When cholera appeared on Elu Landry's estate, he evacuated half the slave village, sent the evacuees to live in the sugarhouse, and set some of them to whitewashing the quarters with lime. Rachel O'Connor, whose plantation was in the Bayou Sara sugar region, wrote to her brother David Weeks at his sugar plantation in the Atakapas District, that "almost everyone talks of white washing there Houses, negro cabins, and all, on account of the Cholera being near, as it is recommended among many other preventatives now in circulation." The inference was that she would do it to her buildings.[21]

19. Residence Journal of R. R. Barrow, November 17, 1857.

20. 1847 Plantation Diary of Charles Oxley, Roseland plantation, St. Charles, August 8, 1847, in Kenner Papers.

21. Landry Estate Plantation Diary and Ledger, July 11, 1849, July 12, 1849; Rachel O'Connor to David Weeks, n.d., in Box 30, 1–2, Weeks Papers.

The interior of the slaves' houses was as rude as their exterior: plain board or brick walls; uncovered rafters, battens, and shingles above, bare floorboards below; heat from a single fireplace; light and air by way of wooden-shuttered windows devoid of glass; and a simple wooden door. The occupants of these simple dwellings bore most of the responsibility for decorating them. Sometimes the planters helped, but their assistance was usually minimal.

The bare furnishings—beds, table, and chairs—the plantation's carpenters built at the expense of the estate. Slaves most often slept on wooden box-type beds. Louisa Martin, once a slave on Richard Pugh's Madewood plantation, on Bayou Lafourche in Assumption Parish, recalled that slaves "had nothin but old sawmill beds—wooden beds, chinch [bedbug] harbors." Cornelius "'member[ed] de man what mak [the beds] he wuz a slave carpenter—his name was Dave Parker—he wuz a good carpenter." Slaves usually slept on mattresses stuffed with straw or Spanish moss, which may have contributed to the bedbug problem. It was the recollection of Hite, however, that slaves "slept on wooden beds wid fresh moss mattress. Our bed was kep' clean. Much cleaner den de beds of today [ca. 1940]. Dey was scrubbed ev'ry Saturday. Dere wasn't a chince on one of 'em."[22]

Another style was the rope bed, which had a wooden frame with lengths of rope strung across it, much in the manner of the flat springs in more modern beds; a straw or moss pallet provided a simpler option. Although Cornelius maintained that "dere were enough beds alright," Martin recalled that there were "sometimes four and five in one bed, chillun, you know," and Carlyle Stewart, a former slave on Octavo de La Houssaye's plantation on Bayou Teche near Jeanerette, remembered that as a boy "he got in . . . bed with maw and her five chellin."[23]

The other furnishings slaves had were simple and homemade. In Martin's cabin, they "didn't have nuthin but ole boxes, sawmill timber . . . dey had a table an about four chairs." Cornelius remembered a "home made cupboard, chairs, benches, table—slave carpenter made all ub em." Slaves sometimes received a few other furnishings and utensils at the expense of the plantation. Ellen McCollam, of Ellendale plantation, in Terrebonne Parish, recorded in her diary that in February, 1845, she "received by the Steamboat . . . a Doz[en] Buckets for negros." In October of the following

22. Louisa Martin, interviewed by Octave Lilly, Jr., 1938, Dillard Project, in Marcus Bruce Christian Collection; Cornelius interview; Hite interview.
23. Cornelius interview; Martin interview; Carlyle Stewart, interviewed by Flossie McElwee, 1940, in Louisiana Writers' Project File, Louisiana State Library.

year, she had one of the women field hands, Cinthy, work temporarily at sewing up mattresses that she distributed to the slaves.[24]

Tin buckets and other metalware were among the items most frequently provided. On Samuel McCutcheon's Ormond plantation, in St. Charles Parish, slaves got ovens, pots, spiders (three-legged skillets suitable for placing over an open fire), and tin kettles; on Richard Pugh's Leighton plantation, in Lafourche Parish, slaves received tin buckets. The contract between John H. Randolph and C. A. Thornton in which Thornton pledged to furnish supplies and homes to slaves in return for a share of the sugar crop grown on Randolph's estate (see above, p. 132) also stipulated that Thornton was to provide the slaves with meat, clothes, tools, and utensils. The precise nature of the utensils was not set down, but probably included were buckets and other metal artifacts. Slaves on William Minor's Waterloo plantation, on the Mississippi in Ascension Parish, received such a distribution in January, 1859. In his plantation diary, he recorded that a number of items were issued the slaves, including large pots, skillets, spiders, bowls, and spoons.[25]

Minor listed one item other than metalware which was distributed for household use: bedticking. There was no mention whether the ticking was made up into mattresses beforehand, as on McCollam's estate, but since the slaves received needles and thread at the same time, they may have had to do the stitching-up themselves on their own time. Slaves received drapery goods other than bedticking at the planter's expense. Blankets were regularly distributed, as mentioned in the plantation ledger of Randolph's Nottoway estate. Also recorded there were attempts to cope with the insect problem by giving out mosquito netting. The clothing allotment for the Weeks family's sugar plantation, at Grande Cote Island, included fifty mosquito bars comprising twelve yards of material each; another clothing list for the same plantation recorded that there was an annual issue of both double and single mosquito bars in 1859, in 1860, and in 1861. William T. Palfrey's plantation diary shows that in July, 1844, eight married couples and two single men received mosquito bars and that one was also given to

24. Martin interview; Cornelius interview; Diary and Plantation Record of Ellen E. McCollam, February 4, 1845, October 6, 1846.

25. List of Shoes and Utensils Distributed to Slaves, in 5 Vital Register, 1836–1862, U-158, No. 1087, McCutcheon Papers; Folder 4, in Richard L. Pugh Papers, Department of Archives and Manuscripts, LSU Libraries; Contract Between J. H. Randolph and C. A. Thornton, January 1, 1846, in Randolph Papers; Diary, 1857 (7), January 13, 1857–January 15, 1857, in William J. Minor and Family Papers, Department of Archives and Manuscripts, LSU Libraries.

"Kizzy for her children." "To furnish . . . musquitoe bars for her slaves" was a contractual obligation of Mary Moore when she entered into the partnership with her husband John establishing a sugar plantation.[26]

Perhaps the most extensive documentation of utensils and furnishings can be found in the records of the Gay family's sugar plantation, in Iberville Parish. Much of the customary equipment was regularly supplied the slaves on this plantation: buckets, skillets, pots, and mosquito bars. The records also show, however, a variety of other supplies. The estate record book for 1825 to 1839 listed nineteen slaves each of whom received one set of knives, forks, plates, cups, and saucers, and another twenty-nine who received only plates. In 1843, "12 little boys received barlow knives," and lists of clothing and supplies given the slaves from 1849 to 1859 show that knives were a regular part of the distribution. Other items distributed to the slaves at the expense of the plantation were sifters, coffeepots, coffee mills, cotton cards, and "tin buckets . . . each containing one cup."[27] Slaves on the Gay plantation also received bedding, allocated by family. In January, 1840, fifty-two bedticks were issued, mostly to women identified as "wives of" named male slaves. Single men also received bedticks, which were recorded under their names.[28] On the Gay plantation through the 1850s, slaves received blankets every three years, at the end of the grinding season, in December or January. The standard allocation was one blanket per adult, and one per several children (see Appendix 11). For example, Nathan and Maria, a childless couple, received two blankets, while Jacob Lenox and his wife, Little Jinny, who had four children living with them, received only four blankets. On Randolph's Nottoway plantation there was a similar ration. Each family, according to its size, was issued from two to five blankets, while childless couples received two blankets and single people one. Slaves on Lewis Stirling's Solitude and Wakefield plantations, in West Feliciana Parish, had a comparable issue of blankets in January, 1833. During a brief holiday before the commencement of harvest in October, 1849, Isaac Erwin, owner of Shady Grove plantation, on Bayou Grosse Tete in Iberville Parish, "gave out negro cloths and 1 blanket a piece gave two pare pan-

26. Diary, 1857 (7), January 13, 1857–January 15, 1857, in Minor Papers; Diary and Plantation Record of Ellen E. McCollam, October 6, 1846; Ledger, 1862–1865 (Vol. VIII), in Randolph Papers; Folder 260, Vol. X, Notebook, 1859–1877, in Weeks Papers; Plantation Diary, 1842–1859, 1867 (Vol. XVII), in Palfrey Account Books; Contract Between Mary C. Moore and John Moore, January 23, 1847.

27. Estate Record Book, 1825–1839 (Vol. VII), Estate Record Book, 1831–1845 (Vol. VIII), Plantation Record Book, 1849–1860 (Vol. XXXVI), all in Gay Papers.

28. Estate Record Book, 1831–1845 (Vol. VIII), in Gay Papers.

taloons a coat and 1 shirt to Men. 1 Frock and two slips to women and 1 blanket a piece." He did not mention providing blankets for children. A different allocation pattern, with each slave—man, woman, or child—receiving a blanket, prevailed on the Stirling family's Wakefield estate in the 1850s (Tables 16, 17). The lists differ slightly, in that the one for 1857 records separately the distribution of blankets to mothers for their infant children.[29]

A niggardly blanket issue, one per slave triennially, could only aggravate the hardships wrought by inferior housing and adverse weather. Blankets apparently could wear out in less than two years. In a letter of July 1840, from the Weeks family's plantation on Grande Cote Island, the overseer, John Merriman, wrote that "there is some Blankets here Shall I give them to the most kneedy or is it your intention to furnish Blankets to gow round, it has or will be two years this fall since there has been any given out." William Weeks, in a letter to his mother in December, 1853, related his satisfaction concerning the lot of the slaves on the Grande Cote Island plantation: "I have given out the blankets, they have all plenty of covering and good warm clothes and are as comfortable as most negroes, and a great deal more so than many." His sobering final comment recognized the differential in treatment, and quality of life, within the slave populations on Louisiana sugar plantations.[30]

Families and households were the basis of the plantation distribution system not only in housing and furnishings but also in food and clothing. That affirmed and reinforced the slave family structure. But the reasons for disproportionate allocations among the slave population are not fully explained in the fragmentary documentation available. No reason is given, for example, for issuing twenty-nine slaves on the Gay plantation a plate each at the same time that nineteen other slaves each received a knife, fork, plate, cup, and saucer.[31]

Some allocations rewarded slaves or served as incentives, as in the case of childbearing women. Planters in Louisiana, like those in Jamaica, attempted to promote a high birthrate among the slaves on their estates. On Minor's Southdown plantation in January, 1857, nine "Sucklers . . . g[o]t one cradle

29. *Ibid.;* Ledger, 1862–1865 (Vol. VIII), in Randolph Papers; Ration Book, 1828, 1830–1838 (H-13), in Stirling Papers; Erwin Diary, September 29, 1849; Folders 48, 54, in Stirling Papers.

30. John Merriman to Mary Weeks, July 12, 1840, in Box 8, Folder 28, Weeks Papers; William F. Weeks to Mary C. Moore, December 29, 1853, in Box 22, Folder 92, Weeks Papers.

31. Estate Record Book, 1825–1839 (Vol. VII), in Gay Papers.

TABLE 16

"Blankets given out to the Negroes, October 8, 1854," Stirling
Family's Wakefield Plantation

	Number in Family	Number of Blankets
Long George	11	11
Wilson	10	10
Lindu's house	5	5
Henrietta	9	9
Hannah	4	4
O Joe	2	2
Sambo	6	6
Suckey	2	2
Chaney	8	8
Tompo	1	1
Yanco, Jack, Franswoise, child	4	4
Liddy, Charlotte, child	4	4
Bartlet	2	2
Harry, wife, Chis	3	3
Nelson	9	9
Affy	2	2
Sam Jackson	1	1
Sophy	3	3
Dilily	7	7
Barica	4	4
Sam Brown	5	5
Ervin	11	11
Ginny, Monday	2	2
Levin, 1; Maretta, 5	6	6
George Austin	1	1
Adam	6	6
Allen	4	4
Ellen	4	4
	Continued on next page	

Source: Folder 48, in Stirling Papers.

TABLE 16—*Continued*

	Number in Family	Number of Blankets
Isaac	1	1
Anderson	5	5
Washington	4	4
Alfred	4	4
Julius	1	1
Cecile	1	1
Spencer	2	2
Catrine	1	1

blanket" each, and three got two. Elite groups such as craftsmen and drivers not only benefited from additional food and clothing allowances but also received preferential allocations of furnishings and utensils. But from estate to estate the planter's conception or exercise of his responsibility for equipping slaves at his expense varied.[32]

The internal economy let slaves compensate for deficiencies by buying items for themselves. Some plantation owners kept the books of the slaves' accounts, recording their income and expenditures and listing the items they purchased and sold. Moreover, the planters often acted as intermediaries, supplying the slaves with items which they had ordered and deducting the cost from the accounts. Their account books provide information on the sorts of items the slaves bought because of the failure of the plantation to supply them.

Often slaves had to purchase their own tableware. Cornelius recalled that tin dishes, knives, and forks were not supplied on the Lyle plantation but were bought by the slaves. Apparently the slaves there were not issued any tableware whatever, because, aside from having to buy dishes and cutlery, they made their own wooden trays and gourd cups. On the Wilton plantation, near Convent, in St. James Parish, slaves used the money they earned to purchase knives, blankets, baskets, and tin cups. On Randolph's planta-

32. Rachel O'Connor to A. T. Conrad, April 12, 1835, in Box 6, Folder 22, Weeks Papers; Diary, 1857 (7), January 3, 1857, in Minor Papers.

TABLE 17

"BLANKETS GIVEN OUT, DECEMBER 25, 1857,"
STIRLING FAMILY'S WAKEFIELD PLANTATION

	For Whom
2 to Eveline	Sidney, Ervin
1 to Lindu	Rosallie
2 to Charlotte	Mary, Celia
1 to Cecile	Virgil
2 to Phoebe	Bartlet, Julius
2 to Frozine	York, Patterson
1 to Sarah	Ned
1 to Isabel	Charles
1 to Clarinda	Georgiana
1 to Affey	Hannah
1 to Henrietta	Albert
1 to Margaret	Thomas
1 to Maretta	Leven
1 to Maria	Judy
1 to Rose	Cinthia
1 to Lucy	Allen
1 to Harriet	Martin
1 to Easter	Richard

SOURCE: Folder 54, in Stirling Papers.

NOTE: This list is followed by one for the distribution of blankets to the remaining slaves on the plantation, similar to the list reproduced in Table 16.

tion in October, 1851, Long William was debited 18 cents for a tin bucket, and three weeks later a slave named Fort purchased a tin bucket for 18.75 cents.[33]

33. Cornelius interview; Daily Journal, 1848, in Bruce, Seddon, and Wilkins Plantation Records; Journal—Plantation Book, 1847–1852 (Vol. V), in Randolph Papers.

The daybook of Erwin's plantation, in Iberville Parish, itemized the income and expenditures of some seventy-five slaves, all but six of whom were men. Their purchases of utensils and furnishings included bedspreads at $1.50 each, buckets at 25 cents apiece, coffeepots at 75 cents each, and knives and forks at $1.25 per set. There was also a notation that "Alfred Cooper bought . . . furniture," although the kind and cost were unspecified. Among items purchased by the slaves on the same plantation three years previously were tallow and spermaceti candles and knives. The same pattern of earnings and expenditures continued on this plantation until the Civil War.[34]

The journal of Alexis Ferry, a planter in St. James Parish, provides a more detailed picture. Twenty-nine male slaves, using money earned cutting wood, purchased items such as glazed, gilt, and yellow bowls, cups and mugs, chairs, and yellow pots. The list, compiled by a French-speaking overseer whose strong point was apparently not literacy, contained words of dubious etymology. Items to which he referred may be containers ("contenit") and saucers ("secousse de tasse"). Other sets of accounts not only show the inadequacy of plantation supplies but also shed light on the structure of sugar plantation slave life and on the dynamics of the internal economic system. George Lanaux' plantation journal for his Bellevue estate, in Plaquemines Parish, shows that in 1851 slaves purchased, among other things, knives at twenty-five cents each, spoons at fifty cents a dozen, and tinware—probably sheets of tin ("ferblanc")—at thirty-five cents per item, out of money they accumulated by cutting wood and raising corn. In the next four years, they bought portable ovens ("four de campagne") at eighty-five cents each, kettles ("chaudiere") at forty cents each, and locks.[35] The purchase of locks is particularly interesting, because, as in Jamaica, the legal status of slaves as chattels without property rights is difficult to reconcile with the kind of ownership asserted by locks. Slaves recognized their de facto status as owners and property holders, and this was also recognized and normally not transgressed by whites on the estates even though it had no de jure basis. Frederick Law Olmsted, visiting a Georgia rice plantation, saw in many of the slave houses "closets with locks and keys" and observed that when the slaves were absent from their houses they "locked their outer doors, taking the keys with them." Louisiana slaves probably took similar

34. Daybook, 1843–1847 (Vol. V), in Gay Papers.

35. Journal, 1842–1865, 1877 (Vol. I), in Alexis Ferry Journals, Department of Archives and Manuscripts, Tulane University Libraries; Ledger, 1851–1856, Bellevue (Vol. XVIII), in Lanaux Papers.

precautions, since locks of several kinds were purchased on the Lanaux plantation: ordinary locks at 75 cents, and complex six-piece ones ("serrure francais de 6 pces") at a dollar each. Slaves on Benjamin Tureaud's Brule, Houmas, and Bagatelle plantations, in the parishes of Ascension and St. James, also purchased locks at 60 cents apiece, as well as such items as buckets at 30 cents each, wire at 25 cents and twine at 37.5 cents per pound, tin at 30 cents per sheet, and mosquito bars for 80 cents each.[36]

Slaves as a rule purchased necessities, the most functional of furnishings, kitchenware, and tableware. As the gilt and glazed bowls bought by slaves on Ferry's plantation illustrate, however, there were instances of slaves equipping their homes more elaborately. In the main, the internal economy that enabled slaves to acquire "luxury" items functioned outside governance by the planter. The marketing system whereby orders were placed through the planter was supplemented by transactions with traveling traders and at markets.

Slaves could acquire much from peddlers and merchants. Traveling salesmen plied the highways and waterways of the Louisiana sugar region, trading and selling various wares. Martha Stuart, who had been a slave on a Black Creek plantation, recalled that slaves had "pictures on the wall" in their houses and would either "send off and buy 'em" or else acquire them from "picture men [who] come thru the country."[37] It was possible for slaves to make many of the household goods they lacked. Cornelius recalled that the wooden trays and gourd cups they used were made by the slaves themselves. Both Stuart and Cornelius remembered they had wooden tubs in which they bathed, and that they were made "by de men, em sawed off barrels." Slaves could also trade for household goods with other slaves on the estate.[38]

Just as the planters' allocations of housewares created inequities, so did the internal economy. Only some slaves could afford candles, which were not normally part of the rations the planter provided. In the words of Martin, the only slaves who had "candles [were] jus dem what was able." She continued, "Us po folks didn't know what candles was." Her cabin was lit by an "old tin pan wid piece of rag and grease." Carlyle Stewart's family

36. Olmsted, *A Journey,* 422; Ledger, 1851–1856, Bellevue (Vol. XVIII), in Lanaux Papers; Ledger, 1858–1872, in Tureaud Papers.
37. Stuart interview. A description of slaves going to Sunday market in Plaquemine is contained in Rev. P. M. Goodwyn to Edward Gay, August 27, 1860, in Box 29, Folder 255, Gay Papers. The letter appears in full above, p. 68.
38. Cornelius interview; Stuart interview.

could not afford to buy candles, but his mother made their own from beef tallow, and Cornelius recalled "de women slave ma[d]e candles—ma[d]e de wicks on de spinnin wheels." Stuart also recalled that slave women made candles.[39]

The system heavily favored slaves with skills, in positions of privilege, or of superior physical abilities or mental aptitude. The houses of slaves no doubt ranged from adequately equipped to the sort found by Olmsted in north Louisiana. "Several of them," Olmsted wrote, "were very destitute of furniture—nothing being perceptible but two very dirty beds, and a few rude stools." The tragedy was that those most likely to suffer from such squalor were those least able to endure it—the old and the young, the infirm and the disconsolate.[40]

The food that slaves ate was cooked either communally or by the family or household. Slave cooks prepared some meals, especially breakfast, in a communal kitchen. On some plantations, they prepared other meals for single slaves, the old, the indolent, orphans, and others in want. Families, however, usually cooked at least the main meal of the day, the evening meal, in their own homes. Although Cornelius mentioned that some of the slave cabins had "mebbe a kitchen in de back," it was more usual for cooking to be done in the larger of the two rooms in the cabin, the one containing the fireplace. Both Louise Downs, a former slave on Dr. Louis Perkins' sugar plantation, in East Baton Rouge Parish, and Martin remembered the big back logs burning in the fireplaces, in which the slave women prepared food for their families in pots, kettles, spiders, and ovens. The slaves perhaps ate at a table set with the cutlery and crockery they had acquired.[41]

The slaves supplemented their diet with food they grew in the kitchen gardens close to their cabins: they rarely received more than a limited ration of pork and corn at the planters' expense. Within the confines of their small kitchen plot, which was often fenced, they also kept their livestock and poultry, and in their gardens they grew a variety of crops for their table. Participation in the internal economy also enabled them to purchase food.[42]

The labors of elderly slaves, along with the work of others during the

39. Martin interview; Stewart interview; Cornelius interview; Stuart interview.
40. Olmsted, *A Journey*, 629–30.
41. Cornelius interview; Louise Emily Downs, interviewed by Octave Lilly, Jr., 1938, Dillard Project, in Marcus Bruce Christian Collection; Martin interview.
42. For lists of rations distributed to slave families, see, for example, Memorandum Books, 1848–1865 (Vol. VIII), 1853–1858 (Vol. IX), 1856–1858 (Vol. X), all in Alexandre E. De Clouet Papers, Department of Archives and Manuscripts, LSU Libraries.

evenings, at midday dinner breaks, and over weekends could yield rich rewards from the fertile alluvial soil of the Mississippi floodplain. But certain conditions militated against the slaves' pursuing this activity zealously, in much the same way as the conditions kept the slaves from repairing and refurbishing their houses and building furniture. The onerous work schedule, especially during the sugar harvest, when night work was demanded of the workers, meant that they had neither the time nor the physical or mental resources to labor strenuously in their gardens. Even the aged slaves were pressed into service during harvesttime. Labor demands differed from plantation to plantation and influenced how conscientious slaves were about tending their gardens.

Small livestock and pet animals could be found in all slave villages and, apparently, in or around most slave houses. Slaves' domestic animals, both cats and the "quarter dogs" the traveler Thomas Bangs Thorpe found in "extraordinary numbers," roamed the houses and gardens. Hite recalled that "de quarters had cat holes fo' cats to com in an' out." [43]

Even within one slave plantation society, even on a single plantation, the quality of slaves' housing differed greatly. Houses were well or ill constructed, furnished in larger or smaller measure, and repaired with varying frequency and effect. Throughout the Louisiana sugar region, however, slaves' housing displayed a basic similarity. Planter control over certain areas created a general consistency throughout Louisiana, which differed in fundamental ways from how things were in Jamaica: the control was firmest in construction patterns, materials, spacing, and the responsibility for building and repair. Nonetheless, in both societies there emerged similar patterns deriving from the relationship between the slaves and their homes. In both societies, the slaves assumed extensive command over what happened in and to their houses. Despite amorphous questions concerning property rights, for most practical purposes the slaves largely determined life and living patterns in the quarters and behaved as property owners. The privacy of slaves' homes was generally inviolable, and their use of locks secured them against intruders and incursions. Even though estates in both societies had house-search policies, these appear not to have been widely used save in emergencies. [44]

43. Thorpe, "Sugar and the Sugar Region," 746–67; Hite interview.
44. Lord Balcarres to the Duke of Portland, August 3, 1795, in Hardwicke Papers (Vol. DLXVIII, Add. 35916), British Library, London; David Ewart, Westmoreland, Jamaica, to Lord Penrhyn, December 8, 1808, December 10, 1808, in Penrhyn Castle Papers (MS 1495). Louisiana planters had house-search policies simi-

As in Jamaica, slaves in Louisiana conducted themselves in ways that show they held their houses in special regard. Although they did not endow their homes with the overt religious and sepulchral importance Jamaican slaves did, on the secular level there was considerable similarity between the two societies. The houses were the setting for peculiarly slave-centered activities on both family and community levels—activities that lay outside the province of the planter and the plantation system. Hite recalled that "de slaves had a gud time in dere quarters. Dey play guitar, danced fo de light went out. Dey put skin over a barrel fo a drum. Dey talked er bout de master's business in dere quarters too. . . . Dey married . . . an had big affairs in dere quarters." Cornelius related how the whites respected the privacy of the slaves' community activities: "De people in de big house did n't come down to our cabins fo' our celebrations—dey come down sometimes, but not on no special days." She also remembered that the slaves "dance[d], jigged . . . [on] Satiday nite—in de slave cabins."[45]

Whites had little say over these activities, and even those they tried to proscribe were carried on clandestinely within the confines of the quarters. Slaves who ran away from the plantation and hid in nearby woods or swamps would return to the quarters at night to visit with relatives and be fed. Although their presence was rarely betrayed, planters frequently sought to discover them. McCollam, in a diary notation for April, 1847, mentioned that "Ester [was] whipped for not telling that she heard Kit (who had run away) talking in the yard." The quarters provided slaves security to engage not only in private slave-centered activities but also in activities that threatened the very institution of slavery.[46]

Louisiana's slaves, like Jamaica's, had customary rights that enabled them to accumulate and dispose of not only landed but also personal property. The slaves in Louisiana spent a considerable portion of any revenue they brought in on the purchase of clothing. Whether or not they purchased ready-made items, the styles of their "best" clothing conformed to the general dictates of fashion in the region. The syncretic influences, so important in determining the styles of such clothing in Jamaica, were less apparent in Louisiana. Like other facets of slavery in the United States, the creolization of clothing styles was further advanced, and it was reflected in the homogenization of fashions throughout society. Nevertheless, there is

<hr />

lar to those mentioned by Kenneth Stampp in *The Peculiar Institution: Slavery in the Ante-Bellum South* (New York, 1956), 149.

45. Hite interview; Cornelius interview.

46. Diary and Plantation Record of Ellen E. McCollam, April 20, 1847.

evidence of an exaggerated Creole style of clothing in William Howard Russell's *My Diary North and South,* which describes the slaves' Sunday clothes as "strangely cut" and "wonderfully made."[47]

The extent and the nature of clothing purchases by slaves show that it was essentially an autonomous activity of great importance to both slave societies. Some slaves managed to buy clothing of high quality, cut in the most elegant styles. At the Gay family's sugar plantation, in Iberville Parish, the slaves' purchases in 1844 included a "Fine Summer Coat," bought at the cost of three dollars by a field hand named Lee, and a "Fine Russian Hat bt. in N. Orleans" for three dollars by another field hand, Elias. Alfred Cooper bought two "Elegant Bonnets" at two dollars each, presumably for his wife, Dido, and his sixteen-year-old daughter, Louisiana. Three years earlier, the account of William Sanders, another slave, was debited by an unrecorded amount for a fur hat, black shoes, and a calico dress for his wife, while Patrick bought a pair of boots and a watch costing fifteen or twenty dollars, Hercules paid ten dollars for a roundabout jacket of blue or black cloth, a dark-colored umbrella, and a waistcoat, Ned Davis made a purchase of a fur hat, a roundabout, and an umbrella, and Samuel Todd bought a white "cambrice" dress for his wife. Similar purchases continued on the Gay estate until the Civil War.[48]

In 1848, slaves on Ferry's plantation bought, among other things, expensive lengths of cloth ("aunes coutes") and a fine dress ("robe bontenit"). In the early 1850s on Lanaux' Bellevue estate slaves paid $2.50 each for oilcloth winter coats, and $1.25 a pair for "log cabin" trousers; a cashbook for Colonel W. W. Pugh's Woodlawn plantation, in Assumption Parish, lists a charge of $12.50 to the slave Woodson for a silk dress for Rachel.[49]

Hite recalled that her mother raised corn, sold it at fifty cents per barrel, and "bought good clothes wid de money, nothing but silk dresses." Although Hite's mother undoubtedly bought more than silk dresses, the frequency of references throughout the slave narratives to the fine clothing slaves bought to wear on days off suggests that the purchase of finery was not unusual (Figure 24).[50]

More typically, though, the slaves spent their earnings on plainer and less

47. Russell, *My Diary,* 373.
48. Daybook, 1843–1847 (Vol. V), Memorandum Book, 1840–1841 (Vol. XXVIII), both in Gay Papers.
49. Journal, 1842–1865, 1877 (Vol. I), in Ferry Journals; Ledger, 1851–1856 (Vol. XVIII), in Lanaux Papers; Cashbook for Negroes, 1848–1855 (Vol. VI), in W. W. Pugh Papers.
50. Hite interview.

expensive clothing for town, market, church, holiday, and special occasion. On one of Tureaud's estates, the slaves spent some of the money they earned through the internal economy on shoes, hats, hose, shirts, pants, dresses, and handkerchiefs, as well as on a variety of cloths such as cottonade, check, cotton, and calico. In the ledger for 1858–1859 are the names of ninety-eight male slaves, all but two of whom accumulated money over the period, the sums ranging from a dollar to seventeen dollars. Well over half of the ninety-eight, including the two nonearners who received goods on credit, made expenditures on clothing. Only eight of the thirty women in the ledger earned any money, and of them only three spent any on cloth or clothing, the other five withdrawing their earnings in cash. Virtually all the 106 slaves who earned money during this time withdrew at least part of their earnings in cash, and probably some of it went to purchase clothing off the plantation.[51]

The Gay plantation's slave accounts for 1844 itemized clothing purchases other than luxury items. In a slave community that two years previously had numbered 267 persons, 86 of whom were males over the age of sixteen years, 77 slaves—71 men and 6 women—earned a combined $900.125, some of which they applied toward cloth and clothing. Here, too, virtually all the slaves withdrew part of their earnings in cash. Apart from a few pieces of ready-made clothing, the slaves bought mostly lengths of cloth: calico, domestic, white cotton, brown linen, and cottonade. In 1844, almost every slave family on the Gay plantation earned money or received credit, which it partly invested in clothing for holiday and Sunday wear.[52]

A slave wedding that took place on Howard Bond's Crescent Place sugar plantation, near Houma, in Terrebonne Parish, described in the diary of Bond's wife, Priscilla ("Mittie") Munnikhuysen Bond, illustrates how fashionable the dress in the nuptials of what were probably two favored house slaves could be: "Had a wedding here tonight, two of the servants got married. . . . The bride looked quite nice dressed in white, I made her turbin of white swiss-pink tarlton [tarlatan] & oranges blossoms. . . . The groom had a suit of black, white gloves, & a tall beaver. The bride dressed in white swiss, pink trimmings & white gloves. The bride's-made & groom's-man dressed to correspond." The bride's ornate headwear is undoubtedly to be laid to the times, since turbans "were the most popular head-dresses of women [in the United States] during the first half of the nineteenth century," rather than to the influence of a clothing heritage peculiar to

51. Ledger, 1858–1872, in Tureaud Papers.
52. Daybook, 1843–1847 (Vol. V), in Gay Papers.

the slave population. The rest of the clothing described was very much a la mode.[53]

Although Hite's recollection of the fine clothing worn by slaves at weddings closely matched Bond's recounting, she underscored the oddity of elaborate ceremonies. "Sometimes de slaves would have marriages lak de people do today wid all de same trimmings. De veil, gown an ev'rything," Hite recalled. "Dey married fo de preacher an had big af'fairs in dere quarters. Den sometime dey would go to de master to git his permission an blessings." She added, however, "Shucks som of dem darkies didn't care er bout master, preacher or nobody dey just went an got married."[54]

Clothing purchases followed the basic principles of the internal economy's operation, with decisions concerning the extent and direction of expenditure resting with the slaves. Stuart declared that slaves could buy "any kind er dress [they] wanted to get." Hite acknowledged that some plantation owners were averse to seeing slaves spend for personal adornment but that the purchases then took place clandestinely. She recalled that "we sold old clothes to darkies who had mean masters. Dey had to hide 'em though."[55]

The extent of slave purchases hung not only on the predilections of the slaves but also on the amount of money they had to spend. When Stuart observed that slaves could have as "many [dresses] as [they] wanted, many as [they] could buy," the final qualification was the important one. Although, according to Stuart, "De oversee used to tell us, you darkies . . . got better clothes den ma wife and chillun's got," slaves relatively inactive in the internal economy wore only what was distributed at the expense of the plantation.[56]

Slaves sometimes received special Sunday clothing as gifts from the planter. McCollam mentioned that, in addition to the regular distribution of work clothes, she "gave out to the negro women each a new dress and handkerchief as a Christmas present." Hite recalled that "on Christmas master would give his slaves presents," and "dey would be clothes most of de time." Better-quality clothing may also have been given on the occasion of a wedding. Martin remembered that slaves, "w'en dey wante to git married dey'd go to de white folks and dey'd give em fine clothes to wear"—as

53. Diary, 1857–1869, in Priscilla ("Mittie") Munnikhuysen Bond Papers, Department of Archives and Manuscripts, LSU Libraries; Elisabeth McClellan, *History of American Costume, 1607–1870* (1904; rpr. New York, 1969), 638.
54. Hite interview.
55. Stuart interview; Hite interview.
56. Stuart interview.

the Bonds gave at least part of the bride's ensemble in the slave wedding Priscilla Bond wrote about.[57]

As in Jamaica, planters in Louisiana customarily purchased the slaves' work clothes and bore the entire cost. The materials most common in Louisiana for that kind of clothing were woolens and a variety of cottons such as denim, calico, cottonade, "lowell," and a twill called jane or jean. Less frequently Louisiana planters distributed osnaburg, fustian, and linsey-woolsey. Julia Woodrich, who had been a slave on a Louisiana sugar plantation, recalled that "the missus wove the cloth," but that was not usual. Planters usually bought commercially woven cloth.[58]

The clothing issued to slaves in both Jamaica and Louisiana included accessories, like hats and kerchiefs, in addition to the trousers, skirts, frocks, and coats. But slaves on Louisiana plantations received shoes and sometimes socks, whereas Jamaican slaves worked barefoot. On the whole, slaves on Louisiana sugar plantations received larger clothing allocations than Jamaican slaves. Moreover, distribution was more frequent, usually twice a year, as compared with the common once a year in Jamaica. Still, it is doubtful whether Louisiana slaves were better outfitted, since they needed extra winter protection. One of the annual issues was selected to be wearable during the hot, humid Louisiana summer, the other during the cold and damp winter months, when frost and snow, unknown in Jamaica, were a perennial threat. The lighter-weight clothing was handed out in spring or early summer and the heavier in the fall or early winter.

For summer the clothes were usually cotton. Each man received a pair of pants and a shirt, each woman a dress and a chemise. If slaves did not get ready-made apparel, lengths of cotton material were given to them and they were expected to make their own. Headgear, usually kerchiefs for women and straw hats for men, were also included in the warm-weather distribution. From the records of John Moore's Magill plantation, it is possible to estimate the quantities of material necessary. A letter to Moore from his overseer, William Lourd, includes a "list of clothing for a suit a piece, 31 grown women—6 small girls, which will take 241 yds for frocks & for chemise 105 yds, close calculation. 35 men will take for pantaloons 105 yds, nine small boys, will take 18 yds—making 123 yds for pantaloons, and the same quantity of stuff for shirting." Each adult female slave, that is, re-

57. Diary and Plantation Record of Ellen E. McCollam, 1847–1851; Hite interview; Martin interview; Diary, 1857–1869, in Bond Papers.

58. Julia Woodrich, interviewed by Flossie McElwee, 1940, Louisiana Writers' Project File, Louisiana State Library.

ceived seven yards for a frock and three yards for a chemise, each adult male slave three yards for a shirt and three for a pair of pants. Young girls, by which Lourd meant early adolescents, each received four yards for a frock and two yards for a chemise; their male counterparts were given two yards for making a shirt, and another two for a pair of pants. Younger children on Magill plantation were given clothing less frequently. Lourd stated that "the children can do without clothes till fall as I gave them all a suit a piece last fall."[59]

On other sugar estates the allowances were comparable. On Randolph's Nottoway plantation, summer clothing, usually issued in mid-March, comprised pants and a shirt for each man, and a dress, or a dress and a chemise, for each woman, all of which were ready-made. Lengths of cloth for a similar outfitting were given the slaves on David Magill's plantation, different kinds of cotton to be used for the various kinds of clothing: the men received twilled cotton for pants, the women denim for dresses, and both plain cotton for shirts or chemises.[60]

The usual practice, mentioned in many plantation journals, was to issue slaves all their summer clothing at one time, that is, on a particular day in spring or early summer. Planters also gave the slaves most of their heavier winter issue on a single day late in the year. It was, however, more common for slaves to receive supplemental allocations of clothing for the winter than for the summer. On Randolph's plantation, for example, the slaves usually received their winter distribution of a shirt, two pairs of pants, and a pair of shoes for each man, and a dress, a chemise, and a pair of shoes for each woman, in mid-October. The ledger entries, however, disclose that as the winter progressed, other articles were distributed, such as "extra shoes" and "josies" (short jackets), given to the women in January and February, and "woollen jackets and socks," passed out in November. Some planters chose to give supplemental lengths of cloth that the slaves themselves made up.[61]

In the standard winter clothing issue on the Weeks family's Grande Cote Island plantation, the slaves received kersey, a coarse, ribbed woolen material that in 1857 cost twenty-seven cents a yard (Table 18). The standard adult issue of kersey for each man or woman that year was seven yards. Philip Hicky, on his Hope estate, used linsey-woolsey for slaves' heavier clothing, and Hite recalled the "thick yarn clothes" that slaves on Lan-

59. William Lourd (overseer), Magill plantation, to John Moore, February 20, 1862, in Box 38, Folder 185, Weeks Papers.

60. Ledger, 1862–1865 (Vol. VIII), in Randolph Papers; Cashbook, 1856–1859 (Vol. XII), in Weeks Papers; Estate of D. W. Magill, in Box 58, Weeks Papers.

61. Ledger, 1862–1865 (Vol. VIII), in Randolph Papers.

TABLE 18

STANDARD WINTER CLOTHING ISSUE FOR EACH SLAVE ON GRANDE COTE
ISLAND ESTATE

	Cotton Shirting (yds.)	Woolens (yds.)	Shoes (prs.)
Men	3	6	1
Women	6	6	1
Boys (adolescents)	2.5	5	1
Girls (adolescents)	6	5	1
Small children[a]	2	0	0

SOURCE: "Clothing Assessments for Grande Cote," in Box 42, Folder 260, David Weeks and Family Papers, Department of Archives and Manuscripts, LSU Libraries.

[a] Small children received two yards of cotton shirting apiece in both the fall and the spring.

dreaux' Trinity plantation wore in the wintertime. Rachel O'Connor, a slaveholder in the Bayou Sara sugar region, referred to the fabric she used for slaves' heavy clothing as blanket cloth, and the records of numerous other plantations merely cite "woollen cloths" in describing the winter issue.[62]

Only the children did not receive shoes as part of their regular clothing allowance. The shoes handed out to the adults were either purchased readymade or made on the plantation. Either way, they were crudely constructed, but especially if fabricated on the estate. Charles Gayarré's account of life on a Louisiana sugar plantation referred to the crude cobbling techniques. Slaves, he noted,

62. "Clothing Assessments for Grande Cote," in Box 42, Folder 260, Weeks Papers; Ally Meade to Mary C. Moore, October 2, 1857, in Box 30, Folder 149, Weeks Papers; Cashbook, 1856–1859 (Vol. XII), in Weeks Papers; Philip Hicky, Hope estate, to Morris Morgan, July 12, 1859, in Philip Hicky and Family Papers, Department of Archives and Manuscripts, LSU Libraries; Hite interview; Rachel O'Connor to David Weeks, November 20, 1833, in Box 4, Folder 17, Weeks Papers.

protected their feet with what they called *quantiers* made in this way. The negro would plant his foot on an ox-hide that had undergone a certain preparatory process to soften it. Armed with a flat and keen blade, another negro would cut the hide according to the size and shape of the foot, leaving enough margin to overlap the top of it up to the ankle. Holes were bored into it, and with strips of the same leather this rustic shoe was laced tight to the foot. It was rough and unsightly, but wholesome, like the French sabot or wooden shoe. The foot, in a woollen sock, or even bare, when encased in a quantier stuffed with rags or hay, was kept remarkably warm and dry.[63]

Cornelius recalled that on the plantation where she was a slave the men made the work shoes "wid beef hide." Apart from commenting that the shoes were "heavy," she spoke of neither their quality nor the skill with which they were fabricated. There were instances in which men skilled in the craft of shoemaking were employed to supply a plantation. Hite recalled that on Landreaux' sugar estate "dere was a big brick house fo' de shoemaker shop. De shoemaker was cullored. He was free. His name was Beverly. He tanned de hides an' did ev'rything. Even teached de darkies, dat is, de young ones." Some planters hired skilled slaves from other plantations to cobble, as when "Mr Billards negro man Edmund came to make shoes" for the slaves on William Palfrey's plantation.[64]

Many planters, however, chose to buy commercially made "negro shoes" for the slaves. Those were of crude construction, and the "ponderous ill-made" footwear seen by Russell was, as likely as not, of this type. It is improbable that the contract the penitentiary in Nashville, Tennessee, had with the Gay plantation in 1840 for making shoes at fifty cents a pair furnished the slaves with well-crafted footwear. Although the retail price for "negro shoes" was somewhat higher if purchased through the usual commercial outlets—$1.00 to $1.25 per pair in the 1840s and 1850s—the quality probably did not differ markedly.[65] The shoes issued to field hands were often called "russet brogans" in recognition not only of the coarse construc-

63. Charles Gayarré, "A Louisiana Plantation of the Old Regime," *Harper's New Monthly Magazine,* LXXIV (1887), 610–11.

64. Cornelius interview; Hite interview; Plantation Diary, 1860–1868, 1895 (Vol. XVIII), in Palfrey Account Books.

65. Russell, *My Diary,* 380; Box 6, Folder 51, in Gay Papers; "W. Emerson's a/c for Boots & Shoes for Southdown & Waterloo for 1849," in Diary, 1850 (4), in Minor Papers; Journal—Plantation Book, 1847–1852 (Vol. V), in Randolph Papers; Box 5, Folder 48, in Stirling Papers.

tion but also of the condition and color of the leather, which had retained its brown hue through tanning. On a number of larger plantations, however, better-quality black shoes were purchased for domestic slaves. Included in the distribution for 1854 of "negro shoes" on the Stirling family's plantation were "House Servants Black Shoes" of various sizes, and Hite recalled that "de master brought his house people shoes from France. Dey had to look gud, caise de master had plenty of company."[66]

Domestics and field workers wore shoes, but hands employed in ditching and in woodcutting in the swamps abutting the plantations sometimes received boots. Because both jobs involved extended periods standing in water, some of the slaves assigned to the jobs, as on the Gay family's plantation, received "ditching boots."[67]

The slaves received shoes once or twice a year, depending on the plantation and, within the estate, on the slaves' sex and age. When planters issued only one pair a year, it was usually part of the fall clothing ration. Elu Landry gave the slaves shoes in October, 1848, and November, 1849; on a plantation of the Stirling family's, between 1859 and 1861 the shoe issue occurred each October.[68] A different system prevailed on the Gay family's estate. Between 1849 and 1853, slave men of working age received two pairs of shoes each year, usually in February and October, while some slave women received only one pair and others two. There is nothing to indicate a basis for the unequal distribution, but demonstrable need may have played a part in the allocation. Some of the women may have been doing light work, perhaps because they were pregnant or suckling, and consequently did not require the ration accorded field hands. Need seems to have been the determining criterion on Randolph's plantation, a ledger of which carries, without further explanation, the entry "Extra shoes given out." The ledger cataloging the shoes passed out on the Gay family's estate for 1859 and 1860 shows that slaves received shoes on numerous occasions, presumably when they needed them. Maunsell White said that he gave the slaves on his Deer Range plantation "2 pr. & sometimes 3 pair in the course of the year depending much on their quality."[69]

66. "Negroe Shoes given out in 1854," in Box 8, Folder 48, Stirling Papers; Hite interview.

67. Estate Record Book, 1831–1845 (Vol. VIII), in Gay Papers.

68. Landry Estate Plantation Diary and Ledger; "List of Negroes Coats & Shoes," in Box 10, Folder 59, Stirling Papers.

69. Plantation Record Book, 1849–1860 (Vol. XXXVI), in Gay Papers; Ledger, 1862–1865 (Vol. VIII), in Randolph Papers; Ration Book, 1859–1863 (Vol. XC), in

The records do not reveal whether it was a specific policy on the Gay plantation to concede shoes less frequently to elderly and adolescent slaves than to working adults or if the youths and the old wore out their shoes less quickly. Young children usually went without shoes. Stewart recalled that as children "we didn't have no shoes." The clothing allocation of slaves on the Weeks family's sugar estate also shows that small children did not get shoes (Table 18).[70]

Sometimes slaves whose shoes wore out before a scheduled distribution had to do without. That would have happened more often when slaves received one rather than two pairs a year. A reason for putting the annual distribution in the fall may have been to let slaves whose shoes wore out go barefoot in the more clement summer months, when the work of weeding and laying the crop by was somewhat less taxing. But the want of shoes could occur at times capable of causing the slaves a great deal of discomfort. John Craighead wrote from his plantation, in Iberville Parish, to his partner, Andrew Hynes, that, with the temperatures near freezing, he was "about to commence making Sugar without . . . shoes for the negroes."[71]

Faced with the prospect of going barefoot in inclement weather, some slaves sought to extend the life of their shoes by caring for them as Cornelius recalled. To preserve the leather and make the shoes more supple and comfortable, the slaves "greas[ed] shoes wid meat skin en put on pot blackenin." The use of blackening may have been to emulate the appearance of the shoes worn by house slaves.[72]

When Louisiana planters failed to distribute clothing twice a year, it caused them or their representatives some concern. W. W. Lawless, overseer on Charles Mathews' Chaseland plantation, on Bayou Lafourche, wrote to the owner, "I have no stuff as yet for the summer clothing for the Negroes & the Seamstresses here have nothing to do & will be late to get the clothing made." Mary Weeks's overseer, John Merriman, reported that at her Grande

---

Gay Papers; Maunsell White, Deer Range, to Charles H. Mason, Esq., editor of *Economist,* Cannelton, September 14, 1849, in White Letterbook.

70. Plantation Record Book, 1849–1860 (Vol. XXXVI), in Gay Papers; Stewart interview; "Clothing Assessments for Grande Cote," in Box 42, Folder 260, Weeks Papers.

71. John B. Craighead, Iberville, to Colonel Andrew Hynes, Nashville, October 1, 1837, in Box 5, Folder 41, Gay Papers.

72. Cornelius interview. Similar practices prevailed in other rural populations. Thomas Hardy mentions a "piece of flesh, the characteristic part [penis] of a barrow-pig [castrated boar] which the country-men used for greasing their boots" (*Jude the Obscure* [1895; rpr. New York, 1978], 33).

Cote Island plantation "the Negro clothing is very indiferent stuff and I think the quantity insufficient as I have received only two hundred and thirty yards—I also received some Bore Stuf, but no cotton for tops, nor none for shirting, do you wish the men to have jackets this season."[73] Self-interest motivated the planters' concern. Planters who had slave seamstresses on the plantation did not want them to be idle for lack of cloth, and they realized that the slaves would be healthier and work better if suitably outfitted. It is as likely that the slaves, deprived of what they considered their due in clothing, would have shown their displeasure, perhaps by adversely affecting the plantations' productivity through job actions. Overseers and planters always underestimated at their peril the power of slaves. Planters, if they wanted the estate to run efficiently, had to recognize and respect what was often a very delicate balance of reciprocal rights and obligations regarding privacy, holidays, property and its disposal, and the other established routines of plantation life.

Ceceil George, who went as a slave from a cotton plantation in South Carolina to a sugar plantation in St. Bernard Parish, Louisiana, recalled that "in de ole country [South Carolina] dey had spinning wheels made dere own cloth—made gloves, caps for de head. . . . In dis country [Louisiana], dey give yo' de ole clothes, one pair shoes a year, no stockin's an' in de winter, sometimes yo' so cold—Lawd . . . have mercy!"[74] Contemporary travelers and commentators disagreed on the adequacy of the slaves' clothing. Accounts range from the description of slaves "with their bodies half exposed to the severest of cold weather" and the comments by James Pearse on their "scanty dress" to the observation of Solon Robinson that they were "all neatly dressed" and the remark of William Howard Russell that their clothing "seemed heavy for the climate." Although the comments undoubtedly reflect the writers' antipathy to or sympathy for slavery, in such an extensive plantation system the slaves must have experienced a wide range in the adequacy of their outfitting.[75]

Some plantations made additional allotments of items like hats, socks, and outer- and undergarments. George may have complained that slaves on La Houssaye's plantation were given "no stockin's," but White ordered for his Deer Range estate "20 doz. of knit woollen socks for [the] negroes,"

73. W. W. Lawless (overseer) to William C. Leich, Bayou Lafourche, March 21, 1858, in Box 2, Folder 20, Mathews Papers; Merriman to Weeks, July 12, 1840, in Box 8, Folder 28, Weeks Papers.

74. George interview.

75. Franklin (La.) *Planter's Banner*, August 2, 1849, p. 1; James Pearse, *A Narrative of the Life of James Pearse* (Rutland, Vt., 1825), 83; Kellar, *Solon Robinson*, II, 167; Russell, *My Diary*, 380.

specifying that he wanted the larger and better quality that sold for $1.50 to $2.25 per dozen. White also wrote of having "splendid over coats made for the people that work in the Field, Blue & green of a large size, so that they last them 3 years." Rachel O'Connor also issued slaves overcoats ("good warm blanket coat[s]") for winter wear, and on other plantations, slaves received similar outer garments or shorter coats and jackets such as round-abouts and "joseys." Included in the slaves' clothing allocations on Minor's Southdown plantation for 1850 were a pair of woolen socks, a nightshirt, and a pair of cotton drawers. The slaves on Randolph's Nottoway plantation got, in addition to the regular fall allocation, josies, woolen pants, jackets, and socks at scattered times during the winter months. Winter headgear usually meant felt or glazed hats or woolen caps for the men, and woolen caps or kerchiefs suitable to be tied turban style for the women (Figures 25–32).[76]

The supplemental distributions frequently favored certain groups of slaves. Moses Driver, a slave driver on the Gay estate, received "woolen pantaloons" in addition to the allowance given the other slaves on the plantation. A year before, of the fifty-one men supplied with winter clothing, ten received "pantaloons only," thirty-three "coats only," and six "pantaloons and coat," one a frock coat, and one a roundabout.[77]

That the care of sick slaves included supplying them with extra clothes is shown by the increased demand for flannel, and the consequent increase in its cost, in New Orleans during the cholera epidemic of 1832. A. T. Conrad wrote to his sister Mary Weeks that planters were providing their slaves with flannel, to be worn "next to the skin," and woolen socks in order to prevent infection. That had caused flannel to become scarce in the city.[78]

Louisiana planters, like their Jamaican counterparts, rewarded fecund slave women. O'Connor, for instance, gave a calico dress to each slave woman on her estate who bore a child.[79]

76. George interview; Maunsell White, New Orleans, to Dr. Thos. E. Wilson, Louisville, November 9, 1848, White to Bracewell, August 10, 1849, both in White Letterbook; O'Connor to Weeks, November 20, 1833, in Box 4, Folder 17, Weeks Papers; Ledger, 1862–1865 (Vol. VIII), in Randolph Papers; Diary, 1850 (4), in Minor Papers.

77. Memorandum Book, 1840 (Vol. XXVII), Estate Record Book, 1831–1845 (Vol. VIII), both in Gay Papers.

78. A. T. Conrad, New Orleans, to Mary Weeks, October 28, 1832, in Box 4, Folder 14, Weeks Papers.

79. Rachel O'Connor to A. T. Conrad, April 12, 1835, in Box 6, Folder 22, Weeks Papers.

Codification of slave laws throughout the early nineteenth century aimed at ensuring the provision of "adequate" clothing for Louisiana's slaves. Contracts for the hiring-out or external employment of slaves usually included stipulations about their clothing. A series of contracts from 1844–1847 between Randolph, of Nottoway estate, and C. A. Thornton for the use of Thornton's slaves on Randolph's plantation included such specifications. A partnership contracted in 1847 between William Weeks, Alfred C. Weeks, and Mary C. Moore "for the purpose of cultivating and carrying on a Sugar plantation on Grande Cote in the Parish of St. Mary" specified that "the Slaves working hands furnished by the parties together with their children and such as may be old and infirm . . . shall be clothed, fed, and receive all necessary medical attendance, at the Expense of the partnership and shall [be] humanely treated." Between 1857 and 1859, John Moore, a St. Mary Parish sugar planter, hired out two adult male slaves and a twenty-six-year-old female slave, along with her two infant children, to William Cary for five hundred dollars a year and clothing, feeding, good care, and payment for medical attention. There was also the stipulation requiring Cary to treat the slaves "as a good master should and not [to put them to] any work to jeopardize life or limb." Although these contracts did not spell out exactly what constituted adequate clothing, it is possible to infer that since the convention of a semiannual distribution was so entrenched, it set the standard of adequacy.[80]

Clothing the slaves was not a heavy financial burden on the planters. John Palfrey, who had a sugar plantation on the German Coast just west of New Orleans, calculated that in 1815 the cost of clothing a ten-year-old slave girl for the previous four and a half years was $22.50, that is, $5.00 a year. For adult slaves, the cost would have been somewhat higher. Shoes cost from $1.00 to $1.25 per pair, and boots around $2.00 or a little more (see above, pp. 156–57). Randolph bought men's jackets in 1860 at "$3.50 less 10 pr. ct." each, and a couple of years previously he had paid $210.43 for "65 Suits of Kerseys [*i.e.,* winter suits] for negro men," that is, about $3.25 a suit. Clothing bills for Uncle Sam plantation in the late 1850s itemized kersey pants for men at $1.25 per pair, kersey coats at $2.50 each, kersey pants for children at $1.125, kersey coats for children at $2.00, lowell (cotton) pants at $1.00, heavy "log cabin" pants at $1.50, shirts ranging from 60 cents for lowell twill to 50 cents for flannel, and "Campechy" hats (straw hats from Mexico) at $2.00 per dozen. Presumably, the flannel shirts issued to slaves

80. Box 1, Folder 6, in Randolph Papers; Box 14, Folder 40, Box 34, Folder 168, both in Weeks Papers.

on Tureaud's Houmas and Whitehall plantations in 1852 were superior to those of the slaves on Uncle Sam estate, since they cost $1.25 each.[81]

The cost was considerably less if planters bought cloth and had it made into apparel on the plantation, and it was still less if the cloth was spun and woven on the estate. White calculated that in 1849 he was paying an average of 12.5 cents per yard for cottonade, jean, and lowell cloth; six years later, John Randolph paid somewhat less than 10 cents a yard (550 yards for $53.25) for "Cotton sheeting from the Penitentiary," where he also bought twenty pounds of thread for $5.00. In 1860, Stirling's Wakefield plantation bought seven-eighths weight osnaburg at 11 cents a yard and four-fourths weight at 13 cents. The heavier kersey cloth used for winter clothes sold for 27 cents a yard in 1857; twenty-five years earlier linsey-woolsey had cost 50 cents a yard and wool cloth 45 cents a yard. When these prices are considered in connection with the annual yardage given slaves—summer issue about ten yards for a woman and six yards for a man, winter issue about twelve yards for a woman and nine yards for a man, with lesser amounts for children—the expense of clothing slaves presents itself as modest.[82]

At least one planter, however, devised a plan to decrease further her expenses for slaves' clothing. O'Connor, who owned a plantation in the Bayou Sara sugar region north of Baton Rouge, was in 1835 "buying negro crops [corn] at five bitts pr. barrel, out of which [the slaves] buy their summer clothing for themselves." She did not mention those slaves who, by reason of age, infirmity, or inability, either did not grow crops or had a poor harvest. They presumably would have received a supplemental allocation at the plantation's expense, been cared for by other members of the slave community, or possibly made do with one set of clothing per year, spending the summer months clad in worn-out garments.[83]

On some large plantations, slave seamstresses worked year round sewing up clothing. Hite recalled "winter clothes was made in summer an' summer clothes was made in winter . . . by old lady Betsy Adams . . . de seam-

81. John Palfrey to Chew and Relf, New Orleans, October 16, 1815, in Box 1, Folder 5, William T. Palfrey and Family Papers; Plantation Book, 1853–1863 (Vol. VI), in Randolph Papers; Box 1, in Uncle Sam Plantation Papers; Box 1, Folder 2, in Tureaud Papers.

82. Maunsell White to Charles H. Mason, September 14, 1849, in White Letterbook; Plantation Book, 1853–1863 (Vol. VI), in Randolph Papers; Plantation Diary, October 2, 1831–February 25, 1833, in Box 9, Folder 58, Stirling Papers; Meade to Moore, October 2, 1857, in Box 30, Folder 139, Weeks Papers.

83. Rachel O'Connor to Mary Weeks, December 14, 1835, in Box 6, Folder 23, Weeks Papers.

stress." Sewing up slave clothing was not the only work done by seam-stresses: they were often responsible for making clothing for the planter and his family, and for other domestic duties. Braxton Bragg, a Louisiana sugar planter and later a Confederate general, apparently did not use the skilled seamstress on his estate for making slave clothing. In a letter to his wife, Bragg mentioned that "Rose is a fine looking girl, 18 yrs, said to be faithful trusty house girl and fair seamstress. Nancy also sews, and one of the field hands makes negro clothing." In 1861, Richard Pugh, a Lafourche Parish sugar planter, paid eight hundred dollars for a "Black Woman, Louise, aged about 34 yrs—a superior french Cook, Washer & Ironer, fluter & Seam-stress." Louise's skills were probably applied to the cuisine and wardrobe of the Pugh family, while less accomplished bondswomen sewed the clothing for slaves on his plantation.[84]

Through the mid-1850s on the Weeks family's Grande Cote Island plan-tation six slaves worked to sew the men's summer clothing. In one year, Charity, Phoebe, and Mary made nineteen sets of shirts and pants of the first size, Nancy, Silvia, Nelly, and Charity made thirty-four sets of the sec-ond size, and Silvia sewed twenty-four pairs of boys' pants. On the Grand Cote Island estate, the slaves worked under the direction of the planter's wife, who provided bolts of cloth and paper patterns. The slave seam-stresses cut the cloth according to the patterns and quantities required, then stitched up the garments.[85]

On Andrew and Ellen McCollam's relatively small Ellendale sugar plan-tation, the approximately twenty-five slaves did not warrant putting slave seamstresses to work full time making clothing. As on other estates of simi-lar size, the slaves employed in sewing also performed other plantation work, mostly of a routine nature. A series of entries in Ellen McCollam's plantation diary provides evidence of that:

[August 5, 1847]	Took Cinthy in to make up the negro clothing
[August 16, 1847]	Cinthy commenced sewing again. She left off last Monday to make brick.
[September 13, 1847]	Cinthy and Chatty sewing.
[October 2, 1847]	Cinthy sewed three days and a half.

84. Hite interview; Braxton Bragg to his wife, February 10, 1856, in Braxton Bragg Papers, Department of Archives and Manuscripts, LSU Libraries; Folder 3, in Richard L. Pugh Papers.

85. Notebook, 1853–1857 (Vol. IX), in David Weeks and Family Papers—The Weeks Hall Memorial Collection; William F. Weeks to John Moore, August 5, 1855, in Box 26, Folder 112, Weeks Papers.

The fall issue of clothing, on which Cinthy and Chatty worked, was distributed on October 17, 1847. In the following two years, two or four slave women alternated between sewing slave clothing and doing field work. Two cryptic entries in the diary are witness, perhaps, to the inadequacy of the clothing distributed:

[August 23, 1848]   Had 8 shirts stolen out of the wash
[September 10, 1849] I had a pair of sheets table cloth stollen out of
                     the garden

No mention is made of the items' recovery, or of a culprit's being apprehended.[86]

After distribution, care of the slaves' clothing was their responsibility. In this, too, there was no uniformity in observers' accounts. Russell observed slaves with their "stockings worn away," and a correspondent for the Franklin *Planter's Banner* remarked on slaves whose clothing was "thick with filth exuded from their skins." On Stirling's plantation there was evidence of a greater concern for hygiene. The plantation journal for 1851 made note that on Tuesday, October 21, 1851, while "Men & boys were employed putting dirt Round the Matlas of Seed Cane . . . the Women and Girls [were] washing up their Clothes." Three former slaves, Cornelius, Stuart, and Downs, all recalled that the slaves were responsible for washing their own clothing. Stuart remembered that pieces of apparel were soaked at "a big wash place at de bayou, a great big spring," and she mentioned that slaves "press[ed] 'em dey ownself." The clothes the slaves pressed, however, were probably Sunday garments. Jamaican slaves also took responsibility for the care of their clothing. William Beckford observed that Jamaican slaves washed their clothes at riverbanks, where they also performed their personal toilet, and J. B. Moreton wrote that female slaves were responsible for washing clothes and that the "black women take of beating and rubbing the clothes with stones and stumps of grass to save the expense of soap," with the result that clothes wore out "amazing fast."[87]

It is possible to conceive of the material culture of the slaves on sugar plantations in both Louisiana and Jamaica as disclosing two dimensions: that for

86. Diary and Plantation Record of Ellen E. McCollam.
87. Russell, *My Diary*, 380; Franklin (La.) *Planter's Banner,* August 2, 1849, p. 1; Cotton Record Book, 1833–1838, 1851–1859 (H-13, Vol. XIV), in Stirling Papers; Cornelius interview; Stuart interview; Downs interview; Moreton, *West India Customs,* 98, 150; William Beckford, *A Descriptive Account,* I, 230.

which the influences were largely centered in the planters, and that for which they were centered more fully in the slaves. Wide variations existed in the aspects of material culture influenced by the planter, both between the two regions and within them: Jamaican planters took on different responsibilities from those their Louisiana counterparts assumed, though there was little consensus among the planters of either region about just what their responsibilities were. The extent to which slaves influenced their material culture, inasmuch as it depended primarily on the level of their participation in the internal economy, varied both inter- and intraregionally, but variations apart from extent were much smaller.

In slave housing, the planter-centered dimension included many differences in construction patterns, materials, spacing, and the responsibility for building and repair. Climate and geography had an effect on both the type of shelter necessary and the availability of construction materials. Demographic considerations also had an impact: after the closure of the slave trade to Jamaica in 1808, planters on the island assumed some of the responsibilities for housing that their Louisiana counterparts adopted in the later post-slave-trade era of the sugar boom. The high rate of absentee ownership among Jamaican planters may have exacerbated the plight of slaves on the island, since their domestic comfort likely received shorter shrift from an attorney or overseer preoccupied with the short-term profits sought by a British-based estate owner. In Louisiana, slaves lived and worked on a plantation that was an integral part of an independent nation-state, not a colony, under a planter whose life, heritage, and interests were rooted not in a mother country thousands of miles distant but in the land that was worked for sugar.

Some aspects of the slaves' material culture were influenced by the varying degrees of planter solicitude or neglect within and between the regions. A survey of the clothing given slaves on sugar plantations in Jamaica and Louisiana does not yield easy, broad generalizations: the diversity of the slaves' apparel overshadows any patterns. Planters always issued work clothes but exhibited little consensus on what was necessary or adequate, and sometimes even flouted legal requirements regarding the matter. The same irregularities and problems are evident in connection with the tools, utensils, furnishings and other such goods the planters distributed.

Much greater uniformity marked the slave-influenced aspects of the material culture. In both Louisiana and Jamaica the slaves assumed significant responsibility for their houses, and there emerged patterns of dominion, territoriality, independence, and property rights. Houses and villages provided the focus for a wide range of activities, all typified by a kind of autonomy fundamentally antagonistic to the principles of slavery. Although these activities had no legal sanction, they were prevalent in both Jamaica and Louisiana. They represented the creative and active development of people in circumventing their bondage and structuring the institution of slavery to their own designs. The development of the slave-centered dimension in housing clearly shows the limits of power even in as coercive an institution as slavery. In real terms, as opposed to theoretical ideal structures, there can be no monopoly of power.

Despite the differences in the degree of participation in the internal economy, a consistency existed in the kind of influence individual slaves exerted and in the aspirations they harbored. Slaves able to earn money chose similar commodities to purchase. They especially appear to have bought clothing so as to make a formal distinction between the part of their lives they spent functioning as enslaved laborers and the part over which they had greater control, on days off and holidays and from sundown to sunup. When working for the planter, slaves never wore the clothes they bought for themselves, and those slaves who could afford to do so, divested themselves of planter-supplied garb in favor of their own clothes when their time was their own.

The direction of the expenditures that slaves made permits an understanding of how they defined themselves and what they construed as self-improvement. For all sugar plantation slaves, money was scarce and earning it difficult, and yet, however much the slaves procured, they consistently gave priority to the same items in their spending.

CONCLUSION

The slaves' independent economic activities on the sugar plantations of Jamaica and Louisiana provided the material foundations for their family and community life. In making possible a degree of economic autonomy and enabling slaves, to some extent, to distance themselves from planter control, the systems of production and marketing developed within the internal economies redefined slave-planter relations while establishing unique patterns of life within the slaves' communities and providing an independent material basis for their society and culture.

The recent historiography of slavery has emphasized how slaves differentiated between their lives from sunup to sundown, as plantation laborers, and their lives from sundown to sunup, when, relatively free of planter control, they developed systems of family and community relations and engaged in cultural, artistic, and religious pursuits. The probability that an independent economic system was present in every slave plantation community in the two regions, however, renders the bifurcation of the day into "sunup to sundown" and "sundown to sunup" inadequate to the complexity of slaves' lives, since a division also existed between laboring for the planter and laboring for themselves and their families, a prerogative they zealously asserted and defended.

A survey of the internal economy on the sugar plantations enhances our insight into the private lives of people who showed remarkable tenacity in transcending the oppression of their bondage and securing significant measures of independence from it. The slaves' economic initiatives demonstrate their power even over the commodity they were enslaved for—their labor—and the monetary rewards garnered by participants in the economy conferred on them a financial competence that could have a pronounced effect on their life-styles.

Slaves engaged planters in an ongoing struggle over the terms of their bondage. While planters held out inducements or, more commonly, resorted to coercion and punishment to extract labor from the men, women, and children they held as slaves, the slaves adopted strategies to resist their enslavement. At times their resistance aimed at escape from, or overthrow of, the "peculiar institution," but more often it sought to improve their lives on the plantation through changes in their working conditions and more secure control over their "private" lives within family and community. Their leverage arose from the dominion they had over the hours during which they did no work for the plantation, over territory in the quarters and grounds on which they dwelt and raised crops and livestock, and over the accumulation and disposition of personal goods and earnings.

Plantation slaves normally had some discretionary time. Although the planters conceded them some, if not all, of the time they had free of plantation duties out of the wish, especially in Jamaica, to get them to raise what they needed for their subsistence, the slaves proved adept in turning the attempt at exploiting them to their own advantage, by using remissions from plantation labor to develop independent economic systems. The amount of time off could vary, depending on crop and season, and it at times barely let the slaves recuperate from the work they were performing.

Undoubtedly the planters gained from the economic enterprise of slaves on their plantations. When the slaves consumed some of the food they raised and purchased clothing for themselves, they lifted some of the planters' responsibilities. Besides, the slaves' moneymaking ventures also provided the planters with cheap and convenient supplies of goods and services. Nonetheless, the internal economy plainly cannot be viewed as being in the main a scheme by planters to manipulate the slave labor force.

The diversity and ubiquity of the slaves' economic activities testify to the creative initiative of their communities in Jamaica and Louisiana. Despite the severe hardships of labor, diet, clothing, housing, discipline, and illness, the slaves managed to participate in, and to a large extent determine the form of, vigorous internal economies. They succeeded because of their extraordinary efforts and sacrifices. None of the money they earned came easily; the work they performed to get it required physical effort, all the more draining on top of the grueling plantation labor expected of them.

The amount of money a slave earned could fluctuate considerably from week to week and year to year, and there were often sizable disparities between the earnings of slaves, even on a single plantation. The significance of the private economy to slave life and the slave community rests less on the quantities of money accumulated than on its social implications. Participation in the internal economy fostered slave initiative at odds with the subservience characteristic of much of plantation life. The decision making and choices exercised within the economy contradicted the premises of slavery: in the economy's operation, the slaves made planting, harvesting, and marketing decisions, chose how and when to spend the earnings they accumulated, assessed how to apportion their free time, and weighed the advisability of this or that theft.

Participation in the internal economy affected the lives of the sugar plantation slaves of Jamaica and Louisiana on the individual, family, and community levels. Individually, slaves experienced rewards derived from a work regimen that was self-motivated and self-organized and whose proceeds went to those who labored. Slaves mastered the arts of husbandry and became proficient in the skills of barter and marketing both as retailers and consumers. Accompanying the material benefits of the internal economy were the psychological compensations derived from exercising freedom of action.

As many of the plantation accounts chronicling the economic activities of the slaves on sugar estates reveal, the efforts were organized by and for the family. The family, or network of immediate kin, appears to have been the basic unit of economic action in the two regions.[1] Members of slave families contributed to the economy of the family unit according to their dispositions and abilities. Elderly slaves, whose plantation duties were often reduced, tended the kitchen gardens and livestock and operated cottage industries, and children had responsibility for light chores, while the stronger adults bore the burden of the heavier labor. The preferences exhibited by slaves in their purchasing also consistently reflected the primacy of family. The purchases they made and the manner in which, and the reason why, they made them reveal how they sought to improve themselves, and to what and to whom they gave priority.

At the community level, the moneymaking ventures slaves engaged in afforded an economic foundation for the development of African-American slave culture. Standards and styles of clothing, furnishings, food, and drink, central to the development of the culture, depended heavily on the slaves' economic independence, as did moments of social life that included gambling and music making. The slaves' religious participation was also af-

---

1. Sidney Mintz and Richard Price come to the same conclusion in *An Anthropological Approach to the Afro-American Past: A Caribbean Perspective* (Philadelphia, 1976), 38: "Small kin groups provided a basis for economic cooperation, [and] were able to develop within some of the most oppressive slave systems."

169

fected by the financial competence they derived from their internal economy. Just as they offered obeah practitioners remuneration, so too they supported other religious establishments through contributions in the collection plate.[2]

Private economic activities were an important underpinning of slaves' community and family life not only in Jamaica and Louisiana but also in other New World plantation societies. Neville Hall, in his study of how the slaves in the Danish Virgin Islands used their free time, points out that at the weekly Sunday market in Christiansted, St. Croix, "the available market produce were, overwhelmingly, the result of the slaves' creative initiative in the use of their 'free' time, particularly in the cultivation of their provision grounds."[3] Ira Berlin tells how slaves on cattle pens in the Carolina and Georgia low country in the early eighteenth century secured "time for their own use." Berlin writes that "the insistence of many hard-pressed frontier slaveowners that their slaves raise their own provisions legitimated this autonomy. By law, slaves had Sunday to themselves. Time allowed for gardening, hunting, and fishing both affirmed slave independence and supplemented the slave diet. It also enabled some industrious blacks to produce a small surplus and to participate in the colony's internal economy, establishing an important precedent for black life in the lowcountry." Slaves developed their private economies when the Georgia and Carolina low country was an underdeveloped frontier region. As Berlin remarks, however, "Blacks kept these prerogatives with the development of the [rice] plantation system." If anything, the growth of townships, and the tendency of plantations to staple monoculture, "enlarged the market for slave-grown produce." In some cases, rice plantation slaves took their goods to market, but in others, "planters traded directly with their bondsmen, bartering manufactured goods for slave produce." Berlin decides that "planters found benefits in slave participation in the lowcountry's internal economy," but that "the small profits gained by bartering with their bondsmen only strengthened the slaves' customary right to their garden and barnyard fowl." The development of an independent economy continued until the abolition of slavery.

2. Mary Turner describes how, in the late eighteenth and early nineteenth centuries, Jamaican slaves who were converted to Christianity by the recently arrived mission churches, used "their ability to earn money and buy goods . . . to contribute to their church and achieve status within it" (*Slaves and Missionaries: The Disintegration of Jamaican Slave Society, 1787–1834* [Urbana, Ill., 1982], 47).

3. Neville Hall, "Slaves Use of Their 'Free' Time in the Danish Virgin Islands in the Later Eighteenth and Early Nineteenth Century," *Journal of Caribbean History,* XIII (1980), 29.

"By the Civil War," Berlin finds, "lowland slaves controlled considerable personal property—flocks of ducks, pigs, milk cows, and occasionally horses—often the product of stock that had been in their families for generations." Berlin stressed the importance of free time in helping create a true community among the slaves. "Participation in the lowcountry's internal economy," he says, "provided slaves with a large measure of control over their lives. The autonomy generated by truck gardening and the task system provided the material basis for lowland black culture."[4]

Philip D. Morgan has shown that the task system of labor that emerged on plantations in the South Carolina and Georgia low country was conducive to the development of extensive internal economies and the accumulation of property by slaves. "By the middle of the nineteenth century it is correct to speak of a significant internal economy," Morgan asserts, and he holds that it rested most heavily on stock raising and crop production. Participation by low-country slaves in the internal economy "afforded a measure of autonomy, . . . fed individual initiative and sponsored collective esteem." Low-country slaves also experienced the "merits of collective solidarity . . . in familial form," he says, since "when laboring in their plots, slaves could work in cooperative units of their own choice, and these generally took the form of family groups."[5] Morgan provides evidence for the autonomy of the low-country slaves' internal economy by showing that "slave property was not only being produced and exchanged but also inherited. . . . The property rights of slaves were recognized across proprietorial boundaries as well as across generations." The ways in which the internal economy enabled low-country slaves to accumulate and bequeath their wealth and property not only "strengthened the family unit" but also "involved slaves in a way of life that was at distinct variance with their ascribed status."[6]

Nigel Bolland's study of slavery on logwood estates in British Honduras (Belize) shows "that slaves maintained a degree of control over their family and community life" that enabled them to develop their own economic

4. Ira Berlin, "Time, Space, and the Evolution of Afro-American Society in British Mainland North America," *American Historical Review,* LXXXV (1980), 57, 65, 66.

5. Philip D. Morgan, "The Ownership of Property by Slaves in the Mid-Nineteenth-Century Low Country," *Journal of Southern History,* XLIX (1983), 402, 414, 418–19.

6. Philip D. Morgan, "Work and Culture: The Task System and the World of Low-Country Blacks, 1700–1880," *William and Mary Quarterly,* XXXIX (1982), 592; Morgan, "The Ownership," 419.

system. A description of Honduran slave life from 1788, cited by Bolland, commented that slaves on logwood estates were "ever accustomed to make Plantation as they term it, by which means they support their wives and children, raise a little Stock and so furnish themselves with necessaries." Although slaves consumed some of what they raised, they also "participated in a rudimentary marketing system where some of their produce was taken into the town of Belize for sale."[7]

Rebecca Scott avers in her 1985 study of the abolition of slavery in Cuba that "records of purchases of animals and produce from slaves are common in surviving plantation account books of the second half of the nineteenth century" and that "contemporary observers also suggested that the cultivation of provision grounds was a very general phenomenon." In her "economic and social interpretation of the significance of production for sale," Scott suggests that "cultivation [by slaves] of provision grounds represented opportunity for initiative, relatively unsupervised labor, and a source of funds—a limited 'personal economy.'"[8]

The works of Berlin, Morgan, Bolland, Hall, and Scott emphasize the active, creative participation of slaves in the formation and operation of the internal economy. Low-country rice plantation slaves had "prerogatives" and "rights" concerning their private economies which gave them both "autonomy" and "control over their lives" and "benefited them economically and socially"; logwood plantation slaves' "control over their family and community life" enabled them to develop a "marketing system" in British Honduras that involved transporting and selling goods in the colony's townships. The internal economy of sugar plantation slaves in the Danish Virgin Islands arose from the "slaves' creative initiative in the use of their 'free' time," just as the growth of a "personal economy" resulted from the opportunities opened up to Cuban sugar plantation slaves when they "obtain[ed] access to land and were able to produce crops."[9]

More recently, the conference "Cultivation and Culture: Labor and the Shaping of Slave Life in the Americas," held at the University of Maryland in April, 1989, brought together a number of scholars who have studied dimensions of the independent economic activities of slaves. Notwith-

7. Nigel Bolland, "Slavery in Belize," *BISRA Occasional Publication,* VII (1979), 4, 11.

8. Rebecca Scott, *Slave Emancipation in Cuba: The Transition to Free Labor, 1860–1899* (Princeton, 1985), 16–17.

9. Berlin, "Time, Space," 57, 65–66; Morgan, "Work and Culture," 597; Bolland, "Slavery in Belize," 4, 11; Hall, "Slaves Use," 29; Scott, *Slave Emancipation,* 16–17.

standing disparities of time, place, crop, and labor norms, the findings of Hilary Beckles, for Barbados, Woodville Marshall, for the Windward Islands, Dale Tomich, for Martinique, Mary Turner, for Jamaica, Richard Price, for Suriname, John Campbell, for the South Carolina up-country, and John Schlotterbeck, for piedmont Virginia, affirm the pervasiveness of slaves' economies and their importance not only within the slave community but also within the larger plantation society.[10]

Links can also be discerned between the internal economies of slave populations and the structure of post-Emancipation economies. Sidney Mintz and Douglas Hall have established "how the peasant economy and its marketing pattern [in post-Emancipation Jamaica] originated within the slave system." They conclude that "after Emancipation, many new markets would appear, and the scope of economic activity open to the freedmen would be much increased. But Emancipation, insofar as marketing and cultivation practices were concerned, widened opportunities and increased alternatives; apparently it did not change their nature substantially." An extensive peasant economy founded on the slave provision-ground system emerged when slaves were freed in Jamaica, and the direct economic affiliations that persisted between the plantation system and many freedmen were similarly influenced by experiences derived from the internal economy's operation. The acumen with which Jamaican freedmen conducted their wage negotiations in the immediate post-Emancipation era testifies to the understanding of fiscal affairs they gained from conducting their internal economy while slaves. A similar connection can be perceived between the slaves' internal economy and the structure of the economies created by Louisiana freedmen after Emancipation. Although many freedmen continued to work on the sugar plantations, for wages, the terms and conditions of employment that they negotiated with the planters enabled them to retain access to the provision grounds they had worked during slavery and thus to perpetuate the private and self-directed economic systems they had developed then. Like their Jamaican counterparts, the newly freed Louisiana sugar plantation workers drew on the financial proficiency they had learned as slaves in conducting their internal economies, and their labor negotiations displayed a

10. The proceedings of this conference are published in a special number of *Slavery and Abolition*, XII (May, 1991), entitled "The Slaves' Economy: Independent Production by Slaves in the Americas" and edited by Ira Berlin and Philip Morgan; it is reprinted as *The Slaves' Economy: Independent Production by Slaves in the Americas*, ed. Ira Berlin and Philip D. Morgan (London, 1991), and *Cultivation and Culture: Labor and the Shaping of Slave Life in the Americas*, ed. Ira Berlin and Philip D. Morgan (Charlottesville, Va., 1993).

sound grasp of the economic issues bearing on their circumstances and also provided clear evidence of the importance they gave to their independent economic pursuits.[11]

Rebecca Scott sees much the same thing in Cuba. The internal economy developed by slaves on Cuban sugar plantations involved "exchanges [that] required masters to deal with slaves in terms of money rather than strictly in terms of forced labor," and consequently, Scott asserts, what slaves learned as participants in their market economy "could affect the way they would behave during and after emancipation."[12] Morgan finds that for slaves in the Georgia and South Carolina low country "the task system and its concomitant domestic economy [made] possible the freed person's adaptation to freedom without the blessings of the former masters." The skills and property low-country slaves acquired through participation in the internal economy profoundly influenced their transition to freedom.[13]

The centrality of the internal economy to the free-time pursuits of slaves on Louisiana and Jamaica sugar plantations suggests that, after Emancipation as much as before, the slaves, their families, and their communities not only accrued material benefits from their moneymaking endeavors but also settled into persisting individual life-styles and relationships with kin and fellow slaves that contributed to the maintenance of discrete social structures.

Mintz and Douglas Hall assert that "it is upon the polinks [provision grounds] that the foundations of the free peasantry [of Jamaica] were established." Neville Hall finds that "in the Danish Virgin Islands, the slaves by the use of the discretionary time, legally and illegally at their disposal, had created certain modes of being and behaviour that were distinctly theirs." He holds that "by emancipation they had created a culture, neither wholly African nor yet European, retaining, adapting, borrowing and adopting."[14]

The internal economy also brought slaves into contact with the free population of the plantation societies in relationships markedly different from those between taskmasters and slave laborers. The slaves exercised considerable power over those with whom they traded. Their influence and control over the free population suggest that the internal economy also

11. Sidney Mintz and Douglas Hall, "The Origins of the Jamaican Internal Marketing System," *Yale University Publications in Anthropology*, LVII (1960), 18, 24.

12. Scott, *Slave Emancipation*, 17.

13. Morgan, "Work and Culture," 599.

14. Mintz and Hall, "The Origins," 9; Hall, "Slaves Use," 42.

played an integral role in the formation of white culture in slave plantation societies. An investigation of the internal economy permits an understanding not only of the private world of the slaves but also of the dominion they had over the lives and society of those who enslaved them.[15]

15. Mintz and Richard Price, *An Anthropological Approach*, 16.

FIGURE 1 A print of a West Indian slave woman on her way to Sunday market. Among the wares she is carrying are sugarcane, pineapples, poultry, a calabash, and a bottle. The clothing and accessories worn to market could be elaborate for both men and women.

From *West India Scenery,* by Richard Bridgens (London [1836?])

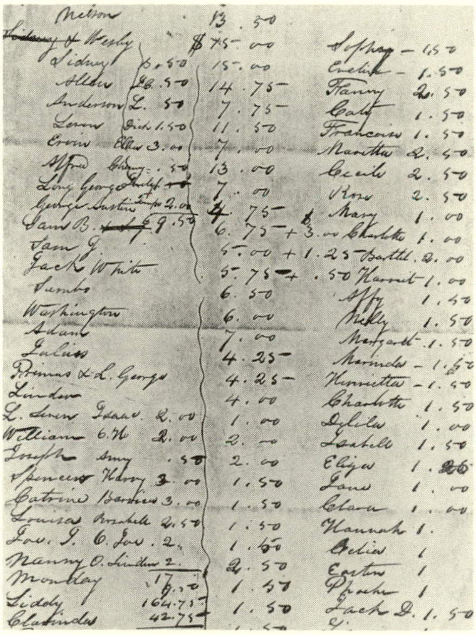

FIGURE 2 A manuscript leaf under the heading "Money paid the Negroes" from the estate of Lewis Stirling and his family, around 1855. The amount distributed came to $258.50.

From Lewis Stirling and Family Papers, Department of Archives and Manuscripts, Louisiana State University Libraries.

FIGURE 3 Thatched wattle-and-daub housing in Jamaica, about 1860. In the background at the left is a partially daubed house. The wattles are the dark horizontals, and the light-colored material on top of them is daub.
From *Picturesque Jamaica,* by Adolphe Duperly (Kingston [1890s]), 67

FIGURE 4 Detail of thatched wattle-and-daub house in Jamaica, about 1860
From *Picturesque Jamaica,* by Duperly, 67

FIGURE 5 A print of Roehampton estate, in Jamaica. Slave houses are regularly spaced in rows at right.
From *A Picturesque Tour in the Island of Jamaica,* by James Hakewill (London, 1825)

FIGURE 6 A print of Old Montpelier estate, in Jamaica. Slave houses are irregularly clustered in the woods behind the sugar mill, at right.
From *A Picturesque Tour,* by Hakewill

FIGURE 7   Jamaican yabbas, made during slavery. The Asante influence on construction and design was strong.
By permission of the Archaeological Museum, Spanish Town.

FIGURE 8   A print of slaves in Antigua planting canes. The women are in skirts, chemises, and turbans, and the men in shirts, pants, and caps or hats. The two drivers supervising the work wear stylishly cut coats. Jamaican patterns of dress were much the same.
From *Ten Views in the Island of Antigua,* by William Clark (London, 1823)

FIGURE 9   A print of slaves feeding sugarcane into a windmill. The women are wearing full-length skirts, half- to three-quarter-length tops, and turbans. The man unloading canes from the cart, at right, is in pants, a shirt or short jacket of a different color, and what appears to be a woolen cap. The driver, left-center foreground, is dressed in a manner superior to that of the field slaves. He has on a glazed hat, a shirt, a jacket, and pants, and appears to be wearing shoes. The white man, extreme left foreground, is probably an overseer.

From *Ten Views in the Island of Antigua,* by Clark

FIGURE 10   A print of slaves cutting and loading sugarcane. The driver, right foreground, has an extremely elaborate costume: nattily cut jacket and trousers, a ruffled neckerchief, and in his hand, a tall glazed hat.

From *Ten Views in the Island of Antigua,* by Clark

FIGURE 11   A print of estate hands at the backbreaking work of holing a cane field. The men appear to be wearing their full annual issue of work clothes: pants, a shirt, and either a woolen cap or a hat. The driver, standing, foreground, has a cutaway jacket, a high collar and neckerchief, and trousers and a hat.
From *Ten Views in the Island of Antigua,* by Clark

FIGURE 12   The party dress of male and female slaves. The ornate turban of the woman dancing, center, typifies the difference from working attire.
A. Brunias, *A Negro Festival Drawn from Nature in the Island of St. Vincent,* 1810 (?)

FIGURE 13 The contrast between work clothes and Sunday best in Jamaica.

From *Jamaica: Its Past and Present State,* by James Phillippo (London, 1843), 230.

FIGURE 14 Men and women celebrating a Junkanoo, or John Canoe, festival. The women are bejeweled for the occasion.

I. M. Belisario, *French Set Girls,* 1830s. Courtesy of the National Library of Jamaica.

FIGURE 15 Men and women in their best clothing, in the mid-1840s. The women are all wearing beads.

Mission Station in Antigua, West India Committee, London

FIGURE 16 Slaves dressed for a dance. Everyone is decked out, although shoeless. One of the ornate turbans is topped by a broad-brimmed hat.

A. Brunias, *Slave Dance in Dominica,* 1810 (?)

FIGURE 17 Housing on the Gay family's plantation, in Iberville Parish. The house, of Creole design and probably constructed in the 1870s, is one of the last that remain of the rows of houses in Figure 18.

FIGURE 18 Rows of double cabins on the Gay family's plantation. Construction may have been after the Civil War, but the building pattern and regular spacing are similar to those found in earlier slave villages on Louisiana sugar plantations.

Photograph, *ca.* 1906, in National Register of Historic Places, Louisiana Historical Preservation and Cultural Commission, Department of Culture, Recreation, and Tourism, Baton Rouge.

FIGURE 19 Two-story brick slave houses on Woodland plantation, in Plaquemines Parish. The design was unusual for the Louisiana sugar region.
From *Louisiana Plantation Homes,* by William Darrell Overdyke (New York, 1965), 204. By permission of Crown Publishers.

FIGURE 20 Rectangular brick double cabin, built around 1850 on Evan Hall plantation, in Assumption Parish.

FIGURE 21   Two double cabins on Evan Hall plantation

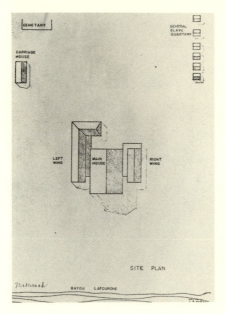

FIGURE 22   Plan of the Pugh family's Madewood plantation, on Bayou Lafourche in Assumption Parish. Regularly spaced double slave cabins are at top right.
From National Register of Historic Places, Louisiana Historical Preservation and Cultural Commission.

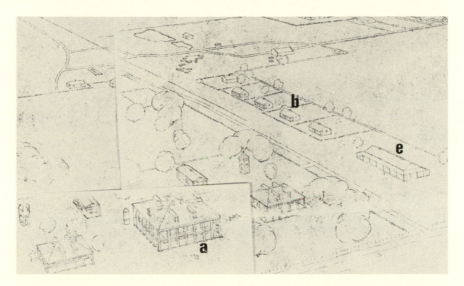

FIGURE 23   Plan of Uncle Sam plantation, in St. James Parish. Regularly spaced double cabins (**b**) are close to the slave hospital (**e**) and the planter's house (**a**).
From Historic American Buildings Survey, LA 74, Department of Archives and Manuscripts, LSU Libraries.

FIGURE 24   A print, "Winter Holydays in the Southern States: Plantation Frolic on Christmas Eve," accompanying the article "Christmas in the South" that Thomas Bangs Thorpe wrote for *Frank Leslie's Illustrated Newspaper.* Sandy Bill and Aunt Patsy, purportedly slaves on the estate of a "wealthy planter of Louisiana," are dancing to the accompaniment of banjo and fiddle. The finery includes the women's collared full blouses, dresses, shawls, and kerchiefs, and the men's coats, short jackets, high-collared shirts, and neckerchiefs. The women's tignons—madras handkerchiefs bound turbanlike around the head—were a fashion in the French sugar islands of Martinique and Saint Domingue, and they resembled the toques worn by female slaves in Jamaica.
From *Frank Leslie's Illustrated Newspaper,* December 26, 1857, p. 62

GATHERING THE CANE.

FIGURES 25–30   The work clothes of sugar plantation slaves in Louisiana. The men are in jackets, shirts, trousers, woolen caps, and wide-brimmed straw hats, the women in full skirts, chemises, and turbans.

From "Sugar and the Sugar Region of Louisiana," by Thomas Bangs Thorpe, in *Harper's New Monthly Magazine,* VII (1853), 746–67.

FIGURE 25

FIGURE 26

Figure 27

Figure 28

FIGURE 29

FIGURE 30

FIGURE 31   Louisiana slaves harvesting cane
From the sketch *The Sugar Harvest in Louisiana,* by Alfred R. Waud. Courtesy of the Historic New Orleans Collection.

FIGURE 32   Transporting cane to the mill
From *The Sugar Harvest in Louisiana,* by Waud. Courtesy of the Historic New Orleans Collection.

APPENDIX 1

SLAVE HOUSEHOLDS ON OLD MONTPELIER ESTATE, AUGUST 1, 1825

REFERENCE NUMBER ASCRIBED FOR THIS STUDY	NUMBER IN HOUSEHOLD	NAMES OF SLAVES, WITH NAMES OF ANY FAMILIES OR DEPENDENTS
1	4	William Miller, Catherine Ellis, William Smart, Thos. Stewart Miller
2	3	Mary Richards 1st, Robert Innes 2nd, Liddy Campbell
3	4	David Richards 2nd, Jane Taylor, Emily Dodd, Ellen Clift
4	3	Martin McPherson 2nd, Eliz. Johnson, Mary Henry
5	6	Sally Grey, John Thomas, David Miller, Henry, Christmas, Geddes
6	3	Elizathe, Rose, James Dukey
7	5	Mary Dawes, John Jones, Quacon, Murdoch, Mary Irwin
8	9	Robert Innes 1st, Sarah Miller 1st, Wm. Spence, Margaret Rose, Mary Campbell 1st, Wm. Love, Mary Johnson, Rosey Warren, Sally, [Sarah Miller's freeborn children]
9	2	Nancy Bell, Thomas Beckford

Continued on next page

SOURCE: "Minutes of Evidence taken before the Select Committee of the House of Lords appointed to inquire into the Law and Usages of the several West India Colonies in relation to the Slave Population . . . ," in *British Sessional Papers: House of Lords,* 1831–32, CCCVI, 82–89, 1376–93.

REFERENCE NUMBER ASCRIBED FOR THIS STUDY	NUMBER IN HOUSEHOLD	NAMES OF SLAVES, WITH NAMES OF ANY FAMILIES OR DEPENDENTS
10	1	Bessy Kemp (free)
11	3	John McPherson, Sarah Richards 1st, William Lansdale
12	6	William, Thos. Cloe, M. Hilton, A. Hedley, F. Hedley, Bell Hedley
13	2	James Ellis 2nd, James Fayers
14	1	William Kemp
15	7	R. Watt, J. Richards 1st, W. Sharp, Ann Drummond, J. Cunningham, Margaret Bowen, Coomba
16	2	Joe Savage, Bessy Savage
17	7	Mary Campbell 2nd, Wm. Thompson, A. Duncan, J. Lawrence, J. Queen, A. Rose, Nelly Vaughan
18	3	Robert Bowen, Ann Dood, Tabra
19	3	William Bennet, Sarah Johnson, Pinkey Ellis
20	2	William Hilton, Charlotte Johnson
21	5	Martin McPherson 1st, Bessy Ellis 4th, Bessy Ellis 6th, George McPherson, William McPherson
22	3	Ann Galloway, Mary Walker, Richard Ball
23	2	Cicero, Sarah Richards 2nd
24	4	Mary Price, Hugh Hamilton, John Hamilton, May Hamilton
25	5	Catherine Price, Thos. Whildale, Isabella Malcolm, Henry, Charlotte (all living at New Montpelier)
26	7	Bessy Fraser, Isabella Monsey, M. A. Paton, Wm. Smithson, R. Smithson, Eliza Smithson, S. Thompson
27	3	John Miller 1st, Henry Waite, Francis Inverarity
28	3	Liddy Bridgen, Charles Hall, Louisa Fryers

Continued on next page

Reference Number Ascribed for This Study	Number in Household	Names of Slaves, with Names of Any Families or Dependents
29	1	Davey
30	6	Billy Richards, Maria Ferguson, Richd. Darlaston 1st, Coelia, Billy, George Malcolm
31	4	Grace Curton, William Rose, John Savage, Henry A. Savage
32	8	Bessy Warren, Eliz. Warren, Ellen Warren, Wm. Tomlinson, Richard Warren, Catherine Thompson, Benoba 2nd, Thisbe
33	3	Mary Galloway, Rob. Galloway, Liddy Stirling 2nd
34	4	William Buckford 1st, Rosey Brown, Chas. Campbell, Mary Miller 3rd
35	4	Elizabeth Ellis 1st, Joe, Charles Thomas, Charles Palmer
36	3	George Ellis 3rd, Famer, Sarah Ellis
37	5	Cath. Thompson 1st, Rob. Rose 1st, Peter Goodwin, Sarah Lewis, Fidelia
38	1	Thomas Lewis Goodwin
39	6	Gilian Sharpe, Nancy Front 1st, Sarah Bennett Aren, Richard, John, Sarah Darlaston
40	2	Eleanor Harvey, Jane Jackson
41	3	William Paton, Charlotte Miller, Mary Ann Ellis 2nd
42	2	Leonard, Margaret Nutter
43	2	James Richard 1st, Jeanny Ellis
44	2	Francis Williams, Betsy Ellis
45	6	Bessy Richards (free), Charles Howard 2nd, Eliza Ellis, Archibald Barker, Peggy Richards, Mary Cogan
46	1	Mary Ann Forrest
47	2	William Squires, Sally Ellis

Continued on next page

REFERENCE NUMBER ASCRIBED FOR THIS STUDY	NUMBER IN HOUSEHOLD	NAMES OF SLAVES, WITH NAMES OF ANY FAMILIES OR DEPENDENTS
48	3	Becky Ellis, Queen Ellis, Douglas, [William Squires]
49	6	George Ellis 1st, Nancy Front 2nd, Robert Barrett, Eliza Fisher, Sylvanas, Frederick
50	7	Bessy Ellis 2nd, Ann Ellis 2nd, Amelia Ellis, Cushe Malcolm, George Thomas, Sanst, Judy, [George Ellis 1st]
51	4	Scott Ellis, Lizzy Miller, Sabina James, Polly Milon
52	2	William Richards 1st, Mary Ann Ellis 1st
53	1	Bessy Ellis 2nd, [William Richards 1st]
54	1	Esther
55	3	Gatty Ellis, Robert Ellis 2nd, Sammy
56	2	William Johnson, Mary Ellis 2nd
57	3	Peggy Ellis 2nd, John Baillie, John Perry
58	2	Leonard Parkinson, Mary Parkinson
59	2	David Richards 1st, Molly Ellis
60	3	William Purkis, Sarah Richards 3rd, Agnes Miller
61	1	Nelly Goodwin
62	5	Jane Wedderburn, Jane Richards 2nd, George Ellis 2nd, Bessy Ellis 5th, Mary Kemp 2nd
63	2	William Richards 2nd, Nancy Frail
64	5	Charles Rose, Ann Ellis 1st, Mary Rose 2nd, Beck Galloway, Rose Ellis
65	(1)	George Palmer (invalid, always in hospital)
66	5	Peggy Ellis 1st, Margaret Lewis, Grace, Giles Miller, Rachael Scarlett
67	2	Baltimore, David Richards 3rd
68	4	Edward Richards, Liddy Stirling 1st, Donald, Rachael Morris
69	3	Ginger Scott, Kitty Lard, Charles Morris

Continued on next page

REFERENCE NUMBER ASCRIBED FOR THIS STUDY	NUMBER IN HOUSEHOLD	NAMES OF SLAVES, WITH NAMES OF ANY FAMILIES OR DEPENDENTS
70	5	William Galloway, Polly Miller 1st, Joseph Bowen, Richard Dixon, Rodney
71	2	Jess Ellis, Hawke
72	3	John Watson, Bessy Ellis 1st, George Watson
73	2	Peter Richards, Jane Brown
74	2	Monimia, Mary Forrest
75	2	James Hedley, Ann Miller 1st
76	1	Mary Wilson
77	2	Mary Miller 1st, Margaret Anderson, [James Hedley]
78	5	Billy Maulsby, Mary White, William Richards 3rd, John Miller, Rebecca Maulsby
79	2	Fanny Walker, James Richards 2nd
80	2	Bob Miller, Sarah Richards 4th
81	7	Wm. Campbell 1st, Sarah Brigett, Geo. Bowen, Ann Miller 3rd, Gren, Susan Campbell, Leak
82	1	Mary Lewis 1st, [David Richards 2nd]
83	2	Wm. Geo. Miller, Sarah Miller 2nd
84	5	Philip A. Scarlett, Jenny Miller Ellis, Richan Ellis 2nd, Robert Rose 2nd, Dublin Malcolm
85	1	John Ellis 3rd
86	3	Wm. Walker, Mary Rose 1st, Cynthia
87	4	Barrett, Harriet Miller, James Harvey, Marlborough
88	2	Rob. Ellis 1st, Ann Frought
89	5	Mary Ann, Rose, Polly, Aimwell, Fraser
90	3	Eliz. Payne, Mary Miller 2nd, Mary Campbell
91	3	Wm. Campbell 2nd, Ann Miller 2nd, John Froy
92	2	Prince Ellis, Fanny Hill
93	2	George Wood, Charlotte Howard

Continued on next page

REFERENCE NUMBER ASCRIBED FOR THIS STUDY	NUMBER IN HOUSEHOLD	NAMES OF SLAVES, WITH NAMES OF ANY FAMILIES OR DEPENDENTS
94	3	John Hilton, Mary Kemp, Jackey
95	1	Behaviour
96	2	Charles Ellis, Lizzer Ellis
97	2	John Hoddle, James Hibbert
98	1	Mary Hedley
99	3	Ellis Howard, Nancy Cunningham, Mary Ann Price
100	2	Charles Howard 1st, Liddy Ellis
101	3	Edward Miller, Jane Miller 1st, Wallace
102	1	Peter Inverarity
103	2	James Miller, Temperance
104	7	Jane Baillie, Richard Darlaston 2nd, Elizabeth Ellis 2nd, Rachael Baillie, Mary Sage, Fergusson, William Whittingham
105	4	John Ellis 1st, Bessy Grace, Beneba 1st, Fanny Bowen
106	5	Dodd, Susan Richards, Richard Ellis 1st, William Wiggan, Garrolt
107	5	Nancy McIntosh, Ann McIntosh, Margaret Brown 2nd, Jack, William Atkinson
108	4	John Ellis 2nd, Mary Howard, Queen Ellis 2nd, Robert Cross
109	2	William Lawrence, George Reid
110	4	James Ellis 1st, Miles Frail, Lord Howard, Angaley
111	1	Mary Thompson
112	3	Thomas Miller, Margt. Brown, Jane Miller
113	1	Margaret Ellis
114	1	John Wilson
115	1	Nancy Ellis
116	1	Rosey Ellis
117	1	George Howard

Continued on next page

REFERENCE NUMBER ASCRIBED FOR THIS STUDY	NUMBER IN HOUSEHOLD	NAMES OF SLAVES, WITH NAMES OF ANY FAMILIES OR DEPENDENTS
118	1	Charley
119	1	Sawney (watchman, no house)
120	2	Baillie, Quamina (watchmen, no houses)
121	1	Roberts Wright (at the wharf, no house)
122	1	Thomas Ellis (at the wharf, no house)
123	1	George Ellis (at the wharf, no house)
124	1	Mary Ann Forest (free)
		AT MONTPELIER FARM
125	4	Charles Brain, Charlotte Watt, Mary Thomson, Eliza John
126	2	Samuel Miller, Mary Ellis
127	5	Richard Barrett, Jane Hughes, Mary Fraser, Robert Anderson, Miller
128	1	Watty Adams
129	1	Mary Gould
130	2	Mary Fowler, Sarah Miller 3rd
131	1	James Allen
132	2	Amelia Grant, Wm. Green
133	1	Harry Frail
134	1	Jacob Chambers
135	3	Willm. Beckford, Ann Mounsey, William
136	1	Bessy Robson
137	(1)	John (runaway, 1814)

Total of 401 slaves on Old Montpelier (including one who has been a runaway for eleven years)

Total of 135 households on Old Montpelier (excluding one runaway and one invalid always in hospital)

Continued on next page

SLAVE HOUSEHOLDS ON NEW MONTPELIER ESTATE, AUGUST 1, 1825

REFERENCE NUMBER ASCRIBED FOR THIS STUDY	NUMBER IN HOUSEHOLD	NAMES OF SLAVES, WITH NAMES OF ANY FAMILIES OR DEPENDENTS
201	4	Charles Rose Ellis, Charles Henry Ellis, Janet Ellis, Jane Thompson
202	3	Ellen Ellis, John Scarlett, Richard Darlaston
203	2	John Hamilton, Bessy Thomas
204	6	John Stokes, Edward Hamilton, Sam Murray, Eliz. Miller, Cath. Hamilton, Jenny Payne
205	6	George Ellis 1st, George Browne, Patrick Kelly, Malcolm, Eliza Payne, Sarah Ellis
206	4	Richard Green, Wm. Green, Bessy Morris, Ellen Walker
207	3	William Warren, Richard Warren, Fanny Richards
208	4	John Palmer, Edward Payne, Ann Palmer, Mary Hughes
209	5	William Perkis, Robert Ellis, Harriet Ellis, Ann Ellis, George Gartritt
210	5	William Palmer, Alex Palmer, Helena Ellis, Francis Ellis, Batty Palmer
211	6	Jas. Stephenson, Simon Stephenson, John Parry, Molly Stephenson, Mary Wadd, Bessy Stephenson
212	3	David Richards, Adam Ellis, Catherine Smart
213	7	George McKenzie, Rob McKenzie, Thomas Walker, Jane Ellis, Cath. Ellis, Bessy Lee, Susan Besley
214	3	Thomas Harvey, Philip Ellis, Sarah Richards
215	1	John McLean
216	5	Chas. Barrett, Sam. Kerr, Mary Ann Ellis 2nd, Eliz. Warren, Ann Warren

Continued on next page

REFERENCE NUMBER ASCRIBED FOR THIS STUDY	NUMBER IN HOUSEHOLD	NAMES OF SLAVES, WITH NAMES OF ANY FAMILIES OR DEPENDENTS
217	7	William Parr, John Parr, James Parr, William Bailey, George Parr, Chas. Miller, Beams
218	3 (4)	Charles Beckford, Beckey Richards, Queen Price (Edward Reid [ref. 280] living in this house)
219	3	John Griffiths, James Dunbar, Hazar Miller
220	4	James Palmer, Davy Ellis, William Aughie, Judy Ellis
221	6	William Ellis, John Payne, James Marshall, Dolly Hamilton, Anny Ellis, Eliza Ellis
222	2	Dennis Lagourgue, Barnet Lagourgue
223	3	James Watcon, Henry Percy, Amelia Scarlett
224	2 (3)	Ann Parkinson, Candice (Letitia Hamilton [ref. 278] living in this house)
225	6	Sam. Reid, Grace Cotton, Bessy Scott, Ann Beckford, Elizabeth Payne, Catherine Miller
226	6	Thomas Parke, Ellis Parke, Queen Price, Fanny Hamilton, Julina Parke, Henrietta Ellis
227	6	Abram Miller 1st, Abram Miller 2nd, Lucinda Ellis, Queen Ellis, Eve Richards 2nd, Minerva Miller
228	4	Robert Campbell, Mary Campbell 1st, Liddy Campbell, Ann Campbell
229	5	Robert Smart, Calypso Lagourgue, Margt. Richards, Susan Miller, Martin Richards
230	5	Bob Lagourgue, Bob Miller, John Robt. Ellis, Eliza Lagourgue, Jenny Miller
231	5	Moses Richards, Robert Douglas, Thomas Bell, Bell Ellis, Rachael
232	2	Walter Smith, Laurie Lagourgue
233	6	William Miller, Adam Smart, Toby Richards, Eliza Smart, Louisa, Lucy Richards

Continued on next page

REFERENCE NUMBER ASCRIBED FOR THIS STUDY	NUMBER IN HOUSEHOLD	NAMES OF SLAVES, WITH NAMES OF ANY FAMILIES OR DEPENDENTS
234	7	James Murray, William Murray, Sharp Hamilton, William Love, George Murray, Mary Ann Murray, Sarah Murray
235	5	Priscilla Murray, Jane Murray, Rose Murray, Eliza Murray, Bessy
236	2	Mary Campbell 2nd, Marina
237	4	John Rook, Robert Rose, Mary Bernard, Ellen Gordon
238	3	Anderson Hamilton, Charlotte Bernard, Grant
239	5	John Ellis, George Ellis, Dolly Ellis, Rose Miller 2nd, L. McKenzie
240	3 (7)	George Malcolms, Ann Scarlett, Seaky Ellis (Andrew Beckford, David Ellis, Fanny Ellis, Phoebe Palmer [ref. 279] living "with Sucky [*sic*] Ellis")
241	2	Louisa Ellis, Becky Jones
242	4	George Hamilton, Wm. Fairclough, Patience Ellis, Marg. Lagourgue
243	3	Billy Hutchin, Juliet Lagourgue, Catherine Palmer
244	6	William Richards 1st, Beckford Hamilton, Duncan Anderson, Susan Campbell, Eliza Fisher, Susan Mitchell
245	3	George Otty, Catherine McIntosh, Bessy Rose Ellis
246	4	George Miller, John Christie, Rosey Miller 1st, Isabella Richards
247	3	Chas. Delaney, Julia Ellis, Flora Ellis
248	3	George Jones, Mary Howard, Grace Hamilton
249	3	Wm. Helton, Jas. Walker, Maria Malcolm
250	3	Sam Lee, Edward Rose, Mary Rose
251	3	James Williamson, Thomas Ellis, Sarah Thompson

Continued on next page

REFERENCE NUMBER ASCRIBED FOR THIS STUDY	NUMBER IN HOUSEHOLD	NAMES OF SLAVES, WITH NAMES OF ANY FAMILIES OR DEPENDENTS
252	5	Henry Williamson, Toby Brown, Sam Lee, Amelia Brown, Matilda
253	3	Wm. Walker, Patrick Ellis, Bella Ellis
254	4	Francis Ellis, Allick Campbell, Charles Palmer, Betty Parkinson
255	5	John E. Payne, Alex Ellis, Liddy Ellis, Susanna Barrett, Grace Ellis
256	4	Peter Scarlett, Thomas Warren, Peter, Molly James
257	8	Saml. Beckford, Lawrence Beckford, Wm. Beckford, Ellen Beckford, Modest Beckford, Mary, Becky, Catherine
258	3	James Hamilton, Mary Ann Ellis 1st, John Richards
259	2	Rebecca Ellis, Billy
260	4	John Hood, Lettice, Bessy McLean, Patient Malcolm
261	3	John Howard, Charles Howard, Becky Ellis
262	2	James Ellis, Leah Ellis
263	3	Richard Miller, Eve Richards, Abigail Ellis
264	3	Nero, Amelia Richards, Susan Richards
265	2	Nancy Francis, Rose Miller
266	3	George Williams, James Anderson, Sarah Johnson
267	3	William Grignon, Mary Allen, John Allen
268	1	Joe Richards
269	2	Sally Hamilton, John McCall
270	1	Mary Anderson
271	1	Flora Ellis
272	2	William Richards 2nd, Sarah Scarlett
273	2	Jack Miller, Peachy
274	3	Robt. Gardner, Thos. Hill, Rebecca Jenkins

Continued on next page

REFERENCE NUMBER ASCRIBED FOR THIS STUDY	NUMBER IN HOUSEHOLD	NAMES OF SLAVES, WITH NAMES OF ANY FAMILIES OR DEPENDENTS
275	2	Mary Ann Wilson, Mary Martin
276	4	Molly Taylor, George Willis, Becky Hamilton, Peter Beckford
277	4	Robin, Dodd, Allen, Mary Ann Ricketts (3 watchmen, no houses)
278	1	Letitia Hamilton (living with Ann Parkinson [ref. 224])
279	4	Andrew Beckford, David Ellis, Fanny Ellis, Phoebe Palmer (all living with Sucky Ellis [ref. 240])
280	1	Edward Reid (living with C. Beckford [ref. 218])
281	1	Neil Malcolm (watchman, no house)
282	5	Davy Grant, Wm. Lindsay, Mary Reid, Molly Aitken, Fowler Ellis
283	1	Jacob Richards (watchman, no house)
284	2	Rosanna Ellis, Queen Howard
285	2	Ben Lagourgue, Dorothy Lagourgue
		AT MONTPELIER FARM
286	1 (2)	William Miller
287	1	Charles Ellis (living with William Miller [ref. 286])
288	1	Joseph Gray
289	1	John James
290	1 (3)	Peter Richards
291	1	Dennis (living with Peter Richards [ref. 290])
292	1	Kent (living with Peter Richards [ref. 290])
293	1	Cecilia
294	1	Judith Creeman
295	1	Betty
296	1	Charlotte Lagourgue

Continued on next page

REFERENCE NUMBER ASCRIBED FOR THIS STUDY	NUMBER IN HOUSEHOLD	NAMES OF SLAVES, WITH NAMES OF ANY FAMILIES OR DEPENDENTS
297	1	Betty Jones
298	1	James Beckford
299	1 (2)	Mary Richards
300	1	Jane Fraser (living with Mary Richards [ref. 299])
301	1	Ellen Barker

Total of 320 slaves on New Montpelier

Total of 94 households on New Montpelier (with slaves living in other slaves' houses included in the household where they reside)

APPENDIX 2

NUMBER OF LIVESTOCK OWNED AND ACREAGE OF GARDENS CULTIVATED BY SLAVES ON OLD MONTPELIER ESTATE, AUGUST 1, 1825

Reference Number	Number in Household	Cows	Steers	Heifers	Bull Calves	Cow Calves	Total Horned Stock	Hogs	Poultry	Acres	Rods	Perches
									Livestock		Extent of Gardens	
1	4	1	0	0	0	1	2	4	11	0	0	0
2	3	1	0	0	1	0	2	0	20	0	0	20
3	4	1	0	1	2	1	5	9	8	0	0	30
4	3	2	0	1	0	2	5	0	7	0	0	30
5	6	2	0	0	1	1	4	4	6	0	0	20
6	3	0	0	1	0	0	1	0	0	0	0	20
7	5	2	0	0	0	1	3	0	8	0	0	20
8	9	1	3	2	0	0	6	1	15	0	0	2
9	2	1	0	0	0	1	2	1	10	0	0	20
10	1	1	0	1	0	0	2	1	0	0	0	0
11	3	0	0	0	0	0	0	0	4	0	0	4
12	6	1	0	0	1	1	3	3	15	0	0	20
13	2	1	1	0	0	1	3	4	6	0	0	5
14	1	1	0	1	0	0	2	0	1	0	0	4
15	7	2	0	0	1	0	3	1	3	0	0	10
16	2	1	1	0	0	0	2	0	0	0	0	30

17	7	5	0	0	2	1	8	2	12	1	0	0
18	3	1	0	0	1	0	2	0	0	0	0	4
19	3	1	0	1	0	0	2	5	4	0	0	4
20	2	0	0	0	0	0	0	0	1	0	0	1
21	5	1	0	0	1	0	2	1	4	0	0	30
22	3	1	0	1	0	0	2	3	6	0	1	0
23	2	0	0	0	0	0	0	1	5	0	0	20
24	4	2	0	1	1	1	5	2	20	0	0	0
25	5	1	0	1	0	0	2	0	0	0	0	0
26	7	3	0	1	0	0	4	3	30	0	0	0
27	3	1	1	1	0	0	2	0	7	0	2	0
28	3	0	0	0	0	0	1	1	12	0	0	20
29	1	1	0	1	1	0	2	0	4	0	2	0
30	6	0	1	0	0	0	1	1	11	0	0	10
31	4	0	0	1	0	0	1	3	5	0	0	4
32	8	2	1	1	0	2	6	13	30	1	2	0
33	3	1	0	0	1	1	3	0	5	0	0	20
34	4	1	0	1	0	0	2	1	10	0	0	0
35	4	1	0	1	0	0	2	10	12	0	2	0
36	3	0	0	0	0	0	0	2	10	0	0	10
37	5	2	1	0	2	0	5	0	8	0	0	10
38	1	0	0	0	0	0	0	2	7	0	0	5
39	6	2	0	0	1	0	3	1	20	0	0	10

Continued on next page

Source: "Minutes of Evidence taken before the Select Committee of the House of Lords appointed to inquire into the Law and Usages of the several West India Colonies in relation to the Slave Population . . . ," in *British Sessional Papers: House of Lords*, 1831–32, CCCVI, 82–89, 1376–93.

Appendix 2—*Continued*

Reference Number	Number in Household	Cows	Steers	Heifers	Bull Calves	Cow Calves	Total Horned Stock	Hogs	Poultry	Acres	Rods	Perches
				Livestock						Extent of Gardens		
40	2	1	1	0	0	0	2	2	6	0	0	20
41	3	2	0	0	0	1	3	8	3	0	0	20
42	2	0	0	0	0	0	0	0	4	0	0	30
43	2	1	0	0	0	0	1	2	4	0	2	0
44	2	0	0	0	0	0	0	0	0	0	0	0
45	6	1	0	1	0	0	2	3	2	0	0	20
46	1	0	0	0	0	0	0	0	1	0	0	2
47	2	2	1	0	1	1	5	7	4	0	0	20
48	3	0	0	0	0	0	0	0	0	0	0	0
49	6	1	0	0	0	0	1	1	13	0	0	10
50	7	0	0	1	0	0	1	3	18	0	2	0
51	4	0	0	0	0	0	0	0	0	0	0	10
52	2	1	1	0	0	1	3	3	15	0	0	5
53	1	0	0	0	0	0	0	0	5	0	0	5
54	1	0	0	0	0	0	0	0	0	0	0	2
55	3	0	0	0	0	0	0	0	1	0	0	10
56	2	0	0	1	0	0	1	0	0	0	0	2
57	3	1	1	0	0	0	2	1	7	0	0	0
58	2	1	0	1	0	0	2	4	6	0	0	20

59	2	0	0	0	0	0	0	0	2	0	0	30
60	3	0	0	1	0	0	1	0	5	0	0	30
61	1	1	0	0	0	0	1	1	10	0	0	10
62	5	0	2	1	0	0	3	11	0	0	0	20
63	2	0	0	0	0	0	0	1	4	0	0	10
64	5	2	1	0	1	0	4	10	4	0	0	10
65	1	0	0	0	0	0	0	0	0	0	0	0
66	5	2	1	1	0	0	4	0	4	0	2	0
67	2	0	0	0	0	0	0	0	4	0	0	5
68	4	1	0	0	0	0	1	2	3	0	0	4
69	3	1	0	0	0	0	1	1	12	0	0	20
70	5	2	0	0	0	2	4	0	4	0	1	0
71	2	1	0	0	0	0	1	2	4	0	1	0
72	3	0	0	1	0	0	1	2	0	0	0	30
73	2	1	0	0	0	0	1	1	12	0	0	10
74	2	0	0	0	0	0	0	0	7	0	0	10
75	2	0	0	0	0	0	0	3	3	0	0	10
76	1	0	0	0	0	0	0	0	0	0	0	10
77	2	0	0	0	0	0	0	2	3	0	0	30
78	5	0	0	0	0	0	0	0	20	0	0	5
79	2	2	0	0	0	0	2	0	7	0	0	4
80	2	0	0	0	0	0	0	0	5	0	0	4
81	7	2	1	1	0	1	4	4	3	0	0	10
82	1	0	0	0	0	0	0	0	0	0	0	10
83	2	0	0	0	0	0	0	0	4	0	0	10
84	5	1	0	0	0	1	2	1	12	0	0	10
85	1	1	1	0	1	0	3	0	0	0	0	0

Continued on next page

Appendix 2—*Continued*

| | | Livestock | | | | | | | | Extent of Gardens | | |
Reference Number	Number in Household	Cows	Steers	Heifers	Bull Calves	Cow Calves	Total Horned Stock	Hogs	Poultry	Acres	Rods	Perches
86	3	0	0	0	0	0	0	0	0	0	0	5
87	4	0	0	0	0	0	0	1	4	0	0	1
88	2	0	0	0	0	0	0	0	4	0	0	5
89	5	0	0	0	0	0	0	0	0	0	0	4
90	3	1	0	0	1	0	2	1	8	0	0	20
91	3	1	1	0	0	1	3	0	2	0	0	10
92	2	0	0	0	0	0	0	0	0	0	0	5
93	2	0	0	0	0	0	0	2	7	0	0	20
94	3	0	0	0	0	0	0	1	3	0	0	10
95	1	0	0	0	0	0	0	0	3	0	0	1
96	2	0	0	0	0	0	0	0	10	0	0	2
97	2	0	0	0	0	0	0	0	0	0	0	20
98	1	0	0	0	0	0	0	0	3	0	0	10
99	3	0	0	0	0	0	0	1	10	0	1	0
100	2	0	0	0	0	0	0	0	3	0	0	20
101	3	0	0	0	0	0	0	1	6	0	0	10
102	1	0	0	0	0	0	0	1	8	0	0	10
103	2	0	0	0	0	0	0	0	4	0	0	10
104	7	2	0	1	0	1	4	0	7	0	0	20

105	30	0	0	2	0	1	0	0	1	0	0	4
106	2	0	0	1	2	1	0	0	1	0	0	5
107	0	0	0	8	9	1	0	0	1	0	0	5
108	10	0	0	4	1	0	0	0	0	0	0	4
109	2	0	0	2	0	1	0	0	1	0	0	2
110	20	0	0	3	1	1	0	0	1	0	0	4
111	20	0	0	6	1	0	0	0	0	0	0	1
112	10	0	0	3	9	0	0	0	0	0	0	3
113	20	0	0	2	0	0	0	0	0	0	0	1
114	10	0	0	0	1	1	0	0	0	0	0	1
115	10	0	0	2	0	0	0	0	0	0	0	1
116	10	0	0	1	0	0	0	0	0	0	0	1
117	0	0	0	0	0	0	0	0	0	0	0	1
118	0	0	0	4	0	0	0	0	0	0	0	1
119	0	0	0	0	0	0	0	0	0	0	0	1
120	0	0	0	4	0	0	0	0	0	0	0	2
121	0	0	0	0	0	0	0	0	0	0	0	1
122	0	0	0	0	0	0	0	0	0	0	0	1
123	0	0	0	0	0	0	0	0	0	0	0	1
124	20	0	0	0	0	0	0	0	0	0	0	1

AT MONTPELIER FARM

125	20	0	0	5	1	0	0	0	0	0	0	4
126	0	2	0	20	0	0	0	0	0	0	0	2
127	0	1	0	50	0	1	0	0	1	0	0	5
128	20	0	0	20	0	0	0	0	0	0	0	1
129	0	1	0	4	1	1	0	0	1	0	0	1

Continued on next page

Appendix 2—*Continued*

Reference Number	Number in Household	Cows	Steers	Heifers	Bull Calves	Cow Calves	Total Horned Stock	Hogs	Poultry	Extent of Gardens		
										Acres	Rods	Perches
130	2	0	0	0	0	0	0	1	10	1	1	0
131	1	0	0	0	0	0	0	0	2	0	0	0
132	2	0	0	0	0	0	0	1	20	0	0	20
133	1	0	0	0	0	0	0	0	20	0	0	0
134	1	0	0	0	0	0	0	0	2	0	0	10
135	3	0	0	0	0	0	0	0	20	0	1	20
136	1	0	0	0	0	0	0	0	1	0	0	20
137	1	0	0	0	0	0	0	0	0	0	0	0
Total	401	77	19	34	20	23	173	190	856 [a]	17	0	28

[a]In the source, this appears as 358.

NUMBER OF LIVESTOCK OWNED AND ACREAGE OF GARDENS CULTIVATED BY SLAVES ON NEW MONTPELIER ESTATE, AUGUST 1, 1825

Reference Number	Number in Household	Livestock								Extent of Gardens		
		Cows	Steers	Heifers	Bull Calves	Cow Calves	Total Horned Stock	Hogs	Poultry	Acres	Rods	Perches
201	4	4	1	1	3	1	10	16	32	1	0	31
202	3	3	0	1	2	1	7	0	16	0	1	15
203	2	2	1	0	0	1	4	6	24	0	3	26
204	6	3	0	1	0	3	7	0	20	0	2	32
205	6	0	0	1	0	0	1	3	20	0	2	35
206	4	0	0	0	0	0	0	1	15	0	1	30
207	3	0	0	2	0	0	2	10	12	0	0	36
208	4	2	0	2	0	0	4	2	12	0	1	0
209	5	1	0	0	1	0	2	3	11	0	0	36
210	5	1	0	0	0	1	2	1	10	0	1	10
211	6	0	0	0	0	0	0	5	6	0	0	30
212	3	1	0	0	0	0	1	7	5	0	0	35
213	7	1	0	0	0	1	2	6	26	0	1	0
214	3	1	0	1	0	0	2	0	5	0	1	16
215	1	0	0	0	0	0	0	0	12	0	0	36
216	5	0	0	0	0	0	0	12	15	0	1	0
217	7	3	1	0	1	1	6	6	15	0	1	20

Continued on next page

213

Appendix 2—*Continued*

Reference Number	Number in Household	Cows	Steers	Heifers	Bull Calves	Cow Calves	Total Horned Stock	Hogs	Poultry	Acres	Rods	Perches
								Livestock		Extent of Gardens		
218	3 (4)	0	0	0	0	0	0	5	6	0	0	25
219	3	0	0	0	0	0	0	0	5	0	0	28
220	4	0	0	0	0	0	0	1	15	0	0	22
221	6	1	0	1	0	0	2	22	14	0	1	23
222	2	0	0	0	0	0	0	1	3	0	0	26
223	3	1	0	0	1	0	2	2	10	0	1	10
224	2 (3)	0	0	0	0	0	0	1	14	0	0	30
225	6	1	0	0	0	0	1	8	14	0	1	0
226	6	0	0	0	0	0	0	2	6	0	0	25
227	6	0	0	0	0	0	0	0	4	0	1	10
228	4	0	0	0	0	0	0	1	12	0	1	15
229	5	0	0	0	0	0	0	0	10	0	0	35
230	5	0	0	0	0	0	0	0	3	0	0	28
231	5	0	0	0	0	0	0	1	6	0	0	29
232	2	0	0	0	0	0	0	2	7	0	0	30
233	6	0	0	0	0	0	0	0	12	0	0	25
234	7	0	0	0	0	0	0	3	14	0	0	0
235	5	0	0	1	0	0	1	0	3	0	1	35
236	2	0	0	0	0	0	0	0	3	0	0	32

Entry												
237	4	0	0	0	0	0	0	0	5	0	0	25
238	3	0	0	0	0	0	0	2	6	0	1	30
239	5	1	1	1	1	0	4	8	18	0	2	8
240	3 (7)	0	0	0	0	0	0	3	4	0	1	15
241	2	0	0	0	0	0	0	5	10	0	1	0
242	4	0	0	0	0	0	0	0	16	0	1	10
243	3	0	0	0	0	0	0	0	3	0	0	0
244	6	0	0	0	0	0	0	6	0	0	1	20
245	3	1	0	1	0	0	2	0	3	0	0	30
246	4	1	0	1	1	0	2	0	6	0	0	35
247	3	1	0	0	0	0	2	0	0	0	0	32
248	3	0	0	0	0	0	0	0	0	0	1	0
249	3	1	0	0	0	0	1	6	10	0	1	25
250	3	0	0	0	0	0	0	0	0	0	0	35
251	3	1	0	0	1	0	2	4	2	0	0	32
252	5	0	0	0	0	0	0	0	2	0	0	25
253	3	0	0	0	0	0	0	4	3	0	0	30
254	4	1	0	0	0	0	1	0	5	0	1	28
255	5	0	0	0	0	0	0	13	15	0	0	0
256	4	0	0	0	0	0	0	1	12	0	1	33
257	8	0	0	0	0	0	0	13	15	0	0	10
258	3	0	0	0	0	0	0	0	0	0	1	25
259	2	0	0	0	0	0	0	0	10	0	0	30
260	4	0	0	0	0	0	0	0	10	0	1	15
261	3	0	0	0	0	0	0	0	0	0	0	30
262	2	0	0	0	0	0	0	1	15	0	0	32
263	3	0	0	0	0	0	0	0	0	0	0	15

Continued on next page

Appendix 2—*Continued*

Reference Number	Number in Household	Cows	Steers	Heifers	Bull Calves	Cow Calves	Total Horned Stock	Hogs	Poultry	Acres	Rods	Perches
		Livestock								Extent of Gardens		
264	3	0	0	0	0	0	0	0	10	0	0	0
265	2	0	0	0	0	0	0	0	0	0	0	28
266	3	0	0	0	0	0	0	0	0	0	0	36
267	3	0	0	0	0	0	0	0	0	0	0	0
268	1	0	0	0	0	0	0	0	12	0	1	0
269	2	0	0	0	0	0	0	0	2	0	1	0
270	1	0	0	0	0	0	0	0	0	0	0	0
271	1	0	0	0	0	0	0	0	7	0	0	0
272	2	0	0	0	0	0	0	1	5	0	1	10
273	2	0	0	0	0	0	0	0	0	0	0	35
274	3	0	0	0	0	0	0	0	5	0	0	30
275	2	0	0	0	0	0	0	0	0	0	0	0
276	4	0	0	0	0	0	0	0	4	0	0	25
277	4	0	0	0	0	0	0	0	0	0	0	0
278	1	0	0	0	0	0	0	0	0	0	0	0
279	4	0	0	0	0	0	0	4	4	0	0	0
280	1	0	0	0	0	0	0	0	0	0	0	0
281	1	0	0	0	0	0	0	0	6	0	0	0

282	5	0	0	0	0	0	0	8	0	2	1	0
283	1	0	0	0	0	0	0	0	0	0	0	0
284	2	0	0	0	0	0	0	0	25	0	0	0
285	2	0	0	0	0	0	0	5	0	0	0	0

At Montpelier Farm

286	1 (2)	0	0	0	0	0	0	20	0	1	0	0
287	1	0	0	0	0	0	0	0	0	0	0	0
288	1	0	0	0	0	0	0	2	20	0	0	0
289	1	0	0	0	0	0	0	4	0	0	0	0
290	1 (3)	0	0	0	0	0	0	2	10	0	0	0
291	1	0	0	0	0	0	0	0	0	0	0	0
292	1	0	0	0	0	0	0	0	0	0	0	0
293	1	0	0	0	0	0	0	10	10	0	0	0
294	1	0	0	0	0	0	0	0	0	2	0	0
295	1	0	0	0	0	0	0	1	16	0	0	0
296	1	0	0	0	0	0	0	4	10	0	0	0
297	1	0	0	0	0	0	0	9	15	0	0	0
298	1	0	0	0	0	0	0	0	0	1	0	0
299	1 (2)	0	0	0	0	0	0	17	20	1	0	0
300	1	0	0	0	0	0	0	2	20	0	0	0
301	1	0	0	0	0	0	0	2	20	0	0	0
Total	320	32	4	14	11	9	70	211	718 [b]	22	1	36

[b] In the source, this appears as 720.

APPENDIX 3

ACREAGE OF PROVISION GROUNDS AND TOTAL ACREAGE OF GROUNDS (INCLUDING GARDENS) CULTIVATED BY SLAVES, OLD MONTPELIER ESTATE, AUGUST 1, 1825

REFERENCE NUMBER	NUMBER IN HOUSEHOLD	ACREAGE OF PROVISION GROUNDS			TOTAL ACREAGE OF GROUNDS (INCLUDING GARDENS)			TYPES OF PROVISIONS	STATE OF GROUNDS AS DESCRIBED
		ACRES	RODS	PERCHES	ACRES	RODS	PERCHES		
1	4	5	2	0	5	2	0	Plantains, cocoas, yams, corn	Clean and in pretty good order
2	3	4	2	0	4	2	20	Plantains, cocoas, yams, corn	Part clean, part foul
3	4	5	3	0	5	3	30	Plantains, cocoas, yams	Good provisions; part clean, part foul
4	3	2	3	0	2	3	30	Plantains, cocoas, yams	Provisions good, but rather foul; a part newly planted
5	6	5	2	0	5	2	20	Plantains, cocoas, yams, corn	In good order; part newly planted
6	3	3	0	0	3	0	20	Plantains, cocoas, yams, corn	In good order; part new and clean
7	5	1	1	0	1	1	20	Plantains, cocoas, yams, corn	In good order

8	9	13	3	0	13	3	2	Plantains, cocoas, yams, corn, coffee	Provisions in general excellent and in good order
9	2	3	2	0	3	2	20	Plantains, cocoas, yams, corn	Generally in good order
10	1	2	0	0	2	0	0	Plantains, cocoas, yams	Provisions good, but foul
11	3	3	0	0	3	0	4	Plantains, cocoas, yams	In general pretty good and clean
12	6	3	0	0	3	0	20	Plantains, cocoas, yams, corn	In good order, and clean
13	2	1	3	0	1	3	5	Plantains, cocoas, yams, corn	Very good
14	1	0	2	0	0	2	4	Plantains, cocoas, yams	Pretty good
15	7	2	0	0	2	0	10	Plantains, cocoas, yams, corn, coffee	In general pretty good
16	2	1	0	0	1	0	30	Plantains, cocoas, yams	Part clean, part foul
17	7	8	1	0	9	1	0	Plantains, cocoas, yams, corn	Generally in good order
18	3	1	0	20	1	0	24	Plantains, cocoas, yams	Part clean, part foul
19	3	3	0	0	3	0	4	Plantains, cocoas, yams, corn	Pretty good
20	2	1	0	0	1	0	1	Plantains, cocoas, yams, corn	Pretty good
21	5	1	1	0	1	1	30	Plantains, cocoas, yams	Clean, and generally in good order

Continued on next page

SOURCE: "Minutes of Evidence taken before the Select Committee of the House of Lords appointed to inquire into the Law and Usages of the several West India Colonies in relation to the Slave Population . . . ," in *British Sessional Papers: House of Lords*, 1831–32, CCCVI, 82–89, 1376–93.

Reference Number	Number in Household	Acreage of Provision Grounds			Total Acreage of Grounds (Including Gardens)			Types of Provisions	State of Grounds as Described
		Acres	Rods	Perches	Acres	Rods	Perches		
22	3	1	1	0	1	2	0	Plantains, cocoas, yams, corn	In good order
23	2	3	0	0	3	0	20	Plantains, cocoas, yams, corn	Good
24	4	3	1	0	3	1	0	Plantains, cocoas, yams, corn	In good order; part newly planted
25	5							(Living at New Montpelier)	
26	7	2	3	30	3	1	30	Plantains, cocoas, yams, corn	In general pretty good
27	3	1	3	30	1	3	30	Plantains, cocoas, yams	In pretty good order
28	3	4	3	0	4	3	20	Plantains, cocoas, yams	In good order
29	1	0	2	0	1	0	0	Plantains, cocoas, yams	Good, and very clean: excellent garden
30	6	2	0	20	2	0	30	Plantains, cocoas, yams, corn	Good, but rather foul
31	4	1	3	0	1	3	4	Plantains, cocoas, coffee	Good, but foul
32	8	10	3	0	12	1	0	Plantains, cocoas, yams, corn	In general good
33	3	2	0	0	2	0	20	Plantains, cocoas, yams, corn	Good

34	4	1	3	30	1	3	30	Plantains, cocoas, yams, corn	Middling
35	4	2	3	0	3	1	0	Plantains, cocoas, yams; in garden, coffee, arrowroot, tobacco, cassava	In good order and clean
36	3	5	0	20	5	0	30	Plantains, cocoas, yams, corn	Good, but rather foul
37	5	3	0	20	3	0	30	Plantains, cocoas, yams, corn	In general good
38	1	2	0	0	2	0	5	Plantains, cocoas, corn	In good order
39	6	5	2	0	5	2	10	Plantains, cocoas, corn	In general pretty good
40	2	2	1	3	2	1	23	Plantains, cocoas, yams	Good
41	3	4	0	20	4	1	0	Plantains, cocoas, yams, corn	Good, and generally clean
42	2	1	0	0	1	0	30	Plantains, cocoas, corn	Old and foul
43	2	2	0	20	2	2	20	Plantains, cocoas, yams, corn	Middling
44	2	0	1	0	0	1	0	Plantains, cocoas, yams	New and clean
45	6	4	3	0	4	3	20	Plantains, cocoas, yams, corn	In general pretty good
46	1	1	0	0	1	0	2	Plantains, cocoas, yams, corn	Part good; part poor and foul
47	2	1	2	0	1	2	20	Plantains, cocoas, yams, corn	In good order
48	3	1	0	0	1	0	0	Plantains, cocoas, yams	Good
49	6	1	2	0	1	2	10	Plantains, cocoas, yams	Provisions good, and in good order

Continued on next page

Appendix 3—Continued

Reference Number	Number in Household	Acreage of Provision Grounds			Total Acreage of Grounds (Including Gardens)			Types of Provisions	State of Grounds As Described
		Acres	Rods	Perches	Acres	Rods	Perches		
50	7	2	2	0	3	0	0	Plantains, cocoas, yams	Provisions good; part clean, part foul
51	4	2	2	0	2	2	10	Plantains, cocoas, yams, corn	Good
52	2	2	0	0	2	0	5	Plantains, cocoas	Part good, part foul
53	1	1	0	0	1	0	5	Plantains, cocoas, yams, corn	Very good and clean
54	1	0	0	0	0	0	2		
55	3	0	2	0	0	2	10	Plantains, cocoas, yams, corn	Good; part clean, part foul
56	2	1	2	30	1	2	32	Plantains, cocoas, yams, corn	Good
57	3	3	1	20	3	1	20	Plantains, cocoas, yams, corn	Good, but rather foul
58	2	3	0	0	3	0	20	Plantains, cocoas, yams	Provisions good, and in good order
59	2	3	0	0	3	0	30	Plantains, cocoas, yams	Generally good
60	3	1	2	0	1	2	30	Plantains, cocoas, yams	Middling
61	1	0	3	0	0	3	10	Plantains, cocoas, yams, corn	Part clean, part foul

No.								Provisions	Condition
62	0	3	4	20	2	4	5	Plantains, cocoas, yams, corn	Good, and pretty clean
63	10	2	2	0	2	2	2	Plantains, cocoas	Good provisions, but rather foul
64	10	3	6	0	3	6	5	Plantains, cocoas, yams, corn	Provisions good; part rather foul
65	0	0	0	0	0	0	1	Plantains, cocoas, yams, corn	Middling
66	30[a]	0	2	30	2	1	5	Plantains, cocoas, yams, corn	Mostly old and foul
67	5	2	0	0	2	0	2	Plantains, cocoas, yams, corn	Pretty good
68	4	0	2	0	0	2	4	Plantains, cocoas, yams	Good
69	20	2	1	0	2	1	3	Plantains, cocoas, yams	Good
70	0	1	2	0	0	2	5	Plantains, cocoas, yams	Good; part newly planted
71	0	3	3	0	2	3	2	Plantains, cocoas, yams, corn	Mostly old and foul
72	30	3	1	0	3	1	3	Plantains, cocoas, yams	Good
73	10	2	2	0	2	2	2	Plantains, cocoas, yams, corn	Pretty good; part foul
74	10	1	1	0	1	1	2	Plantains, cocoas, yams, corn	Part clean, part foul
75	30	2	2	20	2	2	2	Plantains, cocoas, yams, corn	Middling
76	10	3	0	0	3	0	1	Plantains, cocoas	Newly planted; pretty good
77	30	0	3	0	0	3	2	Plantains, cocoas, yams	Good

Continued on next page

[a]Corrected from source.

Appendix 3—*Continued*

Reference Number	Number in Household	Acreage of Provision Grounds			Total Acreage of Grounds (Including Gardens)			Types of Provisions	State of Grounds as Described
		Acres	Rods	Perches	Acres	Rods	Perches		
78	5	2	3	0	2	3	5	Plantains, cocoas, yams, corn	Good and clean
79	2	2	3	0	2	3	4	Plantains, cocoas, yams, corn	Pretty good
80	2	1	2	0	1	2	4	Plantains, cocoas, yams	Good
81	7	2	2	0	2	2	10	Plantains, cocoas, yams, corn	Good
82	1	1	3	0	1	3	10	Plantains, cocoas, yams	Provisions good, but getting old and foul
83	2	0	3	0	0	3	10	Plantains, cocoas, yams, corn	Very good and clean
84	5	1	2	0	1	2	10	Plantains, cocoas, yams, corn	Good; pretty clean
85	1	0	2	2	0	2	2	Plantains, cocoas, yams, corn	Rather foul
86	3	1	2	0	1	2	5	Plantains, cocoas, yams, corn	Middling
87	4	1	2	20	1	2	21	Plantains, cocoas, yams, corn	Part clean, part foul
88	2	3	1	0	3	1	5	Plantains, cocoas, yams, corn	Provisions good, but rather foul

No.								Crops	Condition
89	5	1	1	0	1	1	4	Plantains, cocoas	Provisions good, but foul
90	3	1	3	0	1	3	20	Plantains, cocoas, yams, corn	In good order
91	3	6	1	0	6	1	10	Plantains, cocoas, yams	Very good and clean
92	2	1	2	0	1	2	5	Plantains, cocoas	Rather foul
93	2	0	3	0	0	3	20	Plantains, cocoas, yams, corn	Good and clean
94	3	2	0	0	2	0	10	Plantains, cocoas, yams, corn	Good generally
95	1	0	0	0	0	0	1		
96	2	1	2	0	1	2	2	Plantains, cocoas, yams, corn	Newly planted and clean
97	2	0	2	30	0	3	10	Plantains, cocoas, yams, corn	Good
98	1	0	1	0	0	1	10	Plantains, cocoas	Good
99	3	1	1	0	1	2	0	Plantains, cocoas, yams, corn	Good
100	2	1	0	20	1	1	0	Plantains, cocoas, yams, corn	Rather foul
101	3	1	0	0	1	0	10	Plantains, cocoas, yams, corn	In good order
102	1	1	2	0	1	2	10	Plantains, cocoas, yams	Generally good
103	2	0	0	20	0	0	30	Plantains, cocoas, yams	Rather poor
104	7	8	0	0	8	0	20	Plantains, cocoas, yams, corn	In tolerable order
105	4	1	3	0	1	3	30ᵃ	Plantains, cocoas, yams, corn	Clean
106	5	4	3	0	4	3	2	Plantains, cocoas, yams, corn, coffee	Middling

Continued on next page

Appendix 3—*Continued*

Reference Number	Number in Household	Acreage of Provision Grounds			Total Acreage of Grounds (Including Gardens)			Types of Provisions	State of Grounds as Described
		Acres	Rods	Perches	Acres	Rods	Perches		
107	5	2	2	0	2	2	0	Plantains, cocoas, yams	Good, but foul
108	4	3	2	0	3	2ᵃ	10	Plantains, cocoas, yams	Part good, part foul
109	2	4	3	0	4	3	2	Plantains, cocoas, yams, corn	Good provisions, but foul
110	4	2	2	0	2	2	20ᵃ	Plantains, cocoas, yams, corn	Very good
111	1	0	0	0	0	0	20	Plantains, corn	Good
112	3	2	0	0	2	0	10	Plantains, cocoas, yams, corn	Good
113	1	1	0	0	1	0	20	Plantains, cocoas, yams	Middling
114	1	2	2	0	2	2	10	Plantains, cocoas, yams	Good
115	1	0	0	0	0	0	10		
116	1	0	0	10	0	0	20	Plantains, cocoas, yams	Good
117	1	0	0	0	0	0	0		
118	1	2	2	0	2	2	0	Plantains, cocoas, yams	Good
119	1	0	0	0	0	0	0		
120	2	2	2	0	2	2	0	Plantains, cocoas, yams	Good
121	1	0	0	0	0	0	0		
122	1	1	2	0	1	2	0	Plantains, cocoas, yams	Middling

123	1	1	2	0	1	2	0	Plantains, cocoas, yams	Middling
124	1	1	2	0	1	2	20	Plantains, cocoas, yams, corn	Good
At Montpelier Farm									
125	4	2	0	0	2	0	20	Plantains, cocoas, yams	Good; part old and foul
126	2	3	0	0	3	2	0	Plantains, cocoas, yams, corn	Very good
127	5	3	0	0	3	1	0	Plantains, cocoas, yams, corn	Good; part newly planted
128	1	2	1	0	2	1	20	Plantains, cocoas, yams	Good and clean
129	1	1	1	0	1	2	0	Plantains, cocoas, yams, corn	Part clean, part foul
130	2	2	3	0	4	0	0	Plantains, cocoas, yams, corn	In good order
131	1	1	1	0	1	1	0	Plantains, cocoas, yams, corn	Very good, and in general clean
132	2	0	3	0	0	3	20	Plantains, cocoas, yams, corn	In good order
133	1	1	2	0	1	2	0	Plantains, cocoas, yams, corn	Rather foul; part new and clean
134	1	2	0	0	2	0	10	Plantains, cocoas	Good
135	3	0	0	0	0	1	20	Plantains, cocoas, yams	Good
136	1	0	0	0	0	0	20	Plantains, cocoas, yams	Good
137	1	0	0	0	0	0	0		
Total	401	310	0[a]	35	327	1[a]	23		

Continued on next page

ACREAGE OF PROVISION GROUNDS AND TOTAL ACREAGE OF GROUNDS (INCLUDING GARDENS) CULTIVATED BY SLAVES, NEW MONTPELIER ESTATE, AUGUST 1, 1825

Reference Number	Number in Household	Acreage of Provision Grounds			Total Acreage of Grounds (Including Gardens)			Types of Provisions	State of Grounds as Described
		Acres	Rods	Perches	Acres	Rods	Perches		
201	4	4	2	0	5	2	31	Plantains, cocoas, yams, corn	Good and clean
202	3	2	2	0	2ᵃ	3	15	Plantains, cocoas, yams	Good and clean
203	2	4	1	0	5	0	26	Plantains, cocoas, corn	Part clean, part foul
204	6	2	2	0	3	0	32	Plantains, cocoas, yams, corn	Good and clean
205	6	4	0	0	4	2	35	Plantains, cocoas, yams, corn	Middling
206	4	1	2	0	1	3	30	Plantains, cocoas, corn	Part clean, part foul
207	3	2	2	0	2	2	36	Plantains, cocoas, yams, corn	Good and clean
208	4	3	2	0	3	3	0	Plantains, cocoas	Good and clean
209	5	4	1	0	4	1	36	Plantains, cocoas, yams, corn	Good and clean
210	5	3	2	0	3	3	10	Plantains, cocoas	Good and clean
211	6	3	0	0	3	0	30	Plantains, cocoas, yams, corn	Good and clean
212	3	1	1	0	1	1	35	Plantains, cocoas, yams	Good and clean

213	7	2	2	0	2	3	0	Plantains, cocoas, corn	Good and clean
214	3	4	2	0	4	3	16	Plantains, cocoas, yams, corn	Very good and clean
215	1	1	2	0	1	2	36	Plantains, cocoas	Very good and clean
216	5	2	2	0	2	3	0	Plantains, cocoas, yams, corn	Tolerable; good and clean
217	7	3	2	0	3	3	20	Plantains, cocoas, yams, corn	Good and clean
218	3 (4)	1	1	0	1	1	25	Plantains, cocoas, yams	Part clean, part foul
219	3	1	3	0	1	3	28	Plantains, cocoas, yams, corn	Good and clean
220	4	1	0	0	1	0	22	Plantains, cocoas	Rather neglected
221	6	3	3	0	4	0	23	Plantains, cocoas, yams, corn	Part good and clean, part foul
222	2	0	2	20	0	3	6	Plantains, cocoas	Good and clean
223	3	2	3	0	3	0	10	Plantains, cocoas	Good and clean
224	2 (3)	0	3	0	0	3	30	Plantains, cocoas	Good and clean
225	6	2	3	0	3	0	0	Plantains, cocoas, yams	Good and clean
226	6	2	2	0	2	2	25	Plantains, cocoas, corn	Part good and clean, part neglected
227	6	1	2	20	1	3	30	Plantains, cocoas	Not very clean
228	4	2	2	0	2	3	15	Plantains, cocoas	Good and clean
229	5	2	2	0	2	2	35	Plantains, cocoas, yams, corn	Good and clean
230	5	0	3	30	1	0	18	Plantains, cocoas, yams, corn	Part clean, part foul
231	5	2	0	30	2	1	19	Plantains, cocoas, yams, corn	Good and clean

Continued on next page

Appendix 3—*Continued*

Reference Number	Number in Household	Acreage of Provision Grounds			Total Acreage of Grounds (Including Gardens)			Types of Provisions	State of Grounds as Described
		Acres	Rods	Perches	Acres	Rods	Perches		
232	2	1	2	0	1	2	30	Plantains, cocoas, yams, corn	Good and clean
233	6	1	2	0	1	2	25	Plantains, cocoas, yams, corn	Good and clean
234	7	7	0	0	7	1	0	Plantains, cocoas, yams, corn	Good and clean
235	5	0	2	20	0	3	15	Plantains, cocoas, yams	Good and clean
236	2	1	0	0	1	0	32	Plantains, cocoas, yams, corn	Good and clean
237	4	1	1	0	1	1	25	Plantains, cocoas	Not very clean
238	3	1	2	0	1	3	30	Plantains, cocoas, corn	Good and clean
239	5	2	1	0	2	3	8	Plantains, cocoas, yams	Good and clean
240	3 (7)	3	2	0	3	3	15	Plantains, cocoas, yams, corn	Good and clean
241	2	3	0	0	3	1	0	Plantains, cocoas, corn	Good and clean
242	4	1	0	20	1	1	30	Plantains, cocoas, yams	Tolerable
243	3	0	2	0	0	2	0	Cocoas, corn	Good and clean
244	6	2	2	0	2	3	20	Plantains, cocoas, yams	Very good and clean
245	3	0	1	0	0	1	30	Plantains, cocoas	Very foul

246	4	1	3	20	2	0	15	Plantains, cocoas, corn	Good and clean
247	3	2	0	0	2	0	32	Plantains, cocoas, corn	Good and clean
248	3	1	0	0	1	1	0	Plantains, cocoas, yams, corn	Neglected
249	3	2	3	0	3	0	25	Plantains, cocoas, yams, corn	Very good and clean in general
250	3	2	2	0	2	2	35	Plantains, cocoas	Good and clean
251	3	1	2	0	1	2	32	Plantains, cocoas, yams, corn	Good and clean
252	5	1	2	0	1	2	25	Plantains, cocoas	Good and clean
253	3	1	1	0	1	1	30	Plantains, cocoas	Rather foul
254	4	1	2	0	1	2	28	Plantains, cocoas, corn	Good and clean
255	5	2	1	0	2	2	0	Plantains, cocoas, yams, corn	Good and clean
256	4	1	2	20	1	3	13	Plantains, cocoas, corn	Good, but rather foul in some parts
257	8	3	2	0	3	3	10	Plantains, cocoas, yams, corn	Clean and good
258	3	1	1	0	1	1	25	Plantains, cocoas	Rather neglected
259	2	0	2	0	0	2	30	Plantains, cocoas, yams	Good and clean
260	4	1	0	0	1	1	15	Plantains, cocoas	Good and clean
261	3	0	0	0	0	0	30	Fed from the overseer's store	Good and clean
262	2	1	0	0	1	0	32	Plantains, cocoas, yams	Neglected
263	3	0	2	35	0	3	10	Plantains, cocoas, yams, corn	Tolerable; a small part rather foul
264	3	0	2	0	0	2	0	Plantains, cocoas	Rather foul

Continued on next page

Appendix 3—Continued

Reference Number	Number in Household	Acreage of Provision Grounds			Total Acreage of Grounds (Including Gardens)			Types of Provisions	State of Grounds as Described
		Acres	Rods	Perches	Acres	Rods	Perches		
265	2	0	1	0	0	1	28	Plantains, cocoas, corn	Good and clean
266	3	0	1	0	0	1	36	Cocoas, corn	Tolerable
267	3	0	2	0	0	2	0	Plantains, cocoas	Very foul
268	1	0	2	0	0	3	0	Plantains, cocoas, yams	Good and clean
269	2	1	0	0	1	1	0	Plantains	Good and clean
270	1	0	2	0	0	2	0	Plantains, cocoas	Good and clean
271	1	0	2	0	0	2	0	Cocoas, corn	Tolerable
272	2	1	0	0	1	1	10	Plantains, cocoas	Good and clean
273	2	0	2	0	0	2	35	Plantains, cocoas, yams, corn	Tolerable
274	3	0	3	30	1	0	20	Plantains, cocoas	Tolerable
275	2	0	2	0	0	2	0	Plantains, cocoas	Rather neglected in some parts
276	4	0	2	0	0	2	25	Plantains, cocoas	Rather foul
277	4	0	0	0	0	0	0	Fed from the overseer's store	
278	1	0	1	0	0	1	0		
279	4	1	0	0	1	0	0	Plantains, cocoas, yams, corn	Good and clean

No.							Crops	Condition
280	1	0	0	0	0	0	0	Plantains, cocoas, corn	Good and clean
281	1	0	3	0	0	3	0	Plantains, cocoas, yams, corn	Good and clean
282	5	2	1	0	2	3	0		
283	1	0	1	20	0	1	20	Plantains, cocoas, corn	Part clean, part foul
284	2	0	2	0	0	2	25	Plantains, cocoas, yams, corn	Very foul
285	2	0	1	30	0	1	30	Plantains, cocoas, corn	Good and clean

At Montpelier Farm

No.							Crops	Condition
286	1 (2)	0	3	0	1	0	0	Plantains, cocoas, yams, corn	Good and clean
287	1	0	0	0	0	0	0		
288	1	1	0	0	1	0	20	Plantains, cocoas	Good and clean
289	1	0	2	0	0	2	0	Plantains, cocoas	Good and clean
290	1 (3)	0	1	0	0	1	10	Plantains, cocoas	Very foul
291	1	0	2	0	0	2	0	Plantains, cocoas, yams, corn	
292	1	0	0	0	0	0	0		
293	1	1	0	0	1	0	10	Plantains, cocoas, yams, corn	Very foul
294	1	0	0	0	0	2	0	Plantains, cocoas, yams, corn	In good order throughout
295	1	0	0	0	0	0	16		
296	1	1	2	0	1	2	10	Plantains, cocoas, yams, corn	Part clean, part foul
297	1	0	0	0	0	0	15	Plantains, cocoas, yams	Good and clean

Continued on next page

Appendix 3—*Continued*

Reference Number	Number in Household	Acreage of Provision Grounds			Total Acreage of Grounds (Including Gardens)			Types of Provisions	State of Grounds as Described
		Acres	Rods	Perches	Acres	Rods	Perches		
298	1	0	0	0	0	1	0	Plantains, cocoas, yams, corn	Good and clean
299	1 (2)	2	3	0	3	0	20	Plantains, cocoas, yams, corn	Good and clean
300	1	2	0	0	2	0	20	Plantains, cocoas, yams, corn	
301	1	0	0	0	0	0	20	Plantains, cocoas, yams, corn	Good and clean
Total	320	157	0	15	179	2	11		

APPENDIX 4

BALES OF MOSS SENT BY SLAVES ON THE GAY ESTATE FOR SALE IN ST. LOUIS, 1849–1861

	1849	1850	1851	1852	1853	1854	1855	1856	1857	1858	1859	1860	1861	Total Number of Years Involved	Total Number of Bales Sent
Wm. Sanders	3	3	2											3	8
Scipio	3	3	1	2	4	1	3	5	1	2	3	5		12	33
Jerry	2					1	5	2		1		2		6	13
Nathan	3	1	2	1										4	7
Levi	3	2	1			3	2	5		1	3	2	1	10	23
John, Charlotte	2													1	2
Little Moses	4	1	4		2			1						5	12
Henry Hynes	1	1	2	1	1	1	2	3	1	1	3	2		12	19
Gus	3	1	1			1					1	1		6	8
Austin	3	2	1			1	4	4		1	4	3		9	23
Isaac	1	2												2	3

Continued on next page

SOURCE: Moss Record Book, 1849–1861 (Vol. XXXV), in Edward J. Gay and Family Papers, Department of Archives and Manuscripts, Louisiana State University Libraries.

	1849	1850	1851	1852	1853	1854	1855	1856	1857	1858	1859	1860	1861	TOTAL NUMBER OF YEARS INVOLVED	TOTAL NUMBER OF BALES SENT
Joe Bell	3			1	1	2	2	3						6	12
Ned	4	2												2	6
App	1	2	5		2	4	3	9		3	3		4	10	36
Daniel	3		1		1	2	2	2		2	2	3		9	18
Little Jacob	2	2	2	1	1	1		5		1				8	15
Bill Garner	2		1					3						3	6
Bill Moss	2	1	3		2	2	3	5	1		6	2	1	11	28
Perry	3	1	3	1	2	3	4	10	1	4	4	4		12	40
John	4	1	1			1								4	7
Little Ben	5		1								2			3	8
Ben Fuller	2													1	2
Toney	2		2	2	1	4	2	2		1				8	16
John Gipson	1		1	1	1	2	1	6		1			1	9	15
Louis Bell	1													1	1
Henry Holbrook	2													1	2
Israil	2	3		1		6	1				1	2		7	16
Yellow Augustus	1		2				2	3				2		5	10
Black Augustus	1				1	1		3		2				5	8
Jessie	1													1	1

Tom Bell	3	3	2	2	3	4	4	4	2	1	3	11	30
Little John White	1											1	1
John White	1											1	1
Ceazer	2			2	2	3	4	4	1		5	10	22
Viney, Penelope	1	1	1	2	2	1	2					6	8
Augustus	1		1						2			3	4
Mack	1	1	1	1	1	1	2		1			6	7
Elias	2	2	1	1	4	2	2	7	1	5	3	9	27
Harriet	1											1	1
Ben	5	5	2	3	1	5	10	10	10	2	1	12	48
Henry	1											1	1
Absolom	1											1	1
David	1											1	1
Jacob	1	1							1		1	5	5
Isaac	3	2			2						1	4	7
Ned Davis	1	1	1	2	2	2	1				1	7	9
Simpson	1	1	1	4	5	6		1	5		5	10	30
Ferdinand	1	1	1	2		3		1			10	9	21
Jim Banks	1	1	2	1	2	3			2	1	3	8	15
John Hynes	2	1	1		3	1					1	7	10
Sam Todd, Augustus	1											2	2
Sam	3			1								2	4
Geo. Green	2	2	2	3	2	5		1	1		3	9	20
Rachael	1		1									2	2
Charles	2				1	1					2	4	6
Peyton	2	1		1	3	3	3			1	2	8	15
Drummer John	1			2	2	2	1					5	9

Continued on next page

Appendix 4—*Continued*

	1849	1850	1851	1852	1853	1854	1855	1856	1857	1858	1859	1860	1861	Total Number of Years Involved	Total Number of Bales Sent
Geo., Austin		1												1	1
Sophia		1						2						2	3
Anica		1												1	1
Ritta		1												1	1
Sam Brown		1												1	1
George		1												1	1
Nancy, Henry		1												1	1
Patrick		1	5		3	8	6	15			1			7	39
Alfred		1	1			1	4	3		1	3	2		8	16
Tom		1	1				1							3	3
Bill Chase		1	1			1	1	5		1	2	1		8	13
Lucy		1						1	1					3	3
Josiah			1		1									2	2
Peter Purnell			1											1	1
Emily			1								1			2	2
Charity Moses			1											1	1
Little Austin			3											1	3
Jim Tunley			1	2										2	3
Jim Thornton			3			3		1						3	7

Davy Thornton	1	2							2	3
Penelope, Ritter	1	1							2	2
Horace	1	2	4	5		1	1	1	7	15
Ned Dickerson	1	2	1	4	4	1	4	1	8	18
Henderson	1	2	2	1			3		5	9
Julia	1								1	1
Bill Dock	1	1	2	4	2	2	1		8	14
Geo. Tunley	1								1	1
Levin	1		1						3	3
Sugar Charles	1								1	1
Tom Yellow	1	1							2	2
Henna	1	1							2	2
Clarissa	1	2		1					3	4
Woodson	1	2	2	4	1		2		6	12
Toby	1	1	1	2			2	1	6	8
Sam Satin	1		1	2		1	2		5	7
Bill Thornton		2	1						2	3
John Garner		1	2	1	2	2	2	1	7	11
Moses		6	4	5	1	7	5		7	29
Jacob Lenox		2	2	1			1		4	6
Sophy		1							1	1
Dick, Andrew		2							1	2
Jim Shallowhorn		2	1	2		1			4	6
Margaret		2							1	2
Rainey		2							1	2
Ann		1							1	1
Harry Tunley		2	2	2	1	1	1	1	6	8

Continued on next page

	1849	1850	1851	1852	1853	1854	1855	1856	1857	1858	1859	1860	1861	TOTAL NUMBER OF YEARS INVOLVED	TOTAL NUMBER OF BALES SENT
London						2	2					1		3	5
Little Austin						1	3	2		1	1	1		6	9
Abram							1							1	1
Caroline							1							1	1
Ambrose							1	1						2	2
Joe Penny							1	1			5	3		4	10
Becky							1	1				1		3	3
Polly Ann, Anna Green							1							1	1
Melissa							1	1						2	2
Little Perry							1	2						2	3
Adeline							1							1	1
Gracy							1							1	1
Jacob King							1							1	1
Geo. Black								1		1		1		3	3
Julian								1						1	1
Rachel Shallowhorn								1		1				2	2
Dick								2		1				2	3

Jinny Lenox	1	1				1	1
Hacket	1	1			2	3	4
Hamilton		1			1	2	2
Joe Archy		1	10	1	1	4	13
Brooks		1			1	2	2
Little App		1	1			2	2
Martin			1			1	1
Jenny			1		1	2	2
Little Alfred			1		3	2	4
Chas. Tunley			1			1	1
Perry Moses			2		1	2	3
Providence			3	1	5	3	9
Elizabeth W			1		1	2	2
Ben Tate					3	1	3
Overton					1	1	1
Perry's George					1	1	1
Tamar, Louisa					1	1	1
Eliza Moses					3	1	3
Harry					2	1	2
Sally Ann					1	1	1
Silas					1	1	1
Mary Jackson					1	1	1
George Archy				1	1	2	2
Mary Naylor					1	1	1
Lewis					3	1	3

Continued on next page

Appendix 4—*Continued*

	1849	1850	1851	1852	1853	1854	1855	1856	1857	1858	1859	1860	1861	TOTAL NUMBER OF YEARS INVOLVED	TOTAL NUMBER OF BALES SENT
Nancy												1		1	1
Enoch												1		1	1
Sidney												1		1	1
New Jerry												1		1	1
Henry Scipio													1	1	1
H. Fanny													1	1	1
Total	96	71	80	24	56	117	122	200	10	56	108	142	19		1,101

Total number of slaves involved, 1849–1861: 160 (119 men, 41 women)

APPENDIX 5

EARNINGS AND EXPENDITURES OF SLAVES ON THE TUREAUD ESTATE, 1858 – 1859

	APPROXIMATE AMOUNT EARNED	HOW EARNED	HOW SPENT
Aaron Butcher	$170	Wood, corn	Tobacco, flour, cotton cloth, shoes, cash withdrawal
Abraham	16	Wood, corn	Tobacco, flour, shoes, cash withdrawal
Adam	64	Wood, corn	Tobacco, cotton cloth, shoes, handkerchiefs, meat, cash withdrawal
Albert	13	Wood, corn	Tobacco, cash withdrawal
Aleck Evans	26	Wood, corn	Tobacco, shoes, meat, a lock, hogsheads, cash withdrawal
Alex	12	"Paid by him"	Tobacco, cotton cloth, shoes, meat, sheet tin, a lock
Alfred	105	Wood, corn	Tobacco, flour, cotton and checked cloth, shoes, hose, meat, cash withdrawal
Bazil	44	Corn	Tobacco, flour, cash withdrawal

Continued on next page

SOURCE: Ledger, 1858–1872, in Benjamin Tureaud Papers, Department of Archives and Manuscripts, LSU Libraries.

	Approximate Amount Earned	How Earned	How Spent
Ben Russel	$24	Wood, corn	Tobacco, flour, shoes, cash withdrawal
Bill Busley	45	Wood, corn	Tobacco, cotton cloth, handkerchiefs, meat, cash withdrawal
Bill Polley	14	Wood	Cash withdrawal
Bill Siddon	160	Wood, corn	Tobacco, flour, shoes, hose, cash withdrawal
Billy Buck	3	Wood	Tobacco, shoes, hat, cash withdrawal
Bob Stuart	54	Wood, corn	Tobacco, flour, shoes, meat, cash withdrawal
Brower	14	Wood	Tobacco, thread, calico cloth, shoes, handkerchiefs, hose, shirt, pants, meat, cash withdrawal
Carlos	19	Wood	Cotton cloth, shoes, handkerchiefs, pants, cash withdrawal
Charles Anderson	36	Corn, hogsheads	Tobacco, handkerchiefs, meat, cash withdrawal
Charles Johnson	15	Wood	Tobacco, flour, shoes, cash withdrawal
Charles Pennington	19	"Cash recd. from him"	Tobacco, cotton cloth, handkerchiefs, cash withdrawal
Charles Yellow	2	Wood	Tobacco, flour, cotton cloth, shoes, handkerchiefs, hat, hose, meat (total cost, $15.50)

Continued on next page

	APPROXIMATE AMOUNT EARNED	HOW EARNED	HOW SPENT
Chasteen Smith	$24	Wood, corn	Shoes, meat, cash withdrawal
Cooper	28	Wood	Tobacco, flour, thread, cotton and checked cloth, shoes, cash withdrawal
Curry	23	Wood, corn	Tobacco, shoes, handkerchiefs, meat, cash withdrawal
Daniel	7	"Cash recd."	Shoes, cash withdrawal
David Big	0		Tobacco, shoes, meat (all on credit)
David Ingram	26	Wood, corn	Tobacco, flour, shoes, meat, cash withdrawal
David Little	32	Hogsheads	Tobacco, cotton cloth, shoes, cash withdrawal
David Rock	75	Wood, corn	Tobacco, flour, shoes, meat, cash withdrawal
David Smith	56	Wood, corn	Tobacco, cotton cloth, flour, shoes, meat, cash withdrawal
Dick Sawyer	14	Wood, corn	Tobacco, flour, shoes, cash withdrawal
Ely	13	Wood	Handkerchiefs, pants, cash withdrawal
Felix	1	Wood	Cash withdrawal
Frank	18	Wood, corn, bricks	Flour, shoes, cash withdrawal
George Johnson	17	Wood, corn	Shoes, meat, a lock, cash withdrawal

Continued on next page

	APPROXIMATE AMOUNT EARNED	HOW EARNED	HOW SPENT
George Little	$38	Corn	Tobacco, flour, cash withdrawal
Grimage	35	Wood, hogsheads	Tobacco, flour, cotton and calico cloth, shoes, handkerchiefs, meat, cash withdrawal
Gustus	49	Wood, corn	Tobacco, flour, shoes, handkerchiefs, meat, cash withdrawal
Hampton Turner	49	Wood, corn	Tobacco, flour, shoes, handkerchiefs, meat, cash withdrawal
Harrison	22	Wood	Shoes, handkerchiefs, cash withdrawal
Henry Camphor	28	Wood, corn	Meat, cash withdrawal
Henry Davis	85	Wood, corn	Tobacco, flour, shoes, meat, cash withdrawal
Henry Hite	12	Wood, corn	Tobacco, shoes, handkerchiefs, cash withdrawal
Henson	14	Wood	Tobacco, cash withdrawal
Horace	9	"Cash recd. from him"	Tobacco, shoes, cash withdrawal
Isaac Big	4	"Cash recd. from him"	Tobacco, shoes, meat, bucket
Isaac Fabre	12	Wood, corn	Cash withdrawal
Jack Locket	25	Wood	Tobacco, flour, cotton, checked, and calico cloth, shoes, handkerchiefs, meat, cash withdrawal

Continued on next page

	Approximate Amount Earned	How Earned	How Spent
James Anderson	$47	Wood, corn	Shoes, cash withdrawal
James Siddon	17	Wood	Tobacco, cotton cloth, shoes, hat, cash withdrawal
James Thomas	36	Wood, corn	Tobacco, flour, cotton cloth, shoes, hose, mosquito bar, cash withdrawal
Jesse Big	110	Wood, corn	Tobacco, flour, cotton cloth, shoes, shirt, meat, mosquito bar, cash withdrawal
Jesse Little	53	Wood, corn	Tobacco, flour, shoes, handkerchiefs, hose, wire, twine, a lock, cash withdrawal
John Brannum	7	Wood	Flour, shoes, handkerchiefs, cash withdrawal
John Johnson	28	Wood, "cash recd. from him"	Tobacco, flour, shoes, meat, cash withdrawal
Jonas	36	Wood, hogsheads	Tobacco, flour, shoes, meat, cash withdrawal
Lewis Benjo	22	Wood	Tobacco, flour, shoes, meat, cash withdrawal
Lewis McCargo	43	Wood, corn	Tobacco, flour, shoes, cash withdrawal
Liedge	10	Corn	Flour, cash withdrawal
Lunkey	21	Wood, corn	Tobacco, cotton cloth, shoes, cash withdrawal

Continued on next page

	Approximate Amount Earned	How Earned	How Spent
Madison	$26	Wood, corn	Tobacco, flour, shoes, handkerchiefs, meat, cash withdrawal
Martin	12	Wood	Cotton cloth, shoes, cash withdrawal
Mitchell	146	Wood, corn, "cash recd."	Tobacco, shoes, handkerchiefs, hose, shirts, meat, cash withdrawal
Moses	10	"Cash recd. from him"	Tobacco, shoes, handkerchiefs, cash withdrawal
Moses Jones	23	Corn	Tobacco, shoes, handkerchiefs, meat, cash withdrawal
Nash	0		Flour, checked cloth, handkerchiefs, meat (all on credit)
Nat Johnson	13	Wood	Tobacco, flour, shoes, cash withdrawal
Nat Russel	28	Wood, corn	Tobacco, flour, shoes, handkerchiefs, meat, mosquito bar, cash withdrawal
Nathan Black ("defunct 1859")	15	Wood, corn	Tobacco, flour, cash withdrawal
Nathan Morris	44	Wood, corn	Tobacco, flour, shoes, hose, meat, cash withdrawal
Nathan Yellow ("defunct 1859")	33	Corn	Tobacco, flour, shoes, handkerchiefs, hose, checked cloth, meat, cash withdrawal
Ned	94	Wood, corn	Tobacco, rice, shoes, meat, cash withdrawal

Continued on next page

	APPROXIMATE AMOUNT EARNED	HOW EARNED	HOW SPENT
Nick	$68	Wood, corn	Tobacco, cotton and calico cloth, shoes, handkerchiefs, hose, meat, cash withdrawal
Oliver	35	Corn	Cash withdrawal
Peter Bladen	7	Wood	Cash withdrawal
Peter Little	15	Wood, corn	Flour, cash withdrawal
Peter Preston	22	Wood, corn	Tobacco, flour, shoes, meat, a lock, cash withdrawal
Perry Reed	36	Wood, corn	Tobacco, flour, thread, shoes, dress, meat, cash withdrawal
Perry Walley	62	Wood, corn	Tobacco, cotton cloth, shoes, mosquito bar, cash withdrawal
Philip	3	Wood, "cash recd."	Tobacco, shoes, hat
Richard	1	"Cash recd."	Tobacco
Rodolphe	15	Wood, "cash recd."	Tobacco, flour, shoes, meat, cash withdrawal
Ruffin	3	Baskets	Shoes, cash withdrawal
Sam Cook	81	Wood, corn	Tobacco, flour, cotton-ade, linen and checked cloth, shoes, handker-chiefs, meat, cash withdrawal
Sampson	20	Wood, "cash recd."	Tobacco, shoes, dress, meat, cash withdrawal
Simon	13	Wood, corn	Cash withdrawal

Continued on next page

	Approximate Amount Earned	How Earned	How Spent
Snowden	$34	Wood, corn, shuck collars	Tobacco, flour, cotton and checked cloth, shoes, handkerchiefs, hose, cash withdrawal
Spencer	63	Wood, corn	Tobacco, shoes, meat, cash withdrawal
Stephen	14	Wood, hogsheads	Tobacco, shoes, handkerchiefs, hose, meat, cash withdrawal
Thomas	8	Hogsheads	Shoes, cash withdrawal
Tom Big	25	Wood, corn	Tobacco, flour, shoes, meat, cash withdrawal
Tom Brown	32	Wood, corn	Tobacco, flour, cash withdrawal
Tom Chizem	10	Wood	Shoes, cash withdrawal
Tom Scott	98	Wood, corn	Tobacco, cotton cloth, shoes, meat, cash withdrawal
Washington Bright	12	Corn	Tobacco, thread, calico and checked cloth, shoes, mosquito bar, cash withdrawal
Washington McGuinis	27	Wood	Tobacco, flour, cotton, cottonade, calico, and checked cloth, shoes, hose, dress, a lock, cash withdrawal
William Bill	10	Wood, corn	Tobacco, handkerchiefs, meat, cash withdrawal

Continued on next page

	APPROXIMATE AMOUNT EARNED	HOW EARNED	HOW SPENT
Willis	68	Wood, corn	Tobacco, flour, shoes, child's shoes, shirt, meat, cash withdrawal
Yolle	69	Wood, corn	Tobacco, flour, shoes, cash withdrawal
Total for 98 men	$3,296		
Anna Old	$28	56 days' work for the plantation	Cash withdrawal
Catherine Old	1	Wood	Hat
Elsy	18	35 days' work for the plantation	Flour, shoes, cotton, calico and checked cloth, dress, meat, cash withdrawal
Harriet	5	"Paid by her"	Tobacco, flour, calico and checked cloth, shoes, meat
Mathilda Big	10	700 pumpkins	Cash withdrawal
Phoeby	19	Corn	Cash withdrawal
Sarah Dom	22	44 days' work for the plantation	Cash withdrawal
Winny Big	24	48 days' work for the plantation	Cash withdrawal
Total for 8 women[a]	$127		
Total for all slaves	$3,423		

[a] Of the 30 women in the ledger, 22 had neither debits nor credits recorded.

Continued on next page

Prices Paid by Slaves

Blue buckets	$0.30 each	Pants	$2.00 per pair
Calico cloth	0.50 per 5 yards	Sheet tin	0.30 per sheet
Checked cloth	1.05 per 7 yards	Shoes	1.45 per pair
Cotton cloth	1.00 per 7 yards		1.30 per pair
Cottonade	0.30 per yard		1.10 per pair
Flour	4.60 per barrel		0.55 per pair (children's)
Handkerchiefs	0.20 each	Thread	0.10
Hose	0.15 per pair	Tobacco	0.30 per pound
Locks	0.60 each	Twine	0.375 per pound
Meat	1.05 per 16 pounds	Wire	0.25 per pound
Mosquito Bar	0.80 each		

APPENDIX 6

EARNINGS AND EXPENDITURES OF SLAVES ON THE GAY ESTATE, 1844

	Amount Earned	How Earned	How Spent
Front Place			
z Jacob Lenox	$38.80	Pumpkins, fodder, corn, services as sugar maker	Flour, herring, cash withdrawal
z Armstead	8.00	Fodder, corn	Flour, cash withdrawal
z Moses (driver)	2.00	Corn	Cash withdrawal
z Jim Pipkin	3.50	Fodder, corn	Cash withdrawal
z Wm. Sanders	23.25	Corn, services as 2nd sugar maker	Flour, umbrella, man's saddle, cash withdrawal
z Henry Holbrook	9.00	Fodder, corn	Cash withdrawal
z Big Washington	21.00	Corn	Cash withdrawal
y Sam'l Brown	11.50	Pumpkins, fodder, corn	Bedspread, cash withdrawal
x Scipio	12.25	Fodder, corn	Flour, cash withdrawal
z Tom Bell	19.50	Pumpkins, corn	Flour, herring, goose, coffee, cash withdrawal
y Little Ben	1.00	Moss	Cash withdrawal
z Joe Sims,			
z Henderson	20.50	Corn	Cash withdrawal

Continued on next page

Source: Daybook, 1843–1847 (Vol. V), in Gay Papers.

Note: z = male head of household; y = single male; x = son in a male-headed household; w = son in a female-headed household; v = female head of household; u = husband and wife, joint account; t = daughter in a female-headed household; r = single female; q = unknown; (?) = family relationship uncertain from available data.

Appendix 6—*Continued*

		Amount Earned	How Earned	How Spent
z	Harry Tunley	$20.00	Molasses barrels, corn	Flour, mackerel, domestic cloth, bucket, cash withdrawal
x (?)	Yellow Daniel	13.625	Corn	Coffee, cash withdrawal
y	Ram George	7.50	Corn	Cash withdrawal
y (?)	Toney	1.00	Fodder, corn	Cash withdrawal
y	Bob Ross	12.00	Fodder, corn	Flour, cash withdrawal
z	Jim Banks	4.00	Corn	Domestic cloth, cash withdrawal
z	Lawrence	11.00	Corn	Flour, cash withdrawal
z	Pollard	5.00	Corn	Flour, cash withdrawal
y	Charles Carroll	1.875	Fodder	Cash withdrawal
z	Bill Garner	7.00	Fodder, corn, services as engineer	Flour, calico cloth, cash withdrawal
z	Jim Tunley	4.25	Molasses barrels, half day's work for the plantation, iron hoops	Cottonade and brown linen cloth, cash withdrawal
z	Little Moses	9.00	Fodder, corn, moss	Flour, cash withdrawal
y	Isaac Bell	2.50	Corn	Cash withdrawal
x	Alcade	2.75	Corn	Cash withdrawal
x	Jerry	2.80	Corn	Flour, calico cloth, cash withdrawal
v	Aunt Milly	4.00	Paid by her	Flour
z (?)	Augustus Josiah	6.00	Credit	Flour
w	Lee	4.00	Credit	"Fine summer coat" at $3.00, cash withdrawal
z	Alfred Cooper	53.405	Molasses barrels	Flour, calico cloth for daughter Louisiana, calico and cotton cloth, furniture, 3 buckets, 2 coffee pots, 2 sets of knives and forks at

	Name	Amount		
z	London	$4.50	Corn	$1.25 each, 2 "elegant bonnets" at $2.00 each, cash withdrawal
y	Elias	4.00	Credit	Coffee, cash withdrawal; "Fine Russian Hat bt. in N. Orleans" for $3.00, money due on clothes
x	Little London	4.00	Credit	Flour
z	Nathan	4.00	Credit	Flour
x	Alexr	4.00	Credit	Flour
x	Yellow Davy	4.00	Credit	Flour
z	Josiah	4.00	Credit	Flour, coffee
q	Little David	2.00	Corn	Cash withdrawal

Back Place

	Name	Amount		
z	Patrick	82.00	Pumpkins, fodder, corn	Mackerel, bedspread, cash to Aunt Julia, cash withdrawal
z	Hercules	10.30	Fodder, corn, 5 months' watching	Flour, cash withdrawal
z	Absolem	15.50	Fodder, corn	Mackerel, bedspread, cash withdrawal
z	Davy Stump	25.80	Fodder, corn, molasses sold for meat	Flour, coffee, ham, cash withdrawal
z	Martin	29.87	Fodder, corn, molasses sold for meat	Flour, herring, cash withdrawal
z	Edmund,			
z	Sam Henderson	27.65	Fodder, corn, molasses sold for meat	Flour, herring, cash withdrawal
v	Polly Sanders	23.90	Pumpkins, fodder, corn	Flour, coffee, cash withdrawal
z	Big Austin,			
y	Jacob	31.15	Pumpkins, fodder, corn, hay	Flour, bedspread, cash withdrawal
z	John White	5.50	Fodder, corn, hay	Coffee, cash withdrawal

Continued on next page

Code		Amount Earned	How Earned	How Spent
z y (?)	Perry, Washington	$25.50	Fodder, corn	Cash withdrawal
z	Alfred	1.00	Credit	Cash withdrawal
y	Little Austin,	18.50	Fodder, corn	Flour, cash withdrawal
z	Alfred			
u	Clarissa,	3.80	Hay	White cotton cloth, cash "To Clarissa—$ lent for Emily wedding"
u	Toney			
w	Ned Teagle, Toney	24.25	Corn, molasses sold for meat	Flour, coffee, cash withdrawal
z	Henry Bias	5.50	Fodder, hay, molasses sold for meat	Cash withdrawal
y	Clem	20.00	Moss, services setting kettles	Coffee, cash withdrawal
y	Bill Chase	9.50	Fodder, corn	Cash withdrawal
z	Ned Davis	14.00	Fodder, corn	Flour, coffee, cash withdrawal
z	Joe Engineer	15.00	Services as engineer	Flour, cash withdrawal
y	Cook Dick	5.00	Services	Flour, coffee
y	Simpson	26.50	Pumpkins, fodder, corn	Calico cloth, cash withdrawal
y	Kenawa Moses	8.10	Hay, molasses sold for meat	Domestic cloth, meat, cash withdrawal, "Meat for your children"
z	Bill Moss	5.00	Fodder, corn, hay	Cash withdrawal
y	Little Washington	12.00	Molasses sold for meat	Cash withdrawal
y	Big Ben	11.80	Fodder, corn, eggs	Cash withdrawal

t	Adeline	$ 2.00	Hay	Cash withdrawal
w	Mack	2.00	Hay	Cash withdrawal
q	William,			
q	Anna	2.00	Hay	Cash withdrawal
r	Long Susan	3.00	Corn	Cash withdrawal[a]
y	Yellow Toney	1.00	Credit	Cash withdrawal
y	John White	18.50	Unrecorded	Unrecorded
	"Additional to Hercules, J Lenox & others say"	45.00	Unrecorded	Unrecorded
	Total	$900.125		

[a] A line drawn through this entry implies its deletion and suggests that Long Susan was no longer on the plantation.

Prices Paid to Slaves

Corn	$0.50 per barrel	Molasses sold for meat	$8.00–11.50 per barrel
Eggs	0.125 per dozen	Moss	3.00–6.00 per bale
Five months' watching	5.00	Pumpkins	0.02 each
Fodder	0.01 per bundle	Services as engineer	10.00, 5.00
Half day's work		Services as fireman	5.00
(e.g., Sunday work counting hoop poles)	0.25		
Hay	2.00 per load	Services as 2nd sugar maker	15.00
Iron hoops	1.25 each	Services as sugar maker	30.00
Molasses barrels	1.00 each	Services setting kettles	10.00

Continued on next page

Appendix 6—*Continued*

Prices Paid by Slaves

Bedspreads	$1.50 each	Geese	$0.50 each
Brown linen cloth	0.25 per yard	Ham	0.05 per pound
Buckets	0.25 each	Herring	1.00 per box
Calico	0.10 per yard	Mackerel	7.00 per half barrel
Coffee pots	0.75 each	Meat	0.04 per pound
Cottonade cloth	0.25 per yard	Men's saddles	10.00 each
Domestic cloth	0.10 per yard	Umbrellas	1.00 each
Flour	5.00 per barrel	White cotton	0.10 per yard

APPENDIX 7

"ACCOUNT WITH THE NEGROES FOR 1851" ON NOTTOWAY ESTATE

	PURCHASE RECORDED	PRICE
January		
L. Alfred	1 pair boots	$2.00
Moses	-d[itt]o-	2.00
Coley	-do-	2.00
Caeser	-do-	2.00
Long William	-do-	2.00
Bob	-do-	2.00
Bill Billaps	-do-	2.00
L. George	-do-	2.00
Stephen	-do-	2.00
Cooper William	-do-	2.00
Anthony	-do-	2.00
Ben	-do-	2.00
Peter M.	-do-	2.00
Lee	-do-	2.00
Minny	-do-	2.00
Jacko	-do-	2.00
Washington	-do-	2.00
February		
Frank	-do-	2.00
Henry Green	-do-	2.00
L. Rosetta	1 pair shoes	1.00

Continued on next page

SOURCE: Journal—Plantation Book, 1847–1852 (Vol. V), in John H. Randolph Papers, Department of Archives and Manuscripts, LSU Libraries.

	Purchase Recorded	Price
March 2		
Frank	1 pound tobacco	$0.25
Long William	1 molasses barrel	1.25
Nick	2 molasses barrels	2.50
May 3		
H. Green	1 barrel flour	4.00
Moses	-do-	4.00
L. William	-do-	4.00
Lennon	-do-	4.00
Lee	-do-	4.00
Bob	-do-	4.00
Billy R.	-do-	4.00
Gus	-do-	4.00
L. Alfred	-do-	4.00
Minny	-do-	4.00
B. Alfred	-do-	4.00
Frank	-do-	4.00
Sampson	-do-	4.00
Henry Cris	-do-	4.00
Reuben	-do-	4.00
L. George	-do-	4.00
B. Peter	-do-	4.00
John	-do-	4.00
Taswell	-do-	4.00
Coley	-do-	4.00
Henry Cooper	-do-	4.00
William Cooper	-do-	4.00
Old Bill	-do-	4.00
		paid 3.00
Anthony	-do-	4.00
Bill Billaps	-do-	4.00
Jack	-do-	4.00

Continued on next page

	Purchase Recorded	Price
Harry	-do-	$ 4.00
George Carptr.	-do-	4.00
Caeser	-do-	4.00
Green	-do-	4.00
May 18		
Tom	1 pair russets	1.00
Toby	-do-	1.00
June 1		
Big Peter	1 plug tobacco	0.25
Frank	-do-	0.25
August 2		
Moses	1 pair shoes	1.00
Caeser	1 plug tobacco	0.25
Bob	-do-	0.25
August 10		
Mahala	1 pair shoes	1.00
		charged to George
Susan	-do-	1.00
		charged to Gus
Green	-do-	1.00
August 17		
Big Peter	1 plug tobacco	0.25
Frank	-do-	0.25
Bill Billaps	1 pair boots	2.00
September 7		
Washington	1 plug tobacco	0.25
William Cooper	-do-	paid 0.25[a]
		Continued on next page

[a] A line drawn through this entry deletes it from the record.

	Purchase Recorded	Price
Alfred BlkSmith	-do-	$ 0.25
Little Alfred	-do-	0.25
Gorgo (little)	-do-	0.25
Reuben	-do-	0.25
Big Alfred	1 pair shoes	1.00
Anthony	-do-	1.00
Sampson	-do-	1.00
Lee	-do-	1.00
Nick	-do-	1.00
Lennon	-do-	1.00
Taswell	-do-	1.00
Dice	-do-	1.00
Yellow Jack	-do-	1.00
Toby	-do-	1.00
Noel	-do-	1.00
Little Henry	-do-	1.00
Henry Green	-do-	1.00
Jacko	-do-	1.00
September 20		
Coley	-do-	1.00
Tom Woodruff	-do-	1.00
October 5		
Long William	1 pair boots	2.00
Long William	1 pair shoes (for Leana)	1.00
Washington	1 pair boots	2.00
Bob	1 plug tobacco	0.25
Henry Green	-do-	0.25
Long William	1 tin bucket	0.18
Little George	1 pair shoes	1.00

Continued on next page

	PURCHASE RECORDED	PRICE
October 26		
Frank	1 plug tobacco	$0.25
Washington	–do–	0.25
L. Alfred	–do–	0.25
Lee	–do–	0.25
Fort	1 tin bucket	0.1875
November 18		
William (Cooper)	1 plug tobacco	0.25
December 17		
"Gave Dicey, L Anny, Silla, a pair of shoes."		

APPENDIX 8

CONDITION OF SLAVE HOUSING ON OLD MONTPELIER ESTATE, AUGUST 1, 1825

REFERENCE NUMBER	NUMBER IN HOUSEHOLD	CONDITION OF HOUSING AS DESCRIBED
1	4	A good new house, boarded, Spanish walled, and shingled; kitchen and hogsty
2	3	Two houses: one boarded walls and shingles, good; the other wattled and thatched, very indifferent[a]
3	4	Very good house, boarded floor and walls shingled; kitchen
4	3	Houses old but pretty good, boarded walls and thatched
5	6	Very good house, wattled and plastered, shingled; kitchen, hogsty
6	3	Very good house, wattled, plastered, and shingled; kitchen
7	5	Good house, boarded walls and floor, shingled; good kitchen
8	9	Three houses: two of them wattled, plastered, and shingled, very good; the other pretty good, wattled and thatched; kitchen and hogsty
9	2	House wattled and thatched, needs repairs
10	1	House wattled and thatched, pretty good
11	3	House wattled and thatched, old, open, and very bad

Continued on next page

SOURCE: "Minutes of Evidence taken before the Select Committee of the House of Lords appointed to inquire into the Law and Usages of the several West India Colonies in relation to the Slave Population . . . ," in *British Sessional Papers: House of Lords,* 1831–32, CCCVI, 82–89, 1376–93.

[a] All houses listed as wattled are also plastered inside and out.

REFERENCE NUMBER	NUMBER IN HOUSEHOLD	CONDITION OF HOUSING AS DESCRIBED
12	6	House pretty good but needs foundation built around one end
13	2	New house, Spanish walled and shingled
14	1	House old and decayed
15	7	House old and decayed
16	2	Good house, wattled, plastered, and thatched, but shingles ready to shingle it
17	7	Pretty good house, wattled, plastered, and thatched
18	3	Good house, boarded walls and shingled
19	3	Tolerable house, boarded walls and shingled; needs a foundation
20	2	House wattled and thatched, small and bad
21	5	House wattled and thatched, very bad; foundation gone; falling down
22	3	Old house, rather bad, wattled and shingled; a small new house
23	2	Pretty good house
24	4	A new house, Spanish walled, floored, and shingled
25	5	(Living at New Montpelier)
26	7	House old, wattled, plastered, shingled but getting out of repair
27	3	A new house, wattled and shingled, not quite finished; another small house, wattled and shingled
28	3	Boarded walls and thatched, indifferent
29	1	A hut
30	6	Good stone house, shingled
31	4	Wattled and thatched, open and bad
32	8	Three houses: one very good, wattled, plastered, and shingled; the other two wattled, plastered, and thatched; all with boarded floors
33	3	An old and ruined house; new one raised and thatched but needing a foundation

Continued on next page

Reference Number	Number in Household	Condition of Housing as Described
34	4	Wattled and thatched, old, but pretty good
35	4	Wattled and shingled, pretty good
36	3	Wattled and thatched, indifferent
37	5	Wattled and thatched, very indifferent; foundation needs repair
38	1	Very good, wattled, plastered, boarded floor, and shingled
39	6	Small and old; a new house now raised and shingled, not wattled
40	2	Wattled and thatched, small and bad; a new one, Spanish walled and shingled but not quite finished
41	3	Spanish walled and thatched, pretty good
42	2	Wattled and thatched, old and bad
43	2	Walls bad, shingled roof, pretty good
44	2	Wattled and thatched, pretty good
45	6	Spanish walled, boarded floor, shingled; very good kitchen
46	1	Wattled and plastered, shingled, pretty good
47	2	Very bad, falling down
48	3	Small, wattled, and thatched, very indifferent
49	6	House pretty good but needs wattle and thatch in some places; other good house shingled, in need of some wattles
50	7	Two houses: one pretty good; the other very open and indifferent
51	4	Good house, wattled and plastered, boarded floor; another house, old and bad
52	2	Wattles of the house pretty good, but shingles rotten; good kitchen
53	1	House old and very bad
54	1	Old and very bad; one now raising but not wattled or roofed yet
55	3	House old but pretty good; wattled, plastered, and thatched
56	2	Boarded and thatched, low, and very indifferent

Continued on next page

REFERENCE NUMBER	NUMBER IN HOUSEHOLD	CONDITION OF HOUSING AS DESCRIBED
57	3	Good, boarded and shingled
58	2	House small but pretty good
59	2	Good stone house, shingled; belongs to Lord Howard and Angaley
60	3	Boarded walls and shingled, good
61	1	House lately walled and thatched, good
62	5	New house raised and nearly shingled, not wattled; old house, wattled and thatched, bad
63	2	Good stone house, shingled
64	5	Good stone house, shingled; new kitchen
65	1	No house; invalid always in the hospital
66	5	Good stone house, shingled
67	2	Wattled and thatched, pretty good
68	4	Good house, wattled, plastered, and shingled
69	3	House pretty good, wattled and thatched; good kitchen
70	5	House shingled, old and indifferent
71	2	Walled and plastered, open and bad
72	3	One with pretty good roof, wattles bad; other better, boards, and walls shingled
73	2	Good house, wattled, plastered, and shingled
74	2	House old and open, wattled and thatched
75	2	Wattled and thatched, pretty good
76	1	Small but newly raised, good
77	2	House walled and thatched, good
78	5	House small, boarded walls and thatched, indifferent
79	2	Wattled, plastered, and thatched, good
80	2	Wattled and thatched
81	7	Wattled and thatched, very indifferent
82	1	New house, wattled and shingled
83	2	Wattled and thatched, indifferent
84	5	Wattled and thatched, middling; other house wattled and thatched, bad and in need of repairs

Continued on next page

Reference Number	Number in Household	Condition of Housing as Described
85	1	Wattled and plastered, pretty good, but in need of foundation
86	3	Wattled and thatched, very bad and falling down
87	4	Boarded walls and thatched, very indifferent
88	2	Good stone house, shingled
89	5	Boarded walls, shingled, very good
90	3	House very bad, falling down
91	3	Boarded walls and shingled, good
92	2	Wattled and thatched, old and bad; a new house raised and thatched, not wattled
93	2	House small, old, and bad, wattled and thatched
94	3	Wattled and thatched, low and very bad
95	1	Good stone house, shingled
96	2	Boarded and thatched, open and old
97	2	Wattled and thatched, open and very bad
98	1	Wattled, plastered, and shingled; needs repairs
99	3	An old and indifferent house; new house Spanish walled and shingled
100	2	Wattled and thatched, old and bad
101	3	One old and bad; one newly raised and shingled, not yet wattled
102	1	Good stone house, shingled
103	2	Boarded and thatched, very bad and tumbling down
104	7	One old house uninhabited; new one very good, with walls, floor, and partition, shingled
105	4	Two houses old and indifferent, boarded and thatched
106	5	Boarded walls and thatched, low but pretty good
107	5	Good stone house, shingled

Continued on next page

REFERENCE NUMBER	NUMBER IN HOUSEHOLD	CONDITION OF HOUSING AS DESCRIBED
108	4	Old house very bad; other newly raised and shingled, not yet wattled
109	2	Wattled and thatched, old and very indifferent
110	4	Good stone house
111	1	Wattled and thatched, bad and open
112	3	Wattled, thatched, open, and very indifferent
113	1	Boarded and thatched, bad; needs foundation, wattling
114	1	Boarded and shingled, pretty good
115	1	Small and bad, in need of thatching
116	1	Wattled and thatched, old and indifferent
117	1	Stone hut, shingled (watchman)
118	1	Boarded walls and thatched, pretty good
119	1	(Watchman, no house)
120	2	(Watchmen, no houses)
121	1	(At the wharf, no house)
122	1	(At the wharf, no house)
123	1	(At the wharf, no house)
124	1	Boarded floor, shingled; needs repairs
		AT MONTPELIER FARM
125	4	Wattled, plastered, and shingled, good
126	2	Wattled, plastered, and thatched, good
127	5	Three houses wattled and plastered, good
128	1	Wattled, plastered, and shingled, good
129	1	Wattled, plastered, and shingled, good
130	2	Wattled, plastered, and shingled, good
131	1	Wattled, plastered, and shingled, good
132	2	Wattled, plastered, and shingled, good
133	1	Wattled, plastered, and shingled, good
134	1	Wattled, plastered, and shingled, good
135	3	Wattled, plastered, and shingled, good
136	1	Wattled, plastered, and shingled, good
137	1	(Runaway, 1814)

Continued on next page

CONDITION OF SLAVE HOUSING ON NEW MONTPELIER ESTATE, AUGUST 1, 1825

REFERENCE NUMBER	NUMBER IN HOUSEHOLD	CONDITION OF HOUSING AS DESCRIBED
201	4	Three houses, all good: one of stone; one Spanish walled; one wattled[a]
202	3	Good house, wattled
203	2	Good, wattled and shingled
204	6	Two houses: one Spanish walled and shingled; other wattled and thatched
205	6	Two houses, wattled and thatched
206	4	Good house, wattled and thatched
207	3	Good, wattled and shingled
208	4	Tolerable, thatched
209	5	Good, wattled and thatched
210	5	Good, wattled and shingled
211	6	Tolerable, wattled and thatched
212	3	Good, wattled and thatched
213	7	Good, wattled and thatched
214	3	Good, wattled and thatched
215	1	Good stone house
216	5	Good, wattled and thatched
217	7	Good, wattled and thatched
218	3 (4)	Good, wattled and thatched
219	3	Good, wattled and shingled
220	4	Tolerable, wattled and thatched
221	6	Good, wattled and thatched
222	2	Good, stone and shingled
223	3	Good, wattled and thatched
224	2 (3)	Good, wattled and thatched
225	6	Good, wattled and thatched
226	6	Good, wattled and thatched

Continued on next page

[a]All houses listed as wattled are also plastered inside and out.

REFERENCE NUMBER	NUMBER IN HOUSEHOLD	CONDITION OF HOUSING AS DESCRIBED
227	6	One tolerable, wattled and thatched; other bad, wattled and thatched
228	4	Good, wattled and thatched
229	5	Good, stone and shingled
230	5	Good, stone and shingled
231	5	Good, stone and shingled
232	2	Good, stone and shingled
233	6	Good, stone and shingled
234	7	Good, stone and shingled
235	5	Good, wattled and thatched
236	2	Good, stone and shingled
237	4	Good, stone and shingled
238	3	Tolerable, wattled and thatched
239	5	One good, one tolerable, and one very bad, all wattled and thatched
240	3 (7)	One tolerable and one very bad, both wattled and thatched
241	2	One house bad, wattled and shingled; other good, wattled and shingled
242	4	Tolerable, wattled and shingled
243	3	Bad, wattled and thatched
244	6	Good, wattled and thatched
245	3	Good, wattled and shingled
246	4	Good, stone and shingled
247	3	Good, stone and shingled
248	3	Bad, wattled and thatched
249	3	Good, wattled and thatched
250	3	Tolerable, wattled and thatched
251	3	Good, wattled and thatched
252	5	Tolerable, wattled and thatched
253	3	Good, wattled and thatched
254	4	Good, wattled and thatched
255	5	Good, wattled and thatched
256	4	Tolerable, wattled and thatched

Continued on next page

REFERENCE NUMBER	NUMBER IN HOUSEHOLD	CONDITION OF HOUSING AS DESCRIBED
257	8	Good, stone and shingled
258	3	Good, stone and shingled
259	2	Bad, wattled and thatched
260	4	Tolerable, wattled and thatched
261	3	Bad, wattled and thatched
262	2	Good, wattled and thatched
263	3	Good, stone and shingled
264	3	(Nero a watchman; others living with friends)
265	2	Good, stone and shingled
266	3	Good, wattled and thatched
267	3	Bad, wattled and thatched
268	1	Bad, wattled and thatched
269	2	Good, stone and shingled
270	1	Good, stone and shingled
271	1	Good, stone and shingled
272	2	Good, thatched and wattled
273	2	Good, stone and shingled
274	3	Bad, wattled and thatched
275	2	One good, wattled and shingled; another bad, wattled and thatched
276	4	Good, stone and shingled
277	4	(Three watchmen, no houses)
278	1	(Living with Ann Parkinson)
279	4	(Living with Sucky Ellis)
280	1	(Living with C. Beckford)
281	1	(Watchman, no house)
282	5	One good, wattled and thatched; other tolerable, wattled and thatched
283	1	(Watchman, no house)
284	2	Good, stone and shingled
285	2	Good, stone and shingled
		AT MONTPELIER FARM
286	1 (2)	Good, wattled and thatched

Continued on next page

REFERENCE NUMBER	NUMBER IN HOUSEHOLD	CONDITION OF HOUSING AS DESCRIBED
287	1	(Living with C. Ellis)
288	1	Good, wattled and thatched
289	1	Good, wattled and shingled
290	1 (3)	Good, wattled and thatched
291	1	(Living with Peter Richards)
292	1	(Living with Peter Richards)
293	1	Good, wattled and thatched
294	1	Good, wattled and thatched
295	1	Good, wattled and thatched
296	1	Good, wattled and thatched
297	1	Good, wattled and thatched
298	1	Good, wattled and thatched
299	1 (2)	Good, wattled and thatched
300	1	(Living with Mary Richards)
301	1	Good, wattled and thatched

APPENDIX 9

CLOTHING ISSUED TO SLAVES ON HARMONY HALL ESTATE, FEBRUARY 2, 1798

	Status[a]	Osna- burg (yds.)	Blue Baize (yds.)	Blan- keting (yds.)	Osna- burg Frocks	Blue Frocks	Blan- ket Frocks	Osna- burg Shifts	Osna- burg Coats	Osna- burg Trous- ers	Blue or Blanket Trous- ers	Hats	Caps	Needles
Spize (+ "A Jacket & Pantaloons")	DR	12										1		
Lisbon	AF	7	2.5									1		
Dago	AF	7			1	1							1	
Cuffee	AF	7	2.5									1		
James	AF				1								1	
Bob	AF	6	2.5										1	
Bob cor[omantyn(tee) African]	AF	6										1	1	
Random	AF	7											1	
Jasper	AF	7	2.5									1		
Wilks	AF	7	2.5									1		
Hope	AF	7												
Phillip	AF							1				1	1	
George	AF				1									
Charles	AF				1	1				1			1	
Harry	AF	7										1		
Tom	AF				1								1	
Fortune (runaway)	WF													

Name	Type					
Adam	WF	7				1
Peter	WF	7				
Ritchard	WF		1			1
Cato (+ "A Jacket")	WF		1		1	1
Joe (+ "A B Jacket")	WF		1		1	1
Sam	WF		1			1
Leander	CB		1			1
Pitt	CB		1			1
Marbro	CB		1			1
Will (+ "J[acket] & T[rousers]")	CB		1			1
Quashie (+ "J[acket] & T[rousers]")	CB		1			1
Gosport (+ "J[acket] & T[rousers]")	CB		1			1
Cuffie	CB		1			1
Joe R. Castle (+ "A Jacket")		8			1	
Parson (+ "J[acket] & T[rousers]")	HB		1	1	1	
Bumper (+ "J[acket] & T[rousers]")	HB		1	1	1	
Rodney	YA		1	1	1	

Continued on next page

SOURCE: Harmony Hall Estate Papers (7/56-1), in Jamaica Archives, Spanish Town.

[a] AF = able field hand; AW = able woman; CB = field and cattle boy; CH = child; DR = driver; GI = girl; HB = houseboy; SB = small boy; WF = weak field hand; WW = weak woman; YA = yaws victim.

Appendix 9—*Continued*

	Status[a]	Osna-burg (yds.)	Blue Baize (yds.)	Blan-keting (yds.)	Osna-burg Frocks	Blue Frocks	Blan-ket Frocks	Osna-burg Shifts	Osna-burg Coats	Osna-burg Trous-ers	Blue or Blanket Trous-ers	Hats	Caps	Needles
Charles (+ "J[acket] & T[rousers]")	YA												1	
Jamie	YA				1									
Adam	SB				1									
Peter	SB				1									
Julinna	AW	7	4				1						1	
Betty	AW	7	4				1						1	
Abigail	AW	7	4				1							6
Ancilla	AW			4				1	1					
Minerva	AW	7	4				1					1		6
Fanny (washer)	AW	7	4									1		6
Nancey (cook)	AW	7	4									1		6
Hannah	AW	7	4				1							6
Rachael (yaws victim)	AW	7						1	1				1	5
Eve (sores sufferer)	AW	7	4										1	5
Charity	AW	5						1					1	
Bessy (doctress)	AW	7	4					1	1				1	6
Jeany	WW						1	1	1				1	5
Flora	WW						1	1	1				1	
Patience	WW						1	1	1				1	
Lettuce	WW						1	1	1				1	

Hellena	WW	7	4	1		1	1	5
Amy	WW				1	1	1	5
Cleony	WW	7	3.5				1	5
Mumboe	WW	7	3.5				1	5
Princess	WW				1	1		
Clarissa	GI				1	1		
Frances	GI				1	1		
Clarissa cor[omantyn(tee) African]	GI							
Pussey	GI				1	1		
Lavina	CH				1	1		
Eve	CH				1			

APPENDIX 10

"LIST OF HOUSES NEEDED FOR ACCOMMODATION OF NEGROES, 1856," ON THE GAY ESTATE

Extract from Plantation Record Book, 1849–1860 (Vol. XXVI), in Gay Papers:

No.

1. App [Absalom] & family consisting of Eliza, Leah, App [Absalom, Jr.] [husband, wife, two children]
2. Dick & Milly [husband, wife]
3. Levin & Anica [husband, wife]
4. Ned Davis, Sally, Armas [husband, wife, one child]
5. Big Austin, Lizzy, Wm [husband, wife, one child]
6. Little Austin, Phoebe, Patsy [husband, wife, one child]
7. Alfred, Cynthia, Abram, Hacket, Philis, Com [husband, wife, four children]
8. Charles, Lizzy, Penelope, Andrew [husband, wife, two children]
9. Levi, Adeline, Gracy, Henry [husband, wife, two children]
10. Drummer John, Ailsy, Frank [died 1854] [husband, wife]
11. Black Augustus, Mary Biddy [husband, wife]
12. Yellow Augustus, Horace, Margaret [father, two children]
13. Jerry, Viney, Lucy, Alfred [husband, wife, two children]
14. Woodson, Comfort, Adam [husband, wife, one child]
15. Geo. Green, Maria, Anna, Henderson [husband, wife, two children]
16. Caroline Lenox, Anna [mother, one daughter]
17. Joe Bell, Betsy [husband, wife]
18. Scipio, Becky, Henry [husband, wife, one child]
19. Jim Thornton, Betty, Violet, John [husband, wife, two children]

Continued on next page

20. Bill Chase
21. Bill Garner, Henna, Sally Ann, John [husband, wife, two children]
22. Bill Moss, Susan, Harriet, Lavinia, Priscy [husband, wife, three children]
23. Ben, Emily, Horace, Hamilton, Eady, Lizzy [husband, wife, four children]
24. Thornton, Melissa, Bill Thornton, Enoch [husband, wife, two children]
25. Jim Shallowhorn, Patsey, Rachel, Becky [husband, wife, two children]
26. Harry Tunley, Lucy, Fanny, Biddy, Henry, Charles, Polly [husband, wife, five children]
27. Sugar Charles, Nancy [husband, wife]
28. Simpson, Caroline, Sally Ann [husband, wife, one child]
29. Moses, Charity, Easter, Perry [husband, wife, two children]
30. House for old men & young men without homes[:] Joe Penny, Jim Babe, Peter, Sam Henderson, Ceazar Naylor, Daniel, Ferdinand, Armas, Sam Satin, Jim Tunley
31. Ceazar, Nancy [husband, wife]
32. Tom Bell, Charity, Sophy, George [husband, wife, two children]
33. Maria, Mack, Charlotte [mother, son, granddaughter]
34. Bill Dock, Louisa, Matilda, Henna, Lavinia [husband, wife, three children]
35. Tom, Eliza [husband, wife]
36. Julian, Edmund [two males]
37. Peyton, Rachel, Ellen, Josiah [husband, wife, two children]
38. Ned Dickinson, Rinda, Gracy, Polly Ann [husband, wife, two children]
39. Perry, George, Laura [father, two children]
40. Henry Hynes, Mary, Joe, Sally Ann [husband, wife, two children]
41. Jake Lennox, Jenny, Henna, Jake, Aleck [husband, wife, three children]
42. Henderson, Patsy, Harry, Jim, Lucy [husband, wife, three children]
43. Jim Banks
44. Elias, Rainy [two males]
45. Joe Hynes, Tulip [husband, wife]
46. John Gibson, Ritta [husband, wife]

Continued on next page

47. Maria (Nathan), Victor [mother, child: Maria was the wife of Nathan; Nathan died in 1854]

48. Mary Jackson, Foxall, Toby [mother, two children]

49. Viney, Rinda [mother, daughter]

25 Double houses of which we have 18
Bill Garners house's left 1

APPENDIX 11

"BLANKETS DELIVERED JANUARY 14, 1840," ON THE GAY ESTATE

Extract from Estate Record Book, 1831–1845 (Vol. VIII), in Gay Papers:

Moses, Beckey	2
Rachel Shallowhorn, 5 Children, Wm Sanders, Scipio & Daniel	5
Phoebe & 3 children	2
Big London, Elsey & 5 children, Little London & Major	4
Jim Tunley, Amy Brice & one child	2
Harry, Lucy & 3 children	3
Julia Ann, Alcade	2
Jacob Lenox, Little Jinny & 4 children	4
Caroline	1
Suckey Holbrook, Henry Holbrook	2
Little Charity, Little Moses & 4 children	4
Aunt Milly (1), Linda (1)	2
Dutch Betsey	1
Sue	1
Mary & 1 child	1
Frankey	1
Alfred, Dido & 4 children	4
Isaac, Anica	2
Bill Garner, Henna & 2 children	3

Continued on next page

NOTE: Numbers in parentheses alongside names indicate that blankets were issued individually, although the persons named were bracketed together.

Tom Bell, Charity, 3 children, Joe Bell	4
Sophia (1), Joe (1)	2
Becky	1
Aunt Violet, Davy	2
Henderson, Patsy	2
Amstead & Viney	2
Mary Mouse	1
Charlotte & children	2
Lucy & children	2
Lawrence, Suckey Elias & 2 children	3
Jim Banks, Amy Gilchrist	2
Jim Pipkins, Aunt Sally	2
Saml. Todd, Minta	2
Peter Purnell, Nancy, Mary Ann, Maria	4
Pollard, Charlotte	2
Lewis Bell, Polly (2), Mahala Ann & Oliver (1)	3
Lewis & Davy	1
Aunt Phillis, Coon Charles	2
Lee	1
Nathan, Maria	2
Louisa	1
Miller Billy	1
Elias	1
Hukey	1
Saml. Jenkins	1
Isaac Blacksmith	1
Drummer John	1
Ennells	1
Ben Gray	1
Toney	1
Saml. Jones	1
Aunt Marjery, Rachel	2
Esther, Joe	2
Leaven King (1), Jacob (1), Elsey & Jane (1), Comfort (1)	4
Suckey Sigh, Rachel & 2 children, Josiah, Augustin	5

Continued on next page

282

Cooper Peter	1
Yellow Augustin	1
Sugar Charles	1
Ceasar Naylor	1
Isaac Ball (1), Cromwell (1)	2
Alex	1
Rob Ross	1
Long Susan	1
Jerry	1
Yellow Daniel	1
Little Polly & 4 children	3
Tamer	1
Big Washington	1
Granny Jinny	1
Ram George	1
Patrick, Charity, Martha, Mary, Caroline	5
Thornton, Melissa, Jane, Jim	4
Maria, Mark	2
Aunt Julia	1
Ned, Polly	2
Ann, Harriet	2
Rainey, Davy Stump	2
Polly, Emily	2
Clarissa, Toney	2
Cook Dick	1
Emily	1
Penny, Martin, Harriet, Joe, Jackson	5
Aunt Gray, Adeline	2
Minerva, Henry Bias	2
Aunt Prissa, Susan, Bill Moss	3
Aunt Aggy, Ned & 4 children	3
Rachel Butter, Edmond	2
Fanny Beard, John White	2
Jane, Joe	2
Ellen & 3 children	2

Continued on next page

Appendix 11—*Continued*

Eliza, App	2
Maria Henderson, Sam Henderson	2
Bill Chase	1
Hercules	1
Kenawa Moses	1
Big Ben	1
Austin, Washington, Alfred, Simpson, Doc William, Pale	6
Cynthia	1

ESSAY ON BIBLIOGRAPHY
AND HISTORIOGRAPHY

The paucity of slave testimony hampers the study of black slavery. Where such testimony exists—the United States is undoubtedly the most richly endowed in it of the New World's onetime slave societies—it is in the form of either published accounts of exceptional individuals, or reminiscences of former slaves taken many years after Emancipation. The comparative study of black slavery must, therefore, rely heavily on records left by slaveholders. Planters throughout the Americas left copious records: plantation documents, government testimony, published histories, reminiscences and accounts, newspaper and journal articles and advertisements, wills, mortgages, inventories, correspondence, paintings and drawings. All of these materials, if used circumspectly, aid in understanding the "peculiar institution."

In conformity with the adage that, for the historian, truth is not in accounts but in account books, this study has, wherever possible, relied on manuscript plantation records. Planters, in their public testimony, incorporated the biases of their attitudes to slavery and race. In their plantation records they did not grind that ax: they were concerned merely with tabulating work schedules, crop production, weather, slave fertility and morbidity and mortality, thefts, runaways, punishments, and the like. As unadorned chronicles of the day-to-day occurrences on the sugar estates, the plantation records are less prone to distortion than other sources of information.

The absentee ownership of some of the plantations both helps and hinders the historian. Many Jamaican planters did not live on the island but, remaining in Britain, delegated operational responsibility to attorneys, managers, and overseers. Because the distant owners had to be kept informed of the state of the crop, the slaves, and the buildings, the papers of planter families often contain extensive chronicles of the organization of the plantations sent by the appointed managers. The families, however, lived throughout the British Isles, and the records they left are accordingly scattered. Research in the manuscript collections of Jamaican sugar estates necessitates travel all over Britain and Jamaica. Louisiana sugar planters, by contrast, usually lived on their estates, and the plantation records remain for the most part within the state, with the largest repository at the Department of Archives and Manuscripts of the Louisiana State University Libraries. When relevant materials are located elsewhere, such as in the Southern Historical Collection, at the University of North Carolina at Chapel Hill, microfilm copies are often available in archives in Louisiana.

The cultivation and processing of sugar frequently involved the labor of scores, even hundreds, of slaves on a plantation. The extensive organization required for that resulted in an abundance of records cataloging every aspect of life and labor on the estates. What is more, the records cover extended periods. The large plantations in both Jamaica and Louisiana had a permanence and durability far surpassing that of smaller agricultural holdings. In both societies the large sugar estates not only lasted through decades of slavery but also often continued under the same owners after Emancipation.

The records of a number of Jamaican sugar estates offer sustained detail. The Nathaniel Phillips Papers cover a fifty-five-year period, from 1759 to 1814, and contain personal and business correspondence, probate records, and an exceptional body of accounts and papers for Phillips' Pleasant Hill and Phillipsfield estates. Included are tables of slaves' ages, occupations, and valuations, listings of slave births and deaths and causes of death, schedules of work, and accounts of crops. The correspondence between Phillips, an absentee owner through most of the period, and his delegates supplies extensive detail.

The Penrhyn Castle Papers cover a 125-year period, from 1709 to 1834, and include a wealth of information about the Pennant family's Kupius, King's Valley, and Thomas River estates. The correspondence between the absentee owners, especially Lord Penrhyn and G. H. D. Pennant, and their attorneys, David Ewart and Rowland Fearon, are full of references to the treatment of slaves, and slave lists and plantation accounts tell much concerning the regulation of the estates and the lives of the laborers.

A series of plantation books for Worthy Park estate, running from 1783 to 1845, illustrates the comprehensive nature of the records kept by sugar planters. These books, of which Michael Craton has made good use in *A Jamaican Plantation: A History of Worthy Park, 1670–1970* (with James Walvin; London, 1970) and *Searching for the Invisible Man: Slaves and Plantation Life in Jamaica* (Cambridge, Mass., 1978), include work schedules and lists of food and clothing rations, of slave fertility, morbidity, and mortality, and of runaways and punishments.

Similarly rich in detail over long time spans are the Gale Morant Papers (1731–1845), the Dickinson Family Papers (1745–1801), the Duckenfield Hall Plantation Records (1719–1877), and the William and James Chisholme Papers (1730–1812). Many of the other Jamaican plantation records used in this study are more fragmentary or cover a shorter period of time. Nevertheless, they can be of great value in revealing aspects of slave life. The Harmony Hall records (1797–1799, 1812–1814) evidence changes in clothing allocations to slaves in the late eighteenth and early nineteenth century; the Braco Estate Journal (May, 1795, to November, 1797) gives a daily breakdown of the work slaves performed during a thirty-month period, as well as listings of slave births and deaths and food allocations. The Journal of Somerset Plantation (1782–1786) contains material similar to that in the records of Braco estate. The correspondence between absentee owners and their Jamaican-based agents in the Gordon of Buthlaw and Cairness Papers and the Hamilton of Pinmore Papers clearly shows patterns of interaction between slaves and whites: there are in both sets of papers a number of references to the sale by slaves of goods and services to whites on the estates.

The excellent bibliography compiled by K. E. N. Ingram, *Sources in Jamaican History, 1655–1838: A Bibliographical Survey with Particular Reference to Manuscript Sources* (2 vols.; Zug, Switz., 1976), is an indispensable aid to research on sugar slavery in Jamaica. Ingram provides an exhaustive listing of manuscript materials, their location (and the availability elsewhere of microfilm copies), and a detailed description of their contents.

Unfortunately, there is no comparable bibliography of the abundant manuscript sources for sugar slavery in Louisiana. The planters there, like their Jamaican counterparts, kept painstaking records in regulating the complex organization needed for cultivating and processing sugar on their estates. The plantation manuscripts of Louisiana sugar plantations match those of Jamaican estates in their detail, scope, and coverage of extended periods. Within them are records of life and work that few pre-twentieth-century manuscript sources can rival.

The Edward J. Gay and Family Papers run from the first decade of the nineteenth century, when the founder of the family estate, Joseph Erwin, purchased a gang of slaves, to the outbreak of the Civil War and beyond. (The Gay family still owns the plantation, and it still raises sugarcane there.) The life and labor of slaves on the Gay sugar estate are set down in great detail: quantities of food, clothing, shoes, blankets, bedding, tools, and other utensils issued; slave births, naming mother and child; illnesses and treatments; deaths and their causes, as well as the ages of the deceased; distribution of housing by family, with the age and cash valuation of each slave; work schedules and volume of sugar production; and of particular importance to this study, slave earnings, the manner in which they were produced, and the expenditures they enabled for acquiring goods through the planter. In addition, family correspondence illuminates the slaves' internal economy outside the plantation trading nexus—at markets and with river peddlers.

The Lewis Stirling and Family Papers (1797–1865) also coincide with the full time span of sugar cultivation in Louisiana before the Civil War. The Stirling records predate the family's involvement in raising sugar; the early records show Lewis Stirling, the son of an immigrant Scotsman, building up a gang of slaves through inheritance and purchase. Particularly important for this study are the listings of crops grown by slaves, the amounts of cash they received for them, and the manner in which they spent their realized profit. Herbert Gutman, in *The Black Family in Slavery and Freedom, 1750–1925* (New York, 1976), made excellent use of three registers of slaves (1807–1851, 1846–1865, and 1857–1864) among the Stirling papers. These provide a detailed record of slave births and deaths from the inception of the Stirling family's estates until Emancipation.

The David Weeks and Family Papers (1801–1862) predate that family's involvement in sugar cultivation, and like the Gay and Stirling papers, trace the entire course of sugar slavery in Louisiana, revealing the complexity of slaves' lives under the regime of the "sweet malefactor." Other comprehensive Louisiana sugar plantation records are the William T. and George D. Palfrey Account Books (1832–1868), the Thomas Butler and Family Papers (1830–1869), the John H. Randolph Papers (1844–1864), and the Uncle Sam Plantation Papers (1845–1863).

Less complete and less sustained records, useful for understanding particular facets of Louisiana sugar slavery, are plentiful. The Isaac Erwin Diary is for only four years (1849–1852), but it gives a daily listing of slaves' labor, including holidays and days off, as do the Elu Landry Estate Plantation Diary and Ledger (1848–1849), the Ashland Plantation Record Book (1852), the Samuel McCutcheon Plantation Diaries (1833–1840), the Robert Ruffin Barrow Residence Journal (1857–1858), the Colomb Plantation Journal (1851–1862), and the Journal of Mavis Grove Plantation (1856–1857). The Benjamin Tureaud Papers include a ledger for the years 1858–1859 listing slaves, the amount of money each earned, how it was earned, and what it was used to buy at the plantation store. The Alexis Ferry Journals contain a similar list for 1848.

The structure of the internal economy in Louisiana favors the historian. In Jamaica, the slaves conducted most of their economic activities off the plantation, particularly at market, leaving the transactions unrecorded by planters, but because a large part of the internal economy in Louisiana involved dealings with planters, much was entered into the plantations' records.

Research into sugar slavery in Louisiana is aided besides by a large body of slave testimony. In the late 1930s, two projects—one under the auspices of the Federal Writers' Project of the Works Progress Administration and using only white interviewers, the other mounted through Dillard University and using only black interviewers—undertook to collect reminiscences of the life under slavery. Since the former slaves were recalling events of some eighty years before, the recollections must be used with awareness of the distortions human memory is liable to. The race of the interviewer could itself contribute to distortions, as is clear in the differing responses of Catherine Cornelius to similar questions posed during separate interviews by black and white interviewers. Paul D. Escott, in *Slavery Remembered: A Record of Twentieth-Century Slave Narratives* (Chapel Hill, N.C., 1979), presents a methodology to deal with the biases in slave testimony. The recollections, however, have the potential for revealing dimensions of slave life unseen by planters and therefore unrecorded by them. The clandestine trading of slaves with river peddlers, of which planters gave little account, is documented in the slave narratives, as are intricate details of other aspects of the private lives of slaves. All of the Louisiana slave narratives remain in archives in the state. No comparable body of slave testimony exists for Jamaica, or, for that matter, for any slave societies outside the United States.

Slavery in the British Caribbean colonies ended formally on August 1, 1834; on December 6, 1865, the ratification of the Thirteenth Amendment to the United States Constitution outlawed the institution. Cuba and Brazil were the last bastions of slavery in the Americas. But in 1870 and 1871, legislation in these two societies aimed at gradual emancipation, and on May 13, 1888, the last slaves in the Americas were freed with abolition in Brazil, almost four centuries after black slavery had come to the New World.

The legacy of slavery lives on. The oppression of the African-American descendants of slaves continues to blight the development of New World nations. Racism and discrimination, economic, social, and political, encumber African Americans in freedom, as chains and whips encumbered their enslaved ancestors. Sadly, historiographical tradition has reinforced the oppression. In *British Historians and the West Indies* (London, 1966), Eric Williams attacks the scholarship that has distorted the historical record in order "to justify the indefensible and to seek support for preconceived and outmoded prejudices" (pp. 12–13). C. L. R. James, in *The Black Jacobins* (1938; rpr. New York, 1963), asserts that historiographical tradition has in large measure been the province of a "venal race of scholars, profiteering panders to national vanity" (p. 51). The scholarship arising out of this tradition has been instrumental in propagating consistently biased analyses and, he says, has "conspired to obscure the truth" about slavery and the black experience in the Americas (p. 51). Williams sought, as a principal objective of his scholarship, "to emancipate his [West Indian] compatriots whom the historical writings that he analyses sought to depreciate and to imprison for all time in the inferior status to which these writings sought to condemn them" (*British Historians,* 12–13).

In the United States, for decades after emancipation, racist doctrines permeated scholarship dealing with the "peculiar institution." The writings of Ulrich B. Phillips, long the doyen of the historiography of the United States' slavery, provide the clearest example for this bias, as in his *American Negro Slavery* (New York, 1918). Phillips surely deserves a place among the "Tory historians, regius professors and sentimentalists" condemned by James for "represent[ing] plantation slavery as a patriarchal relation between master and slave" (*Black Jacobins,* 19). Phillips' view of the slave plantation as a "school constantly training and controlling pupils who were in a backward state of civilization" (*American Negro Slavery,* 342–43) failed to confront the terrible realities of the plantation, misrepresented slaves' lives and actions, and because of the dominance of the historiographical tradition of which he was a leader, has been influential in the "deprecation" both of contemporary African Americans and the memory of their slave forebears to which Williams referred.

Phillips' work has remained a force despite the extensive scholarly inquiry into the slavery of the United States in the three-quarters of a century since its publication. Even as recently as 1975, Herbert Gutman commented, in *Slavery and the Numbers Game: A Critique of 'Time on the Cross'* (Urbana, Ill., 1975), on Phillips' enduring effect: "The social history of the enslaved Afro-American remains heavily shrouded by the shadow of U. B. Phillips, a shadow cast by more than that historian's narrow racial assumptions" (p. 7). Gutman claims that the model Phillips used to explain how slavery affected slaves and their descendants—one that sees slave culture as imitating planter culture—even if "freed from its racist assumptions . . . still retains a powerful and wholly negative influence on the conceptualization of the Afro-American historical experience before the general emancipation" (p. 7).

Other historians echo Gutman. In *Slavery: A Problem in American Institutional and*

Intellectual Life (Chicago, 1959), Stanley Elkins observes of Kenneth Stampp's *The Peculiar Institution* (New York, 1956) that, despite its attack on Phillips, Stampp's "strategy . . . was still dictated by Phillips" (p. 21). George Fredrickson and Christopher Lasch claim that historians writing on slavery, despite disagreeing with Phillips' racism, accept what he has defined as the parameters of the debate on slave culture and have "tried to meet him on his own ground" ("Resistance to Slavery," *Civil War History*, XIII [1967], 315–29).

The traditions of Phillips and, regarding the British West Indies, of Thomas Carlyle, in *Occasional Discourse on the Nigger Question* (London, 1853), and James Anthony Froude, in *The English in the West Indies; or, The Bow of Ulysses* (London, 1888), have only recently elicited a sustained challenge. In *Capitalism and Slavery* (London, 1944), Williams brings a comparative perspective to the study of slavery by viewing the development of the slave societies in the Americas within an emergent world capitalist system. According to Ivar Oxaal in *Black Intellectuals Come to Power* (Cambridge, Mass., 1968), the crux of James's argument in his masterly *The Black Jacobins* is that "the ascendancy of the industrial interests w[as] only a necessary precondition for the abolition of slavery, [and] the root cause was not to be found in the interests of the strong, but in the revolt of the weak" (p. 75). James depicted slaves as active and creative, thus challenging Phillips' conception of slave behavior as essentially responsive and reactive to the planter and his agents.

In the decades since Williams' and James' studies and since contemporaneous work by scholars like Herbert Aptheker, Melville J. Herskovits, Richard Hofstadter, and Gunnar Myrdal, the historiography of slavery has undergone tremendous developments. In 1947, Frank Tannenbaum published his seminal study *Slave and Citizen: The Negro in the Americas* (New York, 1947). Like Williams earlier, Tannenbaum demonstrated the promise that comparative methodology held for the historiography of slavery. Subsequently, the scholarship of a host of historians, including Elkins, David Brion Davis, Carl Degler, Elsa Goveia, Marvin Harris, and Magnus Morner, has solidified the position of comparative methodology in the vanguard of the historiography of slavery. Scholarship concerning slavery and the other dimensions of African-American history has also received stimulus and direction from societal and intellectual developments, such as the emergent ideology of the civil rights movement and the reorientation in the disciplines of social history, economic history, and the social sciences.

Throughout the New World, Western European colonizers coerced labor by enslaving Africans and African Americans. The experience of black slaves varied little within the hemisphere. For Africans transported across the Atlantic, often mere chance or temporary market conditions determined their American destination and thus the nationality of their white owners. Slaves did not choose their slaveholders, nor did they define the boundaries of the colonies where they were held in bondage. Slaves' lives as praedial laborers within a plantation system were little affected by the metropolitan affinities of the slaveholders. Historians have too readily accepted the spatial boundaries defined by the slaveholding colonizers. Consequently, the historiography of slavery prior to the development of a comparative perspective has tended to be atomized and parochial. Bias is introduced when a study is defined in terms of only one of the protagonists. A study defined in terms of the spatial boundaries and the metropolitan and institutional affiliations of a set of planters, Catholic Luso-Brazilian, Protestant British North American, or whatever, may obscure continuities in the slavery experience that an alternative methodology can reveal.

Davis based his study in *The Problem of Slavery in Western Culture* (Ithaca, N.Y., 1966) on the premise that "the problem of [black] slavery transcended national boundaries" (p. vii). According to Laura Foner and Eugene Genovese, the editors of *Slavery in the New World: A Reader in Comparative History* (Englewood Cliffs, N.J., 1969), the comparative dimension of slavery scholarship has "introduced an invigorating freshness and a new boldness into historical work" (p. viii) by forgoing narrow confines of a specific national perspective. The methodology has enabled analyses of the relationships of the protagonists, black and white, within slave societies, to the institution of slavery, thus permitting an assessment of what slaves did as slaves and what slaveholders did as slaveholders.

The development of the comparative perspective in the historiography of slavery has not, however, entirely escaped methodological problems. Poor research design detracts from the value of any historical inquiry, but comparative analysis can suffer particularly. Marc Bloch has written that "in order to have historical comparison, two conditions must be fulfilled: a certain similarity or analogy between observed phenomena—that is obvious—and a certain dissimilarity between the environments in which they occur" ("Toward a Comparative History of European Societies," in *Enterprise and Secular Change: Readings in Economic History,* ed. Frederic C. Lane and Jelle C. Riemersma [Homewood, Ill., 1953], 496). Goveia has pointed out that "slavery in the New World has been neither uniform nor static. For it was an economic and social institution that changed both in time and place." Comparative study, she explains, "will only yield sound results if it starts with a methodology which adequately defines whether or not the slave systems to be compared are of the same kind" ("Comment on 'Anglicanism, Catholicism, and the Negro Slave,'" *Comparative Studies in Society and History,* VIII [1966], 328–30).

Determining comparability is but the first step toward the formulation of an adequate research design. Since the emergence of the comparative study of black slavery, there has been considerable debate as to which phenomena provide the best indices of the structure of slave societies. When Tannenbaum chooses in his pioneering study to focus specifically on the heritage of the slaveholders in characterizing slavery in a given New World society, he posits that the important determinants of the form of slave societies were the religion of the slaveholders and the legal traditions and other influences of the mother countries. Tannenbaum has contended that slavery in the Ibero-American colonies was milder because the legislative tradition and dominant religion of Spain and Portugal recognized the "moral personality" of the slaves.

Historians, however, have challenged both the applicability and the suitability of indices based on the metropolitan institutions of the slaveholders. Since, as Goveia points out, "the divorce of law and practice was . . . characteristic" of slave societies in the Americas, analyses of legal statutes and religious dogma may, indeed, tell little about the de facto organization and structure of a society ("The West Indian Slave Laws of the Eighteenth Century," *Revista de Ciencias Sociales,* IV [1960], 104).

Other questions arise whether the indices Tannenbaum chose are sufficient, in and of themselves, to an analysis of slavery. By claiming that the institutional influences he identified determine the structure of the slave systems, Tannenbaum hypothesized a specific chain of causality, one relegating the slave to a passive position. Africans and African Americans, however, brought to the slave societies in which they lived cultures and institutional influences of their own, which contributed to shaping the structure of the societies. The interaction and reciprocal influences of slaves and nonslaves contributed to the development and structure of the slave systems of which they were part.

An adequate understanding of slavery cannot be derived solely from a consideration of the slaveholder and his world. It is imperative to recognize that slaves were, in anthropologist John Szwed's words, "culture bearers and creators" ("The Politics of Afro-American Culture," in *Reinventing Anthropology,* ed. Dell Hymes [New York, 1973], 153–81). But a methodological reorientation designed to incorporate the beliefs and behavior of slaves poses challenges for the historian. Few slaves left personal records; whites rendered most of the documentation available on slavery. The historian cannot proceed oblivious to those records despite their view of slavery from the slaveholders' perspective. The records must be used with care, and with an eye to the biases that riddle them.

Barry Higman demonstrates in his *Slave Population and Economy in Jamaica, 1807–1834* (London, 1976) and *Slave Populations of the British Caribbean, 1807–1834* (Baltimore, 1984) how a wealth of information can be gleaned from, among other sources, census materials such as the Returns of the Registration of Slaves, a triennial compilation of the slave populations in the British West Indies. Russell Menard and Allan Kulikoff in pioneering studies of slavery in the Chesapeake show convincingly that, used with care and sensitivity, legal documentation such as probate records affords tremendous insight into the structure of slave communities, and Mary Turner, Stiv Jakobsson, and Albert Raboteau have illustrated the richness of church and mission records in their work on religion and slavery. Studies such as theirs are in the lead in slavery scholarship. As Michael Craton's analysis of slave rebellions in the British West Indies, Richard Sheridan's study of doctors and slaves, and Hilary Beckles' work on Barbados ably demonstrate, the government documents and parliamentary papers of European nations and their colonial dependencies continue to yield rich resources for historical inquiry, as do hitherto underexamined materials such as court proceedings and records of slave sales.

In investigating how slaves acted in slavery, historians have yet to realize fully the potential that plantation manuscripts hold. Although such records were compiled by whites, they provide a detailed chronicle of the complexity of slaves' lives. The plantation system involved an intricate organization of life and work, the coordination of which necessitated sophisticated record keeping. Planters and their delegates noted daily labor routines, kept punishment rolls, and listed runaways. They kept registers of births and deaths and recorded sickness among slaves. Other accounts reveal dietary, clothing, and housing patterns, as well as expenditures for slaves and payments to and by them. Planters' correspondence and diaries are also rich in detail concerning the activities of slaves. Although these plantation manuscripts view slavery through whites' eyes, they provide invaluable insight into the lives of slaves, the manner in which they organized their family and community, and the impact their actions had on the structure and organization of the plantation.

Plantation records have provided the data for some of the most exciting developments in recent slavery historiography. Even a partial enumeration of such studies shows the extent to which their contribution has dominated the scholarship in recent years both in quantity and methodological orientation. The historiography of slavery in the British Caribbean has been immeasurably enriched by the work of Edward Brathwaite, Richard Dunn, Stanley Engerman, Barry Gaspar, Douglas Hall, Herbert Klein, Woodville Marshall, Sidney Mintz, and Orlando Patterson, as well as of Beckles, Craton, Goveia, Higman, Sheridan, Turner, and others. In *Jamaica Surveyed* (Kingston, 1988), Higman demonstrates the utility and richness of the hitherto neglected source of plantation maps and plans. Scholarship on slavery in Ibero-America and the rest of the non-British West Indies has benefited from the work of Roger Bastide, Frederick Bowser, Robert Conrad, Gabriel Debien, Manuel Moreno Fraginals, Gwendolyn Midlo Hall, Neville Hall, Mary Karasch, Franklin Knight, Colin Palmer, Richard Price, A. J. R. Russell-Wood, Francisco Scarano, Stuart Schwartz, Rebecca Scott, and Dale Tomich, as well as of Mintz, Morner, and others. The historiography of slavery in the United States has been well served by scholarship that has recognized the value of plantation records and has used them with care and discernment to heighten the awareness of the fullness and complexity of slaves' lives. Scholars who have contributed to that scholarship include Paul David, Stanley Engerman, Robert Fogel, Eugene Genovese, Lawrence Levine, Daniel Littlefield, Leslie Howard Owens, Richard Sutch, Peter Temin, and Peter Wood, as well as Gutman, Kulikoff, and Menard.

Scholars have at least partially been able to counteract the white bias inherent in many of the extant manuscripts by seeking out the more direct evidence that the slaves left of their lives in bondage. Both during and after slavery, a steady flow of slave autobiographies chronicled life under slavery. Many of these narratives, along with various other testimony by slaves, provided support for the abolitionist cause and must accordingly be read judiciously. Nevertheless, as John Blassingame has shown, they have tremendous potential for illuminating the slaves' past.

The study of slavery in the United States has benefited immeasurably from the foresight of scholars who recognized the contribution that the recollections of former slaves could make. The effort to collect reminiscences built on projects undertaken at Fisk University in the late 1920s and culminated with the federally sponsored project in the late 1930s. Ultimately, thousands of former slaves gave testimony about their lives. The scope of the questions posed and the size of the cohort interviewed have, as scholars like Escott, Olli Alho, Julius Lester, George

Rawick, and Norman Yetman show, much enlarged the recent understanding of slaves' lives. Even a cursory perusal of the documents can detect the diversity of life and the vitality and creativity that the oppression of servitude could nòt stifle. Rawick found the divergence between the activities of slaves as field laborers and their lives after work and during other time off so striking that he incorporated the dichotomy into the methodology of *From Sundown to Sunup: The Making of the Black Community* (Westport, Conn., 1972):

> The slaves labored from sunup to sundown and sometimes beyond. This labor dominated part of their existence—but only part. Under slavery, as under any other social system, those at the bottom of the society were not totally dominated by the master class. They found ways of alleviating the worst of the system and at times of dominating their masters. They built their own community out of materials taken from the African past and the American present, with the values and memories of Africa giving meaning to the new creation. They lived and loved from sundown to sunup. (Pp. 11–12)

The South African writer André Brink may convey some of the essence of the dichotomy in the words of advice an African woman gave her son in the novel *Looking on Darkness* (New York, 1975): "Joseph, look, inne daytime I work my blerry arse off fo' the white people, but when it gets dark it's our turn. The Lawd give us the night to have a bit of happiness, for the days are hell" (p. 88). The poet LeRoi Jones (Imamu Amiri Baraka), in a stanza that concludes a series of essays entitled *Home* (New York, 1966), captures another dimension of the dichotomy:

> The fair are
> fair, and death-
> ly white.
>
> The day will not save them
> and we own
> the night.
>
> (P. 252)

Much of the activity that Rawick and the others describe went on beyond the ken of whites, and as such rarely found its way into the whites' chronicles. Historians must not only recognize the incompleteness of white testimony on slavery—that it undoubtedly misses much of the family and community life of slaves "from sundown to sunup"—but also discern the importance of uncovering the testimony that slaves left.

Although no other American societies have slave narrative collections equaling those in the United States, slave testimony is still being uncovered, largely by scholars outside the historical profession. The work of anthropologists like Harris, Mintz, Price, and Szwed has disclosed much of value to historians concerning life under slavery. The archaeological studies of Jerome Handler and Frederick Lange, in Barbados, and Higman and Douglas Armstrong, in Jamaica, have shown how much can be learned from excavating the sites of slave villages and graveyards on sugar plantations. Charles Joyner's monograph *Down by the Riverside* (Urbana, Ill., 1984) demonstrates that a great deal can be derived from careful attention to the techniques of folklorists. The potential of these forms of inquiry has not yet been fully realized.

Recent historiography has made heartening progress in penetrating the slavery experience by accepting a methodology and findings that have challenged traditional interpretations of the "peculiar institution." The comparative technique, and the recognition that the slaves were a motive and creative force in determining the structure of slavery, have forced reorientation of the debate.

SOURCES

MANUSCRIPT PLANTATION RECORDS

PLANTATIONS IN JAMAICA

Institute of Jamaica, Kingston

Accounts of Jacob Israel Bernal.
Braco Estate Account Book.
Account Book of Carlton Estate, John Packharnis.
Fyffe Collection.
Georgia Estate Letter Books and Accounts.
Letters of Charles Gordon Gray.
Lady Mary Hamilton's Trust Book.
Harmony Hall Estate Account Book.
Letter of William Hylton.
Account Book of John Morant.
Memorandum Book of Thomas Munro.
Journal of Somerset Plantation.
Spring Plantation Accounts.

Jamaica Archives, Spanish Town

Braco Estate Journal.
Rooke Clarke Papers.
Harmony Hall Estate Papers.
Rose Hall Journal.
Thetford Plantation Book.
Worthy Park Estate Records.

West India Collection, University of the West Indies, Mona, Kingston

Dickinson Family Papers. Microfilm copy of papers that are at Wiltshire Record Office, Trowbridge, Wiltshire, Eng.
Papers of Caleb and Ezekiel Dickinson. Microfilm copy of papers that are at Wiltshire Record Office.

Duckenfield Hall Plantation Records. Microfilm copy of papers that are at Greater London Record Office, Middlesex Records, London.
Holland, Fish-River, and Petersville Plantations Title Deeds.
James Lyon Will and Accounts.
Gale Morant Papers. Microfilm copy of papers that are at Exeter University Library, Exeter, Eng.
Thomas John Parker Papers.
Penrhyn Castle Papers. Microfilm copy of papers that are at University College of North Wales, Bangor.
Nathaniel Phillips Papers. Microfilm copy of papers that are in Slebech Collection, National Library of Wales, Aberystwyth.
William Vassall Letter Books. Microfilm copy of papers that are at Sheffield City Libraries, Sheffield, Eng.

National Library of Scotland, Edinburgh

William and James Chisholme Papers.
Robertson-Macdonald Papers.

Scottish Record Office, Edinburgh

Abercairny Papers.
Airlie Papers.
Hamilton of Pinmore Papers.
Kinloch/Wedderburn Papers.

University of Aberdeen Library

Gordon of Buthlaw and Cairness Papers.

British Library, London

Liverpool Papers.
James Pinnock Diary.

Public Record Office, London

Accounts of Blenheim and Cranbrooke Plantations, Estate of James Moffat, WO 9-48.

Bodleian Library, Oxford University

Barham Family Papers.

PLANTATIONS IN LOUISIANA

Historic New Orleans Collection, Kemper and Leila Williams Foundation, New Orleans

Ashland (Belle Helene) Plantation Journal.
Magnolia Grove Plantation Sale.

Henri de St. Geme Papers.
Appraisal of the Estate of Widow George Webre.

Louisiana Historical Center, Louisiana State Museum, New Orleans

Book of Accounts of the Magnolia Plantation.
Journal of Mavis Grove Plantation.
Plantation Diary of Valcour Aime.

Department of Archives and Manuscripts, Louisiana State University Libraries

Anonymous Planter's Ledger.
Ashland Plantation Record Book.
Priscilla ("Mittie") Munnikhuysen Bond Diary.
Braxton Bragg Papers.
Louis Amedee Bringier and Family Papers.
Bruce, Seddon, and Wilkins Plantation Records.
Robert O. Butler Papers.
Thomas W. Butler Papers.
Thomas Butler and Family Papers.
Alexandre E. DeClouet Papers.
Isaac Erwin Diary.
Nathaniel Evans and Family Papers.
Edward J. Gay and Family Papers.
Philip Hicky and Family Papers.
Patrick F. Keary Letters.
Kenner Family Papers.
Charles Landry Mortgage.
Elu Landry Estate Plantation Diary and Ledger.
George Lanaux and Family Papers.
Moses and St. John Liddell and Family Papers.
Andrew and Ellen E. McCollam Papers.
Samuel McCutcheon Papers.
George Mather Account Books.
Joseph Mather Diary.
Charles L. Mathews and Family Papers.
William J. Minor and Family Papers.
William T. Palfrey and Family Papers.
William T. and George D. Palfrey Account Books.
Pharr Family Papers.
Alexander F. Pugh and Family Papers.
Richard L. Pugh Papers.
Colonel W. W. Pugh Papers.
John H. Randolph Papers.
Slavery Collection.
Lewis Stirling and Family Papers.

Benjamin Tureaud Papers.
Uncle Sam Plantation Papers.
David Weeks and Family Papers.
David Weeks and Family Papers—The Weeks Hall Memorial Collection.
William P. Welham Plantation Records.
Maunsell White Letterbook.

Department of Archives and Manuscripts, Earl K. Long Library, University of New Orleans

Monnot/Lanier Family Collection.

Department of Manuscripts and Archives, University of Southwestern Louisiana Libraries

DeClouet Family Papers.

Department of Archives and Manuscripts, Tulane University Libraries

Robert Ruffin Barrow Papers.
The Bringier Papers (Urquhart Collection).
Burruss Family Papers.
Colomb Plantation Journal.
Jean Baptiste Ferchaud Papers.
Alexis Ferry Journals.
David Rees Papers.
St. Martin Family Papers.
Sebastopol Plantation Papers.
Henry Clay Warmoth Papers.

SLAVE NARRATIVE COLLECTIONS

Marcus Bruce Christian Collection, Department of Archives and Manuscripts, Earl K. Long Library, University of New Orleans.
Federal Writers' Project Files, Melrose Collection, Archives Division, Northwestern State University of Louisiana Libraries.
Louisiana Writers' Project File, Louisiana State Library, Baton Rouge.

MISCELLANEOUS MANUSCRIPT MATERIALS

JAMAICA

Institute of Jamaica, Kingston

Petition of Stephen Fuller.
Robert R. Gillespie Letter.
"The Omnibus; or, Jamaica Scrap Book," by Jack Jingle.
Lemon Lawrence Letter.

Nugent Papers.
Record Book of the Court of the Parish of St. Ann, 1787–1814 (Slave Court).
Annabella Smith Letter.
Simon Taylor Letters.
Philafricanus Letter.
Population of the Sugar Colonies.
Remarks on Wilberforce's Tenth Proposition.
Slave Exports.
Slave Sale.
Slave Sale Broadside.
Slave Sale Receipt.

Jamaica Archives, Spanish Town

Returns of Registrations of Slaves.

Scottish Record Office, Edinburgh

Melville Castle Papers—Dundas.

British Library, London

Clarkson Papers.
Hardwicke Papers.
Liverpool Papers.
Papers Relating to Jamaica, presented by C. E. Long.
Quantity and Value of the Produce of the British West Indies.

Public Record Office, London, England

Colonial Office Documents (CO 134, 137, 140).

LOUISIANA

Historic New Orleans Collection, Kemper and Leila Williams Foundation, New Orleans

Slave Auction Broadside.
Slavery in Louisiana Collection.

Louisiana Historical Preservation and Cultural Commission, Department of Culture, Recreation, and Tourism, Baton Rouge

National Register of Historic Places.
  The Cottage.
  Destrehan Plantation.
  Laurel Valley Plantation.
  Live Oaks Plantation.
  Madewood Plantation.
  St. Louis Plantation.
  Southdown Plantation.

SOURCES

Department of Archives and Manuscripts, Louisiana State University Libraries

D. D. Arden Letter.
Rosella Kenner Brent Papers.
Consolidated Association of the Planters of Louisiana Collection.
Hephzibah Church Book.
Mrs. Isaac H. Hilliard Diary.
Clarissa E. Leavitt Town Diary.
W. L. Martin Papers.
John A. Quitman and Family Papers.
Hudson Tabor and Family Papers.

Louisiana Collection, Louisiana State University Libraries

Historic American Buildings Survey, Survey LA 74 (Uncle Sam Plantation, Convent, St. James Parish), Public Works Administration Program, Federal Project
498-A, Branch of Plans and Designs, National Park Service, United States Department of the Interior.

*Department of Manuscripts and Archives, University of Southwestern Louisiana
Libraries*

Governor Alexandre Mouton Papers.

Department of Archives and Manuscripts, Tulane University Libraries

J. Bart, Jr., Letter.
"History of Evan Hall Plantation," by Henry McCall.
Marie Victoire Ollie Pucheu Slave Sale.

GOVERNMENT DOCUMENTS

JAMAICA

British Sessional Papers: House of Commons.
British Sessional Papers: House of Lords.
Journals of the Assembly of Jamaica.
Report from the Committee on the Commercial State of the West India Colonies. London,
1807. Ordered to be printed July 24, 1807.
*Two Reports (one presented on the 16th of October, the other on the 12th of November,
1788) from the Committee of the Honourable House of Assembly of Jamaica . . . on the
Subject of the Slave Trade, and the Treatment of Negroes . . .* London, 1789. Pub-
lished by order of the House of Assembly, by Stephen Fuller.

LOUISIANA

*The Consolidation and Revision of the Statutes of the State [of Louisiana], of a General
Nature,* prepared by Levi Peirce, Miles Taylor, William W. King, Commission-
ers appointed by the State. New Orleans, 1852.
The Revised Statutes of Louisiana, compiled by U. B. Phillips. New Orleans, 1856.

302

U.S. Bureau of the Census.
Fifth Census of the United States, 1830.
Sixth Census of the United States, 1840.
Seventh Census of the United States, 1850.
Eighth Census of the United States, 1860.

NEWSPAPERS AND JOURNALS

JAMAICA

Anti-Slavery Reporter (London), 1825–36.
Columbian Magazine; or, Monthly Miscellany (Kingston), 1796–1800.
Edinburgh Review, 1802–1929.
Jamaica Journal (Kingston), 1818.
Jamaica Magazine (Kingston), 1812–13.
Jamaica Quarterly and Literary Gazette (Kingston), 1818–19.
Kingston *Daily Advertiser,* 1790.
Kingston *Royal Gazette,* 1780–1840.
Quarterly Review (London), 1809–.
St. Jago de la Vega Gazette (Spanish Town), 1809.

LOUISIANA

Alexandria (La.) *Planter's Intelligencer,* 1829–.
Century Magazine (New York), 1870–1930.
Commercial Bulletin (New Orleans), 1822–84.
De Bow's Review (New Orleans), 1846–80.
Frank Leslie's Illustrated Newspaper (New York), 1855–91.
Franklin (La.) *Planter's Banner,* 1836–63.
Harper's New Monthly Magazine (New York), 1850–1900.
Hunt's Merchants' Magazine and Commercial Review (New York), 1839–70.
Louisiana Chronicle (St. Francisville, La.), 1838–.
Natchitoches (La.) *Herald,* 1837–.
New Orleans *Bee,* 1827–71.
New Orleans *Bulletin,* 1838–.
New Orleans *Daily Picayune,* 1836–1914.
Price Current (New Orleans), 1822–84.
Southern Agriculturalist (Charleston, S.C.), 1828–46.
West Baton Rouge (La.) *Sugar Planter,* 1856–1925.

PRIMARY PUBLISHED MATERIALS

JAMAICA

The American Traveller. London, 1745.
Barclay, Alexander. *A Practical View of the Present State of Slavery in the West Indies.* London, 1826.

Beckford, William. *A Descriptive Account of the Island of Jamaica*. 2 vols. London, 1790.

———. *Remarks upon the Situation of Negroes in Jamaica*. London, 1788.

Bell, Hesketh J. *Obeah: Witchcraft in the West Indies*. 1889; rpr. New York, 1970.

Benezet, A. *A Caution and Warning to Great Britain and her Colonies*. London, 1784.

Bickell, Rev. Richard. *The West Indies As They Are*. London, 1825.

Bridgens, Richard. *West India Scenery*. London [1836?].

Bridges, George W. *The Annals of Jamaica*. 2 vols. London, 1827.

Burke, William, and Edmund Burke. *An Account of the European Settlements in America*. 2 vols. London, 1777.

Caines, Clement. *Letters on the Cultivation of the Otaheite Cane*. London, 1801.

Campbell, Charles. *Memoirs*. Glasgow, 1828.

Carlyle, Thomas. *Occasional Discourse on the Nigger Question*. London, 1853.

Carmichael, Mrs. A. C. *Domestic Manners and Social Condition of the White, Coloured, and Negro Population of the West Indies*. 2 vols. London, 1833.

Clark, William. *Ten Views in the Island of Antigua*. London, 1823.

Coke, Thomas. *A History of the West Indies*. 3 vols. London, 1810.

Collins, Dr. *Practical Rules for the Management and Medical Treatment of Negro Slaves in the Sugar Colonies*. 1811; rpr. New York, 1971.

Conder, Josiah. *Wages or the Whip*. London, 1833.

Cooper, Thomas. *Correspondence between George Hibbert, Esq., and the Rev. T. Cooper relative to the condition of the Negro slaves in Jamaica*. London, 1824. Extracted from *Morning Chronicle*.

———. *Facts Illustrative of the Condition of the Negro Slaves in Jamaica*. London, 1824.

Dallas, R. C. *The History of the Maroons*. 2 vols. London, 1803.

Davy, J. *The West Indies, Before and Since Slave Emancipation*. London, 1854.

De La Beche, H. T. *Notes on the Present Condition of the Negroes in Jamaica*. London, 1825.

Dicker, Samuel. *A Letter to a Member of Parliament*. London, 1745.

Dickson, William. *Letters on Slavery*. London, 1789.

———. *Mitigation of Slavery*. London, 1814.

Duperly, Adolphe. *Picturesque Jamaica*. Kingston [1890s].

Edwards, Bryan. *The History, Civil and Commercial, of the British Colonies in the West Indies*. 3 vols. 1793; rpr. New York, 1972.

Equiano, Olaudah. *The Interesting Narrative of the Life of Olaudah Equiano*. 2 vols. London, 1789.

An Essay Concerning Slavery and the Danger Jamaica Is Expos'd to from the Too Great Number of Slaves and the Too Little Care that is Taken to Manage Them. London [1745?].

Foot, Jesse. *A Defense of the Planters in the West Indies*. London, 1792.

Froude, James Anthony. *The English in the West Indies; or, The Bow of Ulysses*. London, 1888.

Gardner, W. J. *A History of Jamaica*. London, 1873.

Gladstone, John, and James Cropper. *The Correspondence between John Gladstone,*

Esq., M.P., and James Cropper, Esq., on the Present State of Slavery in the British West Indies and in the United States of America. Liverpool, 1824.

Grainger, James. *The Sugar Cane: A Poem.* London, 1764.

Hamel, the Obeah Man. London, 1827.

Harcourt, Henry. *The Adventures of a Sugar Plantation.* London, 1836.

Hibbert, Robert. *Hints to the Young Jamaica Sugar Planter.* London, 1825.

The Koromantyn Slaves; or, West Indian Sketches. London, 1823.

Leslie, Charles. *A New History of Jamaica.* London, 1740.

Letter from a Gentleman in Barbados to his friend in London, on the subject of manumission from slavery. London, 1803.

Lewis, Matthew Gregory. *Journal of a West India Proprietor.* London, 1834.

Ligon, Richard. *A True and Exact History of the Island of Barbados.* London, 1657.

Littleton, Edward. *The Groans of the Plantations.* London, 1689.

Long, Edward. *A Free and Candid Review.* London, 1784.

————. *The History of Jamaica.* 3 vols. 1774; rpr. New York, 1972.

Luckock, Benjamin. *Jamaica: Enslaved and Free.* London, 1846.

[Macauley, Zachary]. *Negro Slavery; or, A View of Some of the Prominent Features of that State of Society as it exists in the United States of America and in the Colonies of the West Indies, especially Jamaica.* London, 1823.

McMahon, Benjamin. *Jamaica Plantership.* London, 1839.

McNeill, Hector. *Observations on the Treatment of Negroes in the Island of Jamaica.* London [1788?].

Madden, R. R. *A Twelvemonth's Residence in the West Indies.* 2 vols. Philadelphia, 1835.

Marly; or, A Planter's Life in Jamaica. Glasgow, 1828.

Martin, Robert Montgomery. *History of the Colonies of the British Empire.* London, 1843.

Mathison, Gilbert. *Notices Respecting Jamaica in 1808–1809–1810.* London. 1811.

Montgomery; or, The West Indian Adventurer. Kingston, 1812–13. By a "gentleman resident in the West Indies."

Moreton, J. B. *Manners and Customs in the West India Islands.* London, 1790.

————. *West India Customs and Manners.* London, 1793.

Negro Slavery. London, 1823–26. By "various authors."

Notes on the Two Reports from the Committee of the Honourable House of Assembly of Jamaica appointed to examine into, and to report to the House, the Allegations and Charges contained in the several Petitions which have been presented to the British House of Commons, on the Subject of the Slave Trade, and the Treatment of the Negroes . . . London, 1789.

Nugent, Lady Maria. *A Journal of a Voyage to, and Residence in, the Island of Jamaica, from 1801–1805.* 2 vols. London, 1839.

Observations Upon the African Slave Trade, and on the Situation of Negroes in the West Indies. London, 1788. By a "Jamaica planter."

Oliver, Vere Langford. *The History of the Island of Antigua.* 3 vols. London, 1894.

Phillippo, James M. *Jamaica: Its Past and Present State.* London, 1843.

Pinckard, George. *Notes on the West Indies.* 3 vols. London, 1816.

Porteus, Beilby. *Tracts on Various Subjects.* London, 1807.

Ramsey, James. *An Essay on the Treatment and Conversion of African Slaves in the British Sugar Colonies.* London, 1784.

————. *A reply to the personal invectives and objections contained in two answers, published by certain anonymous persons, to An Essay on the Treatment and Conversion of African Slaves in the British Colonies.* London, 1785.

Recent, Affecting, and Important Information Respecting the State of Slavery in Jamaica. N.p., n.d. By an "eye witness." Reprinted from Dublin *Evening Mail,* September 30, 1789.

Renny, Robert. *An History of Jamaica.* London, 1807.

Riland, Rev. John. *Memoirs of a West India Planter.* London, 1827.

Roughley, Thomas. *The Jamaica Planter's Guide.* London, 1823.

Schaw, Janet. *Journal of a Lady of Quality.* New Haven, 1921.

Scott, Michael. *Tom Cringle's Log.* 1838; rpr. London, 1915.

Sells, William. *Remarks on the Condition of the Slaves in the Island of Jamaica.* London, 1823.

[Senior, Bernard Martin]. *Jamaica As It Was, As It Is, and As It May Be.* London, 1835.

A Short Journey in the West Indies. London, 1790.

The Slave Colonies of Great Britain; or, A Picture of Negro Slavery drawn by the Colonists Themselves. London, 1826.

Slave Sugar in a Nutshell. London [1850].

Smith, Adam. *An Inquiry into the Nature and Causes of the Wealth of Nations.* London, 1776.

Some Considerations on the Present State of our West India Colonies. London, 1830.

Southey, Thomas. *Chronological History of the West Indies.* 3 vols. London, 1827.

Stephen, James. *The Slavery of the British West India Colonies Delineated.* 2 vols. London, 1824–30.

Stewart, James. *A Brief Account of the Present State of the Negroes in Jamaica.* Bath, 1792.

Stewart, John. *An Account of Jamaica, and Its Inhabitants.* London, 1808.

————. *A View of the Past and Present State of the Island of Jamaica; with Remarks on the Moral and Physical Condition of the Slaves and on the Abolition of Slavery in the Colonies.* 1823; rpr. New York, 1969.

Sturge, Joseph, and Thomas Harvey. *The West Indies in 1837.* London, 1838.

Thome, J. A., and J. H. Kimball. *Emancipation in the West Indies.* New York, 1838.

Williamson, John. *Medical and Miscellaneous Observations Relative to the West India Islands.* Edinburgh, 1817.

Young, William. *The West-India Common-place Book.* London, 1807.

LOUISIANA

Abbott, J. S. C. *South and North.* New York, 1860.

Abdy, E. S. *Journal of a Residence and Tour in the United States of North America, from April 1833, to October 1834.* 3 vols. London, 1835.

Adams, Nehemiah. *A South-Side View of Slavery*. Boston, 1860.

Aime, Valcour. *Plantation Diary of the late Mr. Valcour Aime*. New Orleans, 1878.

Barbe-Marbois, François. *The History of Louisiana*. Philadelphia, 1830.

Bibb, Henry. *Narrative of the Life and Adventures of Henry Bibb, an American Slave*. New York, 1849.

Cable, George W. "Creole Slave Songs." *Century Magazine*, XXXI (1886), 807–28.

———. *Old Creole Days*. New York, 1879.

———. *Strange True Stories of Louisiana*. New York, 1889.

Champomier, P. A. *Statement of the Sugar Crop Made in Louisiana*. New Orleans, 1844–62.

Degelos, Pierre. *Statement of the Sugar Made in Louisiana in 1828 and 1829*. New Orleans [1830?].

———. *Statement of the Sugar Made in Louisiana in the year 1831*. New Orleans [1832?].

Delany, Martin R. *Blake; or, The Huts of America*. Boston, 1970. Serialized in *Weekly Anglo-African*, November, 1861–May, 1862.

Douglass, Frederick. *My Bondage and My Freedom*. New York, 1855.

Featherstonhaugh, G. W. *Excursion Through the Slave States*. London, 1844.

Fenner, Erasmus Darwin, ed. *Southern Medical Reports*. 2 vols. New Orleans, 1849–50.

Fitzhugh, George. *Cannibals All*. Richmond, 1857.

———. *Sociology for the South*. Richmond, 1854.

Gayarré, Charles. *History of Louisiana*. New Orleans, 1885.

———. "A Louisiana Sugar Plantation of the Old Regime." *Harper's New Monthly Magazine*, LXXIV (1887), 606–21.

Grayson, William J. *The Hireling and the Slave*. Charleston, S.C., 1854.

Hamilton, Captain [Thomas]. *Men and Manners in America*. Edinburgh and London, 1833.

Kellar, Herbert Anthony, ed. *Solon Robinson, Pioneer and Agriculturalist: Selected Writings*. 2 vols. Indianapolis, 1936.

Kennedy, Joseph C. G. *Population of the United States in 1860; compiled from the original returns of the eighth census*. Washington, D.C., 1864.

[Kingsford, William.] *Impressions of the West and South during a Six Weeks' Holiday*. Toronto, 1858.

Leon, John A. *On Sugar Cultivation in Louisiana, Cuba, etc., and the British Possessions*. London, 1848.

Martin, François X. *The History of Louisiana, from the Earliest Period*. New Orleans, 1882.

Northrup, Solomon. *Twelve Years A Slave*. London, 1853.

Olmsted, Frederick Law. *A Journey in the Seaboard Slave States*. New York, 1856.

Pearse, James. *A Narrative of the Life of James Pearse*. Rutland, Vt., 1825.

The Pro-Slavery Argument. Charleston, S.C., 1852.

Rost, Judge P. A. *Sugar, Its Culture and Manufacture: Discourse before the Agricultural and Mechanics Association of Louisiana, May 12, 1845*. Hahnville, La., 1876.

Ruffin, Edmund. *The Political Economy of Slavery*. [Washington, D.C., 1857?].

Russell, William Howard. *My Diary North and South*. London, 1863.

The Slave's Lamentation. N.p. [1848?]. By "B.F."

Stroud, George M. *A Sketch of the Laws Relating to Slavery in the Several States of the United States of America*. Philadelphia, 1856.

Thorpe, Thomas Bangs. "Christmas in the South." *Frank Leslie's Illustrated Newspaper*, December 26, 1857, p. 62.

———. "Sugar and the Sugar Region of Louisiana." *Harper's New Monthly Magazine*, VII (1853), 746–67.

Trollope, Frances Milton. *Domestic Manners of the Americans* (1832). Edited by Donald Smalley. New York, 1949.

Weld, Theodore Dwight. *American Slavery As It Is: Testimony of a Thousand Witnesses*. New York, 1839.

SECONDARY MATERIALS

Books

Adamson, Alan. *Sugar Without Slaves: The Political Economy of British Guiana, 1838–1904*. New Haven, 1972.

Alho, Olli. *The Religion of the Slaves: A Study of the Religious Tradition and Behaviour of Plantation Slaves in the United States, 1830–1865*. Helsinki, 1976.

Anstey, Roger. *The Atlantic Slave Trade and British Abolition, 1760–1810*. London, 1975.

Aptheker, Herbert. *American Negro Slave Revolts*. New York, 1943.

———. *To Be Free: Studies in American Negro History*. New York, 1948.

Armstrong, Douglas V. *The Old Village and the Great House: An Archaeological and Historical Examination of Drax Hall Plantation, St. Ann's Bay, Jamaica*. Urbana, Ill., 1990.

Augier, F. R., *et al*. *The Making of the West Indies*. London, 1960.

Aykroyd, W. R. *Sweet Malefactor: Sugar, Slavery, and Human Society*. London, 1967.

Barrett, Leonard E. *The Sun and the Drum: African Roots in Jamaican Folk Tradition*. London, 1976.

Bastide, Roger. *African Civilizations in the New World*. New York, 1971.

———. *African Religions of Brazil: Toward A Sociology of the Inter-Penetration of Civilizations*. Baltimore, 1978.

Beckford, George L. *Persistent Poverty: Underdevelopment in Plantation Economies of the Third World*. New York, 1972.

Beckles, Hilary. *Natural Rebels: A Social History of Enslaved Black Women in Barbados*. New Brunswick, N.J., 1989.

———. *White Servitude and Black Slavery in Barbados, 1627–1715*. Knoxville, Tenn., 1989.

Beckwith, Martha. *Black Roadways: A Study of Jamaican Folk Life*. Chapel Hill, N.C., 1929.

Bell, Kenneth N., and W. P. Morrell, eds. *Select Documents on British Colonial Policy, 1830–1860*. London, 1928.

Bennett, J. Harry. *Bondsmen and Bishops: Slavery and Apprenticeship on the Codrington Plantations of Barbados, 1710–1838.* Berkeley and Los Angeles, 1958.

Berlin, Ira. *Slaves Without Masters: The Free Negro in the Antebellum South.* New York, 1974.

Berlin, Ira, and Ronald Hoffman, eds. *Slavery and Freedom in the Age of the American Revolution.* Charlottesville, Va., 1983.

Berlin, Ira, and Philip D. Morgan, eds. *Cultivation and Culture: Labor and the Shaping of Slave Life in the Americas.* Charlottesville, Va., 1993.

———, eds. *The Slaves' Economy: Independent Production by Slaves in the Americas.* London, 1991.

Berlin, Ira, *et al.,* eds. *The Destruction of Slavery.* New York, 1985. Series I, Vol. I, of Berlin *et al.,* eds., *Freedom: A Documentary History of Emancipation, 1861–1867.*

Black, Clinton. *History of Jamaica.* London, 1958.

Blackburn, Robin. *The Overthrow of Colonial Slavery, 1776–1848.* London, 1988.

Blassingame, John W. *The Slave Community: Plantation Life in the Antebellum South.* New York, 1972.

———. *Slave Testimony.* Baton Rouge, 1977.

Bohannan, Paul, and George Dalton, eds. *Markets in Africa.* Evanston, Ill., 1962.

Botkin, Benjamin. *Lay My Burden Down: A Folk History of Slavery.* Chicago, 1945.

Bowser, Frederick P. *The African Slave in Colonial Peru, 1524–1650.* Stanford, Calif., 1974.

Brady, Terence, and Evan Jones. *The Fight Against Slavery.* New York, 1977.

Brathwaite, Edward. *The Development of Creole Society in Jamaica, 1770–1820.* London, 1971.

Breen, T. H., and Stephen Innes. *"Myne Owne Ground": Race and Freedom on Virginia's Eastern Shore.* New York, 1980.

Brink, André. *Looking on Darkness.* New York, 1975.

Burn, W. L. *The British West Indies.* London, 1951.

———. *Emancipation and Apprenticeship in the British West Indies.* London, 1938.

Burns, Sir Alan. *History of the British West Indies.* London, 1954.

Burns, Robert. *The Complete Works.* Boston, 1863.

Bush, Barbara. *Slave Women in Caribbean Society, 1650–1838.* Bloomington, Ind., 1990.

Campbell, Mavis Christine. *The Dynamics of Change in a Slave Society: A Sociopolitical History of the Free Coloreds of Jamaica, 1800–1865.* Cranbury, N.J., 1976.

Cardoso, Gerald. *Negro Slavery in the Sugar Plantations of Veracruz and Pernambuco.* Washington, D.C., 1983.

Clark, John G. *New Orleans, 1718–1812: An Economic History.* Baton Rouge, 1970.

Clarke, Edith. *My Mother Who Fathered Me: A Study of the Family in Three Selected Communities in Jamaica.* London, 1957.

Clement, William. *Plantation Life on the Mississippi.* New Orleans, 1952.

Comitas, Lambros, comp. *Slaves, Free Men, Citizens: West Indian Perspectives.* Garden City, N.Y., 1973.

Conrad, Alfred H., and John R. Meyer. *The Economics of Slavery, and Other Studies in Econometric History.* Chicago, 1964.

Conrad, Robert E. *Children of God's Fire: A Documentary History of Black Slavery in Brazil.* Princeton, 1983.

Cooper, J. Wesley. *Louisiana: A Treasure of Plantation Homes.* Natchez, Miss., 1961.

Cooper, William J. *Liberty and Slavery.* New York, 1983.

———. *The South and the Politics of Slavery.* Baton Rouge, 1978.

Cox, Edward L. *Free Coloreds in the Slave Societies of St. Kitts and Grenada, 1763–1833.* Knoxville, Tenn., 1984.

Crahan, Margaret E., and Franklin W. Knight, eds. *Africa and the Caribbean: The Legacy of a Link.* Baltimore, 1979.

Craton, Michael. *Searching for the Invisible Man: Slaves and Plantation Life in Jamaica.* Cambridge, Mass., 1978.

———. *Testing the Chains: Resistance to Slavery in the British West Indies.* Ithaca, N.Y., 1982.

———, ed. *Roots and Branches: Current Directions in Slave Studies.* Waterloo, Ont., 1979.

Craton, Michael, and James Walvin. *A Jamaican Plantation: The History of Worthy Park, 1670–1970.* London, 1970.

Craton, Michael, and David Wright. *Slavery, Abolition, and Emancipation—Black Slaves and the British Empire: A Thematic Documentary.* London, 1976.

Craven, Avery O. *Rachel of Old Louisiana.* Baton Rouge, 1975.

Cross, Malcolm, and Arnaud Marks, eds. *Peasants, Plantations, and Rural Communities in the Caribbean.* Guildford, Eng., and Leiden, Neth., 1979.

Curtin, Philip D. *The Atlantic Slave Trade: A Census.* Madison, Wis., 1969.

———. *Two Jamaicas: The Role of Ideas in a Tropical Colony, 1830–1865.* Cambridge, Mass., 1955.

David, Paul A., et al. *Reckoning with Slavery: A Critical Study in the Quantitative History of American Negro Slavery.* New York, 1976.

Davis, David Brion. *The Problem of Slavery in the Age of Revolution, 1770–1823.* Ithaca, N.Y., 1975.

———. *The Problem of Slavery in Western Culture.* Ithaca, N.Y., 1966.

———. *Slavery and Human Progress.* New York, 1984.

Davis, Edwin Adams. *Plantation Life in the Florida Parishes of Louisiana, 1836–1846, As Reflected in the Diary of Bennet H. Barrow.* New York, 1943.

Debien, Gabriel. *Les Esclaves aux Antilles françaises, XVIIe–XVIIIe siècles.* Fort-de-France, 1974.

Deerr, Noel. *The History of Sugar.* 2 vols. London, 1949.

Degler, Carl. *Neither Black nor White: Slavery and Race Relations in Brazil and the United States.* New York, 1971.

De Voe, Thomas F. *The Market Book: A History of the Public Markets of the City of New York.* 1862; rpr. New York, 1970.

Dirks, Robert. *The Black Saturnalia: Conflict and Its Ritual Expression on British West Indian Slave Plantations.* Gainesville, Fla., 1987.

Donnan, Elizabeth. *Documents Illustrative of the Slave Trade to America.* Washington, D.C., 1933.

Drescher, Seymour. *Econocide: British Slavery in the Era of Abolition.* Pittsburgh, 1977.

Duffy, John, ed. *The Rudolph Matas History of Medicine in Louisiana.* Baton Rouge, 1962.

Dunn, Richard S. *Sugar and Slaves: The Rise of the Planter Class in the English West Indies, 1624–1713.* Chapel Hill, N.C., 1972.

Edwards, Melvin R. *Jamaican Higglers: Their Significance and Potential.* Swansea, 1980.

Eisenberg, Peter L. *The Sugar Industry in Pernambuco, 1840–1919: Modernization Without Change.* Berkeley and Los Angeles, 1974.

Eisner, Gisela. *Jamaica, 1830–1930: A Study in Economic Growth.* Manchester, Eng., 1961.

Elkins, Stanley. *Slavery: A Problem in American Institutional and Intellectual Life.* Chicago, 1959.

Eltis, David, and James Walvin, eds. *The Abolition of the Atlantic Slave Trade: Origins and Effects in Europe, Africa, and the Americas.* Madison, Wis., 1981.

Engerman, Stanley L., and Eugene D. Genovese, eds. *Race and Slavery in the Western Hemisphere: Quantitative Studies.* Princeton, 1975.

Escott, Paul D. *Slavery Remembered: A Record of Twentieth-Century Slave Narratives.* Chapel Hill, N.C., 1979.

Fields, Barbara Jeanne. *Slavery and Freedom on the Middle Ground.* New Haven, 1985.

Fischer, Roger A. *The Segregation Struggle in Louisiana, 1862–1877.* Urbana, Ill., 1974.

Fisher, Allan G. B., and Humphrey J. Fisher. *Slavery and Muslim Society in Africa: The Institution in Saharan and Sudanic Africa, and the Trans-Saharan Trade.* London, 1970.

Fogel, Robert W. *Without Consent or Contract: The Rise and Fall of American Slavery.* New York, 1989.

Fogel, Robert W., and Stanley L. Engerman. *Time on the Cross: The Economics of American Negro Slavery.* Boston, 1974.

Foner, Eric. *Nothing but Freedom: Emancipation and Its Legacy.* Baton Rouge, 1983.

Foner, Laura, and Eugene D. Genovese, eds. *Slavery in the New World: A Reader in Comparative History.* Englewood Cliffs, N.J., 1969.

Fontenot, Mary A. *Acadia Parish, Louisiana: A History to 1900.* Baton Rouge, 1976.

Fortier, Alcée. *A History of Louisiana.* New York, 1904.

Fox-Genovese, Elizabeth. *Within the Plantation Household: Black and White Women of the Old South.* Chapel Hill, N.C., 1988.

Fraser, Grace Lovat. *Textiles by Britain.* London, 1948.

Frazier, E. Franklin. *The Negro Family in the United States.* Chicago, 1939.

Freyre, Gilberto. *The Masters and the Slaves: A Study in the Development of Brazilian Civilization.* New York, 1946.

Gaspar, David Barry. *Bondmen and Rebels: A Case Study of Master-Slave Relations in Antigua, with Implications for Colonial British America*. Baltimore, 1985.

Gemery, Henry A., and Jan S. Hogendorn, eds. *The Uncommon Market: Essays in the Economic History of the Atlantic Slave Trade*. New York, 1979.

Genovese, Eugene D. *From Rebellion to Revolution: Afro-American Slave Revolts in the Making of the Modern World*. Baton Rouge, 1979.

――――. *In Red and Black: Marxian Explorations in Southern and Afro-American History*. New York, 1968.

――――. *The Political Economy of Slavery: Studies in the Economy and Society of the Slave South*. New York, 1965.

――――. *Roll, Jordan, Roll: The World the Slaves Made*. New York, 1974.

――――. *The World the Slaveholders Made: Two Essays in Interpretation*. New York, 1969.

――――, ed. *The Slave Economies*. 2 vols. New York, 1973.

Genovese, Eugene D., and Elizabeth Fox-Genovese. *Fruits of Merchant Capital: Slavery and Bourgeois Property in the Rise and Expansion of Capitalism*. New York, 1983.

Goveia, Elsa. *Slave Society in the British Leeward Islands at the End of the Eighteenth Century*. New Haven, 1965.

――――. *A Study on the Historiography of the British West Indies to the End of the Nineteenth Century*. Mexico City, 1956.

Gray, Lewis C. *History of Agriculture in the Southern United States to 1860*. 2 vols. New York, 1941.

Green, William A. *British Slave Emancipation: The Sugar Colonies and the Great Experiment, 1830–1865*. Oxford, 1976.

Gutman, Herbert G. *The Black Family in Slavery and Freedom, 1750–1925*. New York, 1976.

――――. *Slavery and the Numbers Game: A Critique of "Time on the Cross."* Urbana, Ill., 1975.

Hall, Douglas. *Free Jamaica, 1838–1865: An Economic History*. New Haven, 1965.

――――. *In Miserable Slavery: Thomas Thistlewood in Jamaica, 1750–1786*. Basingstoke, Eng., 1989.

Hall, Gwendolyn Midlo. *Social Control in Slave Plantation Societies: A Comparison of St. Domingue and Cuba*. Baltimore, 1971.

Hamshere, Cyril. *The British in the Caribbean*. London, 1972.

Handler, Jerome. *The Unappropriated People: Freedmen in the Slave Society of Barbados*. Baltimore, 1974.

Handler, Jerome, and Frederick Lange. *Plantation Slavery in Barbados: An Archaeological and Historical Investigation*. Cambridge, Mass., 1978.

Hardy, Thomas. *Jude the Obscure*. 1895; rpr. New York, 1978.

Harlow, Vincent T., and Frederick Madden. *British Colonial Developments, 1774–1834: Select Documents*. Oxford, 1953.

Harris, Marvin. *Patterns of Race in the Americas*. Boston, 1964.

Hart, Richard. *Blacks in Bondage*. Kingston, 1980.

Herskovits, Melville J. *The Myth of the Negro Past*. New York, 1941.

————. *The New World Negro: Selected Papers in Afroamerican Studies.* Bloomington, Ind., 1966.

Heuman, Gad J. *Between Black and White: Race, Politics, and the Free Coloreds in Jamaica, 1792–1865.* Westport, Conn., 1981.

————, ed. *Out of the House of Bondage: Runaways, Resistance, and Marronage in Africa and the New World.* London, 1986.

Higman, Barry W. *Jamaica Surveyed: Plantation Maps and Plans of the Eighteenth and Nineteenth Centuries.* Kingston, 1988.

————. *Slave Population and Economy in Jamaica, 1807–1834.* London, 1976.

————. *Slave Populations of the British Caribbean, 1807–1834.* Baltimore, 1984.

————, ed. *Trade, Government, and Society in Caribbean History, 1700–1920: Essays Presented to Douglas Hall.* Kingston, 1983.

Hilliard, Sam Bowers. *Hog Meat and Hoecake: Food Supply in the Old South.* Carbondale, Ill., 1972.

Hoetink, Harry. *Slavery and Race Relations in the Americas: Comparative Notes on Their Nature and Nexus.* New York, 1973.

————. *The Two Variants in Caribbean Race Relations: A Contribution to the Sociology of Segmented Societies.* London, 1967.

Howard, Robert Mowbray. *Records and Letters of the Family of the Longs of Longville, Jamaica, and Hampton Lodge, Surrey.* London, 1925.

Hymes, Dell. *Reinventing Anthropology.* New York, 1973.

Ingram, K. E. N. *Sources in Jamaican History, 1655–1838.* Zug, Switz., 1976.

Jakobsson, Stiv. *Am I Not a Man and a Brother? British Missions and the Abolition of the Slave Trade and Slavery in West Africa and the West Indies, 1786–1838.* Uppsala, 1972.

James, C. L. R. *The Black Jacobins: Toussaint L'Ouverture and the San Domingo Revolution.* 1938; rpr. New York, 1963.

Jones, LeRoi (Imamu Amiri Baraka). *Home.* New York, 1966.

Jordan, Winthrop. *White over Black: American Attitudes Toward the Negro, 1550–1812.* Chapel Hill, N.C., 1968.

Joyner, Charles W. *Down by the Riverside: A South Carolina Slave Community.* Urbana, Ill., 1984.

Kane, Harnett T. *Plantation Parade: The Grand Manner in Louisiana.* New York, 1945.

Karasch, Mary. *Slave Life in Rio de Janeiro, 1808–1850.* Princeton, 1986.

Kiple, Kenneth F. *The Caribbean Slave: A Biological History.* New York, 1985.

Kiple, Kenneth F., and Virginia H. King. *Another Dimension to the Black Diaspora: Diet, Disease, and Racism.* New York, 1981.

Klein, Herbert S. *The Middle Passage: Comparative Studies in the Atlantic Slave Trade.* Princeton, 1978.

————. *Slavery in the Americas: A Comparative Study of Virginia and Cuba.* Chicago, 1967.

Knight, Derrick. *Gentlemen of Fortune: The Men Who Made Their Fortunes in Britain's Slave Colonies.* London, 1978.

313

Knight, Franklin W. *The African Dimension in Latin American Societies*. New York, 1974.

——. *Slave Society in Cuba During the Nineteenth Century*. Madison, Wis., 1970.

Kolchin, Peter. *Unfree Labor: American Slavery and Russian Serfdom*. Cambridge, Mass., 1987.

Kulikoff, Allan. *Tobacco and Slaves: The Development of Southern Cultures in the Chesapeake, 1680–1800*. Williamsburg, Va., 1986.

Laguerre, Michel S. *Voodoo Heritage*. Beverly Hills, Calif., 1980.

Land, Aubrey C., *et al.*, eds. *Law, Society, and Politics in Early Maryland*. Baltimore, 1977.

Lane, Ann J., ed. *The Debate over Slavery: Stanley Elkins and His Critics*. Urbana, Ill., 1971.

Le Gardeur, René J., Jr., *et al. Green Fields: Two Hundred Years of Louisiana Sugar*. Lafayette, La., 1980.

Le Page, Robert B. *Jamaican Creole: An Historical Introduction to Jamaican Creole*. London, 1960.

Leris, Michel, and Jacqueline Delange. *African Art*. London, 1968.

Lester, Julius. *To Be a Slave*. New York, 1968.

Levine, Lawrence. *Black Culture and Black Consciousness: Afro-American Folk Thought from Slavery to Freedom*. New York, 1977.

Lewis, Ethel. *The Romance of Textiles: The Story of Design in Weaving*. New York, 1936.

Lewis, Gordon K. *Main Currents in Caribbean Thought: The Historical Evolution of Caribbean Society in Its Ideological Aspects, 1492–1900*. Baltimore, 1983.

Littlefield, Daniel C. *Rice and Slaves: Ethnicity and the Slave Trade in Colonial South Carolina*. Baton Rouge, 1981.

Litwack, Leon. *Been in the Storm So Long: The Aftermath of Slavery*. New York, 1979.

Long, Anton V. *Jamaica and the New Order, 1822–1847*. Kingston, 1956.

Lucas, J. Olumide. *The Religion of the Yorubas*. Lagos, 1948.

Luraghi, Raimondo. *The Rise and Fall of the Plantation South*. New York, 1978.

McClellan, Elisabeth. *History of American Costume, 1607–1870*. 1904; rpr. New York, 1969.

Mandle, Jay R. *The Plantation Economy: Population and Economic Change in Guyana, 1838–1960*. Philadelphia, 1973.

Marshall, Woodville, ed. *The Colthurst Journal*. Millwood, N.Y., 1977.

Mathieson, W. L. *British Slavery and Its Abolition, 1823–1838*. London, 1926.

Mathurin, Lucille. *The Rebel Women in the British West Indies During Slavery*. Kingston, 1975.

Mayer, Enrique, Sidney W. Mintz, and G. William Skinner. *Los campesinos y el mercado*. Lima, 1974.

Menn, Joseph K. *The Large Slaveholders of Louisiana, 1860*. New Orleans, 1964.

Miller, Elinor, and Eugene D. Genovese, eds. *Plantation, Town, and County: Essays on the Local History of American Slave Society*. Urbana, Ill., 1974.

Miller, Joseph C. *Way of Death: Merchant Capitalism and the Angolan Slave Trade.* Madison, Wis., 1988.

Mills, Gary B. *The Forgotten People: Cane River's Creoles of Color.* Baton Rouge, 1977.

Mintz, Sidney. *Caribbean Transformations.* Chicago, 1974.

————. *Sweetness and Power.* New York, 1985.

Mintz, Sidney, and Richard Price. *An Anthropological Approach to the Afro-American Past: A Caribbean Perspective.* Philadelphia, 1976.

Mintz, Sidney, and Sally Price, eds. *Caribbean Contours.* Baltimore, 1985.

Moody, V. Alton. *Slavery on Louisiana Sugar Plantations.* New Orleans, 1924.

Moreno Fraginals, Manuel. *The Sugarmill: The Socioeconomic Complex of Sugar in Cuba, 1760–1860.* New York, 1976.

————, ed. *Africa in Latin America: Essays on History, Culture, and Socialization.* New York, 1984.

Moreno Fraginals, Manuel, Frank Moya Pons, and Stanley Engerman, eds. *Between Slavery and Free Labor: The Spanish-Speaking Caribbean in the Nineteenth Century.* Baltimore, 1985.

Morner, Magnus. *Race Mixture in the History of Latin America.* Boston, 1967.

Morrissey, Marietta. *Slave Women in the New World: Gender Stratification in the Caribbean.* Lawrence, Kans., 1989.

Myrdal, Gunnar. *An American Dilemma.* New York, 1944.

Nieboer, H. J. *Slavery as an Industrial System.* The Hague, 1900.

Norris, Katrin. *Jamaica: The Search for an Identity.* London, 1962.

Olwig, Karen Fog. *Cultural Adaptation and Resistance on St. John: Three Centuries of Afro-Caribbean Life.* Gainesville, Fla., 1985.

Osofsky, Gilbert, ed. *Puttin' On Ole Massa.* New York, 1969.

Overdyke, William Darrell. *Louisiana Plantation Homes: Colonial and Ante Bellum.* New York, 1965.

Owens, Leslie Howard. *This Species of Property: Slave Life and Culture in the Old South.* New York, 1976.

Oxaal, Ivar. *Black Intellectuals Come to Power.* Cambridge, Mass., 1968.

Palmer, Colin A. *Human Cargoes: The British Slave Trade to Spanish America, 1700–1739.* Urbana, Ill., 1981.

————. *Slaves of the White God: Blacks in Mexico, 1570–1650.* Cambridge, Mass., 1976.

Panamerican Union. *Plantation Systems of the New World.* Washington, D.C.; 1960.

Pares, Richard. *Merchants and Planters.* Cambridge, Eng., 1960.

————. *War and Trade in the West Indies, 1739–1763.* Oxford, 1950.

————. *A West India Fortune.* London, 1936.

————. *Yankees and Creoles: The Trade Between North America and the West Indies Before the American Revolution.* London, 1956.

Parrinder, Edward G. *West African Religion.* London, 1949.

Parry, J. H., and Philip Sherlock. *A Short History of the West Indies.* London, 1956.

Patterson, Orlando. *Slavery and Social Death.* Cambridge, Mass., 1982.

————. *The Sociology of Slavery: An Analysis of the Origins, Development, and Structure of Negro Slave Society in Jamaica.* London, 1967.

Perdue, Charles L., *et al. Weevils in the Wheat: Interviews with Virginia Ex-Slaves.* Charlottesville, Va., 1976.

Phillips, Ulrich B. *American Negro Slavery.* New York, 1918.

————. *Life and Labor in the Old South.* Boston, 1929.

Pitman, Frank W. *The Development of the British West Indies, 1700–1763.* New Haven, 1917.

Postell, William D. *The Health of Slaves on Southern Plantations.* Baton Rouge, 1951.

Price, Richard. *First-Time: The Historical Vision of an Afro-American People.* Baltimore, 1983.

————, comp. *Maroon Societies: Rebel Slave Communities in the Americas.* Baltimore, 1979.

Proctor, Samuel, ed. *Eighteenth-Century Florida and the Caribbean.* Gainesville, Fla., 1976.

Puckrein, Gary A. *Little England: Plantation Society and Anglo-Barbadian Politics, 1627–1700.* New York, 1984.

Raboteau, Albert J. *Slave Religion: The "Invisible Institution" in the Antebellum South.* New York, 1978.

Ragatz, Lowell J. *The Fall of the Planter Class in the British Caribbean, 1763–1833.* New York, 1928.

Ransom, Roger, and Richard Sutch. *One Kind of Freedom.* New York, 1977.

Rawick, George P. *The American Slave: A Composite Autobiography.* 17 vols., 12 vols., 10 vols. Westport, Conn., 1972–78.

————. *From Sundown to Sunup: The Making of the Black Community.* Westport, Conn., 1972.

Rice, C. Duncan. *The Rise and Fall of Black Slavery.* London, 1975.

Ripley, C. Peter. *Slaves and Freedmen in Civil War Louisiana.* Baton Rouge, 1976.

Roberts, George W. *The Population of Jamaica.* Cambridge, Eng., 1967.

Rodney, Walter. *The Groundings with My Brothers.* London, 1969.

Roland, Charles P. *Louisiana Sugar Plantations During the American Civil War.* Leiden, 1957.

Rousseve, Charles B. *The Negro in Louisiana: Aspects of His History and Literature.* New Orleans, 1937.

Rubin, Vera, ed. *Caribbean Studies: A Symposium.* Kingston, 1957.

Rubin, Vera, and Arthur Tuden, eds. *Comparative Perspectives on Slavery in New World Plantation Societies.* New York, 1977.

Russell-Wood, A. J. R. *The Black Man in Slavery and Freedom in Colonial Brazil.* New York, 1982.

Sangster, Ian. *Sugar and Jamaica.* London, 1973.

Savitt, Todd. *Medicine and Slavery: The Diseases and Health Care of Blacks in Antebellum Virginia.* Urbana, Ill., 1978.

Saxon, Lyle. *Old Louisiana.* New York, 1929.

Saxon, Lyle, *et al.,* comps. *Gumbo Ya-Ya: A Collection of Louisiana Folk Tales.* Boston, 1945.

Scarano, Francisco A. *Sugar and Slavery in Puerto Rico: The Plantation Economy of Ponce, 1800–1850*. Madison, Wis., 1984.

Schmitz, Mark. *Economic Analysis of Antebellum Sugar Plantations in Louisiana*. New York, 1977.

Schuler, Monica. *"Alas, Alas, Kongo": A Social History of Indentured African Immigration into Jamaica, 1841–1865*. Baltimore, 1980.

Scott, Rebecca J. *Slave Emancipation in Cuba: The Transition to Free Labor, 1860–1899*. Princeton, 1985.

Scott, Rebecca J., et al., eds. *The Abolition of Slavery and the Aftermath of Emancipation in Brazil*. Durham, N.C., 1988.

Seebold, Herman B. de Bachelle. *Old Louisiana Plantation Homes and Family Trees*. New Orleans, 1941.

Sheridan, Richard B. *The Development of the Plantations to 1750; and, An Era of West Indian Prosperity, 1750–1775*. London, 1970.

————. *Doctors and Slaves: A Medical and Demographic History of Slavery in the British West Indies, 1680–1834*. New York, 1985.

————. *Sugar and Slavery: An Economic History of the British West Indies, 1623–1775*. Baltimore, 1973.

Shugg, Roger W. *Origins of Class Struggle in Louisiana: A Social History of White Farmers and Laborers During Slavery and After, 1840–1875*. Baton Rouge, 1939.

Sitterson, J. Carlyle. *Sugar Country: The Cane Sugar Industry in the South, 1753–1950*. Lexington, Ky., 1953.

Smith, Julia Floyd. *Slavery and Rice Culture in Low Country Georgia*. Knoxville, Tenn., 1985.

Smith, Michael G. *The Plural Society in the British West Indies*. Berkeley and Los Angeles, 1965.

Smith, Robert H. T., ed. *Market-Place Trade: Periodic Markets, Hawkers, and Traders in Africa, Asia, and Latin America*. Vancouver, 1978.

Sobel, Mechal. *Trabelin' On: The Slave Journey to an Afro-Baptist Faith*. Westport, Conn., 1979.

Solow, Barbara, and Stanley Engerman, eds. *British Capitalism and Caribbean Slavery: The Legacy of Eric Williams*. New York, 1987.

Stafford, Earle. *The Basic Jamaica Book*. Etobicoke, Ont., 1977.

Stampp, Kenneth M. *The Peculiar Institution: Slavery in the Ante-Bellum South*. New York, 1956.

Stein, Stanley J. *Vassouras: A Brazilian Coffee County, 1850–1900*. Cambridge, Mass., 1957.

Sterkx, H. E. *The Free Negro in Antebellum Louisiana*. Cranbury, N.J., 1972.

Stuckey, Sterling. *Slave Culture: Nationalist Theory and the Foundations of Black America*. New York, 1987.

Sydnor, Charles S. *Slavery in Mississippi*. New York, 1933.

Szwed, John, and N. Whitten, eds. *Afro-American Anthropology: Contemporary Perspectives*. New York, 1970.

Tannenbaum, Frank. *Slave and Citizen: The Negro in the Americas*. New York, 1947.

Taussig, Charles. *Some Notes on Sugar and Molasses*. New York, 1940.

317

Taylor, Joe Gray. *Louisiana Reconstructed, 1863–1877.* Baton Rouge, 1974.

————. *Negro Slavery in Louisiana.* Baton Rouge, 1963.

Thompson, Edgar T. *Plantation Societies, Race Relations, and the South: The Regimentation of Populations.* Durham, N.C., 1975.

Titus, Noel. *The Church and Slavery in the English-Speaking Caribbean.* Bridgetown, 1983.

Tomich, Dale. *Slavery in the Circuit of Sugar: Martinique and the World Economy.* Baltimore, 1990.

Turner, Mary. *Slaves and Missionaries: The Disintegration of Jamaican Slave Society, 1787–1834.* Urbana, Ill., 1982.

Van Deburg, William L. *The Slave Drivers: Black Agricultural Labor Supervisors in the Antebellum South.* Westport, Conn., 1979.

Waddell, D. A. G. *The West Indies and the Guianas.* Englewood Cliffs, N.J., 1967.

Walvin, James. *Slavery and the Slave Trade: A Short Illustrated History.* Jackson, Miss., 1983.

Ward, J. R. *British West Indian Slavery, 1750–1834: The Process of Amelioration.* Oxford, 1988.

Ware, Charles P., *et al.*, eds. *Slave Songs of the United States.* New York, 1929.

Watson, Karl. *The Civilised Island, Barbados: A Social History, 1750–1816.* Bridgetown, 1979.

Webb, Allie B. W. *Mistress of Evergreen Plantation: Rachel O'Connor's Legacy of Letters.* Albany, N.Y., 1983.

Webber, Thomas L. *Deep like the Rivers: Education in the Slave Quarter Community, 1831–1865.* New York, 1978.

Welmers, Beatrice F., and William E. Welmers. *Igbo: A Learner's Dictionary.* Los Angeles, 1968.

White, Deborah Gray. *Ar'n't I a Woman? Female Slaves in the Plantation South.* New York, 1985.

White, Howard A. *The Freedmen's Bureau in Louisiana.* Baton Rouge, 1970.

Whitten, David O. *Andrew Durnford: A Black Sugar Planter in Antebellum Louisiana.* Natchitoches, La., 1987.

Wiley, Bell I. *Southern Negroes, 1861–1865.* New Haven, 1938.

Williams, Eric. *British Historians and the West Indies.* London, 1966.

————. *Capitalism and Slavery.* London, 1944.

————. *From Columbus to Castro: The History of the Caribbean, 1492–1969.* New York, 1970.

————. *The Negro in the Caribbean.* Manchester, Eng., 1942.

Wood, Peter H. *Black Majority: Negroes in Colonial South Carolina from 1670 Through the Stono Rebellion.* New York, 1974.

Woodman, Harold D., ed. *Slavery and the Southern Economy.* New York, 1966.

Woodward, C. Vann. *The Comparative Approach to American History.* New York, 1968.

Wright, Gavin. *The Political Economy of the Cotton South: Households, Markets, and Wealth in the Nineteenth Century.* New York, 1978.

Wright, Philip. *Knibb "the Notorious": Slaves' Missionary, 1803–1845.* London, 1973.
Yetman, Norman R., ed. *Life Under the "Peculiar Institution."* New York, 1970.

Articles

Anstey, Roger T. "The British Slave Trade, 1751–1807: A Comment." *Journal of African History,* XVII (1976), 606–607.
———. "Capitalism and Slavery: A Critique." *Economic History Review,* XXI (1968), 307–20.
Aufhauser, R. Keith. "Profitability of Slavery in the British Caribbean." *Journal of Interdisciplinary History,* V (1974), 45–67.
———. "Slavery and Scientific Management." *Journal of Economic History,* XXXIII (1973), 811–24.
Bailey, David T. "A Divided Prism: Two Sources of Black Testimony on Slavery." *Journal of Southern History,* XLVI (1980), 381–404.
Banquois, Dora J. "The Career of Henry Adams Bullard." *Louisiana Historical Quarterly,* XXIII (1940), 999–1106.
Bauer, Raymond A., and Alice H. Bauer. "Day to Day Resistance to Slavery." *Journal of Negro History,* XXVII (1942), 388–419.
Beckles, Hilary. "Down But Not Out: Eric Williams' 'Capitalism and Slavery' After Nearly Forty Years of Criticism." *Bulletin of Eastern Caribbean Affairs,* VIII (May–June, 1982), 29–36.
———. "An Economic Life of Their Own: Slaves as Commodity Producers and Distributors in Barbados." *Slavery and Abolition,* XII (1991), 31–47.
Beckles, Hilary, and Karl Watson. "Social Protest and Labour Bargaining: The Changing Nature of Slaves' Responses to Plantation Life in Eighteenth-Century Barbados." *Slavery and Abolition,* VIII (1987), 292—93.
Berlin, Ira. "Time, Space, and the Evolution of Afro-American Society in British Mainland North America." *American Historical Review,* LXXXV (1980), 44–78.
Berlin, Ira, and Philip D. Morgan. "Introduction: The Slaves' Economy—Independent Production by Slaves in the Americas." *Slavery and Abolition,* XII (1991), 1–27.
Blassingame, John W. "Using the Testimony of Ex-Slaves: Approaches and Problems." *Journal of Southern History,* XLI (1975), 473–92.
Bloch, Marc. "Toward a Comparative History of European Societies." In *Enterprise and Secular Change: Readings in Economic History,* ed. Frederic C. Lane and Jelle C. Riemersma, 494–521. Homewood, Ill., 1953.
Bolland, Nigel. "Slavery in Belize." *BISRA Occasional Publication,* VII (1979), 3–36.
———. "Systems of Domination After Slavery: The Control of Land and Labor in the British West Indies After 1838." *Comparative Studies in Society and History,* XXIII (1981), 591–619.
Botkin, Benjamin. "The Slave as His Own Interpreter." *Library of Congress Quarterly Journal of Acquisitions,* II (1944), 37–63.
Brathwaite, Edward. "Jamaican Slave Society." *Race,* IX (1968), 331–42.

Brown, S. E. "Sexuality and the Slave Community." *Phylon,* XLII (1981), 1–10.

Cade, John. "Out of the Mouths of Ex-Slaves." *Journal of Negro History,* XX (1935), 294–337.

Campbell, John. "As 'A Kind of Freeman': Slaves' Market-Related Activities in the South Carolina Upcountry, 1800–1860." *Slavery and Abolition,* XII (1991), 131–69.

Cardoso, Ciro Flamarion S. "The Peasant Breach in the Slave System: New Developments in Brazil." *Luso-Brazilian Review,* XXV (1988), 49–57.

Cassity, Michael J. "Slaves, Families, and 'Living Space': A Note on Evidence and Historical Context." *Southern Studies,* XVII (1978), 209–15.

Cook, Charles O., and James M. Poteet, eds. "'Dem Was Black Times Sure 'Nough': The Slave Narratives of Lydia Jefferson and Stephen Williams." *Louisiana History,* XX (1979), 281–92.

Craton, Michael. "Changing Patterns of Slave Family in the British West Indies." *Journal of Interdisciplinary History,* X (1979), 1–35.

————. "Hobbesian or Panglossian: The Two Extremes of Slave Conditions in the British Caribbean." *William and Mary Quarterly,* XXXV (1978), 324–56.

————. "Jamaican Slave Mortality: Fresh Light from Worthy Park, Longville, and the Tharp Estates." *Journal of Caribbean History,* III (1971), 1–27.

————. "The Passion to Exist: Slave Rebellions in the British West Indies, 1650–1832." *Journal of Caribbean History,* XIII (1980), 1–20.

Curtin, Philip D. "Epidemiology and the Slave Trade." *Political Science Quarterly,* LXXXIII (1968), 190–216.

————. "Measuring the Atlantic Slave Trade Once Again: A Comment." *Journal of African History,* XVII (1976), 595–605.

Debien, Gabriel. "Le Marronage aux Antilles Françaises au XVIIIe siècle." *Caribbean Studies,* VI (1966), 3–44.

De Grummond, Jewell Lynn. "A Social History of St. Mary's Parish, 1845–1860." *Louisiana Historical Quarterly,* XXXII (1949), 17–102.

"Destrehan's Slave Roll." *Louisiana Historical Quarterly,* VII (1924), 302–303.

Devine, T. M. "An Eighteenth-Century Business Elite: Glasgow–West India Merchants, *c.* 1750–1815." *Scottish Historical Review,* LVII (1978), 40–67.

Dupuy, A. "Slavery and Underdevelopment in the Caribbean." *Dialectical Anthropology,* VII (1983), 237–51.

Dunn, Richard S. "A Tale of Two Plantations: Slave Life at Mesopotamia in Jamaica and Mount Airy in Virginia, 1799–1828." *William and Mary Quarterly,* XXXIV (1977), 32–65.

Eder, Donald G. "Time Under the Southern Cross." *Agricultural History,* L (1976), 600–614.

Eltis, David. "The Traffic in Slaves Between the British West India Colonies, 1807–1833." *Economic History Review,* XXV (1972), 55–65.

Engerman, Stanley L. "The Slave Trade and British Capital Formation in the Eighteenth Century: A Comment on the Williams Thesis." *Business History Review,* XLVI (1972), 430–43.

————. "Some Economic and Demographic Comparisons of Slavery in the United States and the British West Indies." *Economic History Review*, XXIX (1976), 258–75.

Foshee, Andrew W. "Slave Hiring in Rural Louisiana." *Louisiana History*, XXVI (1985), 63–73.

Frazier, E. Franklin. "The Negro Slave Family." *Journal of Negro History*, XV (1930), 198–266.

Fredrickson, George M., and Christopher Lasch. "Resistance to Slavery." *Civil War History*, XIII (1967), 315–29.

Furness, A. E. "George Hibbert and the Defence of Slavery in the West Indies." *Jamaican Historical Review*, V (1965), 56–70.

Gaspar, David Barry. "The Antigua Slave Conspiracy of 1736: A Case Study of the Origins of Collective Resistance." *William and Mary Quarterly*, XXXV (1978), 308–23.

————. "Slavery, Amelioration, and Sunday Markets in Antigua, 1823–1831." *Slavery and Abolition*, IX (1988), 1–28.

Genovese, Eugene D. "Materialism and Idealism in the History of Negro Slavery in the Americas." *Journal of Social History*, I (1968), 371–94.

Genovese, Eugene D., and Elizabeth Fox-Genovese. "The Slave Economies in Political Perspective." *Journal of American History*, LXVI (1979), 7–23.

Goodyear, James D. "The Sugar Connection: A New Perspective on the History of Yellow Fever." *Bulletin of the History of Medicine*, LII (1978), 5–21.

Goveia, Elsa. "Comment on 'Anglicanism, Catholicism, and the Negro Slave.'" *Comparative Studies in Society and History*, VIII (1966), 328–30.

————. "Gabriel Debien's Contribution to the History of French West Indian Slavery." In *Papers Presented at the Third Annual Conference of Caribbean Historians, 1971*, 40–48.

————. "The West Indian Slave Laws of the Eighteenth Century." *Revisita de Ciencias Sociales*, IV (1960), 75–105.

Greenfield, Sidney M. "Slavery and the Plantation in the New World." *Journal of Inter-American Studies*, XI (1969), 44–57.

Hall, Douglas. "Absentee Proprietorship in the British West Indies to About 1850." *Jamaican Historical Review*, IV (1964), 15–35.

————. "The Flight from the Estates Reconsidered: The British West Indies, 1838–1842." *Journal of Caribbean History*, X–XI (1978), 7–24.

————. "Slaves and Slavery in the British West Indies." *Social and Economic Studies*, XI (1962), 305–18.

————. "The Social and Economic Background to Sugar in Slave Days." *Caribbean Historical Review*, III–IV (1954), 149–69.

Hall, Neville. "Slaves Use of Their 'Free' Time in the Danish Virgin Islands in the Later Eighteenth and Early Nineteenth Century." *Journal of Caribbean History*, XIII (1980), 21–43.

————. "Some Aspects of the Deficiency Question in Jamaica in the Eighteenth Century." *Jamaica Journal*, VII (1973), 36–41.

Higman, Barry W. "African and Creole Slave Family Patterns in Trinidad." *Journal of Family History,* III (1978), 163–78.

———. "Household Structure and Fertility on Jamaican Slave Plantations: A Nineteenth-Century Example." *Population Studies,* XXVII (1973), 527–50.

———. "A Report on Excavations at Montpelier and Roehampton." *Jamaica Journal,* VIII (1974), 40–45.

———. "The Slave Family and Household in the British West Indies, 1800–1834." *Journal of Interdisciplinary History,* VI (1975), 261–87.

Hofstadter, Richard. "U. B. Phillips and the Plantation Legend." *Journal of Negro History,* XXIX (1944), 109–24.

Inikori, J. E. "Measuring the Atlantic Slave Trade: An Assessment of Curtin and Anstey." *Journal of African History,* XVII (1976), 197–223.

Johnson, Howard. "The Emergence of a Peasantry in the Bahamas During Slavery." *Slavery and Abolition,* X (1989), 172–86.

Kendall, John S. "New Orleans' 'Peculiar Institution.'" *Louisiana Historical Quarterly,* XXIII (1940), 864–86.

———. "Shadow over the City." *Louisiana Historical Quarterly,* XXII (1939), 142–65.

Klein, Herbert. "Anglicanism, Catholicism, and the Negro Slave." *Comparative Studies in Society and History,* VIII (1966), 295–327.

Klein, Herbert S., and Stanley Engerman. "Fertility Differentials Between Slaves in the United States and the British West Indies: A Note on Lactation Practices." *William and Mary Quarterly,* XXXV (1978), 357–74.

Knox, A. J. C. "Opportunities and Opposition: The Rise of Jamaica's Black Peasantry and the Nature of the Planter Resistance." *Canadian Review of Sociology and Anthropology,* XIV (1977), 381–95.

Kolchin, Peter. "Reevaluating the Antebellum Slave Community: A Comparative Perspective." *Journal of American History,* LXX (1983), 579–601.

Kopytoff, Barbara K. "The Early Political Development of Jamaican Maroon Societies." *William and Mary Quarterly,* XXXV (1978), 287–307.

Kulikoff, Allan. "The Beginnings of the Afro-American Family in Maryland." In *Law, Society, and Politics in Early Maryland,* ed. Aubrey C. Land *et al.,* 171–96. Baltimore, 1977.

———. "The Origins of Afro-American Society in Tidewater Maryland and Virginia." *William and Mary Quarterly,* XXXV (1978), 226–59.

———. "A 'Prolifick' People: Black Population Growth in the Chesapeake Colonies." *Southern Studies,* XVI (1977), 391–428.

Leff, Nathaniel H. "Long-Term Viability of Slavery in a Backward Closed Economy." *Journal of Interdisciplinary History,* V (1974), 103–108.

Lichtenstein, Alex. "'That Disposition to Theft, with Which They Have Been Branded': Moral Economy, Slave Management, and the Law." *Journal of Social History,* XXI (1988), 413–40.

Logue, C. M. "Transcending Coercion: The Communicative Strategies of Black Slaves on Antebellum Plantations." *Quarterly Journal of Speech,* LXVII (1981), 31–46.

Lombardi, John V. "Comparative Slave Systems in the Americas: A Critical Review." In *New Approaches to Latin American History,* ed. Richard Graham and Peter H. Smith, 156–74. Austin, Tex., 1974.

McDonald, Roderick A. "Independent Economic Production by Slaves on Antebellum Louisiana Sugar Plantations." *Slavery and Abolition,* XII (1991), 182–208.

———. "Measuring the British Slave Trade to Jamaica, 1789–1808: A Comment." *Economic History Review,* XXXIII (1980), 253–58.

———. "The Williams Thesis: A Comment on the State of Scholarship." *Caribbean Quarterly,* XXV (1979), 63–68.

McDonnell, Lawrence T. "Money Knows No Master: Market Relations and the American Slave Community." In *Developing Dixie: Modernization in a Traditional Society,* ed. Winfred B. Moore, Jr., *et al.,* 31–44. New York, 1988.

McGowan, James T. "Planters Without Slaves: Origins of a New World Labor System." *Southern Studies,* XVI (1977), 5–26.

Malone, Ann Patton. "Searching for the Family and Household Structure of Rural Louisiana Slaves, 1810–1864." *Louisiana History,* XXVIII (1987), 357–79.

Marshall, Woodville. "Metayage in the Sugar Industry of the British Windward Islands, 1838–1865." *Jamaican Historical Review,* V (1965), 28–55.

———. "Peasant Development in the West Indies Since 1838." *Social and Economic Studies,* XVII (1968), 252–63.

———. "Provision Ground and Plantation Labour in Four Windward Islands: Competition for Resources During Slavery." *Slavery and Abolition,* XII (1991), 48–67.

———. "A Review of Historical Writing on the Commonwealth Caribbean Since *c.* 1940." *Social and Economic Studies,* XXIV (1975), 271–307.

Menard, Russell. "From Servants to Slaves: The Transformation of the Chesapeake Labor System." *Southern Studies,* XVI (1977), 355–90.

———. "The Maryland Slave Population, 1658–1730." *William and Mary Quarterly,* XXXII (1975), 29–54.

Mintz, Sidney. "Caribbean Marketplaces and Caribbean History." *Nova Americana,* I (1978), 333–44.

———. "Historical Sociology of the Jamaican Church-Founded Free Village System." *De West-Indische Gids,* XXXVIII (1958), 46–70.

———. "The Jamaican Internal Marketing Pattern." *Social and Economic Studies,* IV (1955), 95–103.

———. "Labor and Sugar in Puerto Rico and Jamaica." *Comparative Studies in Society and History,* I (1959), 273–80.

———. "Peasant Markets." *Scientific American,* CCIII (1960), 112–22.

———. "The Question of Caribbean Peasantries: A Comment." *Caribbean Studies,* I (October, 1961), 31–34.

———. "Slavery and Slaves." *Caribbean Studies,* VIII (1969), 65–70.

———. "Was the Plantation Slave a Proletarian?" *Review,* II (1978), 81–98.

Mintz, Sidney, and Douglas Hall. "The Origins of the Jamaican Internal Marketing System." *Yale University Publications in Anthropology,* LVII (1960), 1–26.

Moreno Fraginals, Manuel. "Slavery and Sugar: The Bitter Aftertaste." *UNESCO Courier,* XI (1981), 10–14.

Moreno Fraginals, Manuel, Herbert S. Klein, and Stanley L. Engerman. "The Level and Structure of Slave Prices on Cuban Plantations in the Mid–Nineteenth Century: Some Comparative Perspectives." *American Historical Review,* LXXXVIII (1983), 1201–18.

Morgan, Philip D. "En Caroline du Sud: Marronage et Culture servile." *Annales— Economies, Sociétés, Civilisations,* XXXVII (1982), 574–90.

———. "The Ownership of Property by Slaves in the Mid-Nineteenth-Century Low Country." *Journal of Southern History,* XLIX (1983), 399–420.

———. "Work and Culture: The Task System and the World of Low-Country Blacks, 1700–1880." *William and Mary Quarterly,* XXXIX (1982), 563–99.

Morgan, Philip D., and Michael Nichols. "Slaves in Piedmont Virginia, 1720–1790." *William and Mary Quarterly,* XLVI (1989), 211–51.

Parry, John H. "Plantation and Provision Ground." *Revista de historia de America,* XXXIX (1955), 1–20.

Patterson, Orlando. "Persistence, Continuity, and Change in the Jamaican Working-Class Family." *Journal of Family History,* VII (1982), 135–61.

———. "Slavery, Acculturation, and Social Change: The Jamaican Case." *British Journal of Sociology,* XVII (1966), 151–64.

———. "Slavery and Slave Revolts." *Social and Economic Studies,* XIX (1970), 289–325.

Phillips, Ulrich B. "A Jamaica Slave Plantation." *American Historical Review,* XIX (1914), 543–58.

Pitman, Frank W. "Slavery on British West India Plantations in the Eighteenth Century." *Journal of Negro History,* XI (1926), 584–668.

Postell, Paul E. "John Hampden Randolph, a Louisiana Planter." *Louisiana Historical Quarterly,* XXV (1942), 149–223.

Price, Richard. "Subsistence on the Plantation Periphery: Crops, Cooking, and Labour Among Eighteenth-Century Suriname Maroons." *Slavery and Abolition,* XII (1991), 107–27.

Pritchard, Walter. "Routine on a Louisiana Sugar Plantation Under the Slavery Regime." *Mississippi Valley Historical Review,* XIV (1927), 168–78.

Pryor, Frederick L. "A Comparative Study of Slave Societies." *Journal of Comparative Economics,* I (1977), 25–49.

Ragatz, Lowell J. "Absentee Landlordism in the British Caribbean, 1750–1833." *Agricultural History,* V (1931), 7–24.

Rankin, David C. "The Tannenbaum Thesis Reconsidered: Slavery and Race Relations in Antebellum Louisiana." *Southern Studies,* XVIII (1979), 5–31.

Reckord, Mary. "The Jamaica Slave Rebellion of 1831." *Past and Present,* XL (1968), 108–25.

Roberts, George W. "A Life Table for a West Indian Slave Population." *Population Studies,* V (1952), 238–43.

Schlotterbeck, John T. "The Internal Economy of Slavery in Rural Piedmont Virginia." *Slavery and Abolition,* XII (1991), 170–81.

Schmitz, Mark, and Donald Schaefer. "Paradox Lost: Westward Expansion and Slave Prices Before the Civil War." *Journal of Economic History,* XLI (1981), 402–407.

Schuler, Monica. "Ethnic Slave Rebellions in the Caribbean and the Guianas." *Journal of Social History*, III (1970), 374–85.

Schwartz, Stuart B. "Resistance and Accommodation in Eighteenth-Century Brazil: The Slaves' View of Slavery." *Hispanic American Historical Review*, LVII (1977), 69–81.

Sheridan, Richard B. "Africa and the Caribbean in the Atlantic Slave Trade." *American Historical Review*, LXXVII (1972), 15–35.

———. "The Crisis of Slave Subsistence in the British West Indies During and After the American Revolution." *William and Mary Quarterly*, XXXIII (1976), 615–41.

———. "The Jamaican Slave Insurrection Scare of 1776 and the American Revolution." *Journal of Negro History*, LXI (1976), 290–308.

———. "Simon Taylor, Sugar Tycoon of Jamaica, 1740–1813." *Agricultural History*, XLV (1971), 285–96.

———. "'Sweet Malefactor': The Social Costs of Slavery and Sugar in Jamaica and Cuba, 1807–1854." *Economic History Review*, XXIX (1976), 236–57.

———. "The Wealth of Jamaica in the Eighteenth Century." *Economic History Review*, XVIII (1965), 292–311.

———. "The Wealth of Jamaica in the Eighteenth Century: A Rejoinder." *Economic History Review*, XXI (1968), 46–61.

———. "The West India Sugar Crisis and British Slave Emancipation." *Journal of Economic History*, XXI (1961), 539–51.

Simmonds, Lorna. "Slave Higglering in Jamaica, 1780–1834." *Jamaica Journal*, XX (1987), 31–38.

Sio, Arnold. "Interpretations of Slavery: The Slave Status in the Americas." *Comparative Studies in Society and History*, VII (1965), 289–308.

Sitterson, J. Carlyle. "The McCollams: A Planter Family of the Old and New South." *Journal of Southern History*, VI (1940), 347–67.

———. "Magnolia Plantation, 1852–1862: A Decade of a Louisiana Sugar Estate." *Mississippi Valley Historical Review*, XXV (1938), 197–210.

———. "The William J. Minor Plantations: A Study in Ante-Bellum Absentee Ownership." *Journal of Southern History*, IX (1943), 59–74.

Stampp, Kenneth M. "Rebels and Sambos: The Search for the Negro's Personality in Slavery." *Journal of Southern History*, XXXVII (1971), 367–92.

Steckel, Richard H. "The Fertility of American Slaves." *Research in Economic History*, VII (1982), 239–86.

———. "Slave Marriage and the Family." *Journal of Family History*, V (1980), 406–21.

Szwed, John F. "The Politics of Afro-American Culture." In *Reinventing Anthropology*, ed. Dell Hymes, 153–81. New York, 1973.

Tandberg, Gerilyn G. "Field Hand Clothing in Louisiana and Mississippi During the Antebellum Period." *Dress*, VI (1980), 89–103.

Tannenbaum, Frank. "The Destiny of the Negro in the Western Hemisphere." *Political Science Quarterly*, LXI (1946), 1–41.

———. "A Note on the Economic Interpretation of History." *Political Science Quarterly*, LXI (1946), 247–53.

Thomas, Robert Paul. "The Sugar Colonies of the Old Empire: Profit or Loss for Great Britain?" *Economic History Review,* XXI (1968), 30–45.

Thrupp, Sylvia. "The Role of Comparison in the Development of Economic Theory." *Journal of Economic History,* XVII (1957), 554–70.

Tomich, Dale. "*Une Petite Guinée:* Provision Ground and Plantation in Martinique, 1830–1848." *Slavery and Abolition,* XII (1991), 68–91.

Tregle, Joseph G., Jr. "Louisiana and the Tariff, 1816–1846." *Louisiana Historical Quarterly,* XXV (1942), 24–148.

Trevor-Roper, Hugh. "Sugar and Slaves." *New Statesman,* January 3, 1964, pp. 13–14.

Turner, Mary. "Slave Workers and Labour Negotiations: Amity Hall, Jamaica, 1805–1832." *Slavery and Abolition,* XII (1991), 92–106.

Wesley, Charles H. "The Emancipation of the Free Coloured Population in the British Empire." *Journal of Negro History,* XIX (1934), 137–70.

White, Alice Pemble. "The Plantation Experience of Joseph and Lavinia Erwin, 1807–1836." *Louisiana Historical Quarterly,* XXVII (1944), 343–478.

White, D. G. "Female Slaves: Sex Roles and Status in the Antebellum Plantation South." *Journal of Family History,* VIII (1983), 248–61.

Whitten, David O. "Lagniappe: Tariff and Profit in the Antebellum Sugar Industry." *Business History Review,* XLIV (1970), 226–33.

———. "Medical Care of Slaves: Louisiana Sugar Region and South Carolina Rice District." *Southern Studies,* XVI (1977), 153–80.

Wolf, Eric R., and Sidney Mintz. "Haciendas and Plantations in Middle America and the Antilles." *Social and Economic Studies,* VI (1957), 380–412.

Woodward, C. Vann. "History from Slave Sources." *American Historical Review,* LXXIX (1974), 470–81.

Yetman, Norman R. "The Background of the Slave Narrative Collection." *American Quarterly,* XIX (1967), 534–53.

Unpublished Works

Bishop, P. A. "Runaway Slaves in Jamaica, 1740–1807: A Study Based on Newspaper Advertisements Published During That Period for Runaways." M.A. thesis, University of the West Indies, Kingston, 1970.

Christian, Marcus Bruce. "The Negro in Louisiana." Typescript in Department of Archives and Manuscripts, Earl K. Long Library, University of New Orleans.

Duncker, Sheila D. "The Free Coloureds and Their Fight for Civil Rights in Jamaica." M.A. thesis, University of London, 1960.

Lathrop, Barnes F. "The Pugh Plantations, 1860–1865: A Study of Life in Lower Louisiana." Ph.D. dissertation, University of Texas, 1945.

McGowan, James T. "Creation of a Slave Society: Louisiana Plantations in the Eighteenth Century." Ph.D. dissertation, University of Rochester, 1976.

INDEX

Page numbers in italics refer to illustrations.